SUCCESSFUL
QUALITATIVE RESEARCH

a practical guide for beginners

VIRGINIA BRAUN
& VICTORIA CLARKE

Los Angeles | London | New Delhi
Singapore | Washington DC

Los Angeles | London | New Delhi
Singapore | Washington DC

SAGE Publications Ltd
1 Oliver's Yard
55 City Road
London EC1Y 1SP

SAGE Publications Inc.
2455 Teller Road
Thousand Oaks, California 91320

SAGE Publications India Pvt Ltd
B 1/I 1 Mohan Cooperative Industrial Area
Mathura Road
New Delhi 110 044

SAGE Publications Asia-Pacific Pte Ltd
3 Church Street
#10-04 Samsung Hub
Singapore 049483

© Virginia Braun and Victoria Clarke 2013

First published 2013

Editor: Michael Carmichael
Editorial assistant: Alana Clogan
Production editor: Imogen Roome
Copyeditor: Neil Dowden
Indexer: Cathryn Pritchard
Marketing manager: Alison Borg
Cover design: Wendy Scott
Typeset by: C&M Digitals (P) Ltd, Chennai, India
Printed and bound by CPI Group (UK) Ltd,
Croydon, CR0 4YY

Library of Congress Control Number: 2012940758

British Library Cataloguing in Publication data

A catalogue record for this book is available from
the British Library

ISBN 978-1-84787-581-5
ISBN 978-1-84787-582-2 (pbk)

For Pene, Marion and Reg, with love

Contents

Acknowledgements

Tempting as it is just to write a long list of names and then lie on the sofa for an hour, for the benefit of the curious reader who, like us, reads the acknowledgements first, we will write something a little more interesting. We apologise in advance to anyone we have forgotten to mention, and to those (many) people whose work has influenced our understanding and practice of qualitative research, but who are not listed here or not cited in the book. (To those of you wondering why you are thanked under 'X' heading and not *also* under 'Y': everyone we mention is only listed once.)

This book's place of conception is an indication of the quality we have aspired to, and hopefully come close to achieving. We wrote our book proposal in the sublime city of Paris, in the summer of 2007, and we thank her for the beauty and inspiration she provided, as well as all the delectable food we happily ate our way through! Although it sometimes feels like we have spent four solid years researching and writing this book, unfortunately chronic health problems (and a chronic inability to say 'no') slowed us down considerably. For this reason, first and foremost we sincerely thank our commissioning editor at Sage, Michael Carmichael, for his patience! We hope it was worth the wait. We also thank Michael for his infectious enthusiasm for the project, and his sterling advice at every stage of the process. To him, and to everyone else involved at Sage: thanks and have a gold star!

Our first foray into writing about methods was a little paper on thematic analysis, published in 2006 in *Qualitative Research in Psychology*, which much to our bemusement has become rather popular. So we must thank Brendan Gough for publishing this paper, and to everyone who has conveyed to us their enthusiasm for it, and the approach and guidelines we outline – your enthusiasm inspired us to write this book!

Anyone who has written a book will know that it is something of an epic undertaking; as one of our colleagues aptly observed, it's like writing a PhD in your 'spare time'. Lots of people have helped directly and indirectly, and in ways big and small. Our thanks go to all those people who, through teaching, supervision, and mentoring, have inspired our love of qualitative research and contributed to our own development as teachers, supervisors and mentors of qualitative research: Nicola Gavey, Karen Henwood, Bruna Seu, Corinne Squire, Mick Billig, Derek Edwards, Celia Kitzinger, Jonathan Potter, Sue Wilkinson (and other members of the Discourse and Rhetoric Group at Loughborough University), Adrian Coyle, Hannah Frith and Kate Gleeson ... Our friends and colleagues at UWE and The University of Auckland, and beyond, have been most excellent in providing direct and indirect support (and some thought-provoking discussions of qualitative research), including Debra Gray, Andrea Halewood, Tim Kurz, Helen Malson, Tim McCreanor, Elizabeth Peel, Paul Redford, Damien Riggs, Merran Toerien, Leonore Tiefer, and Susan Speer, as have various students whose work we have supervised over the years. A special thank-you goes to the students who have taken our research methods classes and taught us how to teach, and write about, qualitative research.

As we conceived this book, we wanted to provide as many real-world material examples as we could, to illustrate *what qualitative research looks like ...* for people who don't know. So we are enormously appreciative to everyone who provided material for the book including our super-duper box authors Sonja Ellis, Sally Wiggins and Brett Smith, and William (Will) Hanson for being brave enough to allow us to make public the first focus group he moderated. (Will did a great job of piloting and conducting the focus group, and helping us to fix a terrible transcript that was supposedly 'professionally' transcribed – beware the bad transcriber!) Thanks to: Barbara Douglas, Panteá Farvid, Nikki Hayfield, Nicola Rance and Gemma Tricklebank for allowing us to use their awesome posters (and a special thanks to Nikki for making our life a lot easier in the final few months of producing this book, by being fabulously organised and supremely capable); Bethany Cooper, Eleni Demetriou, Cassandra Rogers and Katharine Spence for allowing us to use material from their fantastic final year research projects; and Paulette Benton-Greig, Kate Mitchell, Elyse Oberland and Emily Opperman for research assistance; the latter two for your work on the views on pubic hair and experiences of orgasm projects. Since much qualitative research relies on participants, a big thank-you also goes to everyone who participated in the research projects featured in this book, *especially* the six weight and obesity focus group participants, and Dan, Danni, Owen and the four undergraduate students who participated in the body art focus group (and Sophie Gray the moderator's assistant) for their generosity in allowing the groups to be made public. Finally, this book has had various permutations in the last four years, and we kindly thank Irmgard Tischner, who, at one stage, was going to provide some data for the book from her research on experiences of being large.

A special thank-you must go to The University of Auckland library for never letting us down, no matter how seemingly obscure the material we sought; to the Department of Psychology at The University of Auckland for support in various ways; and to Margarete Sandelowski for writing *brilliant* papers on every topic related to qualitative research one could possibly imagine. We almost feel redundant. Thanks to Sara-Jane, Guy, Oliver and Ryann, and to various non-academic friends, for providing some delightful and much needed distractions in the final stages of writing the book, and to Naomi Moller for pep talks and much much more.

Finally, having thanked peers, participants, publisher and Paris, it's time to thank pet, partner and parents! To Toby for being so delightful, and reminding us that books are rubbish and the park, catch and tummy rubs are what it's all about. To David: you probably won't believe it, but we have finished 'the bloody book' and we promise not to write another one ... for a while (and we haven't bought any more cookery books recently either, honest ...); you have been splendid. To Pene for instilling a love of learning and thinking critically about the world; and to Marion and Reg for being proud parents (and for all those trips to the library – they paid off!): this one is for you.

About the authors

Virginia Braun is an Associate Professor in the School of Psychology at The University of Auckland, Aotearoa/New Zealand. She is a feminist and critical psychologist whose research explores the intersecting areas of gender, bodies, sex/sexuality and health. She has worked on projects related to heterosex, sexual health, cervical cancer prevention policy, sexuality and higher education, women's genital meanings and experiences, and female genital cosmetic surgery, and is current involved in a Marsden-funded project related to pornography (with Nicola Gavey & Linda Tyler; University of Auckland). She is also interested in the intersections between academic work and activism, and is involved in The New View Campaign's work around female genital cosmetic surgery. She has an ongoing interest in qualitative research and, with Victoria Clarke, developed a theoretically-flexible approach to thematic analysis. She is currently editor (with Nicola Gavey) of the journal *Feminism & Psychology* (Sage, UK). http://www.psych.auckland.ac.nz/uoa/virginia-braun/

Victoria Clarke is an Associate Professor in Sexuality Studies in the Department of Psychology at the University of the West of England, Bristol, UK. Her research has focused on lesbian and gay parenting, same-sex and heterosexual relationships, sexual practices, sexualities and appearance, sexualities and higher education, and qualitative research methods. She has conducted ESRC and British Academy funded research on same-sex relationships and civil partnership. Her books include *Out in Psychology: Lesbian, gay, bisexual, trans and queer perspectives* (Wiley) with Elizabeth Peel, and *LGBTQ Psychology: An introduction* (Cambridge University Press), with Sonja Ellis, Elizabeth Peel and Damien Riggs. She has developed a theoretically flexible approach to thematic analysis with Virginia Braun. Her current research interests include visible differences/disfigurements and the story completion method. http://people.uwe.ac.uk/Pages/person.aspx?accountname=campus%5Cv2-clarke

SECTION 1

Successfully getting started in qualitative research

Some very important starting information

OVERVIEW

What is qualitative research?
Qualitative research as a paradigm
The emergence of a qualitative research paradigm (in psychology)
What do I need to become a good qualitative researcher?
Why we love qualitative research
Our approach in this book

We're about to introduce you to the wonderful world of qualitative research. It's vast and exciting, full of new areas to discover. We hope you'll learn to love and feel as passionate about it as we do. As we know that won't be the case for everyone, we want you to feel that you *really* 'get' it: that you understand both the purpose and premise of qualitative research, *and*, crucially, that you know how to actually go about doing a qualitative research project. In order for this to happen, you may need to put aside ideas you have about what research is, and approach this field with 'open eyes' – like an explorer who can only understand a completely different culture if they don't view and judge it by the perspectives and values of their own culture.

WHAT IS QUALITATIVE RESEARCH?

The most basic definition of qualitative research is that it uses *words* as **data** (see Chapter 2), collected and analysed in all sorts of ways. Quantitative research, in contrast, uses *numbers* as data and analyses them using statistical techniques. The term qualitative research is used to refer both to *techniques* (of data collection or data analysis) and to a wider **framework** for conducting research, or **paradigm**. Paradigm here refers to the beliefs, assumptions, values and practices shared by a research community (see Kuhn, 1962), and it provides an overarching framework for research. Qualitative research, as we define it, is not just about data and techniques – it's about the application of qualitative techniques within a qualitative paradigm, which is quite different from a quantitative paradigm (see Table 1.1). It has been referred to as **Big Q qualitative research**, and contrasted with **small q qualitative research** (Kidder & Fine, 1987), which is the use of specific qualitative data collection and techniques, not (necessarily) within a qualitative paradigm (see Box 1.1).

Table 1.1   Some *broad* differences between qualitative and quantitative paradigms

Quantitative	Qualitative
Numbers used as data	Words – written and spoken language – (and images) used as data
Seeks to identify relationships between variables, to explain or predict – with the aim of generalising the findings to a wider population	Seeks to understand and interpret more local meanings; recognises data as gathered in a context; *sometimes* produces knowledge that contributes to more general understandings
Generates 'shallow' but broad data – not a lot of complex detail obtained from each participant, but lots of participants take part (to generate the necessary statistical power)	Generates 'narrow' but **rich data**, **'thick descriptions'** – detailed and complex accounts from each participant; not many take part
Seeks consensus, norms, or general patterns; often aims to reduce diversity of responses to an average response	Tends to seek patterns, but accommodates and explores difference and divergence within data
Tends to be theory-testing, and deductive	Tends to be theory generating, and inductive (working *up* from the data)
Values detachment and impartiality (objectivity)	Values personal involvement and partiality (subjectivity, reflexivity)
Has a fixed method (harder to change focus once data collection has begun)	Method is less fixed (can accommodate a shift in focus in the same study)
Can be completed quickly	Tends to take longer to complete because it is interpretative and there is no formula

Adapted (and expanded) from Tolich & Davidson (2003)

BOX 1.1   EXAMPLES OF *SMALL Q* QUALITATIVE RESEARCH

The use of qualitative techniques outside a qualitative paradigm (*small q* qualitative research) happens in different ways:

- A qualitative research project may be conducted in a realist, positivist way, where the values and assumptions of *Big Q* qualitative research are rejected.
- Qualitative methods can be used as a *precursor* for quantitative research. For example, in a study of the effects of the experiences of depression, US professors of psychiatry and nursing James Coyne and Margaret Calarco (1995) conducted two focus groups and thematically organised participants' statements into eight categories, drawing on these to develop a survey, which they used to generate the data they analysed.
- It can be used *alongside* quantitative methods as part of a mixed methods design (see Mertens, 2005). In many **mixed method** designs, the qualitative component may be subsumed within a primarily quantitative, realist project, and it is rarely *Big Q* qualitative research. For instance, in food and farming researcher Charlotte Weatherall and colleagues' (2003) study of UK consumer's perceptions of food, farming and buying locally produced goods, the qualitative data from six focus groups were used to identify consumers priorities when buying food, perceptions of farming/food provision, and interest in local food production, and informed the development of a quantitative survey. The qualitative analysis was presented and interpreted alongside the quantitative results. The analysis described the content of what was said, assuming a direct relationship between what people say and what they believe (and do).
- Qualitative data might be converted to a numerical representation, and analysed *quantitatively*. For instance, public health researchers Mary Story and Patricia Faulkner (1990) collated a selection of episodes of 11 of the most popular US prime-time TV shows and coded the text of those programmes according to food references. The frequency of codes was compared, and was used to determine messages about food and eating presented during prime-time. Overall, they reported 'pervasive' (p. 740) references to food, the majority of which were related to low-nutritional-value snacks, and concluded that the shows and advertising promote poor nutritional practice. The typical method here is content analysis, where qualitative data are coded and analysed numerically, and there is debate about whether it is, or can be, a *qualitative* method. Many say no – for instance, *The Sage Handbook of Qualitative Research* (Denzin & Lincoln, 2005b) barely discusses it; we don't consider it in this book because we want to focus on *wholly* qualitative methods. The quantitative focus in content analysis has been substantively critiqued (Mayring, 2004), and more interpretative forms developed – often referred to as *qualitative* content analysis (e.g. Hsieh & Shannon, 2005; Mayring, 2004), which is similar to **thematic analysis**.

QUALITATIVE RESEARCH AS A PARADIGM

A broad cluster of features and assumptions make up a non-positivist qualitative research paradigm. One thing absolutely fundamental is that it tends *not* to assume there is only one correct version of reality or knowledge. Instead, it comes from a perspective that argues that there are multiple versions of reality – even for the same person – and that these are very closely linked to the context they occur in. Most qualitative researchers would argue that we should not, even *must not*, consider knowledge outside of the context in which it was generated. This refers both to the context of data *generation*, such as an **interview** setting, and to the broader sociocultural and political contexts of the research. New Zealand psychologists Maree Burns and Nicola Gavey's (2004) work on the meanings and **discourses** of body weight, body size and body **practices** provides a nice illustration of this (which they actually built into their **research design**). They contextualised their analysis of the talk of women who practise bulimia through also analysing public health messages promoting 'healthy weight' (as a response to the 'obesity epidemic'), and demonstrated a conceptual linking of 'healthy weight' to slenderness. This common-sense meaning was deployed by women who practised bulimia to explain and justify their purging and compensating practices (e.g. vomiting, excessive exercise): such practices were framed as about obtaining a *'healthy'* (i.e. slim) body. Through contextualising the women's accounts, and specifically analysing public health messages, their analysis provided a compelling insight into the ways something which seems to be a useful message in one domain – that of 'healthy weight' – can actually be deployed in very 'unhealthy' ways in another.

Other elements of a qualitative paradigm include (Silverman, 2000: 8):

- the use of qualitative data, and the analysis of words which are not reducible to numbers;
- the use of more 'naturally' occurring data collection **methods** that more closely resemble real life (compared to other possibilities, such as experiments) – this develops from the idea that we cannot make sense of data in isolation from context;
- an interest in meanings rather than reports and measures of behaviour or internal cognitions;
- the use of inductive, theory-generating research;
- a rejection of the natural sciences as a model of research, including the rejection of the idea of the objective (unbiased) scientist;
- the recognition that researchers bring their **subjectivity** (their views, perspectives, frameworks for making sense of the world; their politics, their passions) into the research process – this is seen as a strength rather than a weakness.

So the qualitative paradigm is quite *different* from the quantitative one. Depending on where you are in your studies, and what you're studying, this might contradict what you've been taught constitutes *good research* – controlled, rigorous, reliable, validated, quantitative and experimental. We're teaching you about a whole different world of research that grew as a response and challenge to the perceived limits of *that* model of research.

THE EMERGENCE OF A QUALITATIVE RESEARCH PARADIGM (IN PSYCHOLOGY)

Quantitative approaches and 'the scientific method' have dominated psychology (in a way that isn't the case in all other social sciences). It's tempting to see the emergence of qualitative research in two ways: a) as a *new* development; and b) as simply offering a *complementary* data collection and analysis toolkit for quantitative psychology. We would warn against both conclusions, and offer a very brief history of qualitative research in psychology to illustrate why.

From the emergence of psychology as a discipline in the second half of the nineteenth century, it has been marked by contestation over the 'appropriate' ways to research and theorise the things we study in psychology. The focus, topic and purpose of psychology itself are similarly contested, but we won't discuss those here. Qualitative ideas and approaches have been part of psychology from its inception. However, first with behaviourism in the early twentieth century, and subsequently with the cognitive revolution in the second half of the twentieth century, quantitative methods employed within a (post)positivist, experimental paradigm dominated the discipline (Ashworth, 2003; Howitt, 2010). Such approaches situated themselves in opposition to the more subjective, interpretative introspective (qualitative) techniques of early psychology, which became classified as 'unscientific' – a criticism of qualitative research which continues to this day, from some quarters, although that of course depends on how we define science itself (Kvale, 1996). What we think of *as* psychology, and indeed how you *do* it, has been strongly shaped by the behavioural and cognitive traditions. Within such approaches, psychology should seek to understand and determine an observable, objective (universal) psychological reality.

The dominance of behaviourism and then cognitive experimentalism meant that it wasn't until the 1980s that qualitative approaches regained a foothold, and subsequently flourished, in some areas of psychology (their history in other social sciences, such as sociology, is different, e.g. Vidich & Lyman, 1994). Their (re)appearance reflected the development of a number of *oppositional* approaches within the social sciences, which challenged mainstream (post)positivist empiricist research design and practice, and the bases on which psychology and the other social sciences theorised and conceptualised their subjects (Ashworth, 2003; Howitt, 2010). Approaches including **feminism** (Crawford & Unger, 2004), **poststructuralism** (Gavey, 1989), **postmodernism** (Gergen, 1990), **social constructionism** (Burr, 2003), **hermeneutics** (Schwandt, 2000) and **phenomenology** (Langdridge, 2007) in different ways questioned or rejected the idea of an observable, independent (singular and universal) reality, with humans understood as *responding to* external and internal influences. Instead, the person was theorised as operating within a subjective, interpreted world, the organisation of which offered a certain version of reality. The relationship between person and context was seen as more fluid and reciprocal, with influence in *both* directions. Qualitative methods were touted as allowing access to people's subjective worlds and meanings, and to groups marginalised (e.g. by their gender, sexuality, race/ethnicity/culture) and often invisible within western psychology. They were seen as crucial for identifying and theorising different *constructed* versions of reality, and for the ways people are both constructed by, and constructors of, reality (see Box 1.2 for a classic example). The use of a qualitative paradigm was in many cases then an implicit and often explicit *rejection* of the values, assumptions and practices of quantitative, experimental psychology (although see Michell, 2004). This rejection was driven from anything from theoretical convictions to political social change agendas.

What we wish to emphasise is that qualitative research has a long, but often marginal, history in psychology, and its strong emergence in certain places (e.g. the UK) in recent decades reflects a shakeup of the very foundations of the discipline. That explains why, in some cases, the response to qualitative research is hostile. You don't need to know much of this history to do qualitative research, but it's important to understand that it's not simply a complementary approach to a quantitative research paradigm, and why this is.

BOX 1.2   A CLASSIC OF QUALITATIVE PSYCHOLOGICAL RESEARCH

British social psychologist Michael Billig's (1978a, 1978b) interview-study of members of the British far-right group the *National Front* provided profound insights into the nature of the organisation, and into the frameworks of meaning and logic that *National Front* members deployed when talking about race, racism and their ideal of a 'white only' Britain. Like many others who have been shown to 'do racism without being racist', *National Front* members often denied they were racist, and instead argued that their position was a logical response to the situation of increased non-white migration to the UK. In simultaneously providing compelling insights into this group, and demonstrating the limitations of social cognitive frameworks (e.g. attitudes) for explaining these insights, Billig's study was at the forefront of the development a *new* approach to social psychology, providing the foundations for the critique and alternative approaches of what would soon become discursive (Potter & Wetherell, 1987) and rhetorical psychology (Billig, 1987) (see Chapter 8).

CONTEXTS OF LEARNING

Reflecting this history, within the psychology undergraduate curriculum, qualitative methods tend to be sidelined in favour of quantitative methods. This occurs even in the UK, where they are required in any British Psychological Society (BPS)-accredited psychology curriculum. If taught, qualitative methods are typically allocated far less time on the curriculum than quantitative methods, and often treated as a single approach, rather than a field as diverse as 'quantitative methods'. They are also often taught *after* quantitative methods and experimental design have been presented. If this is the case, qualitative research often comes as a culture shock (Howitt, 2010) at best; at worst, it is seen as 'unscientific' or as anxiety provoking because it lacks the clarity and control of quantitative research and experimentation, which have often been presented as the pinnacles of research excellence. To become a good qualitative researcher requires a different way of thinking about research.

WHAT DO I NEED TO BECOME A GOOD QUALITATIVE RESEARCHER?

Obviously, there's quite a bit you need to *know* – you'll learn that throughout this book. Do you need a whole lot of technical skills? Not really. If you're a bit of a Luddite (like Victoria), you've found a home in qualitative research! Assuming you know basic word processing, and are familiar with the internet, qualitative research is unlikely to pose technical challenges. However, if you're a tech-savvy gadget kid (which Virginia tries to be), qualitative research also offers you a home. Qualitative research can be conducted low-tech or high-tech, so there's something for everyone. But there is one thing that's really essential: developing a qualitative sensibility.

A QUALITATIVE SENSIBILITY

A qualitative sensibility refers to an orientation towards research – in terms of research questions, and analysing data – that fits within the qualitative paradigm. Certain skills or orientations that make up a qualitative sensibility include:

- an interest in process and meaning, over and above cause and effect;
- a critical and questioning approach to life and knowledge – you don't take things at face value and simply accept the way they are, but ask questions about *why* they may be that way, whose interests are served by them and *how* they could be different;
- the ability to reflect on, and step outside, your cultural membership, to become a cultural commentator – so that you can see, and question, the shared values and assumptions that make up being a member of a particular society – this involves identifying your own assumptions, and then putting them aside (referred to as bracketing them off) so that your research is not *automatically* shaped by these. It is hard to do, but vitally important for being able to get 'deep' into qualitative data;
- the development of a double-consciousness or an analytic 'eye' or 'ear', where you can listen intently, and critically reflect on what is said, simultaneously (e.g. in an interview, being able to focus both on the *content* of what is being said, and

possible *analytic* ideas within it) – this helps produce much better (more complex, richer) data;

- **reflexivity**: critical reflection on the research process and on one's own role as researcher (Finlay, 2002a, 2002b), including our various **insider** and **outsider** positions (Gallais, 2008) – we have insider status when we share some group identity with our **participants** (for example, a *male* researcher researching *men* would be an insider), and outsider status when we do not share some group identity with our participants (for example, a *white* man researching *Asian* men would be an outsider), but for any research, we are likely to have multiple insider and outsider positions;
- good interactional skills – a warm/friendly manner that puts people at ease and helps establish '**rapport**' and 'trust'. This is does not mean you need to be really extroverted or outgoing.

Some of these may come naturally to you; others may be a bit of a struggle. Give them time. In addition, to become a good qualitative researcher, the following need to be added to the qualitative sensibility you have and are developing:

- a basic grasp of some methods of data collection and analysis, which you build to in-depth understanding;
- a conceptual understanding of qualitative approaches.

The skills you will develop in doing qualitative research don't just apply to this field: reading and engaging with information critically; learning to discern and distil out what is vital from a large body of information; active listening; writing and presenting interesting and compelling 'stories' – all these skills will stand you in good stead in the 'real world', as well as in qualitative research.

WHY WE LOVE QUALITATIVE RESEARCH

We love qualitative research: it's rich, exciting, and challenging in lots of ways; it captures the complexity, mess and contradiction that characterises the real world, yet allows us to make sense of *patterns* of meaning. In line with the importance of reflexivity and contextualisation for qualitative research (see Chapter 2), you can find out a bit about why we each love qualitative research, and what we each bring to it as researchers, in Boxes 1.3 and 1.4.

OUR APPROACH IN THIS BOOK

Learning to do qualitative research has been seen by some as akin to riding a bike. British psychologist Jonathan Potter (1997) likened the analytic method **discourse analysis** (see Chapter 8) to a 'craft skill', something that not only takes time to learn, but also requires the 'doing'. This suggests it cannot be learnt by following a recipe,

---

BOX 1.3   MEET VIRGINIA BRAUN

I have been doing qualitative research in psychology for over 15 years, on topics like cervical cancer prevention policy (e.g. Braun & Gavey, 1999), female genital cosmetic surgery (e.g. Braun, 2010), and (hetero)sexual health and 'risk' (e.g. Braun, 2008). What drew me to qualitative research wasn't that I hated statistics; I liked and had always been good at maths and stats. But from my first moments of learning about qualitative research in only a handful of lectures in my undergraduate degree, qualitative research captivated me. I felt it captured ways of knowing, and the richness of real complex lives, in ways that quantitative approaches couldn't, and was compelled to use it. I've never looked back. While I always emphasise that the methods you use *must* be determined by your research question, I find that the questions I have are typically most suited to qualitative approaches – although I do dabble in quantitative research from time to time. A long way on from those first lectures, my passion for qualitative research has only grown.

Qualitative research emphasises that we see things *from a perspective*. So what are some of my influences? As a researcher, I come from both a traditional and non-traditional background. It is 'traditional' in that following a 'bored senseless' gap year, I went to university, completing a bachelors, masters (both at The University of Auckland, Aotearoa/New Zealand), and PhD (at Loughborough University, UK), and then jumped straight into an academic job. And I occupy a raft of categories of privilege: white, middle-class, heterosexual, able-bodied, thin. Yet this surface belies a more complex background that informs my 'lefty' politics and my strong commitment to social justice, and my awareness of and reflection on those positions of privilege. My parents (mother: teacher; father: academic) separated when I was very young; for eight years, to the start of my teens, I lived with my mother (and others) on a very remote hippy commune. It had no electricity or flushing toilets. Road access was a half-hour walk away, but we had no car and there was no public transport. I don't share the pop-cultural knowledge of my peers. I grew up on the margins of western culture, occupying simultaneously positions of privilege and of marginalisation; at primary school, I occupied the lowest social category, and experienced frequent marginalisation and bullying from students and teachers. My experience of white privilege is also tempered by my location: as a Pākehā New Zealander, whiteness cannot be an unproblematic or unquestioned category of privilege – and rightly so! I am part of a collective who have been, and continue to be, privileged as a result of New Zealand's colonised past (and present), which continues to significantly negatively impact Māori, who were colonised by people 'like me'. And I am a woman. Despite my strong, amazing, busy, achieving mother and my alternative secondary school education, it wasn't until university that I discovered feminism. It was a natural fit, and, along with **critical psychology**, provided a framework to bring this all together. I cannot turn off a tendency to critically analyse socially and systemically, rather than individually, **representations** and **constructs** which reinforce inequitable social arrangements, marginalisation and discrimination (and privilege).

BOX 1.4   MEET VICTORIA CLARKE

When I was at school, although I was good at maths and science, I really loved subjects like English literature and history that were less about right and wrong answers and more about interpretation. When studying for my A levels, I was fascinated by debates in sociology about paradigms and methodologies, and critiques of science. So when I began studying psychology as an undergraduate at Brunel University (UK), I was already committed to qualitative and interpretive approaches to research, and their emphasis on the provisional, multiple and context-bound nature of knowledge. In addition, I am drawn to qualitative approaches because they afford us a privileged insight into worlds we have no direct personal experience of – doing qualitative research has allowed me to see ways of life and to hear about experiences that are far removed from my own in rich, vivid detail. Like Virginia, I have been doing qualitative research for over 15 years, on topics such as lesbian and gay parenting (e.g. Clarke, 2001), partner relationships (e.g. Clarke, Burgoyne, & Burns, 2006), and sexuality and appearance (e.g. Clarke & Turner, 2007). Although I am strongly committed to qualitative approaches in general, I'm not, as are many researchers, wedded to a particular qualitative approach; rather my view is that different qualitative approaches can capture something useful and interesting about the complex and messy world in which we all live.

Like Virginia, my research is strongly informed by my left-leaning politics and a commitment to social justice. In many ways my life is shaped by social privilege – as white, as middle class, as a member of a 'respectable' profession like university lecturing – yet these positions of privilege intersect with experiences of social marginality as non-heterosexual, as a woman and, currently, as disabled (by virtue of a chronic health condition). Unlike Virginia, I grew up in fairly conventional circumstances – in the 'burbs with my mother and father. Our outer London, largely working-class town had a large South Asian (Indian sub-continent) immigrant community and I quickly became sensitised to issues of race and racism when I was often the only white child to attend the birthday parties of my South Asian class mates. I was a passionate feminist by my early teens and my passion was further fuelled by a teacher who gave me the books of radical feminists like Sheila Jeffreys to read. I came out as a lesbian in my early twenties, during my undergraduate degree (I now identity as non-heterosexual), and this was highly influential in my choice of lesbian and gay parenting as a topic for my PhD research (at Loughborough University, UK). My training in qualitative research was almost exclusively unpinned by critical frameworks such as feminism, social constructionism, poststructuralism and discourse analysis. This training, combined with my personal commitments to criticality and social justice, means that most of my research is conducted through a critical lens.

or picked up from a 'how to' guide; others feel the same about qualitative research in general. In contrast, some (e.g. McLeod, 2001) argue that clear guidance is vital for demystifying qualitative research, and making it accessible to everyone, and in recent years there has been an increased focus on practical guidance (e.g. Smith, Flowers, & Larkin, 2009). Both positions hold validity: clear guidelines are important for learning, but *doing* qualitative research remains an essential part of the learning process. The point is nicely expressed by a British student talking about his experience of learning qualitative methods: 'the more you do [qualitative research] the better you get, it's practice, it's like art you have to do it to learn it you can't just sit there read a book and think "oh that's how I do it," it's not like you can just pick up a manual and go how do I analyse this, not like with stats' (PD in Shaw, Dyson, & Peel, 2008: 187).

We have designed this book as a *practical* introduction to qualitative research, for people relatively new to the field. It is intended to demystify the process of qualitative research, and help emerging qualitative researchers feel they have a grasp of what they need to do to be a *successful* qualitative researcher. Our experience tells us that practically oriented information and the use of examples from real research projects are crucial for a productive learning experience. Because of this, we do some things differently in this book, compared to most other qualitative teaching guides:

- We prioritise practice over theory; we aim to teach you what you need to know to *do* qualitative research, from design to data collection, analysis and reporting, without deeply engaging with theory. Obviously theory *is* important. It's absolutely *vital* for developing a fuller and deeper understanding of qualitative methods and **methodologies**, and what knowledge we can and cannot generate from the methods we use. But these debates can be inaccessible (and less meaningful) if you first don't have some basic understanding of qualitative data and what you might do with it, analytically. Requiring deep theoretical engagement at the start can actually cloud the process, making qualitative research (in general) harder to understand than it needs to be. In contrast to the usual model of learning theory first, we believe that the theory can more easily become clear, and relevant, to people, through the process of starting to actually *do* qualitative research – that is, 'getting your hands dirty' with data collection and analysis. So we suggest you only need *limited* theoretical knowledge before you jump right in and start doing qualitative research, and for this reason, our discussion of theory is limited to an introduction in Chapter 2, and theory specific to certain analytic approaches in Chapter 8. Once you feel you have understood the basics of what qualitative research is, and how you do it, we encourage you to start to read more deeply into theory (e.g. Burr, 2003; Guba & Lincoln, 2005; Nightingale & Cromby, 1999) to enhance your analytic skills.
- We understand qualitative data analysis as having one of three basic forms or frameworks: searching for *patterns*, looking at *interaction*, or looking at *stories*. We focus on pattern-based analysis, as the most basic and common qualitative approach (in psychology), and teach you to analyse qualitative data within this

patterns framework. We aim to teach 'basic' and 'generic' qualitative research skills and knowledge, which can be applied to different analytic methods. So instead of providing several chapters on different analysis 'methods', we systematically walk you through a basic thematic approach, and compare and contrast this with other approaches, where relevant. This different approach to teaching analysis ensures you understand the core premise and purpose of pattern-based ways of analysing qualitative data, and the similarities and differences between different methods, and their language and concepts.

- We aim to guide you through the entire process of qualitative research. In keeping with our very practical orientation, we do so using lots of 'real' research examples, both in the text itself, and on the *companion website*.

WHO WE'VE WRITTEN THE BOOK FOR

This book is written first and foremost for students learning qualitative research within a (undergraduate or taught postgraduate) psychology degree (we are both psychologists). The book supports a teaching block on qualitative methods, and is designed as a resource for students doing a qualitative research project – from the process of research design to the writing-up of the report. Students learning and doing qualitative research in the context of other social and health disciplines should also find it useful, as will more established researchers encountering or doing qualitative research for the first time. Although we're both psychologists, and a lot of the material orients to psychology, qualitative psychology isn't clearly disciplinary-bound: it bleeds across the boundaries of related disciplines such as sociology, social work, counselling, nursing, education, social anthropology, socio-legal studies and social geography. We therefore use examples from within and outside psychology and we draw from qualitative research around the globe; in fitting with qualitative psychology's emphasis on knowledge as contextual (see Chapter 2), we always note where the research examples are from.

SOME INFORMATION ABOUT OUR TAKE ON THINGS, INCLUSIONS AND EXCLUSIONS

There are a few other specific things that will be useful to know in reading and making sense of this book:

- We're not *neutral* when it comes to qualitative research – we think it's fantastic! But more specifically, we also advocate particular *forms* of qualitative research – those that are contextualist or constructionist in their orientation (see Chapter 2), and typically part of a Big Q approach. Given that, we don't discuss qualitative research used in a (post)positivist (small q) way.
- To give some sense of coherence and comparability, many of our examples come from research related to weight, eating, diet and 'obesity' (including the **focus group** [FG] data we analyse in Chapters 9–11). You'll quickly see we often use the language of *fat*. This might seem shocking to some readers, and may be taken as derogatory. On the contrary, in line with fat politics, fat is

not a 'dirty word' (Wann, 2009) – or indeed a 'dirty' state of embodiment – and in order to counter fat phobia, we must shift from euphemistic language around fatness. Terms like 'obesity', which have the ring of medical neutrality, also are far from neutral, and convey a whole lot of (problematic) values and assumptions.

- Given that qualitative research is a diverse field, and given that this is an introductory textbook, we can't cover everything. Our decisions on what to include and exclude reflect a combination of factors: a) methods that are generally considered to be core in qualitative psychology; b) methods we feel are realistically useable within a limited amount of time; c) methods that require limited resources, and which are thus amenable to student projects; d) methods which don't require a lot of technical expertise; and e) methods which are primarily text based. This means we don't discuss in any depth increasingly popular conversation analytic (e.g. Hutchby & Wooffitt, 2008), discursive psychological (e.g. Edwards & Potter, 1992), **narrative** analytic (e.g. Riessman, 2007) or visual methods (e.g. Frith, Riley, Archer, & Gleeson, 2005), various participatory or action research approaches (e.g. Kemmis & McTaggart, 2005) including memory work (e.g. Willig, 2008) and ethnography (e.g. Griffin & Bengry-Howell, 2008), or methods which can blur qualitative/ quantitative boundaries, such as Q-methodology (e.g. Watts & Stenner, 2005) or repertory grids (e.g. Jancowicz, 2004).
- Throughout the book we refer to small, medium and large projects. To give some examples of what we mean by these terms, we provide examples of student projects from our own universities in Table 1.2.

THE WAY WE'VE STRUCTURED THE BOOK

There are three *types* of questions in qualitative research:

1 your research question(s): what you're trying to find out;
2 the questions you ask participants to generate data (NB: only in qualitative research that collects data from *participants*);
3 the questions you ask of your data, in order to answer your research question(s).

Each of these types of questions is *different*, and they are the focus of different stages in the research process. The book guides you through the entire research process from conceiving and designing qualitative research, through to collecting and analysing qualitative data and writing up, evaluating and disseminating qualitative research, in a more or less sequential order.

- *Section 1: Successfully getting started in qualitative research* deals with some of the basic issues in qualitative research, and covers aspects of planning and design. We recommend *definitely* reading these chapters first if you're (relatively) new to qualitative research, or research at all.
- *Section 2: Successfully collecting qualitative data* covers various methods of data collection. Because interactive methods (where the researcher interacts with participants to generate data) are very common, two chapters are devoted to the

Table 1.2   Sizes of projects in different countries

Country	Small Project	Medium Project	Large Project
UK (Department of Psychology, University of the West of England)	*Final year undergraduate project* • 7½ months part time (PT) • 10,000 word report*	*MSc dissertation* • 1 year PT • 15,000 word report* *MPhil thesis* • 18–36 months full time (FT); • 40,000 word report* *Professional doctorate thesis* • 3 years PT • 30–40,000 word report*	*PhD thesis* • 3–4 years FT • 80,000 word report*
Aotearoa/ New Zealand (Department of Psychology, The University of Auckland)	*Honours dissertation* • 7½ months PT • 8–10,000 word report (length only a guideline)*	*MA/MSc thesis* • 9–12 months FT • 35–40,000 word report	*Professional doctorate (DClinPsy) dissertation* • 3 years PT • 60,000 word report *PhD thesis* • 3–4 years FT • 100,000 word report

*Excludes reference list and appendices

most widely used of these (interview and FGs). We have also included some textual approaches which are *particularly* useful for small-scale, time-limited projects.

- *Section 3: Successfully analysing qualitative data* includes five chapters, first describing the process of **transcription**, then introducing different approaches to analysis and finally moving to a practical discussion and demonstration of the stages of *doing* analysis.
- *Section 4: Successfully completing qualitative research* covers the very important issue of how to ensure that your qualitative research is of an excellent standard, and the dissemination of your results through reports and presentations.

This structure invokes a simple, directional process for qualitative research, from design to completion, like climbing a staircase where you start at one point and finish at the other with no chance of digression. Is qualitative research like this? Not at all, sorry! Qualitative research is instead a *recursive rather than linear* process; it often involves going sideways and backwards, as well as forwards, to reach the answers you're looking for. While you can read the book from end to end, you may also want to move back and forth through it, to match where you are in your learning or research process, and definitely revisit questions of theory (Chapters 2 and 8) as you learn more.

PEDAGOGICAL FEATURES YOU'LL FIND IN THE BOOK

The book contains a range of distinct pedagogical features to assist your learning:

- a succinct *overview* and *summary* of each chapter;
- suggestions for *further resources* relevant to the focus of each chapter (e.g. further reading, online resources, content on the **companion website**);
- *classroom exercises* and *questions for discussion* – usually at least four provided for each chapter;
- *research examples* – demonstrating the use of a particular method;
- *tables* – for easy comparisons and reference;
- *boxes* – to highlight particular bits of information;
- a *glossary* of terms to demystify some of the jargon of qualitative research – the first time a glossary term appears in the text, it will be **emboldened**;
- a set of *research design tables* to aid in determining the scope of your research project and in ensuring an appropriate fit between all aspects of your qualitative project (Tables 3.1–3.3);
- some *material examples* to guide you in producing research materials.

The book is supported and expanded by a thorough **companion website** (www.sage pub.co.uk/braunandclarke) that includes multiple additional resources, including:

- an extensive qualitative data archive (the full **transcript** of the weight and obesity FG we ran for the book; a full transcript and audio file from a second FG on body art; various sample textual **datasets**);
- an extensive collection of material resources which provide examples of different qualitative research documents (some additionally annotated);
- information about an additional textual data collection method (**vignettes**);
- examples of qualitative presentations and posters;
- chapter-by-chapter learning resources, including extended examples of certain boxes and tables;
- self-test multiple-choice questions for each section of the book;
- an interactive flashcard glossary;
- answers to certain chapter exercises;
- links to the Sage journal articles recommended as further reading.

CHAPTER SUMMARY

This chapter:

- provided a brief introduction to what qualitative research is;
- introduced the idea of research paradigms, and outlined a qualitative paradigm;
- briefly summarised the emergence of qualitative research (within psychology);
- explained the all-important qualitative sensibility;

- introduced ourselves and our perspectives;
- introduced the approach and scope of this book.

FURTHER RESOURCES

Further reading:

For accessible introductions to the history and emergence of qualitative psychology, we recommend: Ashworth, P. (2003). The origins of qualitative psychology. In J. A. Smith (Ed.), *Qualitative psychology: A practical guide to research methods* (pp. 4–24). London: Sage.

Howitt, D. (2010). Part 1 Background to qualitative methods in psychology, especially Chapter 2, How qualitative methods developed in psychology. In *Introduction to qualitative methods in psychology*. Harlow: Prentice Hall.

Online resources:

See the *companion website* (**www.sagepub.co.uk/braunandclarke**) for:

- self-test multiple choice questions relating to Section 1;
- the flashcard glossary – test yourself on the definitions of key terms used in this chapter;
- further readings (articles from Sage journals).

Ten fundamentals of qualitative research

OVERVIEW

Qualitative research is about meaning, not numbers
Qualitative research doesn't provide a single answer
Qualitative research treats context as important
Qualitative research can be experiential or critical
Qualitative research is underpinned by ontological assumptions
Qualitative research is underpinned by epistemological assumptions
Qualitative research involves a qualitative methodology
Qualitative research uses all sorts of data
Qualitative research involves 'thinking qualitatively'
Qualitative research values subjectivity and reflexivity
Knowing what you now know, is qualitative research right for your project?

If you're travelling to a completely foreign country, some basic knowledge – such as what language is spoken and what the key aspects of culture and etiquette are – is vital for a successful trip. This chapter provides such an introduction for qualitative research, so that rather than blundering uninitiated into the wilderness of qualitative research, and potentially getting lost or making some fundamental errors, you can walk confidently, with solid ground beneath your feet. We introduce ten basic things you really need to know about qualitative research before you start to do it, and then discuss how you determine the suitability of qualitative research for a project.

Before we begin, it's important to note that qualitative research is a rich, diverse and complex field (see Madill & Gough, 2008). It can aim to do one or more different things: 'give voice' to a group of people or an issue; provide a detailed description of events or experiences; develop theory; interrogate the meaning in texts; identify discourses or demonstrate the discursive features of a text; and/or engage in social critique. Qualitative research is *not* a single thing, although people who don't understand it often treat it as if it were.

QUALITATIVE RESEARCH IS ABOUT MEANING, NOT NUMBERS

In a nutshell, if asked what the *central* thing that distinguishes qualitative research as a field is, our answer would be that it deals with, and is interested in, *meaning*. At its core, qualitative research is about capturing some aspect of the social or psychological world. It records the messiness of real life, puts an organising framework around it and interprets it in some way.

To gain an understanding of what it *is*, it's also helpful to understand what it is *not*. As noted in Chapter 1, qualitative and quantitative research have quite different foci and purposes, and result in quite different knowledge and claims. Box 2.1 provides a useful comparison of two studies on the same broad topic, one using a qualitative approach and one using a quantitative approach; see also Table 1.1 in Chapter 1. Qualitative research is not about testing hypotheses, and not typically about seeking comparisons between groups. This isn't to say you cannot make comparisons in qualitative analysis, but only quantitative methods provide a framework for *testing* difference between groups in any concrete or absolute way. And it does *not* aim for replication, either as a principle, or as the criterion by which the quality of research is established (see Chapter 12). Because of a focus on knowledge as something that comes from, and makes sense within, the contexts it was generated from (see below), qualitative research does not assume the 'same' accounts will always be generated, every time, by *any* researcher.

QUALITATIVE RESEARCH DOESN'T PROVIDE A SINGLE ANSWER

If you love certainty, qualitative research is going to present you with some challenges. Among most qualitative researchers, it's generally agreed upon that there is more than *one* way of making meaning from the data that we analyse, which means there isn't a single 'right' answer. One of the criticisms of qualitative research from some quantitative researchers is that, if that's the case, then our analyses are simply 'made up' and don't tell us anything meaningful; that 'anything goes' in qualitative research. This is emphatically *not* the case. An analysis of qualitative data tells one *story* among many that could be told about the data. The idea that analysis is like a story is a useful concept, but don't think this means it's fictional. Imagine you've gone on holiday with your family. When you come back, your story of the holiday may be quite different to your parents' story – they may have had a fantastic time, while you were bored senseless. Each is an equally true story of the holiday. Qualitative researchers recognise that the data analyses we produce are like such stories – they are partial, and they are **subjective** (see below). But any good analysis needs to be plausible, coherent and grounded in the data. You don't need to be claiming to tell the only or absolute truth to be telling a compelling 'truth' about your data.

QUALITATIVE RESEARCH TREATS CONTEXT AS IMPORTANT

Another key tenet of qualitative research is an appreciation that information and knowledge always come from somewhere. Qualitative data are understood as accounts that are *not* produced in the ether. Instead, they are seen to be produced in particular contexts, by participants who come from, and are located within, specific contexts. What does that mean? It means that, in contrast to the positivist/quantitative ideal of being able to obtain 'uncontaminated' knowledge, with all biases removed, qualitative research recognises that these exist, and incorporates them into the analysis. It recognises the subjectivity of the data we analyse, and the analyses we produce. Subjectivity basically refers to the idea that what we see and understand reflects our identities and experiences – the contexts we've existed in, a concept sometimes also referred to as '*perspectival* subjectivity' (Kvale, 1996: 212). Qualitative research does not treat this subjectivity as **bias** to be eliminated from research, but tends to involve contextualised analysis, which takes this into account.

QUALITATIVE RESEARCH CAN BE EXPERIENTIAL OR CRITICAL

Qualitative research is exploratory, open-ended and organic, and produces in-depth, rich and detailed data from which to make claims. As a field, it can be divided into two broad camps (Reicher, 2000), which we term experiential and critical. **Experiential qualitative research** validates the meanings, views, perspectives, experiences and/or practices expressed in the data. We call it experiential because participants' **interpretations** are prioritised, accepted and focused on, rather than being used as a basis for analysing something else. **Critical qualitative research** takes an interrogative stance towards the meanings or experiences expressed in the data, and uses them to explore some other phenomenon. Typically, it seeks to understand the factors influencing, and the effects of, the particular meanings or **representations** expressed. We call it critical because it doesn't take data at face value. This means that analysts' interpretations become more important than participants'. We'll explain these two camps in a bit more detail.

EXPERIENTIAL QUALITATIVE RESEARCH: TELLING IT 'LIKE IT IS'

Experiential research is driven by a desire to know people's own perspectives and meanings, to 'get inside' people's heads as it were, and to prioritise them in reporting the research. Research becomes a process of collecting such information, and then putting an organising, interpretative framework around what is expressed in the data.

BOX 2.1   COMPARING A QUALITATIVE AND QUANTITATIVE APPROACH

Here we contrast two studies (Christianson, Lalos, Westman, & Johansson, 2007; Herlitz & Ramstedt, 2005) on the same (broad) topic – sexual risk – conducted in the same country (Sweden) to give you a sense of the different sorts of understandings that are generated by quantitative and qualitative research.

Quantitative Study	Qualitative Study
Assessment of sexual behaviour, sexual attitudes, and sexual risk in Sweden (1989–2003) (Herlitz & Ramstedt, 2005).	'Eyes wide shut' – sexuality and risk in HIV-positive youth in Sweden (Christianson et al., 2007).
Research aim: to identify changes in the general Swedish population's attitudes, knowledge, beliefs and behaviours related to HIV/AIDS, over time. Specific hypotheses: a) that sexually risky behaviour would have decreased; b) that attitudes to sex would be more conservative, due to risk of HIV/AIDS.	*Research aim/question*: to explore perceptions of sexual risk taking among HIV positive youth, and their understandings of why they contracted HIV.
Sample: a random sample, stratified for age, was generated from the general population in 1989, 1994, 1997 and 2003 (n = 4000 each year), and a sample in 2000 randomly selected but weighted toward urban dwellers (n = 6000). Overall response rate was 63%, and total n = 13,762.	*Sample*: a **purposive** sample of 10 HIV positive Swedish residents (five female; five male; seven born in Sweden; three born abroad) aged between 17 and 24. Participants were recruited through three HIV clinics/organisations.
Method of data collection: quantitative questionnaire (closed response options), consisting of 85–90 items, delivered by mail to sample. Up to three reminders were sent.	*Method of data collection*: in-depth semi-structured interviews (see Chapter 3); tape recorded; transcribed 'verbatim' (all utterances transcribed as spoken).
Method of data analysis: statistical. Multiple logistical regression, a statistical method that allows determination of the (relative) influence of multiple variables (e.g. age, sex, education level) on a particular outcome (e.g. practising unsafe sex), in order to predict the likelihood of that outcome.	*Method of data analysis*: grounded theory (see Chapter 8). **Coding** and analysis began from the first interview. Analysis involved multiple stages of (open) coding and re-coding and organising the data into core categories and subcategories; for credibility, four participants also read and commented on the preliminary analysis (Chapter 12 discusses **'member checking'**).

Key results: neither hypothesis supported: significant increases in casual sexual contacts without condoms, and multiple partners, between 1989 and 2003; attitudes to 'sex' outside relationships more permissive in 2003 than 1989; attitudes were more liberal, with regard to acceptability of casual sex, than behaviour; youngest participants *more* likely to use condoms for casual sex than older participants.

Conclusions: need for continuous, extensive sexuality education to help reduce sexual risk which can be controlled by behaviour (e.g., condom-use).

This type of research can show: changes in sexual attitudes and practices (at a population level); factors that might predict particular outcomes a researcher might be interested in – can be useful for targeting interventions.

This type of research cannot show: the meanings of different experiences; *why* these changes may have occurred.

Evaluation: this sort of research is useful for mapping large population-level patterns in behaviour – it provides a 'breadth' of knowledge. The focus on association between factors can be very useful for targeting interventions. However, it does not provide 'deep' or 'rich' understanding around sexual attitudes, perceptions of risk, or behaviour, and so cannot offer understandings of *why* people do what they do.

Key results: identified two main clusters of factors that limited the individuals' possibilities for agency in sexual interactions: a) 'sociocultural blinds' referred to factors which make safer sex a hard topic to broach, like the idea that 'being in love' protects you from sexual risk; b) 'from consensual to forced sex' referred to factors within consensual encounters, like pleasure and trust, and coercion, which resulted in risky sex.

Conclusions: the data and analysis emphasise the context-bound nature of sexual experiences and practices, and the way power and gender inflect most experiences. Contrary to the idea that informs health promotion, of a rational agent who makes (informed) choices about their behaviour, these accounts show that agency can be compromised by various factors beyond the individual's control.

This type of research can show: the richness of (reported) real lived experiences; nuances and diversity within accounts; patterns across accounts. Can offer insights into the lived complexity of negotiating safer sex practices. Can help understand how and why young people are at risk for HIV.

This type of research cannot show: general patterns across the population; cause and effect relationships.

Evaluation: this sort of research is useful for providing a compelling sense of what sexual risk/safety (or any other topic) really is like, for individual people in their lives. It provides both rich and deep understandings of the ways people make sense of, and put into practice, scientific 'facts' about sexual risk and safety. While it can inform interventions, it cannot be generalised to *all* people, and so cannot be used to make population-level claims about sexual safety and risk.

There are many reasons why a qualitative approach is more suitable than a quantitative one when trying to understand people's meanings:

- it allows us to retain a focus on people's *own* framing around issues, and their own terms of reference, rather than having it pre-framed by the researcher (e.g. items in a questionnaire);
- it allows a far richer (fuller, multi-faceted) or deeper understanding of a phenomenon than using numbers, not least because the complexity of people's meanings or experiences is revealed and retained in qualitative data;
- reality, meaning and experience for people often tend to be messy and contradictory; qualitative research can 'embrace this messiness' (Shaw et al., 2008: 188). Participants' language can reveal both 'mess' and contradiction in a way quantitative methods cannot;
- as it can be open-ended, exploratory, organic and flexible, it can evolve to suit the needs of the project (such as accommodating unanticipated ideas expressed by participants);
- by collecting and analysing such data, we can find out things that we might never have imagined; things that would be lost using quantitative methods. This means the scope of knowledge and understanding is opened up considerably.

What we can understand with qualitative research is not limited by the researcher's imagination and existing knowledge in the field. Instead, participants' experiences and meanings (personal and wider societal meanings) *drive* experiential qualitative research. For example, researchers wanting to understand more about young women and eating might conduct interviews or focus groups (FGs) to understand the meanings that 'food' has for a small group of young women, the place it has in their lives, and their experiences of eating (or not eating) food, instead of getting young women to complete a quantitative survey about food and eating which would involve them responding to categories and options pre-determined by the researcher.

So experiential qualitative research seeks to make sense of how the world is seen, understood and experienced from the person's perspective. Language is treated as if it provides a window to the person's interior; it is understood as the way people report their experiences, practices and meanings in a straightforward fashion; it is the vehicle researchers use to access and make sense of that inner world. Research often involves what is talked about as 'mapping' or 'giving voice' to 'the rich tapestry of people's lives' – analysis provides 'rich' or 'thick' descriptions of meaning and experience (see Box 2.2).

BOX 2.2   'THICK' OR 'RICH' DESCRIPTION

The idea that qualitative research should provide thick description came from US anthropologist Clifford Geertz's writing about ethnography in the 1970s (Geertz, 1973). Description was 'thick' when contexts of behaviour were described; it was 'thin' when context was excluded. Subsequently taken up in different ways throughout qualitative research, the idea now is often used synonymously with the term 'rich' to refer to detailed descriptions of the object of study, in which the complexity and contradictions of participants' stories of their lives are included.

CRITICAL QUALITATIVE RESEARCH: INTERROGATING THE STORIES WE COLLECT

In critical qualitative research, in contrast, the focus is not on language as a means to get *inside* the person's head, but on language as it is used 'out there' in the world. Its interest is in how language gives shape to certain social realities – and the impact of these. While critical qualitative research is essentially about language as a mode of communication, interest shifts away from only looking at the semantic content (the objects the words refer to). Rather, language is understood as the main mode by which the reality of our world is *created*, and so researchers within this tradition use language to explore the ways different versions of reality are created. They take what is called a constitutive or productive view of language; its central premise is that language creates rather than reflects reality (Weedon, 1997). For example, a project concerned with young women and eating might examine the ways young women talk about food in ways which **construct** distinct categories around different food types and eating patterns and habits (obvious ones might be healthy/unhealthy; good/bad; fattening/non-fattening; controlled/uncontrolled). Unlike experiential qualitative research, critical qualitative research doesn't see such talk as offering a window into how these young women *really feel* about food/eating. Rather, talk is seen as depicting a reality about food that they are *creating* or *constructing* through the way they talk about it, and which reflects broader ways of understanding available in their sociocultural contexts (see Chapter 7 for more on this approach).

Within this approach, research can broadly be divided between that interested in **representation** and **construction** and that interested in **language practice**. An interest in representation and/or construction is an interest in factors which shape or create meaning and the effects and implications of particular patterns of meaning. Language is one of the main means by which representation and construction occur; qualitative research is therefore ideal for researchers interested in these. Qualitative research is used to understand the ways language (or imagery) tells *particular* stories about **research objects**. (Research objects – the things we study – can be concrete things, like clothing, or abstract things, like love.) To continue the previous example, a project concerned with young women and eating might analyse the ways weight and dieting are represented in teen magazines, and the explicit and implicit ideas about food, weight and eating that exist there. One common representation might be of food as something that is a threat to health, self and well-being – with the implication that eating should be approached with caution, with the right types of food consumed in a controlled fashion. A key assumption is that there are numerous ways objects could be represented, and that different representations have different implications for individuals and society (Hall, 1997). For instance, the representations of body size as the result of genetics and hormones or of individual eating and exercise behaviour carry quite different inferences about how a person can or should feel, and indeed behave, regarding their body size. For a fat person, a genetic/hormonal account means that they are seen as not responsible for their fatness; an eating/exercise account makes them potentially responsible and blameworthy. Some research in this tradition involves the practice of **deconstruction** (Norris, C., 2002a; Parker, 1988), whereby texts are 'taken apart' and interrogated for the dominant and hidden assumptions (or oppositions) they rely on.

In terms of *language practice*, qualitative research seeks to examine the ways language is used to create particular versions of reality. The analytic focus ranges widely: some is quite micro, with a focus on the *detail* of language use, such as the function of particular features of talk and texts (Hutchby, 2002). Hong Kong linguist Amy Tsui (1991), for instance, examined the ways the expression 'I don't know' functions in conversation not (just) to express a cognitive state, but to avoid or ameliorate certain delicate activities, such as a disagreement or making an assessment about something (see also Potter, 1997). Some is more macro, and considers the ways language produces a certain version of reality. For example, researchers have examined the ways people deploy different constructions of identity at different points in a conversation, identifying that these serve different purposes for the speaker (as Edley & Wetherell, 1997, show around heterosexual masculinities). For example, consider a fat man talking to a doctor about his desire to lose some weight. At one point in the conversation he may use language which suggests he is an 'in control' independent person who can choose to act in ways which will determine his weight. At another point, he may use language which suggests his fatness is not his 'fault', and that it results from forces beyond his control, such as biology or culture. Each construction has different implications, allowing the doctor to blame him, or not, for his weight, and to feel confident offering one of a range of weight-loss suggestions.

A BRIEF SUMMARY, AND AN INTRODUCTION TO THEORY

So qualitative research is concerned with words, and sometimes images, and is typically either experiential or critical. Each camp contains diverse interests (e.g. the critical camp is concerned with representation, construction or language practices). In whatever form it takes, qualitative research accesses the richness of the worlds we all exist in – whether they are the worlds that exist 'in our heads', or the social and physical worlds external to us. Regardless of which camp it's in, qualitative research overall tends to come from a different theoretical position than quantitative and experimental research. And then different qualitative methodologies also have their own particular theoretical frameworks and do different sorts of things with data. In setting out a framework for research practice, methodology relies on **ontology** and **epistemology** (Ramazanoglu & Holland, 2002). These complicated-sounding words refer, respectively, to theories about the nature of reality or being and about the nature of knowledge. Each demarcates what can and

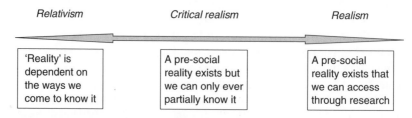

Figure 2.1 The ontology continuum

cannot count as meaningful knowledge and informs our methodology and the process of producing that knowledge. Qualitative research often departs radically from quantitative research in both of these.

QUALITATIVE RESEARCH IS UNDERPINNED BY ONTOLOGICAL ASSUMPTIONS

Ontological positions specify the relationship between the world and our human interpretations and practices. Ontology determines whether or not we think reality exists entirely *separate from* human practices and understandings – including the research we conduct to find such things out – or whether we think it cannot be separated from human practices, and so knowledge is always going to reflect our perspective. There are many variations, which range along a continuum from a view where 'reality' is entirely independent of human ways of knowing about it – what has been described as a 'mind-independent truth' (Tebes, 2005) (known as **realism**) – to a view where reality is entirely depends on human interpretation and knowledge (known as **relativism**) (see Figure 2.1).

Realism assumes a knowable world, which is comprehensible through research – that *the truth* (and there is only one) is 'out there' and can be accessed by the appropriate application of research techniques. In its most extreme or 'naive' version, it has been referred to as 'a correspondence theory of truth' (Madill, Jordan, & Shirley, 2000: 3), where what we observe is assumed to mirror truthfully what is there. Realism is the ontology underpinning most quantitative research, but it rarely informs qualitative research. Relativism, in contrast, argues that there are multiple constructed *realities*, rather than a single, pre-social reality or mind-independent truth, and that we can never get beyond these constructions (Cromby & Nightingale, 1999). Rather than being universal, what is 'real' and 'true' differs across time and context, so that what we can know reflects where and how knowledge is generated. A relativist ontology underpins some qualitative approaches, including some versions of discourse analysis, but it rarely informs quantitative research. Somewhere in between sit *critical realist* positions, now quite commonly adopted in qualitative research, which also invoke a real and knowable world which sits 'behind' the subjective and socially-located knowledge a researcher can access (Madill et al., 2000). Because knowledge is viewed as socially influenced, it is thought to reflect a separate reality that we can only *partially* access. The critical realist position holds that we need to claim that some 'authentic' reality exists to produce knowledge that might 'make a difference' (Stainton Rogers & Stainton Rogers, 1997). For example, we would need to be able to claim that the shame and embarrassment that (some) fat people experience in airline seats (Farrell, 2011) is *real* to produce knowledge that might mean airlines change standard seating sizes. In this position, an external reality (people's feeling of shame) provides a *foundation* for knowledge. A critical realist position underpins a number of different qualitative approaches, including some versions of **thematic analysis**, **grounded theory**, discourse analysis and **interpretative phenomenological analysis** (IPA). These different positions are illustrated by analogy in Box 2.3.

BOX 2.3   ONTOLOGY THROUGH THE LOOKING GLASS

The analogy of looking at a view can be useful to illustrate realism, relativism and critical realism. *Realism* would be akin to looking at a view through a perfect glass window in your house. The information you access from this perfect glass window corresponds exactly to what really is outside – if you go outside, the path and garden you have seen would be there; you can walk along the path, smell the roses, and thus verify the truth of what you have viewed. Your window has given you a way to determine the reality that exists beyond it, a way to measure what is there. *Relativism* is better captured by the idea of prisoners looking at a view from their prison cells. Prisoners housed in different cells will see different views of the world outside the prison, but there is no way of prioritising one prisoner's view as *more real* than another's. Moreover, although the views appear real, they could be a projection or a hologram. A prisoner has no way to ascertain the truth of the information they have about what is outside the prison. It is impossible to step outside to determine if their view corresponds to the real landscape outside; there is no way of measuring the relationship between the physical landscape and the perception of it, and thus no way of knowing how true it is. *Critical realism* would be like looking at a view where the only way to see it is through a prism, so what is seen is nuanced by the shape of the prism (the prism is culture, history, etc.). If you could just get rid of that prism, you'd be able to see what lies behind it (the truth), but you never can get beyond it.

Where you sit on the ontology continuum determines whether you think that you *cannot* remove the process of knowledge production from what you're studying (relativism – we can only ever view the scene from some perspective, and never know if the knowledge we have of it is the only or 'right' one) or whether you think you *can* (realism – we can ascertain the true nature of the scene if only we use the right tools, i.e. look through a *perfect* glass window).

QUALITATIVE RESEARCH IS UNDERPINNED BY EPISTEMOLOGICAL ASSUMPTIONS

The central concern of epistemology is what counts as legitimate 'knowledge': in a world where all sorts of knowledge exist, how do we know which to trust, which are meaningful? As an illustration, consider two ideas about what we are like as persons: personality theory and astrology. Astrology tells us our 'essence' comes from the alignment of astronomical bodies at the time of our birth – most basically, through year (in the Chinese horoscope) or month (in the western horoscope). Both Virginia and Victoria are (western astrological) Librans, which means we have high aesthetic senses, are hopelessly indecisive, hate conflict and crave harmony. Astrology makes predictions on our daily (and indeed lifetime) experiences, based on planetary and other alignment. Such astrological predictions are popular, and feature in most western mainstream media. In contrast, personality theory, developed out of scientific psychology, argues that psychometric testing can determine our location along certain dimensions of personality (the most 'robust' being the 'big five' traits: neuroticism, extraversion, agreeableness, conscientiousness and openness to experience; Digman, 1990). These traits form a stable core essence of who we are as a person, and can be used to predict how we behave in the world. While many in the contemporary west might 'scoff' at astrology (less than a quarter of Britons believe in horoscopes, Gill, Hadaway, & Marler, 1998), and dismiss it as an invalid way to theorise and understand human personality, far fewer would question the validity of psychological science. Barring some 'critical psychologists' (see Burr, 2002), not many westerners question the idea that we each *have* a personality. This is because scientific epistemology is the dominant epistemological position in the west at present: true knowledge is determined by science; other forms of knowledge are framed as biased, untrustworthy and 'unscientific'. So epistemology determines *what* counts as valid, trustworthy, 'true' knowledge within a community and, conversely, what is seen as not valid knowledge. If we lived in a culture where true knowledge was determined not by science, but by astrologers, the theory of personality might be treated with the same derision that astrology is by many people.

So epistemology is about the nature of knowledge, and addresses the question of *what* it is possible to know. What counts as knowledge determines *how* meaningful knowledge can be generated (and what it is seen to represent). Epistemology can also be realist or relativist – a realist epistemological position assumes that it is possible to obtain 'the truth' through valid knowledge production; a relativist epistemological position states that, theoretically, knowledge is always perspectival and therefore a singular, absolute truth is impossible. A basic distinction between epistemological positions is whether we think reality (be that external or personal) is *discovered* through the process of research, or whether we think reality is *created* through the process of research. In one camp, we could characterise the researcher as archaeologist who digs to uncover a reality (knowledge) that exists quite independent of their practice (the [post-] positivist camp). In the other camp, we could characterise the researcher as a sculptor who creates a reality with their sculpture, so is involved in the production *of* that reality (the constructionist camp). We will briefly outline these two broad epistemological positions found within psychology and the social sciences, and a third, **contextualism** (Henwood & Pidgeon, 1994).

POSITIVISM

Positivism assumes a straightforward relationship between the world and our perception of it. Closely aligned with **empiricism**, it separates out the practice of observation, the observer and that which is observed, and requires demonstration of reality through objective (unbiased) collection of data. Valid knowledge is obtained through the application of established scientific methods which control variables and remove various forms of contamination and bias. Appropriate application will discover 'the truth that is out there'. In the social sciences, it would now be hard to find people who adhere to a pure form of positivism; instead a less pure version termed *postpositivism* tends to dominate. **Postpositivism**, which first emerged from the critiques of science by scholars like Karl Popper (Popper, 1959), still holds onto the search for *the truth* and sees this as, by and large, achievable, but acknowledges that researchers are influenced by their contexts, and influence research – that facts are not neutral reflections of the truth, but are theoretically influenced (Clark, 1998; Guba & Lincoln, 2005). Where this differs from constructionist epistemologies is that postpositivist researchers still believe in, and aim to know, that singular truth, and thus seek to control for or remove subjective influences on knowledge production as much as possible. Qualitative research is sometimes undertaken within this paradigm, and some argue that postpositivism should take its place as an appropriate epistemology for qualitative research (Michell, 2004); others disagree.

CONSTRUCTIONISM

Other approaches question idea that knowledge is an objective (or as objective as possible) reflection of reality – but instead see our ways of knowing the world as tied to the (social) world in which we live. *Constructionist* epistemologies argue that the world and what we know of it do not reflect an 'out there' true nature of the world (or an 'in there' true psychology (waiting to be discovered, but that what we know of the world, and ourselves and other objects in the world is constructed (produced) through various discourses and systems of meaning we all reside within (Berger & Luckmann, 1967; Burr, 2003; Gergen, 1985, 1999). As these change, truth changes, meaning there is no *one* truth which a certain method allows access to – there are *knowledges*, rather than knowledge. The terms in which the world is understood are seen to be related to specific social, cultural contexts. Knowledges are viewed as social artefacts, and are therefore seen as social, cultural, moral, **ideological** and political. A critical stance tends to be taken regarding perceived truths and taken-for-granted knowledge. Given this position, there are numerous possible ways to create truths. However, constructionism as an epistemological position is not saying that knowledge is just 'made up' and 'anything goes' (nor that there is nothing 'outside the text', meaning no material or experiential reality exists; Edley, 2001b). What it is saying is that knowledge of how things are is a product of how we come to understand it – for example, the 'knowledge' that people really do have personalities is the product of a long history of theorising 'the person' and personality research, rather than independent fact (Burr, 2002). The process of knowledge production is still (often) empirical in that it is grounded in data, and understanding of some kind is sought. Where this differs from realist and positivist positions is that there is no singular underlying reality that is theorised as providing the *foundation* for true knowledge – constructionism is a non-foundational view of knowledge.

CONTEXTUALISM

Sitting between these poles, and somewhat akin to **critical realism**, contextualism is another epistemology which has a foot in both camps (Henwood & Pidgeon, 1994). Tebes cites Pepper (1942) to describe the central metaphor of contextualism as 'the human act in context' (2005: 216). It can be seen as a version of constructionism (constructionism-[*very*]-lite), in that it doesn't assume a *single* reality, and sees knowledge as emerging from contexts (hence the name) and reflecting the researcher's positions, so that it is local, situated, and therefore always provisional (Madill et al., 2000; Tebes, 2005). But it does retain an interest in understanding *truth*, and hence has a realist dimension. It argues that while no single method can get to *the truth* (Tebes, 2005), knowledge *will* be true (valid) in certain contexts. So it retains a notion of 'the truth' which constructionism rejects.

ONTOLOGY, EPISTEMOLOGY, METHODOLOGY AND METHOD

Ontology and epistemology are far from independent of each other, and they lead into particular methodologies and together constrain the methods that are appropriate for your research. For instance, if you take a relativist/constructionist position where you don't think that 'personality' or 'attitudes' are stable constructs that reside in people's heads and exist independently of context, or the process of finding out about them, you simply cannot 'measure' them using personality tests or attitude scales. Instead of seeing 'personality' or 'attitudes' as individual variables (the realist/positivist take), they can be understood as things which become meaningful as we present ourselves in the world and interact with others, which can be understood, captured and analysed by looking at language and discourse (see Burr, 2002; Potter & Wetherell, 1987). The point here is not that one of these approaches is inherently *right* and one is *wrong* (although many people align with one or the other and indeed think that), but that different sorts of knowledge are generated within different theoretical and methodological frameworks – as US psychologist Jeanne Marecek (2003: 54) has observed, it's about asking (and answering) the question: 'What kind of truth am I interested in hearing?' What's important is coherence within your overall research design (see Chapter 3).

QUALITATIVE RESEARCH INVOLVES A QUALITATIVE METHODOLOGY

Two terms often used interchangeably when talking about research are method and methodology. But they are different. Method refers to a tool or *technique* for collecting or analysing data: the interview and the survey are methods of collecting data; thematic analysis and analysis of variance are methods of analysing data. Methods are quite specific and applied in specific ways. Methodology is broader, and refers to the *framework* within which our research is conducted. It consists of theories and practices for how we go about conducting research. It provides a package of assumptions about what counts as research and how it is conducted, and the sorts of claims you can make about your data. It tells us which methods are appropriate for our research and which are not. Methodology can be understood as a *theory* of how research needs to proceed, to produce valid knowledge about the psychological and social world. It is what *makes our research make sense*, both in terms of design, and in terms of process.

Methodology provides a *framework* for making a series of decisions about your research, including:

- How can participants be selected?
- What methods of data collection and analysis are appropriate?
- Who can or should conduct research?
- What is the role of the researcher?

The obvious question, then, is what are the features of a qualitative methodology? Unfortunately, there's no single answer. One thing you'll quickly learn about qualitative research is that simple straightforward answers aren't that common – sorry! This is because 'qualitative inquiry is rife with ambiguity' (Patton, 2002: 242), because there are lots of methodologies, and because many qualitative data analysis 'methods' are more accurately understood as methodologies. For example, IPA is much more than a method of analysing data – it sets out a whole framework for conducting a study; grounded theory and discourse analysis likewise. Although each qualitative methodology is unique, they share many similar features, like siblings in a big family. And like siblings, some methodologies are more similar than others, and 'get along' better with other methodologies (they share similar core assumptions). This stems from the fact that they all come under the umbrella of a qualitative paradigm (see Box 2.4).

BOX 2.4   METHODOLOGIES AND PARADIGMS

A qualitative paradigm provides the essential – and generic – criteria for what counts as qualitative research. But then each specific methodology varies from this to provide a framework for how an actual study is conducted and the data interpreted. Different methodologies share many features from the generic qualitative paradigm, but not necessarily all, and they may be expressed differently. Think of the relationship as akin to the difference between the generic criteria for making a cake, and the particulars of a specific recipe. A cake generically consists of sugar, butter, eggs, flour and a raising agent. The sugar and butter are creamed, the eggs beaten in and the dry ingredients gently added. The mixture is poured into a single tin, and baked immediately in a pre-heated oven. Almost any cake that is made will resemble this process, but the specifics will vary: butter may be replaced with oil; the eggs may be separated and the whites beaten first; different ingredients (e.g. chocolate, carrots, vanilla) may be added for flavour and texture. The resulting outcome is recognisably a cake, but is not identical to other cakes, either in making or in outcome. Similarly, research conducted using a qualitative methodology like discursive psychology is recognisably qualitative, but quite different from research conducted using a different qualitative methodology, such as IPA (see Chapter 8).

BRIEF SUMMARY

Phew! You've survived a whirlwind introduction to some of the fundamental things you need to know about what qualitative research is and what it is not, and made it through the most complex discussion of theory you'll find in the book. You should by now understand that qualitative research is more than just collecting and analysing qualitative data; it refers to a cluster of different methodologies which offer frameworks for conducting research and producing valid knowledge. What a qualitative paradigm tells us is that useful knowledge can be generated by looking at meaning, with small samples, and that the researcher should not theorise themselves as absent or removed from this process. It also locates knowledge as contextual, and always partial, and as linked to particular theoretical and methodological commitments.

QUALITATIVE RESEARCH USES ALL SORTS OF DATA

Data are the bedrock of the social sciences – they are what we use to answer the questions we have, and generate new and useful understandings of phenomena in the world. Without data, we'd all be theorists. Not that there's anything wrong with being a theorist, but the social sciences are located within an empirical tradition, where knowledge is grounded in data. Qualitative research is just as *empirical* as quantitative, as its knowledge generation is also based on data.

Within qualitative research, the data you collect are relatively 'naturalistic' in the sense that they aren't put into pre-existing categories – they are not pre-coded and categorised at the point of collection (like responses to a scale on a questionnaire would be) (Lincoln & Guba, 1985). The **raw** (uncoded) **data** retain the messiness of real life. However, they are not necessarily 'natural' in that we ourselves often *generate* the data we use (what counts as **naturalistic data** is a debate in some areas of qualitative psychology, e.g. Potter & Hepburn, 2007; Speer, 2002a). The possibilities for data are seemingly endless: the most common – and very useful – methods of data collection are individual interviews (for examples, see Ahmed, Reavey, & Majumdar, 2009; Whitehead & Kurz, 2009) and group discussions (e.g. see Augoustinos, Tuffin, & Every, 2005; Schulze & Angermeyer, 2003) – done face-to-face, over the phone or via email. Data could also come from sources like diaries (e.g. Milligan, Bingley, & Gatrell, 2005); **qualitative surveys** (e.g. Toerien & Wilkinson, 2004); parliamentary debates (e.g. Ellis & Kitzinger, 2002); women's magazines (e.g. Roy, 2008); internet discussion sites (e.g. Wilson, Weatherall, & Butler, 2004); television documentaries (e.g. Hodgetts & Chamberlain, 1999); dinner-time conversations (e.g. Wiggins, 2004); or even the text on a tube of children's toothpaste (e.g. Parker, 1996). Others are increasingly using visual imagery as well – from photo-elicitation techniques, where photographs are used in conjunction with interviews (e.g. Oliffe & Bottorff, 2007), to the use of the visual in its own right (e.g. see contributions to a special issue of *Qualitative Research in Psychology* on this topic, Frith et al., 2005) – but, as noted in Chapter 1, we focus primarily on text in this book.

SO WHAT 'COUNTS' AS DATA?

So with seemingly endless possibilities, how can we know what 'counts' as data? Data come into being either through *production*, where we generate them ourselves by what we get participants to do, or through *selection* from existing materials, such as media reports or blogs. With production, we develop criteria for *how* we generate the data, and *who* we have as participants; with selection, we develop criteria through which we select a particular collection of instances, which become our data. Sampling criteria are covered in the next chapter, alongside the question of *how much data* one needs – a tricky question in qualitative research (Morse, 2000) (see the design tables, Tables 3.1–3.3, in Chapter 3).

NOT ALL DATA ARE CREATED EQUAL

How do you know if data are any 'good'? If they are well selected (see Chapter 3), that's a start. If you can easily see things to say about them, that's a good indication, too. Another aspect that often gets talked about is 'rich' or 'shallow' data – with **rich data** generally better. Shallow or 'thin' data are those which only really access the surface of a topic, the everyday or obvious stories about it; rich data are those which offer a more thorough, thoughtful or unexpected commentary on the topic. Imagine two friends had eaten a meal they'd enjoyed. When you asked what it was like, one said, 'My steak was really good', and the other said, 'I had an asparagus and lemon risotto and it was incredible. It combined different colours, flavours and textures so that it was a whole eating experience, heaven to my eyes, nose and mouth. For me, texture's the most important thing in a meal, even more than flavour. The asparagus was barely cooked while the rice melted, and so it was crunchy and creamy all at once. I couldn't stop eating it, but had to slow down to savour every mouthful so it wouldn't end. The only problem was, they didn't give me enough. It's one of the best things I've ever eaten.' The first description is 'thin'; the second, 'rich'.

Rich data are preferred in qualitative research. They are data which reach below the surface, and allow the researcher to gain a deep understanding of the topic of interest. They can be generated, for instance, by a participant who reflects on their experience in a thoughtful manner (Morse, 2000), by an interviewer who asks critical probing questions, or by text which articulates in depth the dominant meanings about a topic (or goes beyond them). Importantly, richness of data is also determined by context, purpose and mode of data collection: what counts as rich in a qualitative survey would be quite different from what counts as rich in an in-depth interview. Unfortunately, it's hard to provide an absolute definition of what makes data rich, but with experience you will know it when you see it. The weight and obesity FG on the *companion website* contains rich data – see Sally's first extract (starting line 79), and how we coded it for our IPA example (Table 9.3 in Chapter 9) for an example of rich data.

To be *good*, data also have to serve the purpose of the research. What is primarily important is that the data allow you to address your research question (see Chapter 3). To continue the idea of healthy eating, if you are interested in what might stop men from 'healthy eating', for instance (e.g. Gough & Conner, 2006), the best place to start looking is with men themselves, and what they say. Regardless of what data we use, we always need to be able to justify our choice of data: why, and how, did we select or produce them, and why are they useful to enable us to answer our research question?

QUALITATIVE RESEARCH INVOLVES 'THINKING QUALITATIVELY'

Research is a culture, and different cultures exist for different research paradigms and methodologies. After a while you become enculturated, knowing the language and implicitly understanding the norms and practices of a particular research culture. If you've studied much psychology, for instance, you're probably already somewhat enculturated into another research culture: a '"quantitative" culture' (Gough, Lawton, Maddill, & Stratton, 2003: 5), with the scientific experiment as pinnacle of research excellence. This culture includes norms and expectations about hypotheses, objectivity, bias, (statistical) significance, replication, and so on. Reading that form of psychology requires understanding these concepts; conducting that form of research (well) requires putting those into practice; writing it up means using the appropriate language and style. Qualitative research culture is quite different (e.g. see Marecek, 2003) and part of becoming a qualitative researcher is learning to *think qualitatively* (Anderson, 2008; Morse & Richards, 2002). In this section we discuss some of the language and concepts of qualitative research, to start you on that process.

As we've discussed already, the purpose of qualitative research is to understand or explore meaning and the ways people make meaning, rather than to *prove* a theory or determine a relationship between factors. This means that while qualitative research has research questions (see Chapter 3), and aims and objectives (although sometimes expressed in a different language), and even theories it examines, it does not typically have hypotheses which are empirically tested and (dis)proved. So in developing a qualitative orientation and project, you want 'understanding' as your key driver. For instance, your project might have 'understanding fat women's emotional experiences around clothes shopping' (Colls, 2006) as its aim.

Once you have analysed your data, how should you talk about your analytic insights? Quantitative research uses the language of *results* and *findings*, terms which can be problematic for qualitative research, as are words like revealed, discovered and uncovered. This is because they all stem from the (positivist empiricist) model of research as a process of excavation – research as archaeology – where, if you dig deeply, using the appropriate skills and tools, in an organised fashion, you will discover the truth hidden within. Qualitative methods stem from a different model of research, which is more akin to the process of sculpting or patchwork quilting (some suggest the qualitative researcher should be seen as a quilt-maker; Denzin & Lincoln, 2005a). Let's consider the patchwork analogy. You start from a position where you have lots of shapes of material (your data), some of which are similar to others, and some of which are different, and then you work at arranging them in to a particular pattern to tell a particular story (the patterned quilt – i.e. analysis – you produce). This metaphor is useful in dealing with the suggestion that 'anything goes' in qualitative research. While we could make different patterns on our quilt, through using the fabric (data) in different ways, the end product would still represent what we had started with (our raw data). Furthermore, some quilted patterns will 'work' (e.g. look great, be coherent and well organised), while others won't (e.g. look bad, be random or chaotic); all will be constrained by the raw materials – just like with qualitative data analysis. While this is partly a matter of taste, it is not just individual – the community agrees in general on what counts as *good* and *bad* quilting (competitions get judged, prizes get awarded) – there are standards; the same goes for qualitative analysis (see Chapter 12).

One of the best ways to learn the language of qualitative research is through reading qualitative research, but keep in mind that what we've introduced here is best practice for qualitative research reporting. People don't always do this; even very experienced qualitative researchers can find it difficult to 'let go' of their quantitative training, and sometimes academic journals, particularly ones less welcoming to Big Q qualitative research, may require the use of more quantitative language.

QUALITATIVE RESEARCH VALUES SUBJECTIVITY AND REFLEXIVITY

There are two other important issues to grasp before becoming immersed in qualitative research culture. The first of these is subjectivity in research; the second, closely related, is reflexivity. Within a positivist-empiricist model of research, where objectivity is valued, avoiding bias is a prime concern. Bias refers to the idea that the researcher might (inadvertently) have influenced the results, so that they cannot be trusted. This could be through poor sample selection, poor instrument design, or their research practice (for example, the idea of interviewer effects, where characteristics of the interviewer can be shown to influence data collection; e.g. Singer, Frankel, & Glassman, 1983). Within a qualitative paradigm, the question 'How might the research be biased?' fails to make sense, as all research activity is seen as influenced, and the influence of the researcher is just one of many influences, albeit often a significant one.

In the same way objectivity is valued in a quantitative paradigm, subjectivity is positively valued in the qualitative paradigm (e.g. consider books like Fine, 1992; Hollway, 1989). Research is understood as a *subjective* process; we, as researchers, bring our own histories, values, assumptions, perspectives, politics and mannerisms into the research – and we cannot leave those at the door. The topics we find interesting to research, and ways we ask questions about them, the aspects of our data that excite us – these (and many other factors) reflect who we are; our *subjectivity*. Therefore, any knowledge produced is going to reflect that, even if only in some very minor way. The same has to be said for participants in our research; they bring their own experiences, perspectives and values to the research. They're not robots; we're not robots – we're all living, breathing, subjective human beings, partial in our knowledge, and flawed. Is this a problem? The short answer is absolutely not. The model of knowledge in qualitative research is one where a robot would make a terrible researcher; in qualitative research, our humanness, our subjectivity, can be used as a research tool. But to do qualitative research well, and to use subjectivity in this way, it needs to be thought about and considered.

The way to do this is by being reflexive. *Reflexivity* is an essential requirement for good qualitative research (and usefully there are whole books dedicated to helping us become reflexive; e.g. Etherington, 2004; Finlay & Gough, 2003). Reflexivity in a research context refers to the process of critically reflecting on the knowledge we produce, and our role in producing that knowledge. It can be useful to distinguish between two forms of reflexivity – functional and personal (Wilkinson, 1988). Functional reflexivity involves giving critical attention to the way our research tools and process may have influenced the research. For instance, this might include consideration of the ways the stories that people tell about dieting might be influenced by the method we choose – for instance, data collected via FGs or researcher-directed diaries are likely to be different: an FG involves face-to-face interaction and discussion with others, whose comments and bodies might impact on what any one participant shares; a diary invokes a mode of directed yet somehow private, intimate disclosure, where the researcher is less directly present (see Chapters 5 and 6).

Personal reflexivity in research is about bringing the researcher into the research, making us visible as part of the research process – unlike in quantitative research, where the researcher is typically invisible (that robot). At the very least, it might involve acknowledging who we are as researchers (much like Victoria and Virginia did in Chapter 1). More than that, it involves considering how factors like our *embodiment* (our physical bodies and what we do with them) can influence the production of knowledge within research (e.g. Burns, 2003, 2006; Rice, 2009), or how our assumptions can shape the knowledge produced. For example, Virginia (Braun, 2000) examined **heterosexism** (the assumption that everyone is heterosexual) within her doctoral research – both her own and that of her participants – and discussed both how this had 'shut down' possible avenues of inquiry, and the implications for research practice more broadly. Reflexivity is essential in all qualitative research, and can be seen as part of 'quality control' in qualitative research (see Chapter 12). That said, it's not easy to do (particularly if you're embedded in a quantitative research culture), so we encourage you to start this process right away. One way to assist this is to keep a research journal which records your thoughts, feelings, and reflections about your process. We encourage all qualitative researchers – however experienced – to keep a reflexive research journal throughout the process of their research (see Chapter 3).

KNOWING WHAT YOU NOW KNOW, IS QUALITATIVE RESEARCH RIGHT FOR YOUR PROJECT?

Researchers choose their research methodology for a combination of epistemological, political and practical reasons. Epistemology delimits the types of approaches that are possible; politics may guide the researcher towards methods that can give answers that can be used for particular ends; and practical factors, such as our skills and the resources we have, constrain research design in various ways. Even if the questions '*What* do I want to know?' and '*Why* do I want to know that?' drive our research, the questions themselves often already reflect epistemological, ontological and political positionings. For example, if you want to try to understand the July 2011 far-right terrorist attack in Norway, in which Anders Behring Breivik killed 77 mostly teenage Norwegians, by measuring levels of racism in Norway, your research is already situated with a (post)positivist framework; if you wanted to understand this act by analysing the construction of Norwegian national identity among online postings by members of ultra-right-wing organisations, you're situated within a qualitative paradigm. So depending on your theoretical commitments, what you want to know, and why, qualitative approaches might not be suitable. They might not be suitable because you want to establish some sort of relationship between various factors (say between prevalence of depression and race/ethnicity in the US; Riolo, Nguyen, Greden, & King, 2005). Or they might not be suitable because you want to ascertain how common something is within a particular population (e.g. the prevalence of eating disorders in Norwegian adolescents [Kjelsås, Bjørnstrøm, & Götestam, 2004] or in lesbian, gay and bisexual populations [Feldman & Meyer, 2007]). Chapter 3 discusses research questions in more depth.

Once you've identified the benefits of a qualitative approach, then you have to determine which particular approaches within the paradigm are most useful. Some qualitative writers have described an (ideal) process for qualitative research as one of bricolage where the situated, subjective, knowledgeable, inventive researcher selects and uses the best of a wide variety of tools, techniques and theories at their disposal to collect data and tell a story about their research object which answers their research questions (Denzin & Lincoln, 2005a). This book will give you the confidence to understand and use a range of qualitative methods and approaches.

CHAPTER SUMMARY

This chapter:
- introduced ten fundamental things you need to grasp about qualitative research before you start do it, including:
    - knowing that qualitative research is about meaning;
    - recognising that qualitative research doesn't seek a single answer or single truth;
    - recognising that context is really important in making sense of qualitative data;
    - understanding that qualitative research is not a single approach or method, and different forms have different purposes;
    - recognising that ontology *and* epistemology are important for research, and understanding some of the main variations within psychology;
    - grasping the concept of methodology;
    - knowing what different sorts of *data* suit qualitative research, and what constitute 'good' qualitative data;

- o understanding what 'thinking qualitatively' involves;
- o understanding why subjectivity and reflexivity are important;
- discussed how to determine whether qualitative research suits a particular research question.

? QUESTIONS FOR DISCUSSION AND CLASSROOM EXERCISES

1 You are doing research into environmentally sustainable practices (e.g. public transport use, recycling, buying local food, or reducing energy consumption), an increasingly important area of psychological research (Kurz, 2002). Working individually, and based on what you've learned so far about qualitative research, list five reasons why qualitative research might be useful in helping you to understand and increase environmental sustainability. Then, in small groups, generate a list of five possible research topics about environmentally sustainable practices that suit qualitative research methods, and five research topics that *do not*. Feed these back to the class as a whole, and explain why they are or are not suitable for qualitative research.

2 What does it mean to say the researcher in qualitative research is not a robot?

3 From what you know so far, discuss any questions, concerns and criticisms you have about qualitative research. Try to identify what each of these questions, concerns or criticisms relates to. Are you evaluating qualitative research from a quantitative/positivist standpoint?

4 In an article in *Feminism Media Studies*, British-based psychologists Katy Day, Brendan Gough and Majella McFadden (2004) analysed media representations of women and drinking. Read their article. Drawing on this chapter, discuss the ways (both big and small) that their study, as an example of qualitative research, differs from quantitative research.

5 Becoming reflexive as a researcher is really tricky, but it is essential for qualitative research. Spend ten minutes thinking about all the different ways you could affect the research process. First, try to think about visible factors that might lead participants to make presumptions about you (e.g. what do the ways you look and sound suggest about you?). Try to list at least ten of these. Now move to 'invisible' factors – the assumptions that you have about life or the topic of research. Others can't necessarily see these, but they might shape the research in certain ways. An example could be the assumption that being a stay-at-home mother is a sacrifice, because it means paid employment is limited; another could be that the ideal family environment to raise a child is with two (different sexed) parents. Try to identify at least *five* such assumptions. Identifying these factors is the first step to reflexivity. Once you've done this, pair up with someone else in the class (ideally someone you don't know very well). Take turns to chat about what you do at weekends or your favourite films and television programmes for a few minutes, and then try to list five–ten assumptions you might make about them – which might affect how you

would respond to them if you were a research participant. Compare notes: Are their own reflexive observations and your assumptions about them similar? Is there any overlap? Did you make any 'internal' assumptions or are they all external? Discuss the ways these factors may or may not be an influence in qualitative research.

FURTHER RESOURCES

Further reading:

There have been many different ways in which the terrain of qualitative research (in psychology) has been mapped over the years. Three useful works that provide different 'takes' on this, and include discussion of paradigms, epistemology, ontology, methodology and method, are:

Henwood, K. & Pidgeon, N. (1994). Beyond the qualitative paradigm: introducing diversity within qualitative psychology. *Journal of Community & Applied Social Psychology, 4*, 225–238.

Madill, A. & Gough, B. (2008). Qualitative research and its place in psychological science. *Psychological Methods, 13*, 254–271.

Marecek, J. (2003). Dancing through the minefields: toward a qualitative stance in psychology. In P. M. Camic, J. E. Rhodes, & L. Yardley (Eds), *Qualitative research in psychology: Expanding perspectives in methodology and design* (pp. 49–69). Washington, DC: American Psychological Association.

You may want to come back read more about theory at a later point. For a comprehensive and accessible introduction to social constructionism, see: Burr, V. (2003). *Social constructionism* (2nd ed.). London: Psychology Press.

For a briefer introduction to social constructionism, see: Potter, J. (1996). Discourse analysis and constructionist approaches: theoretical background. In J. T. E. Richardson (Ed.), *Handbook of qualitative research methods for psychology and the social sciences* (pp. 125–140). Leicester, UK: BPS Books.

For a critical realist approach to social constructionism, see: Willig, C. (1999). Beyond appearances: a critical realist approach to social constructionism. In D. J. Nightingale & J. Cromby (Eds), *Social constructionist psychology: A critical analysis of theory and practice* (pp. 37–51). Buckingham, UK: Open University Press.

For an introduction to more experiential theoretical frameworks, see: Chapter 2, The theoretical foundations of IPA. In J. A. Smith, P. Flowers, & M. Larkin (2009). *Interpretative phenomenological analysis: Theory, method and research* (pp. 12–39). London: Sage.

For an engaging and accessible account related to subjectivity and research, see: Passions, politics, and power: feminist research possibilities. In M. Fine (2002). *Disruptive voices: The possibilities for feminist research* (pp. 205–231). Ann Arbor: University of Michigan Press.

Online resources:

See the *companion website* (**www.sagepub.co.uk/braunandclarke**) for:

- self-test multiple-choice questions relating to Section 1;
- the flashcard glossary – test yourself on the definitions of key terms used in this chapter;
- further readings (articles from Sage journals).

Planning and designing qualitative research

Research is a planned and designed activity, and qualitative research is no exception: *every* project needs an overall design – you could think of this as the blueprint of the research. Although research design in some qualitative methods texts refers primarily to the *method* of data collection (e.g. an interview study, a story-completion study), we conceptualise it as something far wider. We encourage you to think of design *broadly*, as something which incorporates the goals of your study, the theoretical framework(s), the research questions (which guide you), **ethics**, and the method(s) you will use to generate and to analyse data. Although this might seem like something that doesn't need a lot of attention, we consider it one of the most crucial chapters in the book. Planning any research is vital, and helps determine the feasibility of your ideas and ensure that you don't waste your own time – and the time of any participants – by generating knowledge that cannot help answer a question.

British-based health and counselling psychologist Carla Willig (2001: 21) has noted that 'a good qualitative research design is one in which the method of data analysis is appropriate to the research question, and where the method of data collection generates data that are appropriate to the method of analysis'. This is a good basic definition because it shows that qualitative research is not a linear process. Research question(s), method(s) and even theories all feed into, and inform, each other, and there are many routes to research design (see Box 3.1). Tables 3.1–3.3 can be used to guide research design: one is organised by research question type (see next section); one by methods of data collection (see Chapters 4–6); and one by methods of data analysis (see Chapters 8–11).

BOX 3.1   ROUTES TO RESEARCH DESIGN: EPISTEMOLOGICAL, POLITICAL, TECHNICAL OR PRAGMATIC?

How is the design of a project shaped and determined? In some cases, epistemological commitments may drive your research, and these commitments will determine the whole scope and nature of your project. For example, if you start from a phenomenological theoretical position, which is concerned with lived experienced, this provides an umbrella under which only certain types of questions (about lived experience), methods (interviews or diaries and IPA analysis) and answers fit. In other cases, certain political commitments or objectives will drive your research. For instance, if you're starting from a commitment to improving the situation of women in prison (e.g. Torre & Fine, 2005), your political goals determine the best *form* and type of knowledge (such as qualitative data gathered through observation, interviews and focus groups, within an action research framework), and your questions and analysis. Sometimes your research question itself will determine your methodology and choice of methods. And in others still, your reason for choosing a qualitative method might be determined by technical or pragmatic factors such as the skills you have as a researcher, and the methods you know. If you start from *technical* skills, your research design is limited by what you know and can do, and the research needs to be designed from that centre point. (Bryman, 1988).

The following questions are a useful guide for thinking about qualitative research design (many could also apply to quantitative design):

- What do I want to know?
- Why do I want to know it?
- What assumptions am I making about research, and knowledge (what are my theoretical and methodological positions)?
- What type of data would *best* answer these questions?
- What type of data will *I* use to tell me what I want to know? (The answer to this and to the previous question is not always the same.)
- How much data will I need?
- How will I collect my data?

- *If my research involves participants:*
    - o   Who will I need to collect data from?
    - o   How will I access and recruit those participants?
- How will I analyse my data in order to answer my questions?
- What particular ethical issues do I need to consider?
- Are there any pragmatic or practical factors that I need to take into account?

By the end of this chapter, you should have a sense of the sorts of things you need to know to answer most of these questions. We have kept this chapter as practically oriented as possible. It is intended as a useful resource not only for project design, but also for writing research proposals for assignments, and writing and submitting ethics and funding applications. We encourage you to return to this chapter after you have read some of the chapters on methods of data collection and analysis, to ground your chosen methods in an overall research design.

THE RESEARCH TOPIC AND RESEARCH QUESTIONS

Your research topic and your research question(s) are closely related, but the topic is potentially broader. So you might be interested in young women and physical education as a topic, but your specific research question might be 'What are young women's experiences of physical education at school?' For qualitative research, both the topic and the research question need to 'fit' with the framework you are using (see Chapter 2). Some topics and questions are suitable for qualitative research; others are not. Research questions are important, because they guide the research (both the design of it and the doing of it). Quantitative research starts with a clear and fixed research question; in qualitative research, you also start with a research question, which guides design, but it can also evolve and become refined as a study progresses. Indeed, in some approaches like grounded theory (Charmaz, 2006), this would be expected.

THE SCOPE AND RATIONALE OF YOUR RESEARCH QUESTION

In their guidelines for undergraduate projects, Gough et al. (2003: 5) identify that qualitative research questions 'should have some social relevance and originality'. There's not much point doing research on something we already know everything about! But originality is not necessarily about doing something that's 100 per cent brand spanking new; it's about generating some knowledge that might be new because of topic (a completely new area), the approach (the topic has never been explored in this way, and we can learn something new from it), or context (the topic has never been studied in this place or time and this may generate new knowledge), or sample (the issue has not been explored with this particular sample). It can be some or all of these.

A good example of research that was original in many of these ways was a project Virginia was involved in on sexual coercion among gay and bisexual men (Braun,

Table 3.1 Design by type of research question

Type of research question with real life examples	Suitable types of data	Suitable analytic method	Difficulty Rating*	Suitable size of sample
Experience Such as: women's experience of polycystic ovarian syndrome (Kitzinger & Willmott, 2002); the experiences and needs of men affected by infertility (Malik & Coulson, 2008)	Interviews (both face-to-face and virtual) are ideal; researcher-directed diaries, qualitative surveys and some secondary data sources (e.g. bulletin boards, personal blogs) are also good; focus groups may be appropriate for some research questions	IPA, TA (esp. experiential)	Easy	Small/moderate (large enough to convincingly demonstrate patterns across a date set; small enough to retain a focus on the experiences of individual participants)
Understandings and perceptions Such as: perceptions of the impact of air travel on climate change (Becken, 2007); expert professionals' views of risk in relation to sexual coercion for men who have sex with men (Braun, et al., 2009)	Focus groups, qualitative surveys, story completion tasks, vignettes and some secondary data sources (e.g. bulletin boards, personal blogs), are ideal; interviews are good when the participant has a personal stake in the topic (e.g. black people's views on inter-racial adoption [NB most inter-racial adoptions involve white people adopting non-white children]).	TA, GT, pattern-based DA	Easy	Moderate/large (large enough to capture a range of perspectives; not so large that you are drowning in data)
Practices/accounts of practice Such as: the appearance and clothing practices of non-heterosexuals (Clarke & Turner, 2007); the gendered dynamics of sleep (Hislop & Arber, 2003)	Interviews, focus groups, qualitative surveys, researcher-directed diaries, some secondary data sources (e.g. bulletin boards, personal blogs)	TA, GT, pattern-based DA	Easy/moderate	Moderate/large (large enough to capture a range of accounts; not so large that you are drowning in data)

(Continued)

Table 3.1 (Continued)

Type of research question with real life examples	Suitable types of data	Suitable analytic method	Difficulty Rating*	Suitable size of sample
Influencing factors Such as: identifying the factors that influence people's decisions to continue regular genetic screening (Michie, 1987); factors that influence parents' food purchasing behaviours (Maubach, Hoek, & McCreanor, 2009)	Interviews, focus groups, qualitative surveys, researcher-directed diaries, some secondary data sources	TA, GT	Moderate	Moderate/large (enough to identify relevant influencing factors; not so large that you are drowning in data)
Representation Such as: representations of male and female sexuality in women's magazines (Farvid & Braun, 2006); representations of masculinity and the 'metrosexual man' in men's magazines (Hall & Gough, 2011)	Secondary sources	Constructionist TA and GT, pattern-based DA	Moderate/difficult	Small/moderate
Construction Such as: young people's constructions of eating disorders in a story completion task (Walsh & Malson, 2010); constructions of 'New Zealanders' in accounts of sexual health and risk (Braun, 2008)	Secondary sources, story completion tasks, vignettes, interviews, focus groups, qualitative surveys, researcher-directed diaries	Constructionist TA and GT, pattern-based DA	Moderate/difficult	Small/moderate

Type of research question with real life examples	Suitable types of data	Suitable analytic method	Difficulty Rating*	Suitable size of sample
Language practice Such as: how people construct, manage and undermine 'healthy eating' talk in dinnertime conversations (Wiggins, 2004); how veganism is constructed as 'normal' in online discussions (Sneijder & te Molder, 2009)	Naturalistic data are ideal – both mundane (e.g. audio recordings of someone's home telephone conversations) and institutional (e.g. audio or video recordings of counselling sessions); some secondary data sources (e.g. broadcast media); interviews and focus groups also used	Discursive psychology, conversation analysis and some forms of narrative analysis	Difficult	Small/moderate

*Please note that this is an indication of the *relative* ease/difficulty of using different methods (there is very little about qualitative research is straightforwardly easy!); it is also important to note that some people take to 'difficult' methods like discourse analysis like a 'duck to water'! The difficulties ratings are just intended to provide a general guide.

Table 3.2 Design by method of data collection

Family of Method	Specific versions	Difficulty rating	How much data for a small project?*	How much data for a medium project (or one study in a large project)?*	How much data for a large project?*	Often used in combination with which other data collection methods?	Particularly suitable methods of analysis
Interactive data collection methods	Interviews	Easy/moderate	6–10 interviews	10–20 interviews	20+ interviews	Researcher-directed diaries and vignettes	TA, IPA, GT and pattern-based DA
	Focus Groups	Moderate	2–4 focus groups	3–6 focus groups	10+ focus groups	Vignettes; secondary sources as elicitation tools	TA, GT and pattern-based DA
Participant-generated textual data	Qualitative Surveys	Easy	15–50 surveys	50–100 surveys	100+ surveys	Vignettes, story completion tasks, secondary sources as elicitation tools	TA, IPA, GT and pattern-based DA
	Researcher-directed diaries	Moderate	10–30 diaries	30+ diaries	80+ diaries	Interviews, focus groups	TA, IPA, GT and pattern-based DA
	Story-completion tasks	Easy	15–40 SCTs (for comparative designs, need at least 10 participants in each group)	40–100 SCTs	200+ SCTs	Qualitative surveys	TA, GT and pattern-based DA

Family of Method	Specific versions	Difficulty rating	How much data for a small project?*	How much data for a medium project (or one study in a large project)?*	How much data for a large project?*	Often used in combination with which other data collection methods?	Particularly suitable methods of analysis
Secondary sources	Printed materials, online/ electronic materials, broadcast media and film	Easy	1–100	1–200	4–400+	Focus groups, qualitative surveys; can be used as elicitation tools in interviews, focus groups and qualitative surveys	TA, GT and pattern-based DA; IPA can be used to analyse some types of secondary source (e.g. bulletin boards and blogs) in which people report personal experiences

*The amount of data recommended varies according to the research question and the type of analysis chosen (refer to the other tables for guidance), the richness of the data, and how much each participant contributes (e.g. for diaries and interviews). Sample size may also affect publishability, with smaller samples potentially being seen as inadequate.

Table 3.3 Design by method of analysis (all suitable for small projects)

Method	Difficulty rating	Suitable types of research question	Suitable types of data	Sufficient data for a *small* project	Ideal sample & sampling approach
Thematic Analysis	Easy (especially experiential TA)	Any except language practice (need to map type of TA to type of research question, e.g. constructionist TA for construction questions)	Any, no ideal data	N=6–10 interviews N=2–4 focus groups N=10–50 participant generated textual N=10–100 secondary sources	Any (homogeneous sampling facilitates generating **themes** in small samples)
Interpretative Phenomenological Analysis	Easy	Experience (and understandings and perceptions)	Interviews are ideal; researcher-directed diaries, qualitative surveys and focus groups also used	N=3–6 interviews N=2–4 focus groups N=10–20 qualitative surveys/researcher-directed diaries	Homogeneous
Grounded Theory Lite	Moderate	Any except language practice (although GT generally places more emphasis on social processes than individual experiences); influencing factors is ideal (need to map type of GT to type of research question, e.g. constructionist GT for construction questions)	Any, but interviews are common	N=6–10 interviews N=2–4 focus groups N=10–50 participant generated textual N=10–100 secondary sources	Any (homogeneous facilitates generating categories in small samples)
Pattern-based Discourse Analysis	Moderate	Accounts of practice, representation, construction	Any, no ideal data	N=1–6 interviews N=1–2 focus groups N=10–40 participant generated textual N=1–50 secondary sources	Any (homogeneous facilitates generating patterns in small samples)

Schmidt, Gavey, & Fenaughty, 2009; Braun, Terry, Gavey, & Fenaughty, 2009; Fenaughty, Braun, Gavey, Aspin, Reynolds, & Schmidt 2006; Gavey, Schmidt, Braun, Fenaughty, & Eremin, 2009). This project was *original* in that: the topic was one very little research had previously been conducted on; almost all prior research had been quantitative; it had never been explored in the Aotearoa/New Zealand context; and it examined not only the views and experiences of men themselves, but also the views of professionals who could offer expert opinions, which had not previously been considered. What about *social relevance*? Through the research, an issue that is often silenced could be brought to light, men's experiences could be understood, and factors that may be associated with such sexual coercion could start to be examined and considered for prevention. It had the potential to produce knowledge that social and health agencies and other organisations, including the police, would find useful. It also disrupted the **heteronormativity** in the field of sexual coercion research, which has largely focused – with very good reason – on women's experiences of sexual coercion by men.

What Gough et al.'s (2003) criteria point to is the need to think about the *so what* of our research: what *is* the point of the answers we will generate? Do they take us anywhere further than we were before the research? In designing a project and, specifically writing a research proposal, this 'so what' element should be considered in relation to scholarly literature and to the broader socio-political context. Although Gough et al. highlight a particular aspect of this 'so what' question (social relevance), it's not *just* about doing research which has clear practical application – research can be very impactful without this. It's about thinking about knowledge as *for a purpose* – rather than just for its own sake. Research can have a purpose in various different ways, from critiquing taken-for-granted norms in society, through to identifying a problem and providing a solution to that problem.

This is really about developing a clear *rationale* for your research project. You also need a rationale for the different *elements* of the research, like data collection and analysis methods. So in developing your questions, you need to be able to answer the question of why, and how, the research is interesting and important. Think about how you might answer the question 'Why this study now?'

FORMULATING RESEARCH QUESTIONS

In formulating your research question, you first have to determine that it suits qualitative research, and then what form of qualitative research it suits. In general, qualitative research suits research questions based around the meaning of experiences, and questions concerned with broader meaning-making. It tends to ask 'how...?' rather than 'why...?' questions (Marecek, 2003), the latter being more common in quantitative psychology. However, as the scope of qualitative research is broad, qualitative research questions themselves come in a really diverse range of forms. Table 3.4 provides examples of different research questions and locates them in relation to the different varieties of qualitative research discussed in Chapters 1 and 2.

Table 3.4   Research questions mapped onto modes of qualitative research

Examples of research question	Qualitative focus	Broad approach
How do homeless people in London experience their daily lives (Radley, Hodgetts, & Cullen, 2005)?	Experience or understanding	Experiential
What social and environmental barriers do parents and children see to healthy eating, physical activity and child obesity prevention programmes (Hesketh, Waters, Green, Salmon, & Williams, 2005)?	Perceptions, views and opinions	Experiential
How do co-habiting same-sex couples think about and manage their finances (Burns, Burgoyne, & Clarke, 2008)?	Accounts of practices or behaviours	Experiential
What factors influence the 'poorer' dietary habits of lower compared to higher socioeconomic status people (Inglis, Ball, & Crawford, 2005)?	Identifying factors that influence experiences, behaviours, events or situations	Experiential
How is male and female sexuality represented in women's magazines (Farvid & Braun, 2006)?	Representation	Critical (could be experiential)
What barriers to healthy eating are constructed in the ways men talk about it (Gough & Conner, 2006)?	Construction	Critical
How is prejudice like *racism* (Wetherell & Potter, 1992) or *heterosexism* (Peel, 2001; Speer & Potter, 2000) 'done' in and through language?	Language practice	Critical

Sometimes, the sorts of things we might be interested in just might not work. They might not be able to be answered through qualitative research. An example we come across often is students wanting to do research on media influence. At first it seems obvious – we're enmeshed in the media, and clearly they influence us, otherwise millions wouldn't be spent on advertising each year. But thinking about it a bit more, it's not a good topic for a couple of reasons. The main reason is that it's really difficult to actually find out the sort of information that could answer this question. People aren't necessarily able to identify the influences of the media on their actions, and there's also a strong social norm to be an *individual* who thinks and acts *for themselves*, rather than a 'cultural' dope, in the thrall of the media. And even if people did and could talk about it, we wouldn't be able to claim *definitive* effects, because we'd need a quantitative design to do that. Ways this broad topic *could* be explored from a qualitative approach include researching how people think about certain media or how the media represent a certain issue.

THE FIT BETWEEN QUALITATIVE RESEARCH QUESTIONS, AIMS AND OBJECTIVES

If you have ever filled out a grant application, or have been engaged in positivist/ quantitative research, then you'll be familiar with the concepts of aims and objectives. Research aims specify what the research intends to achieve; they are the purpose of the research. Research objectives are more concrete, and measurable, aspects. Although there's not a perfect overlay, research aims are basically encompassed by your research questions – but the aims might be laid out in more detail and specificity than the research question.

Research objectives fit 'underneath' the research questions/aims, and are more specific. For instance, in one of Virginia's sexual health projects (e.g. Braun, 2008), the aim was to generate detailed new knowledge and ways of understanding the transmission of sexually transmitted infections (STIs), through examining the social contexts of sexual practice (see the Material Examples related to this project on the **companion website**). As a relatively large-scale qualitative project, it had lots of specific objectives. These included the identification of: (a) the meanings of sexual risk, sexual safety and sexual health; (b) the meanings of STIs; (c) framings of STI prevention; (d) discursive and contextual impediments to STI prevention; (e) factors which promote safer sex practices; and (f) the development of recommendations for STI prevention.

MATCHING QUESTIONS TO METHODS AND THEORY

Research questions are also closely linked to methodology, epistemology and ontology (see Chapter 2). Within different frameworks, certain questions make sense and others do not. A mismatch between theoretical frameworks and research questions is a classic error that's easy to make, especially if you're new to an approach. For example, if you are interested in understanding the experience of something for people, you need to approach the research from a *contextualist* perspective, which assumes a truth that can be accessed through language, whether partially or completely (Madill et al., 2000), and you would need to choose your methods to suit this. In contrast, if you are interested in looking at the construction of meaning, you need to approach your research from a *constructionist* perspective (Burr, 2003), which treats language as part of the construction or production of reality. Your data would need to be collected and analysed in an appropriate way. Issues around matches between theory, method, and topic are also relevant to supervisor selection (see Box 3.2).

BOX 3.2   SELECTING A SUPERVISOR FOR A STUDENT PROJECT

For some projects, you'll be in a position to choose a supervisor. It's rare to find the perfect person, who has the exact right methodological, theoretical and topical expertise. So if that isn't the case, don't despair. Try to find someone who works in the (very) broad area you're interested in. For instance, if you wanted to do research on young men's views on exercise and activity, a supervisor who worked in health, sport, or gender research would make sense; even better, they worked in men's or women's health. In terms of methods, you want a supervisor who has experience of supervising and doing qualitative research. For some of the more accessible qualitative analytic approaches (e.g. TA, IPA, GT), it is not essential that they are intimately familiar with a particular approach (e.g. you are keen on TA but they use IPA themselves). Overall, a supervisor who works within a *critical* qualitative framework is likely able to supervise *critical* and *experiential* qualitative projects, as they will typically have been trained in both approaches; a supervisor who only works within *experiential* approaches may not be adequately equipped to supervise *critical* work. On balance, we think that methodological familiarity and fit is probably more important than topic fit, but it also pays to be aware about what is most important to you (e.g. using a particular method or exploring a very specific topic), and to be flexible about the less important bits, in order to get a good fit with your supervisor.

THE IMPLICATIONS OF RESEARCH TOPICS AND QUESTIONS

In thinking about research topics and research questions, it's also important to consider the *ethical* and *political* dimensions of research. We encourage you to ask questions like: in whose interests is this research? Who might have a stake in the outcomes? In what ways – good or bad – might the research be interpreted and/or used? That is, how ethically delicate or politically sensitive is the research? The sexual coercion project discussed above is a good example of research that is very politically sensitive, as it involves identifying a negative feature within an already marginalised community (gay and bisexual men), and one that potentially links to some very negative stereotypes that have existed about gay male sexuality – that gay men are sexually predatory. As such, the research has the potential to be used in quite negative ways; the opposite of what we intended as researchers. We addressed this throughout the project and in presentations and publications. With research which is ethically delicate (discussed later in the chapter) or politically sensitive, it is worth thinking carefully about purpose, and *why* you want to do it, and exploring how much community support there might be for the research. This is vital if you're not a member of the community you are researching. Unless there's a lot of support, it is not a good idea for a first project, and possibly not for any project.

It's also important to remember that not all qualitative research approaches its topic from an 'empathic' perspective, which is about honouring the experiences of those who take part (see Chapter 2). Some research questions take an interrogative or even oppositional stance. Even experiential qualitative research may involve participants whose actions and views are profoundly disturbing and problematic – such as US feminist sociologist Diana Scully's (1994) work on sexual violence, which involved interviewing men convicted and imprisoned for rape.

ISSUES OF DATA SAMPLING

Like any research, qualitative research involves the selection of a data sample we then analyse. In most cases, we won't be sampling *all* instances of talk or text relevant to our research question, so we need to answer questions related to: a) *how much* data we need; b) how we select our sample; and, if we use human participants, c) how we recruit participants. Overall, we need a sample that is *appropriate* to our research question and the theoretical aims of the study, and provides an *adequate* amount of data to fully analyse the topic and answer our questions (Morse & Field, 2002).

SAMPLE SIZE: HOW MUCH DATA? HOW MANY PARTICIPANTS?

Qualitative research tends to use smaller samples than quantitative research, but 'there are no rules for sample size in qualitative inquiry' (Patton, 2002: 244). Sometimes only a *single* participant or text is analysed in depth (e.g. see Crossley, 2007, 2009). A sample size of between 15 and 30 individual interviews tends to be common in research which aims to identify patterns across data (e.g. Gough & Conner, 2006; Terry & Braun, 2011a). More than 50 interviews would constitute a large sample in qualitative participant-based research (Sandelowski, 1995), although in rare cases interview samples are far bigger (e.g. Holland, Ramazanoglu, Sharpe, & Thomson, 1998). However, when your research analyses printed text rather than data generated from participants (see Chapter 6), your sample may well be much larger (see Table 3.2).

Sample size is not a simple question (Sandelowski, 1995). Sample size will be affected by 'what you want to know, the purpose of the inquiry, what's at stake, what will be useful, what will have credibility, and what can be done with available time and resources' (Patton, 2002: 244). Factors like 'the quality of data, the scope of the study, the nature of the topic, the amount of useful information obtained from each participant, the numbers of interviews per participant … and the qualitative method and study design used' (Morse, 2000: 3) also affect how much data you need (see Tables 3.1–3.3 for guidelines around sample size).

One of the concepts that can drive the question of how much data you need for a qualitative study is **saturation**, a concept that developed from grounded theory (Bowen, 2008). Saturation typically refers to the point when additional data fails to generate new information (Morse, 1995; Sandelowski, 1995). In relation to how much data are required to reach saturation, Morse (2000) identified that, in general: a *broader* scope requires more participants; a less accessible, more awkward or sensitive topic may require more participants, as people may have difficulty talking about it; 'shallow' data require more participants; and the less data collected from each participant, the more participants needed. So, for example, a study that explores men's experiences of their bodies (broad topic), using a qualitative survey (relatively 'shallow' data, collected only once), would generally require more participants than a study that explored men's experiences of anorexia (a narrower topic), using repeated in-depth interviews (relatively *rich* data with a lot generated from each participant). What you want to make sure is that you have *enough* data to tell a rich story, but not too much that it precludes deep, complex engagement with the data in the time available (Onwuegbuzie & Leech, 2005).

Saturation remains a widely – if not always accurately (Bowen, 2008; Charmaz, 2005) – used rationale for sample size in qualitative research. However, it is not the only criterion. Saturation invokes a particular model of qualitative research (experiential, more positivist), where data are collected to provide a *complete* and *truthful* picture of the object of study, a theoretical position not all qualitative research subscribes to.

SAMPLING STRATEGIES

So *how* do you sample in qualitative research? In quantitative research, the idea of the random sample predominates, with the aim of **generalisability**, which means you apply the results of a study to the wider population; in qualitative research, the typical approach to sampling is **purposive**, with the aim of generating 'insight and in-depth understanding' (Patton, 2002: 230) of the topic of interest. Purposive sampling involves selecting data cases (participants, texts) on the basis that they will be able to provide 'information-rich' (Patton, 2002: 230) data to analyse. In some cases, your focus might be narrow, such as in experiential research where you want a sample that has experienced a particular phenomenon – such as Scandinavian health researcher Terese Bondas's (2002) study of pregnant Finnish women's experiences of antenatal care, where women needed to be pregnant and receiving such care. In others, your criteria might be far wider, such as in British-based psychologists Merran Toerien and Sue Wilkinson's (2004) study of British women and body hair removal, where participants just needed to be women resident in the UK. Under the broad umbrella of 'purposive' sampling, a range of different sampling strategies can be used (see Box 3.3).

Thinking about sampling requires thinking about inclusion and exclusion criteria for our sample: who or what *do* we want to hear from, and who or what do we *not* want to hear from. Qualitative researchers sometimes aim to sample for *diversity* of perspectives (sometimes referred to as maximum variation or maximum heterogeneity sampling, Fassinger, 2005), *typicality* or *homogeneity* of perspectives, or something in between (Patton, 2002). Importantly, different 'types' of participants are not sampled in qualitative research so that you can generalise to all other people of that 'type'. Qualitative nursing researcher Magarete Sandelowski (1995: 180) expressed this nicely:

> When qualitative researchers decide to seek out people because of their age or sex or race, it is because they consider them to be good sources of information that will advance them toward an analytic goal and not because they wish to generalize to other persons of similar age, sex, or race. That is, a demographic variable, such as sex, becomes an analytic variable; persons of one or the other sex are selected for a study because, by virtue of their sex, they can provide certain kinds of information.

BOX 3.3   SOME COMMON SAMPLING STRATEGIES IN QUALITATIVE RESEARCH

Convenience sampling is a very common approach in participant-based research (Patton, 2002), both qualitative *and* quantitative, and refers to a sample selected because it is *accessible* to the researcher. A typical way of doing this is taking a number or all of those who answer an advertisement for participants. These participants are almost always self-selected and bear *no* necessary relationship to the wider population. The classic convenience sample is the use of undergraduate (psychology) students, a staple in quantitative and indeed some qualitative psychology research, when that research is not intended specifically to examine the experience *of* undergraduate students. Such students are used because they are accessible and convenient for academics or other students. Convenience has been identified as the least rigorous and justifiable sampling method (Sandelowski, 1995).

Snowballing or *friendship pyramiding* are also common techniques, often forming part of convenience sampling. They involve the sample being built up through the networks of the researcher and other participants. The most common form of snowballing is one where the researcher asks participants if they know anyone else who might want to take part (Patton, 2002). The invitation to take part might then either come from the existing participant or from the researcher. This strategy won't necessarily work if you are sampling for a specific experience or condition that might be uncommon or private (e.g. infertility).

Stratification refers to sampling to ensure that the range and diversity of different groups in a population are included in your sample. This could relate to any factor, such as age, race/ethnicity/culture, sexuality, ability and location (e.g. urban/rural). The relevance of the stratification would depend on your research topic and question(s). Variation might be demographic (e.g. age, sex) or phenomenal (e.g. nature or type of experience) or more theoretically driven (Sandelowski, 1995). Stratification is often used in quantitative research to produce a sample matched to proportions in the general population (e.g. 65 per cent white if the population is 65 per cent white; 90 per cent heterosexual if the population is 90 per cent heterosexual); in qualitative research it is more about ensuring that diversity is incorporated into the sample.

In *theoretical sampling*, common in GT, sampling becomes an iterative process, where the burgeoning data analysis and theory development shapes the selection of subsequent participants to elaborate the developing theory (Coyne, 1997; Marshall, 1996). For example, as part of developing a *grounded* theory around the organisation of food and the development of disordered eating within families, British public health researcher Nicola Kime (2008) shifted her sampling frame from different generations, in general, to look at members of three generations *within one family*, in order to better develop and theorise intergenerational influences.

Finally, in some instances, your dataset will have a very specific criterion, meaning you sample for a *specific* event or issue. You would sample *all* or some of the data which met that criterion (Patton, 2002, refers to this as *criterion sampling*) – such as all or some of the parliamentary debates on a certain topic.

So, qualitative research sample selection involves theoretical and pragmatic influences, applied flexibly in a way which is justifiable in the context of your overall research design.

BEYOND 'THE USUAL SUSPECTS'

One factor to keep in mind when sampling is what groups your participants 'represent'. Are they the **usual suspects** – the educated, white, middle-class, straight people who tends to dominate much psychological research (see also Henrich, Heine, & Norenzayan, 2010)? Their dominance as research participants reflects who the majority of western academics and students tend to be, combined with the use of convenience and **snowball sampling**. But all too frequently, such participants are taken to represent *any* participant. They are not seen as having specific locations within the culture, which make them a *certain type* of participant; that is, their responses are not analysed *as* coming from educated, white, middle class, straight people. But they do. Only including the usual suspects can perpetuate their predominance in the psychological knowledge produced: their views and experiences continue to be over-represented.

So how might you sample beyond this – to access 'hidden', **hard to engage** or difficult to reach groups, who are less frequently represented in research? **Hidden populations** are those whose group memberships are not necessarily visible, and/or may be stigmatised in some way, so that known membership of that group may be troubling or threatening for an individual. Such groups may include illicit drug users (Kuebler & Hausser, 1997), people with invisible disabilities (Sturge-Jacobs, 2002) or lesbian, gay or bisexual (LGB) Christians and Muslims (Yip, 2008). Hard to reach or engage groups can overlap with hidden populations. They include groups who might: a) not feel a strong connection to, investment in, or understanding of research (e.g. less educated or poorer communities); or might b) have had very negative experiences of research in the past, such as many indigenous groups including Māori in Aotearoa/New Zealand and Inuit in Canada (Smith, 1999c), and thus feel disinclined to participate; or c) groups who often fall outside sampling pools (e.g. people who live rurally) and so may not be invited to participate in the first place (see Brackertz, 2007; Meezan & Martin, 2003); and d) groups for whom participation may be risky, such as poor non-white lesbian/gay adults who may not be 'out' to their family (e.g. Carrington, 1999). Access to such groups is tricky, and fraught with ethical and political questions, particularly so if you yourself do not occupy those categories (e.g. Wilkinson & Kitzinger, 1996). At the very least, the starting point is to be aware of who your sample *is*, and *what* groups participants are (and are not) members of. Better practice would be to consider who you would like to *include* in your sample, more diversely than just obvious identity categories like age or sex, and consider ways to ensure your research is non-discriminatory (see below).

Many groups who are viewed as hidden, hard to reach or difficult to engage could also be classified as vulnerable participants and in need of extra care in terms of research (Liamputtong, 2007), particularly when researching 'sensitive' topics – topics which are private, personal, and which may discredit or incriminate participants in some way (Renzetti & Lee, 1993). Talking about his experience researching religious LGB people, British-based sociologist Andrew Yip (2008, para 7.1) noted 'the importance of researching meanings and lived experiences sensitively, focusing on being theoretically and culturally sensitive to participants' specificities'. So while there are clear advantages in sampling beyond the usual suspects – both in terms of generating better knowledge, and for 'giving voice' to marginalised people, it's not something that's necessary easy, even for insiders, or to be undertaken naively, and an ongoing reflexive analysis of your role and interpretations as the researcher is even more vital in this context.

Ultimately, your sample is a crucial determinant of what you 'find' with your research. This truth is captured in the title of an article on data collection (Suzuki, Ahluwalia, Arora, & Mattis, 2007): 'the pond that you fish in determines the fish that you will catch'.

RECRUITING PARTICIPANTS

Who our sample is ties directly to *recruitment* – how we find and get participants to take part in our research. Recruitment isn't often discussed in any detail in research publications (notable and useful exceptions include: Arcury & Quandt, 1999; Fish, 1999), so we try to demystify the process a bit here. Participant recruitment ranges from the very easy (rare) through to the extremely difficult (also thankfully rare). Certain topics are going to be easier to recruit for than others. For instance, the topic of men and vasectomy in Aotearoa/New Zealand was very easy for Virginia's doctoral student Gareth Terry (Terry & Braun, 2011a, 2011b) to recruit for – after some media publicity, he was inundated with men wanting to take part. The topic captured a common experience (approximately 25 per cent of men in Aotearoa/New Zealand will eventually have a vasectomy) that men *wanted* to talk about. But there's no easy way to know in advance what topic will be easy or difficult to recruit for so, in general, you should start recruitment as early as you can. If you're in a university context and sampling from a student participant pool, some of these issues are sidestepped.

It's typically easier to recruit the 'usual suspects', unless we have access to groups who fall outside those boundaries (for instance, if we belong to those groups). If we do not, recruitment of such groups can be an involved process: US sociologist Mignon Moore (2006) described an in-depth process of getting to know New York black lesbian communities – which, despite being a black lesbian, she was not part of – for *one year* before she asked about research participation. She identified this group as one that traditional methods of participant recruitment (e.g. flyer advertisements) would not capture, so non-traditional practices were essential for recruitment.

At the very basic level, potential participants need to be informed about the research, through some form of advertising. Advertisements need to be eye-catching, inform participants about the scope of the study, and provide contact details for more information. Thinking creatively about advertising and recruitment can assist in getting the best sample for your project (Box 3.4 lists suggestions and strategies we've used that have been successful). An important point is that regardless of how you advertise, recruitment materials and strategies typically need to be approved under your ethics protocols, so need to be determined early in the design phase.

BOX 3.4   DIVERSE STRATEGIES WE'VE USED FOR RECRUITING PARTICIPANTS

- Putting notices in public spaces, such as around university campus (see the *companion website* for examples).
- Using university participant pools.
- Emailing notices of studies to various listservs and email groups.
- Leaving flyers in locations where those who fit your criteria are likely to see them (e.g. in bridal stores if you want to recruit people about to get married) and recruiting through specific places like doctors surgeries, gyms, churches/mosques/synagogues/temples. While leaving notices or detailed brochures (see the *companion website*) might result in some participants, you might have far more luck if staff are willing to help recruiting (e.g. a GP who is prepared to hand out flyers to potential participants). Obviously this will require relationships to be established – for example, British psychologist Susan Speer collaborated with a psychiatrist in her research with trans people (e.g. Speer & Green, 2008).
- Identifying key people who you can use to recruit for you, such as an individual well-connected with potential participants. For example, Virginia hired a two younger research assistants with wide social networks to recruit for her sexual health study (Braun, 2008).
- Going somewhere potential participants are likely to be, and presenting verbal or written information about your research – including big events like LGBTQ pride or wedding fairs, where you might be able to get a stall to promote the research.
- Approaching organisations to recruit through them (e.g. on-campus clubs/societies, charities, youth groups, support groups, sporting clubs), which might involve speaking at a meeting, or putting notices in the organisations' newsletters or on their websites.
- Using the internet, such as posting notices on different web fora or creating pages on social media sites like Facebook. The internet provides many different possibilities (as well as potential pitfalls) for recruitment (for suggestions, see Gaiser, 2008; Williams & Robson, 2004), offering potential access to different groups of people, including very *specific* or sub-cultural groups (e.g. serious online gamers) you may not otherwise have access to (see Hamilton & Bowers, 2006). It can also enable larger samples.
- Press releases to, or advertisements in, local or specialist media may be useful depending on your country and project scope.

Always check if it's okay before you advertise or try to recruit in these ways, and don't expect you will get everything for free. If using charities, for instance, you may want to volunteer some of your time to say thanks. You should also offer to provide a summary of your project or a copy of your report.

INCENTIVES/'THANK YOU' PAYMENTS

One thing we often get asked is whether we should 'pay' participants in research, or offer some form of compensation. This is a thorny issue, and one we're not resolved on (we disagree, for various reasons). For a start, not all researchers have funding to cover this. Others feel that 'paying' participants completely alters the nature of research endeavour, and suggests that there is no (other) value in being a participant in research. However, participants *do* offer up their time, and may have costs associated with participation (such as travel and childcare), and the time research takes. Offering some form of 'thank you' takes this into account, and so potentially can even make your research more inclusive. On balance, for student projects, we'd say there is no need to offer some recompense; this is especially the case if participants are recruited from a participant pool – credit earned itself is some form of recompense. If some recompense is offered, we would advise keeping it small, and practically oriented (e.g. a £10–25 voucher). Another option sometimes used is a prize draw that all participants are entered into (e.g. 'win a £100 Amazon voucher'). Whether or not any recompense is *advertised* is another tricky question. Ethically, the British Psychological Society (BPS) advises against offering compensation or inducements (financial or otherwise) that might *tempt* participants to be exposed to harm they wouldn't otherwise be exposed to in their everyday lives (Ethics Committee of the British Psychological Society, 2009); not mentioning this up front removes that possibility. However, it also takes away the possibility that recompense allows for more inclusivity in your sample (or aids recruitment).

BEING AN ETHICAL QUALITATIVE RESEARCHER

It should go without saying that our research should be of the highest ethical standards – but what does that mean? Ethics covers our relationships with participants, with academic communities, and with the wider world in which we conduct research, as well as our research practice. Psychology prioritises a deontological approach to ethics, where ethicality tends judged on the basis of our *process* – how we conduct our research – rather than (just) on our *outcomes* – judging ethicality based on outcomes would be a consequentialist approach (Brinkmann & Kvale, 2008). As an extreme example, a deontological approach says it wouldn't be ethical to expose people to HIV, even if you are certain your research would result in a cure for HIV. Ethics should be seen as an integral part of *all* stages and aspects of research, and being an ethical researcher involves not only adhering to the minimum standards set out in ethical *codes of conduct*, but also developing a broader ethical orientation that informs your research practice. Most of the discussion around ethics particularly applies to research with participants, but even textual data collection can raise ethical issues (see Box 6.2 in Chapter 6). The focus on ethics at the level of research participants has been referred to as *micro* ethics; *macro* refers to ethics applied at the level of the society in which research is conducted (Brinkman & Kvale, 2005). In an ethical orientation to research, both would be considered (Lincoln, 2009).

ETHICS CODES, ETHICS COMMITTEES AND
AN ETHICAL ORIENTATION TO RESEARCH

Following the horrors of medical experimentation in Nazi Germany, the first research and practice codes to define ethically acceptable and unacceptable practice were set down during the Nuremberg war-crimes trials, in what became known as the Nuremberg Code (1947). This formed the basis of medical ethics developed by the World Medical Association. Psychology caught up with the game slightly later: the American Psychological Association (APA) produced its first ethics code in 1953 (Fisher, 2009). But it was only after studies like US sociologist Laud Humphrey's (1970) *Tearoom Trade*, and US psychologist Stanley Milgram's (1974) *Obedience to Authority* brought social science ethics to the foreground, did the researcher's ethics become seen as something that needed policing by others; no longer was the researcher, by nature of their position within the academy, deemed able to determine for themselves what was ethical. Since that time, the coverage and detail of ethics has built substantially, and as discussion of the (ongoing) revisions of ethical codes shows (e.g. Fisher, 2009), ethics codes are responsive, living documents.

Ethical codes provide universal principles (and practical standards), but these are applied and interpreted in different ways in different times and places (a good range of different countries' codes have been compiled by the International Union of Psychological Science – http://www.iupsys.net/index.php/ethics/compendium-of-codes-of-ethics-of-national-psychology-organizations). Our practice as researchers is covered by both general codes produced by professional societies and the specific requirements of ethics committees (review boards) within our institutions, which can vary considerably by institution; sometimes it may be covered by ethics committees in places we conduct our research or recruit our participants (e.g. hospitals) – it's important you learn what your local requirements are. The process of applying for, and getting, ethical approval can be very time-consuming, depending on location and research design – for students in the UK, it can be quite quick (two weeks or less); for students in Aotearoa/New Zealand, it typically takes at least a month.

One of the unintended and unfortunate consequences of these ethical requirements is that ethics can be seen as a hoop to jump through, a specific *stage* of research (or even a barrier to research), rather than something that should permeate our whole research practice. Ethics codes should be seen as the *lowest* level of ethical standard required, not the pinnacle to aspire to (Brown, 1997, provides an interesting discussion of this). Instead, we encourage you to think of ethics as 'embedded in the totality of scholarly practice' (Baarts, 2009: 423).

Core ethical requirements

We base our discussion here on the BPS's (2009) *Code of Ethics and Conduct*, which is organised around four principles (respect, competence, responsibility and integrity) under which various 'standards' apply. The Code mirrors others like the APA code in having a combination of aspirational principles – the ideals that inform ethics – and enforceable standards – prescriptions and proscriptions for behaviour (Fisher, 2009). Most standards commonly applicable to research practice fall under the principle of respect. These include: the (general) need to maintain privacy and confidentiality (see Box 3.5); the need to (generally) obtain informed consent from participants and avoid deception; the need for self-determination, which means that participants know about their right to withdraw from research during or after it has taken place.

BOX 3.5   CONFIDENTIALITY, ANONYMITY AND NAMING OF PARTICIPANTS

While the requirements of confidentiality and anonymity seen like a straightforward requirement, and very sensible, they can be complex. Anonymity can be protective of participants, but it can also remove their voice, and might conflict with social justice goals. The balance between such factors depends on the nature of your topic, your participants, and your research aims and intentions (see Guenther, 2009, for a detailed discussion of this issue). Despite the wider debate, in general we recommend **pseudonyms** (fake names) as the best practice for protecting participants' anonymity. But it's important to include information about the rationale around anonymity and confidentiality in participant information sheets, to discuss this with participants, and to allow participants the possibility of choosing their own pseudonym or (if appropriate) to be named, recognising that this can impact on other participants' anonymity. All these practices may need approval from the relevant ethics body. It's important that you tell participants about the *limits* of confidentiality. For example, although law varies internationally, data *can* legally be subpoenaed, and researchers face imprisonment if they don't comply. Furthermore, if participants disclose that they are harming others, or intend to harm themselves (e.g. commit suicide) or others, you have an obligation to report this to the relevant authorities. Although such situations are unlikely, it's important this is clearly specified to participants, so that they aware that there isn't an iron-clad *guarantee* of confidentiality.

Standards included under the principle of competence include awareness of professional ethics, standards of ethical decision-making, and limits of competence, all of which relate to being an ethical researcher. The principle of responsibility covers the general concept of 'doing no harm'. It includes the standard of protection of research participants, which covers a host of factors including the need to minimise risk, to inform participants around risk, and of their rights of withdrawal, and the standard of debriefing of research participants after they have taken part. Debriefing is not common in qualitative research, as it does not typically involve deception, but the practice of finishing data collection by asking participants if they have any questions, providing details of sources of support, and offering participants a brief summary of the research, should they wish to receive it, can be seen as a version of this. Finally, the principle of integrity includes the standard of honesty and accuracy, which basically means we don't misrepresent our data or our participants and we don't use others' work without acknowledging it (plagiarism).

All researchers should familiarise themselves with the relevant ethic codes that they work under. But the core requirements for ethical practice include obtaining informed consent and avoiding deception, maintaining confidentiality and privacy, ensuring participants' right to withdraw (without explanation or negative impact), not subjecting participants to (unnecessary) risks, and being honest and accurate in reporting research results.

'SNAKES IN THE SWAMP'? ETHICS IN QUALITATIVE RESEARCH

So far so good, but when you're doing *qualitative* research, ethics become more complicated, and qualitative research has been a domain in which ethical discussion has broadened and flourished (Brinkman & Kvale, 2005; Lincoln, 2009). Described as 'snakes in the swamp' (Price, 1996: 207), the situation is potentially more uncertain, complex and nuanced than with quantitative designs, partly because of the fluidity of qualitative research designs. So additional or particular concerns arise with qualitative research, and require broader thinking about ethics:

- The potential for harm can be thought of very broadly (see above).
- The potential vulnerabilities of the researchers need to be considered; as we often gather in-depth, detailed data about sensitive issues, we can be traumatised by the data (see Gough et al., 2003).
- Informed consent becomes a more complex issue (Weatherall, Gavey, & Potts, 2002) as qualitative research is quite open-ended and iterative. We often don't know in advance *exactly* how we're going to analyse our data, or the sorts of claims we will make about them. Consent can only be granted to our broad interests/approach, not the final form of analysis, or sometimes even our exact research questions. Informed consent has been termed 'a shorthand promise for an abridged information package' (Weatherall et al., 2002: 534).
- Even the seemingly simple issue of confidentiality is complex. As we display the actual words of real-life individuals, identification becomes more of a possibility. In anonymising data, we have to be sensitive to what might be identifying, and how we might change it to increase anonymity but not change it so much that it alters the meaning substantially (Guenther, 2009). In situations where participants are members of a relatively small community, issues of ethics and anonymity require extra thought (Gavey & Braun, 1997; Williams & Robson, 2004). As anonymity is virtually impossible to *completely guarantee* it's good to be careful in how this is described in material given to participants (see Chapter 5, and the **companion website**, for examples of **participant information sheets** [PISs]). See Chapter 7 for further discussion around anonymising data.
- Recording audio or video data also raises ethical concerns, because voices (and bodies/faces) are more recognisable than printed text, and they are harder to anonymise; it's important that these are kept very securely (in password protected files).
- Interpretations of experience and issues of representation are two other areas that are particularly pertinent for qualitative research. We, as researchers, can tell a *different* story from that told by our participants. Analysis involves interpretation, which is informed by particular subjective and theoretical (and political) lenses. This means the product of our analysis is often far removed from the 'raw data' we receive. Some researchers have written about the anxiety this can cause (e.g. Miles & Huberman, 1994; Price, 1996). The interpretation of data, through analysis, transforms data from the words participants tell us, into a story about those words. That story is *our story* about the data, not the participants' story, and our story may differ from their's. When we as researchers occupy a more 'powerful' position

than our participants (that is, we belong to groups with more social power than they do), representation becomes even more pertinent to consider. Fortunately, a considerable body of literature has discussed the ethics and politics of *representing the other* (e.g. Pitts & Smith, 2007). Some researchers use **participatory methods**, which in some ways sidestep these issues of representation and interpretation, as the participants are active collaborators in the research process (but not completely, see Fine & Torre, 2004).

- Managing dual relationships – knowing those who take part in our research – is potentially more complex in qualitative than quantitative research, due to the extent of contact and the often deeply personal and sensitive nature of the stories participants tell us (see Chapter 4).
- Finally, physical safety needs to be considered, and weighed up carefully in research design, planning and practice (see Box 3.6).

BOX 3.6   RESEARCHER 'SAFETY' AND QUALITATIVE RESEARCH

It's really important that researcher safety – physical, psychological *and* emotional – is taken into consideration as part of research design. This involves thinking about where, when, and how research takes places, and who collects data, as well as what the topic is. For instance, a young woman interviewing straight men about their sexually coercive behaviour, in their homes in the evening, rings all sorts of alarm bells. A really good practice for interviews is a 'buddy' system, where another person has details of the researcher's movements around data collection, but only accesses these if there's a problem. The researcher lets the 'buddy' know when they are doing an interview, and when they'll be finished, and 'checks in' when they are done, through a brief phone call. Such a system may require ethical approval, if it involves someone outside the research team knowing participant details. The numerous other aspects to consider around researcher safety are covered in the UK's Social Research Association guidelines (http://the-sra.org.uk/wp-content/uploads/safety_code_of_practice.pdf) and in Petra Boynton's (2005) practical text, *The research companion*, which covers research from a real-world perspective.

To sum this all up, in qualitative research ethics intersect with the topic of research, the politics of the research, and the values of the researcher, participants, and collaborators. Together this renders them far more complex, in the field, than ethics codes suggest (Baarts, 2009), requiring complex thinking on the part of researchers. This is particularly the case for socially or politically sensitive research topics.

DOING NON-DISCRIMINATORY RESEARCH

Research is not a value-neutral activity. Our lives are filled with values and assumptions, and these can permeate our research practice and lead to discriminatory research. As well as research which confirms negative viewpoints (such as the controversial linking of intelligence to race, genetically, e.g. Jensen, 1969), research is discriminatory when the practice and/or reporting of it contains assumptions which implicitly exclude certain categories of people (e.g. LGB people or non-heterosexuals). This contributes to their further marginalisation within society, and can happen in very subtle ways (see Braun, 2000). Awareness and respect of difference are core ethical requirements; as researchers we have ethical obligations not to be discriminatory in research (e.g. Ethics Committee of the British Psychological Society, 2009), and so need to consider how to avoid it.

In planning and conducting research, you need to think about the ways in which your design, your practice, and your interpretations and presentations may be discriminatory and how they could be *made* non-discriminatory. The APA's *Publication Manual* (American Psychological Association, 2010, see also http://supp.apa.org/style/pubman-ch03.00.pdf) offers useful guidelines for 'avoiding bias' and using inclusive, non-discriminatory language in writing up research; guidelines for avoiding sexism (e.g. Denmark, Russo, Frieze, & Sechzer, 1988) and heterosexism (e.g. Committee on Lesbian and Gay Concerns, 1991) in research have also been developed (see also Chapter 12).

We'll illustrate this with an example. Imagine you're doing a study about couples' experiences of becoming parents. The first thing to be clear about is whether this is about straight couples, or lesbian or gay couples, or *all* couples. In recruiting for a study, you would need to be clear about what couples you want. If you want just to focus on straight couples, be explicit that is the focus (advertise your research: 'straight couples wanted ...'). If you want same-sex couples, be explicit about that (e.g. 'couples [straight or same-sex] wanted ...'). Because we live in a heteronormative society, where 'couple' often refers to, or is interpreted as, *straight* couple, if you recruit generically, you may implicitly exclude lesbian or gay couples – they might assume that it's just straight couples you want, and so not volunteer (on the flipside, they might make a political point *and* volunteer). It would also be important to indicate your own sexuality in the recruitment process as well, so potential participants – especially if lesbian or gay – know whether or not it's research conducted by an insider or an outsider (see Wilkinson & Kitzinger, 1996). If your study was *just* on straight couples, whether intentionally or not, you would also need to avoid heterosexism in the reporting and interpretation of the results. A common example is reference to 'couples' when the research is really about heterosexual couples – for instance with statements like: 'traditional gender roles become more salient for couples, once they are parents'. Better would be: 'traditional gender roles become more salient for *heterosexual* couples, once they are parents'. The same sorts of practices apply around other socially significant categories, like race/ethnicity/culture and class.

A category of discrimination very rarely considered is that of *genderism*, or the assumption that people identify as male *or* female, and *only* one of those, and that they have always done so. Almost all research does this, if it collects demographic information on gender. One of the most basic demographic categories is male/female, but this excludes people who do not identify as male *or* female, or forces them into a box that isn't right. Some researchers include other categories, including 'transgender', 'transman', 'transwoman', or 'other (please specify) _____' (and/or the choice to tick more than one 'gender' option), in order to recognise this diversity (see the examples of demographic forms on the ***companion website***; also Treharne, 2011).

What is at the heart of much this discussion is the way our methods or practices may unintentionally exclude whole groups of people. As researchers it's important to reflect on the presumptions and inadvertent 'biases' in our research and to develop better, more inclusive practices. Reflexivity is vital for reflecting on, learning from, and moving beyond, the discriminatory research practices we almost all (unintentionally) engage in.

Some people feel that such considerations in research (and life) are 'political correctness gone mad' or 'censorship' by the liberal left. Not surprisingly, we disagree entirely! But it's worth explaining *why* this is important. We'll mention three reasons:

- It's important from a 'formal equality' perspective, where all people should be treated the same, but more importantly from an *equity* perspective, where 'equality of outcomes', rather than 'inputs' is key, recognising people don't all start from the same opportunities, so might need to be treated differently to ensure equal end results for everyone.
- It's important from a knowledge perspective: to gain the best possible knowledge, to have a true 'psychology of the people', we cannot exclude certain members of society. Some theorists have even argued that those 'on the margins' of mainstream society can produce better insights than those wholly 'at the centre', because they see things from a different perspective and can shed light on things the more privileged of us can take for granted (Harding, 2004).
- It's important for individual and group well-being. Research (e.g. Herdt & Kertzner, 2006) has comprehensively demonstrated the negative mental, emotional and physical health impacts for individuals who experience marginalisation as a result of belonging to non-dominant categories. If we do not engage in non-discriminatory research, we collude in the 'doing of harm' to such groups within society. This is a broad professional ethical issue.

INFORMATION FOR PARTICIPANTS

Information given to participants in relation to research typically involves: a) some form of information/advertisement (noted above); b) a much more detailed PIS which spells out the scope, and practical and ethical elements of the research; and (except in some cases – which your local guidelines will spell out) c) a Consent Form the participant signs and returns. We have included a range of examples of different forms, some with explanatory annotations, on the *companion website*; Chapter 5 provides examples specific to our weight and obesity focus group. Your institution will have specific requirements that your materials will need to comply with.

COLLECTING DEMOGRAPHIC DATA

We would advocate for the importance of systematically collecting demographic information – which isn't something qualitative researchers are always good at. If we fully believe knowledge is situated, it is important to reflect on the relationship between your results and your sample. Other groups of people might hold very different views or have very different experiences. So you need to have some way of judging the groups your participants 'belong' to – demographic information tells you *something* (but certainly not everything) about your sample. Reporting participant demographics is also ethical, not least as a corrective to the invisibility of a normative sample (made up of the usual suspects), and makes us recognise that *all* participants belong in specific cultural spaces.

The APA (2010) requires researchers to collect enough demographic information to adequately 'describe' their sample. Important demographic information might include people's sex/gender, their age, their racial/ethnic/cultural identifications, their sexuality, their social class, their occupation, their qualifications; exactly what information you ask for depends on your research questions and the types of people you are collecting data from (see the examples on the *companion website*, and in Chapter 5). You need to think about whether you ask people to tick boxes in response to these questions (e.g. 'Which of the following options best describes your race?') or ask people to use their own words to define themselves. Asking people to pick from one of a number of predetermined categories generates data that are very easy to summarise, but people may not feel that they fit into any of the available categories (Treharne, 2011). If you use a list of options, it is important that it is appropriate – many researchers use official categories such as those constructed by the Office of National Statistics in the UK (see www.statistics.gov.uk/). In general, we use tick-box categories or self-definitions (or a mixture of both) depending on how important it is to understand people's self-definitions in relation to the research question. For instance, in a project examining trans people's experiences of prejudice and discrimination that Victoria supervised, it was important to ask people to describe *in their own words* how exactly they identified themselves, as there is no universally agreed on way of naming trans people. The potential dilemma then is how such open-ended descriptions are categorised by the researchers in reporting the results.

Demographic information may be reported in qualitative research to show the diversity of the sample (e.g. 'ages ranged from 24 to 67, with a mean of 53') or it may be used to show particular characteristics of each participant (e.g. 'Mark, a 37-year-old white able-bodied male'), or both. What is crucial is that qualitative research does *not* treat such information as a *variable*: It is not something the data are analysed or interpreted on the basis of. Instead, demographic information is important to show the limits of what we can claim and on what basis we can claim it (it is also relevant to quality criteria; see Chapter 12).

TIMETABLING YOUR RESEARCH

One of the hardest things about research – especially qualitative research – is keeping it on track, and finishing it in good time. There are good reasons for this: recruitment can be difficult; data collection typically takes far longer than we anticipate; transcription (if necessary) is time-consuming; and you just can't imagine how long it takes to analyse qualitative data until you've done it. On top of this, it's also just really difficult to conceptualise and work towards one deadline far in the distance (e.g. a PhD completion three–four years away, or even project deadline eight months away). For this reason, breaking down a project into timetabled chunks – leaving lots of extra time at the end for analysis and writing – is a really good practice. Box 3.7 provides an indication of how long the different elements of research might take and a rough timetabling guide. If you're doing a student project, your timetable will usually be planned and discussed with your supervisor, and they'll be involved in giving feedback on your progress along the way (see Chapter 13).

BOX 3.7   TIMETABLING QUALITATIVE RESEARCH

Below are some indications of the time different aspects of planning and doing qualitative research can take. The size of the project and how much time you commit to it obviously affect these hugely; we've written these for the equivalent of an undergraduate project or honours dissertation, where the person is working about a third of their time on it, over a 7½-month period. NB: these different stages also *overlap*.

Literature/planning: *two months* to collect, read, and process the literature, plan/design a study, and also write a full draft of the introduction/literature review section of the report.

Ethical approval: *one month* or more – depending on your institutional requirements, from writing and putting an application in, until final approval.

Recruitment: *up to two months* (or possibly even more), depending on how 'easy' your sample is to access, and how interesting the topic appears to people.

Data collection: *up to two months* or possibly more. Can be very quick if collecting text-based data, or very slow if trying to schedule focus groups.

Transcription: *one month.* It is quicker for single interviews; much slower for focus groups.

Data analysis: *four months* is probably the minimum you want to have to familiarise yourself with your data, to code it, to analyse it, to discard analyses that don't work, and then to reanalyse it, and then write up the analysis into a coherent narrative, which the scholarly literature is often integrated into.

Writing: *one month.* Writing is integral to the whole process of analysis, so shouldn't be conceived as entirely separate. But in addition, there's all the work in writing a full report, which includes the introduction, conclusion and method sections, not to mention the final editing/polishing of the whole thing. This probably takes at least one a month extra on top of the writing you do when producing your analysis.

That gives you some indication of the time involved at each stage.

(Continued)

BOX 3.7 *(continued)*

Here's how we encourage our students to spread the tasks over a 7½-month project:

Month 1:	Collect and read literature (topic, methodology, etc.).
	Plan and design the study.
	Work on ethics application.
	Start drafting the literature review part of the report.
Month 2:	Work on the literature review.
	If you get ethics approval, start recruitment and data collection.
Month 3:	Recruitment/data collection.
	Transcription or data entry (as relevant).
	Full draft of literature review.
Month 4:	Finish any recruitment and data collection.
	Finish transcription or data entry (as relevant).
	Draft methods section.
	Start analysis.
Month 5:	Analysis. Writing (part of analysis).
	Additional literature searches and reading – in concert with analysis.
Month 6:	Analysis and writing – full draft of the analysis.
	Revise and finalise literature review and method.
	Aim to have a full draft of the project/dissertation by the end of this month.
Month 7:	Revise the analysis and write-up.
	Additional literature searches and reading as necessary.

RESEARCH DESIGN: THE PROPOSAL

All the design elements of a project come together when we develop a proposal, such as a funding application, a research proposal (e.g. for doctoral research), or an ethics application. Writing a proposal is an excellent chance to really crystallise what it is you are trying to do, and why, with a project. A proposal contains many of the elements covered in this chapter (see the ***companion website*** for examples of real research proposals); other aspects, like data collection and analysis methods, are covered throughout the rest of the book (see also Tables 3.1–3.3).

DOCUMENTING YOUR RESEARCH PROCESS

Good record keeping is a key practice for any competent researcher (see Chapter 12), so you should start your record keeping now. Basic requirements for documentation include information about participant recruitment methods, what responses you got and how you followed them up, so you have a record of *who* took part, *how* you recruited them, and *who* didn't take part. They include basic demographic information about the participants, and more general information about data collection (such as location of data collection, time and duration). They also include a record of the relevant stages and process of data analysis (see Chapters 8–11). In some methods, such as grounded theory there is an explicit requirement for **memo** writing that provides a very solid paper trail (see Chapter 9). Basically, your record keeping should provide full and thorough information about what you did, why/how you did it, and what conclusions you came to (and why). This is about keeping an audit-trail of your research process; such information might be relevant when reporting your research (see Chapter 13).

Above and beyond these, as noted in Chapter 2, keeping a research journal is absolutely vital to the development of good qualitative research. In a research journal, the researcher regularly reports, and reflects, on the *progress* and *process* of the research. This is effectively your research *diary*, and is written for you – and it's useful to come back to it, throughout the analysis. It is your resource, and tells the 'other' story of your research, the one *not* typically told in the reporting of your data (if you report your results in a very reflexive manner, then it may be included, and this resource is *crucial*). A research journal often includes discussion of things like:

- Reflections on the process and practice of recruitment and data collection. This might include **field notes** on things such as what an interview felt like when you were doing it, observations of a participant that might offer additional insights into their data.
- Analytic insights that occur during data collection. Box 3.8 offers an example of two entries from one of Virginia's projects that covers these first two.
- The emotional aspects of the research – joy, frustration, anxiety, elation, despair are not unknown experiences for qualitative researchers; our research can profoundly affect us, and our emotional process around this can affect the research (Gilbert, 2001; Hallowell, Lawton, & Gregory, 2005). A diary can be a tool to reflect on, deal with, and learn from the emotional aspects of this process.

Ultimately, it's your tool as a researcher, and should be thought of as one of the means you use to develop a richer, more thoughtful, complex analysis, informed by a reflexive position.

CHAPTER SUMMARY

This chapter:
- identified key elements to think about in relation to qualitative research topics and research questions;
- discussed issues related to sampling and recruitment;
- provided an overview of ethical issues in qualitative research;
- discussed timetabling in relation to qualitative research;
- introduced the importance of thinking of overall design;
- outlined the value of keeping a research journal and documenting your research process.

BOX 3.8   EXAMPLES OF RESEARCHER JOURNAL ENTRIES FROM VIRGINIA'S SEXUAL HEALTH RESEARCH (BRAUN, 2008)

FG4-1, 13/12:

Group with 4 women in their 20s, all unknown to each other. Started off quite slow, and was never as interactive as FG2, but eventually got quite good, they discussed and disagreed. One participant had to leave and we kept going for another 20 mins. I did the demographics at the beginning which worked well because people arrived at different times. The new room was better, too … more spacious. Will have to check the tapes to see how well they picked up, but think it will be fine. Overall, these women were 'pro' safe sex – as condoms – and generally promoted practising it. However, many of them talked of times when they hadn't, and that this had been a 'choice' they had made … In some cases, people talked too generally …

Some key points
o   *Trust among people you know not to have STIs, so they're not as 'risky'*
o   *Trust or not of a partner not to expose you*
o   *Admiration for what 'should be' best practice around sex – ie telling a sexual partner you have an STI at the start of something … demonstrates it is unusual to do this*
o   *The 'slip up' – ie sex without a condom*
o   *Safe sex as really important – but doesn't always happen*
o   *Not having safe sex as a choice – because at the time, other things are more important …*
o   *Sexual health as holistic vs. absence of disease*
o   *Lack of specific knowledge of different STIs, but a general overall knowledge (and of names of STIs) […]*

FG 10-1, 19/1:

This group was far more talkative, although only 3 participants – two of whom were friends. They had a tendency to get off topic, and back onto pet topics (e.g. women getting pregnant to get the DPB [domestic purposes benefit]) and I didn't manage to rein them in as much as I should have. Still, quite a bit was covered. Again, this was a very different group from any of the others. Safe sex as important … didn't really talk much about their own personal experiences – I wonder if I am setting the groups up like this, since I have been saying it's a general discussion … might stop doing that now … I think this is one that will be useful, where some of the themes will be more apparent when the data are analysed. But some things that spring to mind:

Some key issues
o   *Good sex as safe sex*
o   *Not caring about risk – others, not themselves*
o   *Girls as more responsible around sex; safety as gendered*
o   *Lack of self respect and lack of power around sex*
o   *Lack of power around sex and lack of safety*
o   *Safety as not taken-for-granted in the sense that safe sex isn't the bottom-line of sex, it's like 'special' sex that has to be worked for, requested etc …*
o   *STIs as a concern only when you've had one*

❓ QUESTIONS FOR DISCUSSION AND CLASSROOM EXERCISES

1   Research has shown that women who are categorised as 'obese' experience a poorer quality of life than men who are categorised as 'obese', and that they experience higher levels of social stigma (Ferguson, Kornblet, & Muldoon, 2009). Such results stem from a comparative quantitative research design. How could you research women's quality of life and experiences of social stigma related to obesity using a *qualitative* approach? What research question might you ask? Using the design tables (Tables 3.1–3.3), identify the methods that would fit with the research question.

2   In pairs, devise a sampling and recruitment strategy for a study which seeks to understand young people's experiences of starting 'dating'. What sort of sampling strategy would work best, and why? How would you work to ensure that the views beyond those of the 'usual suspects' were (also) included in the study? How would you tackle the question of recruitment?

3   What ethical issues might there be involved in a qualitative study looking at young people's experiences of starting dating? How might this differ between online or face-to-face methods of data collection?

4   Using the qualitative research proposal proforma on the **companion website**, write a proposal for a small (7½-month) qualitative project on a topic of your choice. (This exercise will likely require some familiarity with later sections of the book.)

FURTHER RESOURCES

Further reading:

For an accessible but detailed discussion of the purpose of different types of research, sampling for qualitative research and a range of different modes of research design (NB: some of the language is different to that we use), see: Patton, M. Q. (2002). Chapter 5: Designing qualitative studies. In M. Q. Patton, *Qualitative Evaluation and Research Methods* (3rd ed., pp. 209–258). Thousand Oaks, CA: Sage.

For an excellent overview of qualitative research ethics, see: Brinkmann, S. & Kvale, S. (2008). Ethics in qualitative psychological research. In C. Willig & W. Stainton Rogers (Eds), *The Sage Handbook of Qualitative Research in Psychology* (pp. 262–279). Los Angeles: Sage.

For a detailed overview of ethics in *online* research, see: Wishart, M. & Kostanski, M. (2009). First do no harm: valuing and respecting the 'person' in psychological research online. *Counselling, Psychotherapy, and Health, 5*, 300–328.

For a thoughtful discussion of researcher wellbeing, see: Boynton, P. (2005). Chapter 6: Researcher well-being. In P. Boynton (2005), *The Research Companion: A practical guide for the social and health sciences* (pp. 119–138). Hove: Psychology Press.

To read about researchers talking about the experience of doing (sensitive) qualitative research, a useful starting place is: Dickson-Swift, V., James, E. L., Kippen, S., & Liamputtong, P. (2007). Doing sensitive research: what challenges do qualitative researchers face? *Qualitative Research, 7*, 327–353.

Online resources:

Most ethics codes and guidelines can be found online. Particularly relevant and useful ones include:

- British Psychological Society's *Code of Human Research Ethics* (2010): www.bps.org. uk/sites/default/files/documents/code_of_human_research_ethics.pdf
- American Psychological Association's Ethical Principles of Psychologists and Code of Conduct: www.apa.org/ethics/code/index.aspx
- New Zealand Psychological Society's *Code of Ethics for Psychologists Working in Aotearoa/ New Zealand* (2002): www.psychology.org.nz/cms_display.php?sn=64&pg=2379&st=1
- For the ethics codes of other national psychology organisations, see: http://www.iupsys.net/ index.php/ethics/compendium-of-codes-of-ethics-of-national-psychology-organizations
- Social Research Association's Ethical Guidelines (2003): http://the-sra.org.uk/wp-content/uploads/ethics03.pdf
- British Psychological Society's *Guidelines for Ethical Practice in Conducting Research Online*(2007): http://www.bps.org.uk/sites/default/files/documents/conducting_research_on_the_internet-guidelines_for_ethical_practice_in_psychological_research_online.pdf
- Association of Internet Researchers' Ethics Guide (2002): http://aoir.org/documents/ethics-guide/
- Social Research Association's Code of Practice for the Safety of Social Researchers: http://the-sra.org.uk/wp-content/uploads/safety_code_of_practice.pdf

See the *companion website* (**www.sagepub.co.uk/braunandclarke**) for:
- self-test multiple choice questions relating to Section 1;
- the flashcard glossary – test yourself on the definitions of key terms used in this chapter;
- research material examples – consent forms, participant information sheets, demographic forms, project advertisements for participants, research proposals;
- a qualitative research proposal proforma, to help you write a proposal;
- further readings (articles from Sage journals).

SECTION 2

Successfully collecting qualitative data

Interactive data collection 1: interviews

OVERVIEW

What are qualitative interviews?
When and why would I use interviews?
Designing and piloting the interview guide
Issues to think about in relation to participants
Preparing for the face-to-face interview
Conducting the face-to-face interview
Preparing for and conducting the virtual interview
What to do when interviews go badly

Interviews are everywhere. On any given day, we might listen to an interview with a politician on the radio while eating breakfast, read an interview with a celebrity in a magazine on the bus to university or watch members of the public being interviewed on the local evening news. The social prevalence of interviewing (according to US sociologists Gubrium & Holstein, 2002, we live in an 'interview society') means that interviews are perhaps the most familiar data collection tool both for new qualitative researchers and for participants. Interviews are certainly one of the most common methods of data collection within the social and health sciences (Briggs, 1986), and *the* most common *qualitative* method of data collection. There are a number of different styles of qualitative interviewing, including narrative (Mishler, 1986), active (Holstein & Gubrium, 1995, 1997), grounded theory (Charmaz, 2002) and feminist (Oakley, 1981) approaches. In this chapter we outline a generic approach to qualitative interviewing (that can be adapted according to specific requirements). We define interviewing as a 'professional conversation' (Kvale, 2007), with the goal of getting a participant to talk about *their* experiences and perspectives, and to capture *their* language and concepts, in relation to a topic that *you* have determined (Rubin & Rubin, 1995).

WHAT ARE QUALITATIVE INTERVIEWS?

The semi-structured interview (sometimes called the interview guide approach; Patton, 2002) – our focus in this chapter – is the dominant form for *qualitative* interviews (see Box 4.1). In this approach, the researcher has prepared an interview guide before the interview, but does not rigidly adhere to it, either in terms of the precise word-ing of questions, or the order in which questions are asked. For example, compare a *planned* question from Victoria's research on lesbian and gay parenting ('What do you think about the argument that children need male role models?') with the *actual* question she asked a lesbian couple who talked about their decision to co-parent with a gay male friend ('Is it important for you for your kids to have male input? Is that one of the reasons why you chose a donor?'). Question wording and order are contextual, and responsive to the participant's developing account. In the words of US sociologists Rubin and Rubin (1995: 42), the ideal qualitative interview is 'on target while hanging loose'. Participants are given the opportunity to discuss issues that are important to them and that the researcher hasn't anticipated, and aren't on the interview guide, so the researcher needs to be flexible.

BOX 4.1   STRUCTURED, SEMI-STRUCTURED
AND UNSTRUCTURED INTERVIEWS

Interviews are often divided into three types:

Structured: the questions and the response categories are predetermined by the researcher; this is the commonest type of interview in *quantitative* research.

Semi-structured: the researcher has a list of questions but there is scope for the participants to raise issues that the researcher has not anticipated; this is the commonest type of interview in qualitative research.

Unstructured: the researcher has, at most, a list of themes or topics to discuss with the participant, but the interview is strongly participant-led; this type of interview is used by some qualitative researchers.

What this tripartite typology overlooks is that *all* interviews – indeed all social encounters – are structured in some way. Even in supposedly unstructured interviews, the interviewer (mostly) asks questions and the interviewee (mostly) responds to them. Some researchers have instead distinguished between standardised or closed (quantitative) interviews (where the response categories have been pre-determined by the researcher) and reflexive or open (qualitative) interviews (where the responses are determined, to a greater or lesser extent, by the participant) (Hammersley & Atkinson, 1989). The distinction between these is shown in Table 4.1.

Partly because the qualitative interview arose as a method in response to critiques about the 'depersonalisation' of (then) standard social scientific methods of data collection (Oakley, 1981), face-to-face contact between researcher and participant has typically been viewed as the ideal way to collect interview data; the 'gold standard' (Novick, 2008). **Virtual interviews** are often viewed as a (poor) substitute for face-to-face interviews. However, increasingly, telephone, email and online interviews are regarded as different *types* of interview method, as extensions of the traditional method rather than substitutes for it, which have particular strengths and weaknesses in their own right (Sturges & Hanrahan, 2004). They are seen to provide the qualitative researcher, in the correct circumstances, with effective data generation tools. We discuss both face-to-face and virtual modes of interviewing in this chapter.

In a qualitative interview, the researcher asks the participant a series of (ideally) open-ended questions, and the participant responds *using their own words*. When interviewing face-to-face, the researcher and participant have a spoken conversation, which is typically audio-recorded and the recording is transformed into written text, ready for analysis, through a process of transcription (see Chapter 7). The same basic process applies

Table 4.1 Comparison of standardised and qualitative interviews

Standardised interviews	Qualitative interviews
The ideal interviewer is a 'robot' asking each participant exactly the same questions, in exactly the same way, in exactly the same order	Interviewers, like participants, are individuals with their own particular interview style; question wording and the order in which questions are asked vary according to the personal style of the interviewer and the responses of the participant
All of the questions are prepared in advance	An interview guide is prepared in advance, but the ideal qualitative interview is flexible and responsive to the participant; good interviewers follow up on unanticipated issues and ask spontaneous and unplanned questions
Closed (yes/no) questions are widely used	Open-ended questions are preferred to encourage participants to provide in-depth and detailed responses and to discuss what is important to them
Response categories are determined in advanced by the researcher	The goal of an interview study is to capture the range and diversity of participants' responses, in their own words
Every effort is made to minimise the impact of the interviewer on the participants' responses	The interviewer plays an active role in the interview, co-constructing meaning with the participant. It is neither possible nor desirable to attempt to minimise the interviewer's role. The interviewer should reflect on how their practices and values may have shaped the data produced

for **telephone interviews** (see Burke & Miller, 2001; Miller, 1995); the possibilities of software like Skype for conducting spoken virtual interviews are also being explored (Hay-Gibson, 2009). Virtual *written* interviews can be conducted synchronously (e.g. using instant messaging or chat software) or asynchronously, meaning there is a variable gap between question and response (e.g. via email) (Mann & Stewart, 2002). **Online/ email interviews** require no transcription as the software preserves a record of the interview dialogue.

Some of the guidance we provide in this chapter will seem like rules that *must* be followed. However, ultimately you should aim to develop your own interviewing style (Rubin & Rubin, 1995). A *qualitative* interviewer is not a robot, precisely programmed to conduct every interview according to a set of inviolate rules. Rather, a qualitative interviewer is a human being, with a distinctive personal style, who uses their social skills, and flexibly draws on (and, in some cases, disregards) guidance on good interview practice to conduct an interview that is appropriate to the needs and demands of their research question and methodological approach, the context of the interview and the individual participant (Table 4.1 provides a comparison of qualitative and quantitative interviews).

A well-conducted qualitative interview can generate amazing data, and you'll get rich, detailed and quite often unanticipated accounts if you use the method well (Table 4.2 discusses the strengths and weaknesses of qualitative interviews).

Table 4.2 Summary of the strengths and limitations of (face-to-face) qualitative interviews

Strengths	Limitations
Rich and detailed data about individual experiences and perspectives	*Time consuming for researchers* to organise, conduct and transcribe
Flexible: you can probe and ask unplanned questions	*Lack of breadth* because of smaller sample sizes (compared to a qualitative survey study)
Smaller samples: you often need only a small number of interviews to generate adequate data (see Table 3.2 in Chapter 3)	*Not necessarily ideal for sensitive issues*: some people feel may more comfortable disclosing sensitive information in a group setting or in an anonymous survey
Ideal for sensitive issues: a skilled interviewer can get people to talk about sensitive issues	*Time consuming for participants*: an interview often takes *at least* an hour to complete
Accessible: can be used to collect data from vulnerable groups such as children and people with learning disabilities	*Lack of anonymity*: may be off-putting to some participants, especially those who are 'hard to engage' in research (see Chapter 3)
Researcher control over the data produced increases the likelihood of generating useful data	*Not necessarily 'empowering' for participants*: participants have less control over the data produced (compared to qualitative surveys and email interviews)

WHEN AND WHY WOULD I USE INTERVIEWS?

Interviews are ideally suited to experience-type research questions (see Table 3.1 in Chapter 3). For example, British feminist psychologists Celia Kitzinger and Jo Willmott used interviews to research the experiences of women with polycystic ovarian syndrome (see Illustrative Research Example 4.1). Interviews can also be useful for exploring understanding and perception- and construction-type research questions – such as (supposedly) healthy men's constructions of their health-promoting practices (Sloan, Gough, & Connor, 2010). In this case, they are best suited to exploring understandings, perceptions and constructions of things that participants have some kind of personal stake in – people without a personal stake in a topic are unlikely to generate the rich and detailed responses you want from interviews. Focus groups (FGs; see Chapter 5) or qualitative surveys (see Chapter 6) are better methods when people don't have a personal stake in the topic. Interviews can also be used to explore practice-type research questions, such as the clothing practices of fat women (Colls, 2006). Grounded theorists have used interviews to answer influencing factor-type questions, such as the factors that influence people's decisions to continue regular genetic screening (Michie, McDonald, & Marteau, 1996).

DESIGNING AND PILOTING THE INTERVIEW GUIDE

Good preparation is the key to the successful use of interviews in qualitative research. Your first task is to design your interview guide – the series of questions that will guide your 'conversation' with the participant (see Material Example 4.1; the *companion website* includes other examples of interview guides from our research). A good guide will enable you to build trust or **rapport** with the participant – a key component in interactive data collection (Reinharz, 1993) – so they feel comfortable disclosing personal information to you. Rapport and well-planned questions are important for generating rich and detailed accounts relevant to your research question.

Start developing your guide by brainstorming a list of questions relating to the areas you are interested in (Smith, 1995); if relevant, some or all can be informed by, or adapted from, previous research. Then reflect on the following issues:

Opening and closing questions: start the interview with an introducing question (e.g. 'So erm why don't we start by you telling me something about yourselves and your family?'; see Kvale & Brinkmann, 2009); end the interview with a closing or 'clean-up' question. Clean-up questions allow the participant to raise issues that are important to them that haven't already been covered (e.g. 'I think that's basically everything I had to ask you to talk about, um have you got anything else you'd like to say or any kind of final thoughts or any things you'd like to follow up that I haven't asked you?'). Sometimes clean-up questions trigger really useful unanticipated data.

ILLUSTRATIVE RESEARCH EXAMPLE 4.1

Women's experience of polycystic ovarian syndrome

British feminist psychologists Celia Kitzinger and Jo Willmott (2002) noted that research has failed to explore women's experience of polycystic ovarian syndrome (PCOS), a condition marked by symptoms such as infertility, 'excess' hair growth, irregular or no menstrual cycles, weight gain, acne, male pattern hair loss and excess androgen production. Jo Willmott conducted 30 in-depth, semi-structured, audio-recorded interviews with women with PCOS, all recruited through a national PCOS self-help group (she shared her experiences of living with PCOS with the participants). The participants were largely white (24 white, six non-white) heterosexual women aged between 21 and 42, with a mean age of 29. Interviews were mostly conducted in the women's homes and lasted 45 to 90 minutes. The interview guide 'was deliberately broad based and wide-ranging, and was designed to allow women to tell their own stories, rather than adhering to a strict structure' (p. 350). Prompts, probes and follow-up questions were used to 'elicit breadth and depth in responses' (p. 350). The guide was piloted on two women, and the final version directed women to talk about:

- how they came to be diagnosed with PCOS;
- what their symptoms were and how they dealt with them;
- how they felt about having PCOS and how it affected them;
- issues around disclosing their condition to others.

The authors used thematic analysis (see Chapter 8) to analyse the data and were interested in 'women's qualitative experience of their PCOS, and in the issues they themselves raised in relation to it' (p. 351). They let the data suggest names for **themes**, and took direct quotations from the transcripts to illustrate the kind of data classified by each theme. The analysis was based on the assumption that what women say is evidence of their experience.

Their key finding was the women experienced themselves as 'freaks' and as not *proper* women. The women's concern with 'normal' femininity often focused on hair, periods and infertility:

> *'Bearded ladies and hairy monsters'* – women were upset and embarrassed by their facial and body hair and took steps to remove it; they contrasted their own (perceived) hairy, monstrous bodies with the imagined bodies of normal women.
> *'Irregular women'* – women often experienced their periods as 'freakish' or 'abnormal' because they were irregular; regular periods were desirable either as a sign of womanhood or fertility.
> *'Infertility:"My whole purpose of being a woman was gone"'* – women expressed very strong feelings about actual or possible infertility. Although 'excessive' hair growth and lack of periods was distressing, infertility was 'crushing' and added to women's feelings of 'freakishness' and of not being 'real' women.

Kitzinger and Willmott concluded that the women in their study were challenged in their perceptions of themselves as feminine and as women and called for further research.

MATERIAL EXAMPLE 4.1

Interview guide from Victoria's research on lesbian and gay men parenting (see Clarke, 2006; Clarke, 2007)

- **To start with, I'd like to know more about having children as a lesbian/gay man. Can you tell me what it is like for you? Can you tell me about your family?** (Do you use the word 'family'?) Who counts as your family? For couples: How do you divide up child care? (Is one of you the main carer?)
- **Did you choose to be a parent or did it just happen?** If you chose it, why? (Is your choice related to your sexuality?) Have you always wanted to have children? If it 'just happened' – what do you think/feel about this?
- **Do you think your family is 'different' in some way?** Why? In what way(s)? Why not? Are you raising your children differently? Why? In what way(s)? Why not? What difference (if any) do you think it makes for your children to have two female/male parents/a lesbian parent/a gay parent?
- **Do you think your family/your having children challenges any stereotypes?** Why? Which one(s)? Why not?
- **Can you tell me about any challenges/issues you have faced?** Any challenges/issues specific to being a lesbian/gay parent? How have you resolved them? (Have you resolved them?)
- **What is the most positive thing about raising children as a lesbian/gay man?** The most negative?
- **Have you encountered prejudice (as a lesbian/gay parent/family)?** Have your children? How have you/they dealt with it?
- **Do you discuss your sexuality with your children?** How have they reacted to your sexuality/'coming out' as a lesbian/gay man/_____?
- **What do you think about the argument that children (especially boys/girls) need male/female role models?**
- **What are your hopes for your children's future?**
- **How do your relatives feel about you being a lesbian/gay man (raising children)?**
- **What impact (if any) does lesbian and gay parenting have on the lesbian and gay community?** What impact (if any) does it have on the wider society? Do you go out on the 'scene'; spend time in lesbian and gay community spaces, etc.? Have you ever encountered any hostility in lesbian and gay community because you are a parent? How do you think your life is different from that of lesbians/gay men who don't have children?
- **What advice would you give to a young lesbian/gay man thinking about whether or not to have children?**
- **Is there anything else you would like to add?** Ask me?

Sequencing of questions: organise your questions so that they flow logically and cluster into topic-based sections. Early questions should be less probing, sensitive and direct than later questions. For example, in Victoria and colleagues' research on money management and commitment in first time heterosexual marriage, the interviews started with 'gentle' questions about how the participants met their partners, how and when they decided to get married, what marriage and commitment meant to them, before moving onto to more sensitive questions about the couples' money management practices (Burgoyne, Clarke, Reibstein, & Edmunds, 2006). Another useful hint is to funnel questions: the ideal interview guide is often conceived of as an inverted triangle, moving from the general to the specific. Structuring questions (Kvale & Brinkmann, 2009) can be useful to signal a shift to a new topic area (e.g. 'Er you've already started talking a bit about money and that that's kind of what I'd like to talk about next'). These features can be seen in the interview guide provided in Material Example 4.1, from Victoria's research into lesbian and gay parenting.

Constructing and wording questions: wording is vital for developing effective interview questions. Poorly worded questions (see Box 4.2) can damage rapport and subsequent data collection. Expect to draft and redraft your interview guide: in first drafts questions are often too direct (Smith, J.A., 1995), too closed and too leading. Questions should be redrafted until they are 'gentler and less loaded but sufficient to let the respondent know what the area of interest is and recognize that he or she has something to say about it' (Smith, J.A., 1995: 15). Trying out questions on someone else and asking for advice on level of difficulty and tone (Smith, 1995) is very useful.

Prompts and probes: in addition to your main questions, prompts and probes encourage participants to open up, expand on their answers and provide more detail. In the example interview guides on the **companion website**, the main questions are often bolded and the probes aren't. Notice that the probes are often more explicitly worded than the main questions, but they wouldn't be asked in this way. Probing can also take the form of 'an expectant glance' or an 'um hm, mm, or yes, followed by an expectant silence' (Fielding & Thomas, 2008: 251) or a specifying question (Kvale & Brinkmann, 2009), which spells out the type of further detail required. You don't need to prepare probes for every question, just when you think it would be helpful (Smith, J.A., 1995).

Research questions are not interview questions: in Victoria Clarke and Kevin Turner's (2007) research on non-heterosexual visual identities, the research question was 'What role do dress and appearance play in the development and maintenance of lesbian, gay and bisexual identities?' They didn't pose this question to participants, but asked more focused and concrete questions, such as 'Do you think there is a stereotypical look for gay men?' Participants' responses to such questions allowed Victoria and Kevin to answer their *research* question.

Social desirability: finally, think about whether you are likely to only get obvious, socially desirable responses to particular questions; these may not provide useful data.

Once you have a polished draft of your interview guide, review it by asking yourself the following questions:

- What am I trying to find out with this question? Will it generate that information? Don't make the mistake of confusing opinions and feelings; don't ask 'How do you feel about that?' when you want to know about the participant's views and opinions (Patton, 2002).
- Does this question help me to answer my *research* question?
- Are there (problematic) assumptions embedded in this question?
- What would it feel like if I was asked this question?
- How are participants from different backgrounds likely to feel if asked this question?
- Is this question likely to be meaningful to my participants? This is really important – for instance, the first question on Virginia's sex in long-term relationships interview guide (on the **companion website**) wasn't meaningful to participants, and failed to generate any useful data.

If your interview questions don't stand up to this scrutiny, you'll need to rework them. Time spent honing and refining your guide is important. As British health researcher Jonathan Smith (1995: 12–13) noted:

Producing a schedule beforehand forces you to think explicitly about what you think/hope the interview might cover. More specifically, it enables you to think of difficulties that might be encountered, for example, in terms of question wording or sensitive areas and to give some thought to how these difficulties might be handled. Having thought in advance about the different ways the interview may proceed allows you, when it comes to the interview itself, to concentrate more thoroughly and more confidently on what the respondent is saying.

Testing out your interview guide on a trusted friend or colleague is useful, but in small projects there's limited scope for formal piloting – where interviews are conducted to test the guide but no data are collected. Instead, we recommend thoroughly reviewing your guide after the first few interviews – are you getting the kind of data you need to address your research question? As a *qualitative* interview guide doesn't need to be treated as *fixed* at the start of data collection, it can evolve across the entire data collection process if new issues arise (Charmaz, 2002). Questions might be reworked, or removed, or new questions added to the guide during this review; the entire guide might be reorganised.

ISSUES TO THINK ABOUT IN RELATION TO PARTICIPANTS

Different groups of participants can raise particular issues that need to be considered for interviews:

Interviewing people you know: in qualitative research it is perfectly acceptable to interview someone you know, such as your housemate, a friend or a work colleague;

BOX 4.2   DESIGNING EFFECTIVE INTERVIEW QUESTIONS

Ask open questions: this is the most important guidance for designing effective qualitative interview questions. Open questions, which avoid yes/no answers and encourage participants to provide detailed responses and to discuss what is important to them, are key. Try starting questions with phrases like: 'Can you tell me about ...?', 'How do you feel about ...?', 'What do you think about ...?' At the same time, avoid questions being *too* open and not providing participants with enough direction. For example, from Victoria's lesbian and gay parenting interview study (e.g. Clarke, 2006):

Victoria: Erm I don't know anything about you at all so erm why don't you we start by you saying something about your family and your situation
Mary: Me or Jane ((inaudible))
Victoria: Both of you
Mary: Oh both of us
[...]
Mary: Erm what sort of things do you want to know personal things or how long we've been together
Victoria: Well cos I- I don't know if you've got who's got kids or ((inaudible))
Jane: Right we've got five

Ask 'non-leading' questions: you are interested in participants' perspectives, so avoid putting words into their mouths by asking leading questions. Hypothetical questions (Patton, 2002) that invoke other people's views ('Some people think that ...') or imagined scenarios that project into the future or invite participants to view an issue from someone else's standpoint can be a good way of asking about controversial issues.

Ask singular questions: questions that ask about multiple things can be confusing for participants (which part of the question do they answer first?), and you can miss collecting important data because participants only answer one part of the question. For example (from Virginia's research on sex in long-term relationships, Terry & Braun, 2009):

Virginia: Mmm so what were you, what, when you felt bad what was, what sort of things was it, how did it make you feel, like was it worried about the relationship or about him or about yourself or

Ask short questions: long and complicated questions can be confusing for participants.
Don't ask questions with double-negatives: these can also be confusing ('So you're not not getting married?').

Ask clear and precise questions: avoid ambiguity (especially when asking about intimate and sensitive topics such as sexuality); don't assume that participants will share your understanding of widely used and assumed-to-be commonly understood terms (such as 'sex').

Ask linguistically appropriate questions: ensure the wording of questions and use of terminology is appropriate to your participant group. Avoid using jargon and complex language (you don't want people to feel stupid); also avoid overly simplistic language that leaves your participants feeling patronised. Rubin and Rubin (1995: 19) advise that 'by being aware of your own specialized vocabulary and cultural assumptions, you are less likely to impose your opinions on the interviewees'.

Ask non-assumptive questions: avoid making assumptions about your participants. For example, imagine you are interviewing 'average-sized' women about their feelings about their bodies. If you ask a question like 'Can you imagine how you would feel if you were a size 20?' you indicate that you assume your participant has never been a size 20 – because you ask her to *imagine* what that would be like. Although such presumptions can potentially be damaging to rapport, and result in poorer data, assuming shared knowledge or asking 'presumptive' questions works sometimes (Patton, 2002). But it should not be done *unintentionally*. For example (from an interview with a Muslim couple):

Victoria: Mm-hm what about Christmas? What did you do about Christmas with presents and stuff like that buying presents for each other and?

Farah: Erm ((pause)) we don't actually celebrate Christmas

Victoria: Oh of course of course you don't then

Ask empathetic questions: avoid questions that overtly or covertly criticise or challenge participants ('You're not into country music are you?'), and questions that can be perceived as threatening: 'why' questions can be interpreted in this way (instead of 'Why do you ...?' try 'What are your reasons for ...?').

these are known as 'acquaintance interviews' (Garton & Copland, 2010). But you enter into a 'dual relationship' with that person (e.g. they are your friend *and* a participant), which raises some additional ethical considerations and some inflexible 'dos and don'ts'. Don't use your pre-existing relationship to pressurise someone to participate in your research or to disclose information in the interview. If a friend discloses something in the interview that is new to you, that information should remain confidential to the interview (unless your friend raises it again later). At the same time, don't gloss over (relevant) information that *isn't* new to you; only the audio recorded information counts as data, not the things you happen to know about your friend from other sources. If the person you are interviewing is someone you have a hierarchical relationship with (e.g. you're their therapist or line-manager), you need to be very sensitive to the ways in which your position could be experienced as potentially coercive, even if you don't think it is. The delicacy of this issue is such that ethics committees often require information about pre-existing relationships with participants.

Interviewing strangers: in some ways interviewing strangers is easier than interviewing people you know because you don't have to manage a dual relationship (it may also feel easier for the participant to disclose personal information to a stranger). However, it can be more difficult to establish rapport and feel comfortable having an in-depth and possibly intimate social encounter with someone you don't know. Building rapport and putting the participant at ease are a priority; make sure the participant has more time than the interview will take so you don't have to immediately jump into it, without rapport-building pre-interview chit-chat. Finally, safety is a greater concern when interviewing strangers, especially if interviewing people in their homes (see Chapter 3).

Interviewing across difference: some researchers argue that some participants feel more comfortable disclosing (sensitive) information to someone who is broadly similar to them, meaning that for an effective interview, it is important to 'match' the major social characteristics of the participant and the interviewer (see Sawyer et al., 1995). So, a woman researcher will interview female participants (DeVault, 1990; Reinharz, 1992) and a black male researcher will interview black male participants (obviously, this conceptualisation of 'matching' overlooks the ways in which two women, or black men, can be different; see Riessman, 1987). Sometimes a participant may request, or only agree, to be interviewed by someone from a similar background (see Kitzinger, 1987). This type of interviewer–participant 'matching' may be possible in large, well-funded interview studies; it is rarely practical or possible in smaller-scale research. This means that most qualitative interview researchers have experience of interviewing people who are different from them in important ways. However, 'interviewing across difference' *is* a complex issue, and you should undertake further reading in this area if you plan to do this (e.g. Blee, 1998; Dunbar, Rodriguez, & Parker, 2002; Reinharz & Chase, 2002; Riessman, 1987; Schwalbe & Wolkomir, 2002; Scully, 1994). In interviewing people who are socially marginalised in ways that we are not, we are researching and representing the experiences of the 'other' (see Wilkinson & Kitzinger, 1996) and this requires extra caution and sensitivity (discussed further below). On a practical level, communication can pose challenges: 'even when the interviewer and interviewee seem to be speaking the same language, the words they use may have different connotations' (Rubin & Rubin, 1995: 18). Furthermore, the liberal view of 'pretending difference doesn't exists' is not always helpful: people *are* different, and it is important not to assume that other people experience the world in the way that we do. At the same time, it is also important not to assume that our differences shape *every* aspect of our lives.

Power in interviews: the notion of 'interviewing across difference' draws our attention to the power relationships that shape interviewing. The relationship between researcher and participant is typically conceived of as a hierarchical one (this is more explicit in quantitative and experimental research, where participants were traditionally called 'subjects'), with the researcher in control of the interview. Others argue that control isn't inherent in the position of the interviewer but is something that is achieved between the researcher and the participant in the interview itself (for an excellent discussion of this, see Russell, 1999). Participants may perceive you as an 'expert' and for some participants your status as a researcher will override other aspects of your identity and experience, such as a shared experience of an eating disorder or a shared sexual identity (Clarke, Kitzinger, & Potter, 2004). Some researchers seek to challenge the interviewer–participant hierarchy and empower participants through a process of *empathic* interviewing (see below, and see also Oakley, 1981; Reinharz, 1992). At the very least, it's important to be aware of the exploitative potential of interviews.

Interviewing people who occupy societal positions of greater or lesser power than you adds another dimension to the power relationship between interviewer and participant. You hold a position of power as the researcher, but if you are a (young) student interviewing high-status individuals such as consultant surgeons or heads of large companies, there is potential for you to feel vulnerable, for them to dominate the interview (in ways that are unhelpful) and for you to lose control of the interview (see Odendahl & Shaw, 2002). A number of feminist researchers have shared their experiences of interviewing men and boys and feeling vulnerable as women in the process. For example, Kathryn Lovering (1995: 28), an experienced British school teacher, youth worker and educational psychologist, has written about her experiences of losing control of FG discussions with adolescent boys when the boys' discussion became 'smutty, sexist and oppressive'; 'all I wanted to do was get out of the room as fast as possible!' There are no easy or obvious 'solutions' to such dynamics – simply trying to avoid any power differences is not a solution, and would limit samples to those who reflect the characteristics of researchers (which is already a problem with the dominance of the 'usual suspects' in psychological research; see Chapter 3). The key is to be prepared, to have read about other researchers' experiences (e.g. Edwards, 1990; Lee, 1997; Thomas, 1995; Willott, 1998) and to have given some thought to how you will manage the power dynamics of the interview in advance.

Participant distress: it's not unusual for participants to become distressed when discussing sensitive issues, so don't be too anxious if it occurs. Manage participant distress effectively by *acknowledging* people's distress ('Are you okay? Would you like to stop the interview for a while?') and allowing them to express it, but also 'containing' it within the context of the ongoing interview. Don't stop the interview and start thrusting tissues at people at the merest hint of tears; in our experience people are usually happy to continue the interview after taking a moment to collect themselves. It may be appropriate to back off from a topic that is causing distress, and tentatively returning to it later in the interview ('Would it be okay to talk a bit more about X, or would you rather move onto talking about Y?').

Interviewing vulnerable people: certain groups of people are recognised to be more vulnerable than others, and we recommend that new interviewers only interview groups such as children (see Docherty & Sandelowski, 1999; Eder & Fingerson,

2002), people with learning disabilities (Swain, Heyman, & Gillman, 1998) and older people with dementia (see Russell, 1999; Wenger, 2002) if they have professional experience with the participant group, because interviewing **vulnerable groups** requires additional skills and experience and has different ethical requirements.

PREPARING FOR THE FACE-TO-FACE INTERVIEW

First, if you're new to interviewing, it's really important to test out and practice your interview *technique*: a trusted friend or colleague can help. Interviewing is one domain where practice makes perfect, so don't be put off by critical feedback. Interviewing is challenging. It involves lots of multi-tasking: listening to what people are saying, being attentive to their tone of voice and body language ('Do they seem uncomfortable with this topic; should I back off?'), mentally ticking off questions on your guide as the participant speaks ('They've already addressed question seven, so I don't need to ask that, but I must follow-up on this issue …'), spotting relevant information in participant responses and asking unplanned follow-up questions (Kvale & Brinkmann, 2009), keeping an eye on the recording equipment – the list goes on! Practise your opening blurb (about your study, ethical issues and consent; see below), test out your recording equipment, so you are familiar with exactly how it works, and try to memorise your interview guide as much as possible. That's one less thing to worry about!

PLANNING THE DATA COLLECTION PROCESS EFFECTIVELY

Once you have designed your research materials (interview guide, consent form, participant information sheet [PIS], demographic form; see Chapter 5 and the *companion website* for examples), it's time to plan for data collection. The participant is being very generous with their time and is willing to share with you intimate details of their life, so make participating as easy as possible. Negotiate a time for the interview that is convenient for the participant and be considerate of them in other ways. For example, if you have a horrible cold but feel well enough to conduct the interview, you probably want to give them a chance to decide if they want to be interviewed by a sniffing, coughing researcher! Give participants a clear idea of how long the interview is likely to last so they allow plenty of time. Most qualitative interviews last around an hour, plus about 30 minutes for pre- and post-interview chat, negotiating consent, completing demographic forms and so on, or even longer if you are meeting in the participant's home; we have on occasion spent over four hours with a participant.

Think about scheduling. We do not recommend doing more than one interview in a day for a few reasons. Conducting a good interview requires intense focus, which is tiring, and if you do more than one a day, you can miss asking questions, or following up on points, because the content of different sessions mix in your mind (Rubin & Rubin, 1995). Furthermore, this sort of research can be emotionally draining (Hallowell et al., 2005); not over-doing data collection is part of maintaining your own wellbeing as a researcher.

Ideally, avoid scheduling lots of interviews very close together. If you are transcribing your own interviews, schedule your interviews so that you have time to transcribe each interview as soon as possible after conducting it – interviews are a lot easier to transcribe when they are fresh in your mind (it generally takes about eight–ten hours to transcribe one hour of audio recording thoroughly; see Chapter 7). This also allows you to reflect on, and adjust, your interviewing style and questions before your next interview (Rubin & Rubin, 1995).

LOCATION, LOCATION, LOCATION

Select or negotiate a location for the interview in which the participant feels comfortable and you feel safe (some ethics committees may require certain participants to be interviewed on university grounds). It should be as quiet as possible, with little or no background noise (so you both can concentrate and the recording is crystal clear), little in the way of distractions (e.g. windows with lots of people walking past, posters on the walls), comfortable seats, a table/surface to place the recording equipment on, and convenient for the participant. If participants have concerns about anonymity, and/or don't want anyone they know to find out that they are participating in your study, you need to give extra consideration to a suitable (private) location. It's often easiest to book a room at university; the advantages of such a space are that it's an environment you choose and control, and it's safe. Disadvantages include that it's a somewhat formalised/intimidating setting that some participants may feel uncomfortable in, it can be sterile, it may be hard for some people to find, and parking/access may be an issue for people outside of the university (provide really clear instructions). If you are interviewing people you know, it's often easier to pick a suitable location and safety can be less of a concern (it's okay to interview people you know well in your own home, if this suits the participant). If you are interviewing people you don't know in their homes or workplaces (or in a community centre or *very quiet* café), you need to think carefully about your safety. We recommend the '**safety buddy**' procedure for off-campus interviews (see Chapter 3; see also Boynton, 2005).

If you're going into someone else's space, think about practical issues like pets, children, televisions and housemates. We have encountered aggressive Staffordshire bull terriers, wheezing asthmatic Yorkshire terriers who insisted on sitting on the microphone, house rabbits, housemates who were planning to stay in the interview room to watch television, noisy televisions, screaming toddlers, and so on. If you feel anxiety about dogs or other animals, or have animal-related allergies, check out the pet situation. If possible, schedule interviews for when small children are in day care or in bed. Don't be afraid to politely ask participants to turn off the television for the sake of the recording, or if the interview can be conducted in a private room – if you don't, those 'distractions' may hamper your data collection. Finally, in some cultures such as Māori or Pacific cultures in Aotearoa/New Zealand it is important to take a small gift of food; in other cultural contexts, such as white British culture, this is not expected.

If *you* are organising the interview space, a simple way to help participants feel welcome is to offer refreshments on arrival, and during the interview: tea, coffee or a cold drink, and some sorts of (quiet) snack – like soft biscuits or grapes (avoid noisy snacks; crisps, crackers, apples and food with noisy wrappings are a no-go for interviews; with drinks, although disposable cups are less environmentally friendly than ceramic ones, they don't create a 'bang' when put down beside a microphone). Always provide drinking water. Always have tissues in case the participant becomes distressed. Think about where you position the chairs in the room. Facing each other at an angle so the participant is not sitting directly opposite you is best. Use chairs that are roughly the same height – it can feel rather awkward if you're sitting on a chair that's much higher or lower than the one the participant is sitting in. If there is a table in the room, consider whether it would help or hinder the interview to have a physical 'barrier' between you and the interviewee. Either way, a table is useful for positioning the recording equipment. This might seem like a lot to consider, but these are all aspects of making the participant comfortable, and therefore conducting the most successful interview.

AUDIO-RECORDING VERSUS NOTE-TAKING

Because most qualitative researchers are interested in the detail of participants' responses, and the language and concepts they use in talking about their experiences and perspectives, it is important to have a precise record of the interview. This is best achieved by audio-recording the interview and then producing a transcript of the audio-recording (see Chapter 7). Audio-recorders are now almost all digital, ranging from basic MP3s through to professional-level devices. Quality can be significantly impacted by the microphone. A built-in one may not be high enough quality, so test it and consider an external microphone (if your device allows it). Good quality devices will often have a light to indicate that the device is recording – keep an eye on it throughout the interview. Carry spare batteries and/or plug the device into the mains supply if possible. We recommend using two audio recorders so you have a back-up. The recorder should be positioned close to the participant, without being intrusive – and if interviewing in their space, ask permission before putting your equipment down, especially on an expensive looking coffee table! Always pre-check the equipment. If the interview is in your space, test the audio pick-up from different points in the room and with different speech volumes.

When recruiting participants, ask them to read the PIS before agreeing to be interviewed (the *companion website* has an example of an interview study PIS); it's important that they understand that their interview will be audio-recorded, and that they are both consenting to participate in an interview *and* consenting to being recorded. Virginia has interviewed people in different places around the world who, when she got there, refused to be recorded (saying they hadn't been 'warned' – they had, in the PIS; they just hadn't read it carefully enough). At best this can result in a poorer interview and data, at worst, if audio-recorded data are *crucial* for your analysis, wasted time – both for you and the participant – and expense.

If we rely on written notes as the record of the interview, much of the richness and detail of the interview will be lost. Furthermore, it is difficult to develop rapport with a participant and conduct a successful interview if we are looking down and scribbling away in a notebook rather than focusing on them. But it's wise to make brief notes as you're going to keep a track of things to follow up on, or new questions to ask (tell the participants you might do this so they're not thrown when you start making notes). It is also very useful to make 'field' notes *after* each interview, where you record details of the participant's self-presentation and surroundings, and reflect on your personal reaction to the participant, how you think the interview went, important features of the participant's responses, ideas for data analysis, additional questions to ask in subsequent interviews, things you need to work on with regard to your interview technique, and so on (see Box 3.8 in Chapter 3).

PERSONAL DISCLOSURE

The final thing to consider *before* the interview is your strategy around personal disclosure. Personal disclosures during recruitment can encourage people to participate in your research. If you are a member of the group you are researching and feel comfortable about 'outing' yourself, this can be important information to include on a PIS; likewise, it can be equally important to disclose that you are not a member of the group you are researching (see Asher & Asher, 1999). But what about personal disclosure *in* the interview? A research methods text from the 1960s gave the following advice about personal disclosure in (quantitative) interviews: 'If he [the interviewer] should be asked for his views, he should laugh off the request with the remark that his job at the moment is to get opinions, not to have them' (Selltiz, Jahoda, Deutsch, & Cook, 1965: 576). This strategy is not appropriate in contemporary qualitative interviewing! Some researchers think that personal disclosure is important to establish rapport and to challenge the researcher–participant hierarchy (see Oakley, 1981, for a classic discussion of self-disclosure in interviewing); others think that personal disclosure on the part of the interviewer can create a false sense of intimacy and encourage the participant to over-disclose (Finch, 1984). Whatever your position, this needs to be considered in advance. See Box 4.3 for an example from one of Virginia's PhD interviews where personal disclosure was handled poorly, through lack of preparation (see Chapter 7 for a discussion of transcription notation). If you do make disclosures, though, keep them in check. The interview is not an opportunity for us to talk about ourselves or to form a new friendship (Cotterill, 1992); the disclosure must happen in the framework of a professional interview.

Related to personal disclosure is the issue of personal presentation. Prior to the interview, give some thought to the image you present to participants – for most interviews a relaxed but professional image is appropriate, but this will largely depend on the participant group. You should dress up for some groups (business people) and down for others (students) (see Boynton, 2005).

CONDUCTING THE FACE-TO-FACE INTERVIEW

With everything planned and prepped, you're ready to start interviewing! Needless to say, there are many more things to consider during interviewing, not least managing your own nerves and monitoring potential participant distress.

BOX 4.3   EXAMPLE OF AN INTERVIEWER RESPONDING BADLY WHEN ASKED A QUESTION BY A PARTICIPANT

From the first interview Virginia conducted for her research on women's experiences of their genitalia (Braun & Kitzinger, 2001; Braun & Wilkinson, 2003, 2005):

Kim: What d'you think tell me some stuff about what you think

Int: About

Kim: ((laughs)) About on the subject of vaginas tell me what you know you've been asking me a lot a questions I'm wondering kind of

Int: I have um (.) I'm not actually su- I've been thinking about this and I've been trying to clarify my own thoughts

Kim: Mm

Int: and in terms of doctors I see it very clinically

Kim: Mm yeah

Int: the whole thing an an an an and it's quite interesting I I mean I would only (.) have a woman doctor and I don't know why that is but it's just what I've always

Kim: Yeah

Int: always wanted and I've always done and um (.) so it's quite it's quite interesting um (.) in in that the

Kim: Mm

Int: I mean I d- I would there very much kind of clinicalise it but in terms of other things like um (.) awareness or (.) they're things I'm struggling all these things ((laughs)) I've been asking you are things I'm struggling with myself

Kim: Mm

Int: and I haven't (.) um got any answers ((laughs))...[Virginia's response continues in this vein for quite some time]

OPENING THE INTERVIEW

Once you have greeted your participant and thanked them for agreeing to take part, explain (again) what your research is about, its purpose and why you are conducting it (participants are often interested in our personal motives), and give them the opportunity to ask questions. Emphasise that there are no right or wrong answers to your questions and that you are interested in *their* views; they are the expert on their experiences. Next, negotiate consent – we generally do this by giving the participant a copy of the PIS (if they don't have one to hand) and consent form, talking through the key information on the PIS, and giving them an opportunity to read the PIS and consent form, and ask us any questions. Only then do we invite them to sign the consent form. We give a copy of the PIS and consent form to the participant in case they want to refer to it after the interview.

We would usually then ask the participant to complete the demographic form (reminding them that the provision of such information is voluntary), which gently gets them in the mode of 'being the interviewee' and gives us a final opportunity to re-check our audio-recording equipment. When we're ready to start the interview, we usually ask the participant if they are happy to begin, and for us to switch on the audio-recorder. Once recording, we ask our opening question.

It's important to treat your interview sheet as a *guide* for conducting the interview and asking questions, not a recipe to be followed to the last gram! As we noted and demonstrated earlier, you tailor the wording of questions for individual participants, and the context of the interview; the ordering of questions should be responsive to the participant's developing account. For example, if a participant raises something towards the start of the interview that you planned to ask about later on, it is appropriate to discuss it earlier; similarly, if something has already been covered by an earlier response, don't feel you have to ask the question you have prepared on this topic just because it's on your guide. You should treat interviews as a flexible tool, which are partly planned and partly spontaneous. Some 'rules' for question and guide design can be broken: some planned questions may not be asked and some unplanned (but nonetheless highly relevant) issues may be discussed.

FOLLOWING UP AND GETTING PEOPLE TO TALK

New interviewers need to be wary of the rushed and overly rigid interview. One of the trickiest aspects of interviewing is asking unplanned and spontaneous questions and getting people to open up and talk at length. If the person doesn't seem uncomfortable talking about the topic, but has provided only a very short response to a question, don't automatically rush on to the next question on your guide; stay with the question you have just asked. As well as using silence effectively (see below), to generate richer, more detailed responses, you can ask for examples ('Could you give me an example ...?'), clarification ('What do you mean by ...?'), specific details ('How did that make you feel?') (Rubin & Rubin, 1995), or simply ask for more information ('Can you tell me more about that?'). If necessary, reassure the participant that they are the experts on their experiences, and that their views and opinions are interesting to you. If the participant talks about something that you hadn't planned to ask about but is potentially relevant to your research question, ask more about it. Tailor subsequent questions to the specific circumstances of the participant and to their developing interview narrative. The key to all of this is memorising your interview guide and, more importantly, having a clear sense of your research question, so you can make on-the-spot decisions about whether information is potentially relevant to it and if you should ask for more or move onto the next question. Our students' interviews often start out fairly rushed and rigid (sticking closely to the question wording and order on the interview guide) and become more relaxed and fluid (and produce richer data) as they gain more experience and confidence.

INTEREST VS. EMPATHY

For many qualitative researchers, the key to successful interviewing is to show *interest* in, and to appear non-judgemental about, what the participant is saying. Gaze, body language (a relaxed stance) and non-evaluative guggles like 'mm', 'mm-hm', 'ah-ha' can all be used to convey to the participant that you are actively listening to them and you want them to continue (equally, lots of 'mm's in quick succession can convey that you want them to stop). Some qualitative researchers advocate the value of personal disclosure and the use of evaluative comments like 'Yeah, I know what you mean' or 'Yeah, something similar happened to me' to signal that you agree with what the participant has just said, or that an experience is shared, and to build trust and rapport (see Oakley, 1981). But such an empathic approach assumes participants talk about things you 'agree' with (not all participants do, e.g. Scully, 1994), and becomes tricky if the participant comes to expect your affirmation. For example, Victoria once interviewed a woman who expressed the view that the *Harry Potter* novels were anti-Christian and damaging to children – at the time of the interview, Victoria was reading and loving one of the *Harry Potter* novels. It would have threatened rapport (and thus data collection) *and* been disrespectful, for Victoria to say what she really felt in this moment; instead she showed non-judgemental *interest* in the participant's perspective. This response was appropriate; she was conducting the interview as Victoria-the-researcher, rather than Victoria-the-person. Whether you show interest and/or empathy can depend on the topic and purpose of the interview, the participant group (empathic approaches are best used when you are an 'insider' researcher or interviewing someone you already know; see Garton & Copland, 2010) and your particular interviewing style (see Rubin and Rubin, 1995, for a detailed discussion of the pros and cons of interest versus empathy in interviewing).

AVOIDING 'DOING EXPERT'

While we are 'experts' in the sense that we are trained researchers and know a lot about our research *topic*, the participants are the experts on *their* experiences, views and practices. Yet they may look to us *for* expertise; a very effective way to close down an interview is to assert such authority and 'do expertise' about an issue. As an example, in her lesbian and gay parenting research, Victoria conducted FGs on the meaning of family; in one, a participant expressed uncertainty about whether gay couples could marry. Victoria found herself giving an (unsolicited) mini-lecture on gay marriage – the discussion effectively ground to a halt, and instead of some potentially interesting and useful data about the participants' knowledge of gay marriage, Victoria had her far less useful mini-lecture instead!

USING SILENCE

As any journalist will tell you, a great way to get people to talk is to simply remain silent when someone has finished speaking; they will usually start speaking again, often expanding on what they were saying before, to fill the gap. By remaining silent you effectively give the interviewee permission to continue, and subtly encourage them to do so. We have noticed that many interviews conducted by students (including the first ones we conducted as students) are rather 'rushed' and wooden. Questions have been asked in quick succession, and no silences have been allowed to develop. If you are feeling nervous, the risk is that you will rush the interview to get it over and done with as soon as possible, and a rushed interview is rarely a good interview. It's really useful to learn how to tolerate silence – it might feel like a silence is stretching on for ages, but it will only be a second or two. Of course, don't take it to extremes or it may make the participant uncomfortable.

MANAGING NERVES

It is natural to feel nervous when conducting an interview – it's a new (and rather odd) experience that might involve meeting a new person (will you be able to establish rapport?) and has high expectations associated with it (getting good data). Even though we have both been conducting interviews for over 15 years, we can still find it anxiety provoking. But we have strategies for managing this. Very basically, give yourself enough time to prepare and 'calm' yourself: avoid rushing to an interview, all the while worrying about being late (and invariably getting lost); take time to catch your breath and focus before starting the interview. Practising your interview technique will help with nerves; we have become more confident and less anxious over time. But when we have been visibly nervous, interviewees have generally been very kind, patient and understanding. To a certain extent 'interpersonal' nerves can be alleviated as you can *perform* (and hide behind) the role of a professional researcher and interviewer, with its script and specialist equipment and materials. It also helps to remember that most participants have little understanding of the interview process, and although you may not feel like one, you are an expert by comparison. Even if you are meeting a stranger in their home, you are 'in charge' of the interaction and you guide the interviewee through the process.

CLOSING THE INTERVIEW

Once you have asked all of your questions and you have given the participant the opportunity to add any other information they think is important, it's time to close the interview. A clear end to the interview avoids the participant saying lots of interesting things after you have switched off your audio recorder. When the interview feels like it has come to a natural end, check (again) whether there is anything else the participant wants to add, and then ask specifically if they are happy for the interview to end and for the recording equipment to be stopped. Finally, thank the participant and give them another opportunity to ask you questions about the research. Participants might ask if they will receive the transcript of the interview, a copy of your report, or a summary of the results. Think very carefully about what you can realistically offer and avoid making promises in the 'warm afterglow' of the interview that are difficult to keep. We usually offer to send participants a short (two-page) summary of our results, and this satisfies most people.

PREPARING FOR AND CONDUCTING THE VIRTUAL INTERVIEW

As noted above, telephone, email and online interviews are no longer regarded as (poor) substitutes for face-to-face interviews but as different *types* of interview method, with

---

BOX 4.4   ADVANTAGES OF VIRTUAL INTERVIEWS

Convenient and empowering for participants

- People can participate in the comfort of their own homes or in a location of their choosing (and email interviews can be completed in a participant's own time); these can also be more convenient for researchers.
- Participants may feel a greater sense of control and empowerment (particularly in email interviews) because they can reply to questions when they are ready and have time to reflect on and edit their responses (they are not sitting opposite a researcher who is waiting for a response).

Accessible and (more) anonymous

- Not limited by geography (and email interviews not constrained by time zones); accessible to geographically isolated and dispersed participant groups.
- More accessible for some people with physical disabilities and mobility issues.
- Participants with concerns about anonymity and 'hard-to-engage' groups may be more willing to participate in a virtual interview than a face-to-face one.
- Facilitates the participation of shy people and those who lack confidence in talking face-to-face, and people who feel they express themselves better in writing.

Potentially ideal for sensitive topics

- People may feel more comfortable disclosing sensitive information in virtual interviews because of partial (telephone) or complete (email/online) anonymity and because they are confiding in a non-judgemental machine rather than directly in another person.

---

their own advantages and disadvantages. Boxes 4.4 and 4.5 summarise some of the key advantages and disadvantages of (different types of) virtual interviews (Bowker & Tuffin, 2004; Chen & Hinton, 1999; Evans, Elford, & Wiggins, 2008; Hamilton & Bowers, 2006; James & Busher, 2006; McCoyd & Kerson, 2006; Meho, 2006; Murray & Sixsmith, 1998; Opdenakker, 2006; Sturges & Hanrahan, 2004).

There are a number of important procedural differences between face-to-face and virtual (especially online and email) interviews, so before you begin collecting data you need to think about the following issues:

Length of virtual interviews: Email/online interviews tend to take longer to complete than face-to-face and telephone interviews. Online synchronous interviews can take around 90 minutes to two hours (compared with around an hour for a face-to-face interview); email interviews can unfold over several days, weeks or months depending on the number of questions you have, whether you email your questions all at once or in batches – see below – and on the participant's schedule and other commitments (Meho, 2006). British-based employment and education researchers Nalita

- There is less social pressure and no visual cues to inform judgements about the researcher/participant (and potentially fewer of the complexities associated with interviewing across difference); however, remember your use of language can reveal a lot about your social background, educational experiences, and so on.

Relatively resource-lite
- No need for transcription and no loss of raw data for online/email interviews. For this and others reasons (e.g. no time and money spent travelling to the interview location), virtual interviews are considerably more time- and cost-effective than face-to-face interviews (and with email interviews, it is possible to conduct more than one interview at a time).
- Larger samples are possible (because of the time and costs saved from no travel and, in the case of online/email interviews, no transcription).

Potentially allow more engagement with data during data collection
- Because of the extended time-frame of email interviews, questioning and starting data analysis can co-occur, and the developing analysis can inform the interviews; participants can be invited to comment on the developing analysis (see Chapter 12 for a discussion of respondent validation or 'member checking').
- In online and especially email interviews, researchers have time to formulate prompt and follow-up questions, so the interview can be more responsive to the participant's developing account and there is less chance of missing useful information.

James and Hugh Busher (2006: 414) found that interviews they expected to take two or three weeks 'eventually extended in many cases over several months, because this speed of responses suited participants in the busy press of their daily lives'. For email interviews, it can be helpful (for you and the participants) to set a deadline for completion of the interview (this is particularly important if you are working to a relatively tight schedule).

Participants will be typing rather than speaking: In online/email interviews, reassure participants that correct spelling and grammar are not important and use, and encourage participants to use, acronyms or abbreviations (LOL for laugh out loud, ROFL for rolling on the floor laughing), emoticons (☺ to signal smiling), and underlining and *italics* (for emphasis) as a substitute for non-verbal cues (Murray & Sixsmith, 1998). But be aware that the language of emoticons is not universal; for instance, the Japanese have a different emoticon language from that used in the west, and some countries don't use them (Opdenakker, 2006). The type of

BOX 4.5   DISADVANTAGES OF VIRTUAL INTERVIEWS

Less accessible to some groups

- Potential participants are limited to those with access to a networked computer or mobile device (or telephone); such people tend to be more affluent.
- With online/email interviews, participants need to have a certain level of competence in reading and writing (these types of interviews are potentially less accessible to participants with limited literacy skills); more challenging for participants who type slowly.
- Some people feel they express themselves better when speaking rather than writing (so prefer face-to-face or telephone interviews).

Less convenient for participants

- Online/email interviews are potentially more time consuming than face-to-face and telephone interviews; writing responses takes longer than speaking and for this reason some participants may perceive online/email interviews as more onerous than face-to-face and telephone interviews.

The researcher has less control over the interview

- In online and especially email interviews, participants can edit their responses so data are less spontaneous and 'natural'.
- The context in which the participant is typing their responses, and the ways in which this context shapes their responses, is unknown (e.g. other people may be present; the participant may be switch-tasking and doing other things at the same time as completing the interview).

encouragement that we give participants in face-to-face (and telephone) interviews is also important in online/email interviews (e.g. there are no right/wrong answers; we are interested in *your* experiences and perspectives).

Negotiating informed consent: It is not possible to hand 'virtual' participants a PIS to read or a consent form to sign in the interview. However, this information can easily be emailed or posted to participants. Participants can be asked to (print off and) sign and return a consent form via post, or use an electronic signature and return as an email attachment. For email/online interviews, it can be easier to ask participants to read the consent form and then write or cut and paste a statement of consent into a response. For example: 'I have read the informed consent and have had the opportunity to ask questions. I understand that I can withdraw from the study at any time with no negative effects. My responses confirm my ongoing consent' (McCoyd & Kerson, 2006: 394).

Establishing trust and rapport: It is often assumed that without access to visual cues it can be difficult to establish trust and rapport with participants. Although there may be advantages to remaining anonymous (participants cannot make judgements about you based on your appearance; see Box 4.4), it is important to establish your legitimacy and provide participants with a way of checking who you are (or who

- Anonymity and a greater sense of control may mean that participants in online/email interviews are more willing to stop participating, do not send responses in a timely fashion, or are unfriendly to the interviewer; in email interviews, the distractions and disturbances of everyday life can lead to participants losing the thread of the interview.
- Interviews can be disrupted by technical problems.

Some forms of information (and data) are lost

- It can be difficult to check if participants are who they say they are (particularly with online/email interviews).
- Virtual communication provides the researcher with less information than face-to-face communication. For example, in online/email interviews especially, there is no direct observation of emotion or other visual cues so it can be difficult to interpret delays in responding. In a face-to-face interview, the interviewer can observe whether a participant appears to be upset or struggling to articulate how they feel, and so can make a more informed judgement on how to proceed.

The researcher's ability to respond to participants is limited

- The researcher's ability to refer participants for appropriate (local) support may be limited.
- Virtual (especially online/email) interviews have exploitative potential, encouraging participants to over-disclose sensitive information and be less censored than in face-to-face communication.

Risk to security of data

- Online/email interviews are potentially less secure than face-to-face interviews, so the interview data could be accessed by others and the participants' anonymity and confidentiality compromised.

your supervisor is). For instance, you can direct participants to an official webpage (Madge & O'Connor, 2002) or invite them to make a verifying phone call to the university switchboard where they can ask for you/your supervisor by name; having all your research materials on official letterhead is also helpful. Moreover, personal disclosures (even if they are just about why you are interested in your chosen topic) can help put participants at ease and build a relationship.

Asking questions: Develop an interview guide just as you would for a face-to-face interview (following the same rules of question design). However, there is a lot of room for miscommunication and misinterpretation in virtual interviews, and asynchronous email interviews in particular don't necessarily allow for immediate clarification (and probing). This means that questions in virtual interviews, particularly in email interviews, need to be more self-explanatory than questions in face-to-face interviews. At the same time, avoid providing too much direction as this can narrow and constrain participants' responses.

Sending questions in email interviews: There is no one correct way to send questions in an email interview (although questions should be embedded in an email rather than sent in an attachment; Meho, 2006). Some researchers recommend sending all of your (planned) questions at once and *then* sending any follow-up questions once you have received the participants' initial responses (Hodgson, 2004); others recommend sending questions in batches; others, one question at a time. Sending all your questions at once can lead to shorter interviews (in terms both of the participants' responses and the time it takes to conduct the interview), whereas sending one question at a time (or sending questions in batches) can lead to much longer interviews (again, both in terms of the participant's responses and the time it takes to conduct the interview). For example, US social work scholars Judith McCoyd and Toba Kerson (2006), in their research on women who terminated a pregnancy after a diagnosis of foetal anomaly, sent an initial request for the participants to 'tell their stories', then sent questions in batches of 2–3 customised for a particular participant. Their interviews typically involved 8–14 interactions (interestingly, in general their email interviews were 3–8 pages longer than the face-to-face interviews and 6–12 pages longer than the telephone interviews they conducted for the same study). Tell participants how many questions to expect; some researchers recommend sending the interview guide to participants in advance to allow them time to consider their answers and to maximise the reflective potential of virtual, especially email, interviews (Murray & Sixsmith, 1998).

Preserving the dialogue to aid reflection or prioritising data security to protect anonymity: There are differences of opinion as to whether you should conduct email interviews in ways that preserve the dialogue between you and the participant. For example, James and Busher (2006: 410, capitalisation in original) instructed their email participants as follows: 'It is anticipated that an on-going dialogue will occur. In order to achieve this, please ensure that you answer on top of the message and question sent to you. PLEASE DO NOT ANSWER AT THE BOTTOM OF IT. This will ensure that the sequence of questions is not broken.' The advantages of preserving the dialogue in this way is that you have a chronological record of the interview and you and the participant can scroll back through the dialogue and reflect on their earlier responses (James & Busher, 2009). Other researchers have cut and pasted a participant's responses, cleaned of any identifying information, into a word file and immediately deleted any emails sent by or to participants because of concerns about the security of email interviews (McCoyd & Kerson, 2006). This option may be appropriate for participants with particular concerns about anonymity and confidentiality (either way, it is important to inform participants via the PIS of data-security risks associated with email interviews; Hamilton & Bowers, 2006).

Maintaining momentum: In online/email interviews, it's important to strike a balance between maintaining the momentum of the interview and allowing participants time to reply to your questions. Because you are not face-to-face with the participant and not using guggles to reassure them that you are listening and are interested in what they are saying, explicit acknowledgement and encouragement when you receive responses to questions is important. With email interviews, you can help participants to stay focused on the interview with one or two polite reminders to respond to your questions if you haven't heard from them after a few days (Meho, 2006). Because of the lack of visual cues in all virtual interviews, it can be difficult to know if participants are reflecting on their response, are distracted by another task, or have terminated the interview (Madge & O'Connor, 2002) – always politely check if you are unsure. Long delays in responding to questions could be a sign that participants are uncomfortable or distressed – again, politely check if you think this is case and explore with participants whether they are okay to continue with the interview, would like to take a break, or stop altogether. When conducting email interviews, it is important to plan your time effectively so that you can check email regularly (inform participants if you are going to be away from email for an extended period of time) and respond promptly to participants' emails. Finally, it's important to be aware that it can be difficult to close online/email interviews; although some will have a clear ending, others 'will simply die away' (Mann & Stewart, 2000: 157). Check with the participant whether they want to close the interview and treat a non-response as affirmative.

WHAT TO DO WHEN INTERVIEWS GO BADLY

As discussed above, there are lots of things you need to be aware of, and do, to interview well. Your first few interviews are unlikely to be perfect. Developing interviewing skills is a learning process like any other, and everyone makes mistakes. Each time you conduct an interview, reflect honestly on your performance, and think about how you can improve your skills. It's useful – if somewhat unbearable – to listen to the audio recording or read the transcript of your first interview and discuss it with your supervisor, to develop your interviewing technique.

What is a good interview? Our dream (face-to-face) interview scenario is something like this: the participant is highly motivated, has lots to say, talks freely, is very eloquent and quotable, and stays on topic. Unfortunately, not all participants are like this! If you encounter an unforthcoming participant, keep in mind that even the most skilled and experienced interviewers sometimes struggle to get people to talk; don't instantly blame poor interviewing skills. People can be 'difficult' interviewees in many different ways, beyond reluctance to talk. Rubin and Rubin (1995: 7) argued that interviews are 'wonderfully unpredictable' because participants 'may take control of the interview and change the subject, guide the tempo, or indicate the interviewer was asking the wrong questions. Sometimes interviewees become hostile; sometimes they become overly friendly, threatening, or flirtatious.' Some participants say things that you find offensive; they might ask *you* lots of questions instead of answering yours. The main thing to remember is that an interview doesn't just happen. You, as interviewer, in collaboration with the participant, make it happen. For instance, manage self-disclosures so that the interview doesn't turn into a conversation; gently or firmly steer the interview back on topic (try to find something relevant in what the participant is saying and use that to steer the interview in the right direction – 'You mentioned X, how does that relate to …?'); prepare in advance for how you might react to 'offensive' comments. Remember, your role is to react as a researcher, not *as yourself* (see Flood, 2008).

CHAPTER SUMMARY

This chapter:

- outlined when and why to use interviews and the pros and cons of interviews as a method of qualitative data collection;
- discussed how to prepare for the interview, including designing your interview guide and constructing effective questions;
- outlined issues to consider in relation to participants such as interviewing 'the other';
- discussed how to prepare for and conduct the face-to-face interview, including finding a suitable location and planning strategies around self-disclosure;
- discussed how to prepare for and conduct the virtual interview;
- highlighted some of the things that can go wrong in interviews and how to manage these.

? QUESTIONS FOR DISCUSSION AND CLASSROOM EXERCISES

1   Working in small groups, first identify all the problems with the 'really bad interview guide on partner relationships' below. Second, redesign the interview guide solving the problems you have identified (this could involve discarding some questions and designing new ones). See the ***companion website*** for answers to this exercise.

---

1   If you are not already married, are you planning to get married within the next few years?
2   How many times a week do you have sex with your partner, and do you orgasm every time you have sex?
3   Have you or your partner ever been unfaithful?
4   I love going to the cinema with my partner, do you?
5   Do you have a good time with your partner?
6   Would you go to Relate if you had problems in your relationship?
7   When and how did you meet your partner?
8   Who does most of the cleaning in your house – you or your partner?
9   Do you earn more money than your partner?

2   In groups of three, develop a research question on the broad topic of students' experiences of university life and design a guide for a short interview to address this question (about five main questions plus probes). Nominate one person to take the role of the interviewer, one the role of interviewee, one the role of observer, and conduct an interview. While the interview is being conducted the observer should note down positive and negative aspects of the interview. The observer (and the interviewee) should give constructive feedback to the interviewer. Then, change roles so everyone performs each role.

3   Now you have conducted three interviews with your guide, reflect on how you could improve it. Does the question wording need to be changed in anyway; did some of the questions not work very well; do you need to change the order of questions; do you need more prompts and probes?

4   Repeat exercise 2 using your revised guide, but this time the interviewee should role-play being a 'difficult interviewee' (e.g. asking the researcher lots of questions about their experiences, giving monosyllabic answers, going off topic) – don't tell the interviewer the ways you're going to be difficult; let it come as a surprise! The interviewer's task is to try to manage the difficulties and keep the interview on track. Again, the observer and interviewee should feedback to the interviewer on their performance, and everyone should take a turn in each role.

FURTHER RESOURCES

Further reading:

For useful advice on designing questions, with examples from real interviews, see: Chapter 7, Qualitative interviewing. In M. Q. Patton (2002), *Qualitative research and evaluation methods*, (3rd ed., pp. 339–427). Thousand Oaks, CA: Sage.

For a classic (and much debated – see Cotterill, 1992; Finch, 1984; Malseed, 1987; Ribbens, 1989) discussion of the empathic approach to interviewing, see: Oakley, A. (1981). Interviewing women: a contradiction in terms. In H. Roberts (Ed.), *Doing feminist research* (pp. 30–61). London: Routledge & Kegan Paul.

For a fascinating account of conducting interviews with convicted rapists, see: Chapter 1: A glimpse inside. In D. Scully (1994), *Understanding sexual violence: A study of convicted rapists*. New York: Routledge.

For an overview of the advantages and disadvantages of telephone (versus face-to-face) interviewing, see: Shuy, R. W. (2002). In-person versus telephone interviews. In J. F. Gubrium & J. A. Holstein (Eds), *Handbook of interview research: Context and methods* (pp. 537–555). Thousand Oaks, CA: Sage.

For an overview of online/email interviewing, see: Mann, C. & Stewart, F. (2002). Internet interviewing. In J. F. Gubrium & J. A. Holstein (Eds), *Handbook of interview research: context and methods* (pp. 603–627). Thousand Oaks, CA: Sage.

 Online resources:

See the *companion website* (**www.sagepub.co.uk/braunandclarke**) for:

- self-test multiple choice questions relating to Section 2;
- the flashcard glossary – test yourself on the definitions of key terms used in this chapter;
- examples of research materials for interview-based studies (interview guide, participant information sheet, consent form, transcriber confidentiality agreement);
- answers to the 'really bad interview guide on partner relationships' exercise;
- further readings (articles from Sage journals).

Interactive data collection 2: focus groups

Using a group discussion format has become an increasingly popular way to collect data from participants. The focus group (FG), as it is generally known, as a social science method was developed by Robert Merton and colleagues in the early 1940s (Merton, 1987; Merton & Kendall, 1946), but until the 1990s only really featured in political and market research. Now, after 'rapid growth' (Morgan, 2002: 141), it's become an entrenched and exciting method of data-collection (Farnsworth & Boon, 2010; Morgan, 1997). Initially spearheaded by health researchers (Wilkinson, 2004), FGs are now used extensively across the social sciences to explore topics as diverse as the language of racism (see Augoustinos & Every, 2007), tourists' views of air travel and sustainability (Becken, 2007), and the place and role of alcohol in 'dating' in Sweden (Abrahamson, 2004). This chapter outlines a relatively formal, but not highly structured, style of FG (Morgan, 2002), akin to the style of interview discussed in Chapter 4; as we build on many points raised in Chapter 4, we recommend you read that chapter first. Other types of FGs include less formal mealtime discussions among friendship groups (e.g. Fine & Macpherson, 1992; Speer, 2002b).

WHAT ARE FOCUS GROUPS?

Focus groups are a method where data are collected from *multiple* participants at the same time. They involve a relatively unstructured, but guided, discussion focused around a topic of interest. The person who guides the discussion is called a moderator, rather than interviewer, because they don't just ask questions and get direct responses back; what you're typically aiming for is participants discussing points raised by the moderator among themselves. Usually, the moderator is the researcher or someone external to the group; in some cases (e.g. sometimes with pre-existing groups) FGs can be self-moderating, with the discussion guided by a group member who takes responsibility for moderating the group (e.g. Buttny, 1997). Traditionally, FGs have been an in-person, face-to-face mode of data collection, but like interviews have shifted into the virtual realm in the last decade or so – see Box 5.1. Our focus in this chapter is on face-to-face groups.

BOX 5.1   VIRTUAL FOCUS GROUPS

Like interviews (see Chapter 4), FGs can take many different 'virtual' forms, from a range of typed discussions produced in different online modes (e.g. using chat software, discussion boards, email), to audio(visual) group conversations (e.g. using the telephone, Skype). Moving to a virtual format means groups can either be run where all participants contribute at the same time (synchronous groups), which mimics a face-to-face group, or where participants contribute at different points over an extended period of time (asynchronous groups). Many of the advantages (and disadvantages) of virtual FG methods echo those for virtual interviews (see Boxes 4.5 and 4.6 in Chapter 4), but each form also has its own particularities. If you are considering using a virtual FG method for data collection, you need to be aware of these, and think about how they intersect with the sorts of topics and participants you may be researching.

Virtual FGs offer exciting possibilities (particularly for the tech-savvy), but also particular challenges. We do not discuss them in any more depth, as we do not consider them a 'beginner' method of qualitative data collection. If you are contemplating **virtual focus groups**, to get you started, we recommend reading Gaiser (2008) for an accessible yet thorough introduction to online FGs, including comparisons with face-to-face groups, and Hughes and Lang (2004) for a more in-depth yet still accessible discussion, and then consulting the growing body of scholarship on virtual FGs (e.g. Adler & Zarchin, 2002; Bloor et al., 2001; Burton & Bruening, 2003; Chase & Alvarez, 2000; Fox et al., 2007; Gaiser, 1997; Graffigna & Bosio, 2006; Hoppe et al., 1995; Krueger & Casey, 2009; Liamputtong, 2011; Madge & O'Connor, 2004; Mann & Stewart, 2000; Oringderff, 2008; Schneider, Kerwin, Frechtling, & Vivari, 2002; Silverman, n.d.; Sweet, 2001; Underhill & Olmsted, 2003; Williams & Robson, 2004).

Social interaction among group members is central to the method; it's what distinguishes FGs from methods like interviews or surveys. FGs are potentially complex social situations (Hollander, 2004). In an FG, participants (can) interact with each other to ask questions, challenge, disagree or agree. As you get to see everyday processes of social interaction, the FG reduces some of the artificiality and decontextualisation of many forms of even qualitative data collection (Wilkinson, 1999). Indeed, FGs have been seen as one way of gaining accounts that are more 'naturalistic' – more like regular conversations – than those generated in individual interviews (Wellings, Branigan, & Mitchell, 2000). FG data can reveal the ways the meaning of a topic is negotiated among people, how accounts about a topic are elaborated, justified, and so on, as they are disputed or agreed upon, which has been termed collective sense-making (Frith, 2000; Wilkinson, 1998a). Some say that the method is wasted or even misused if we do not consider the interactive, contextual nature of the data (Hollander, 2004; Kitzinger, 1994b) and the role of group dynamics in the production of FG data (Farnsworth & Boon, 2010) in our analysis; this element is, however, often not analysed in any depth (Webb & Kevern, 2001; Wilkinson, 1998b).

INTRODUCING OUR FOCUS GROUP DATA

Throughout the rest of the book, we provide illustrative and worked examples from an FG we designed and ran specifically for the book. We wanted to replicate as closely as possible the typical student first research experience by focusing on a topic we have not researched before, so we chose 'weight and obesity' as an issue removed from either of our primary research interests. Because students typically collect their own data, after we brainstormed and developed a question guide, we hired a postgraduate student, William (Will) Hanson, to run a FG for us – the first group he had ever moderated. Furthermore, because students typically collect data from other students, we recruited six participants from Victoria's university; all were undergraduate psychology students, and white women, but they ranged somewhat in age (four were school leavers; two were mature students), and in other ways, such as parental status and weight history – two women revealed having previously had gastric-band (weight-loss) surgery during the group. Will piloted the FG guide – informally – with a group of his friends prior to conducting the actual focus group, and we all concluded on the basis of the pilot that only a few minor changes were needed to the FG guide (see Material Example 5.1). The FG was conducted in a room on campus; the audio-recording was transcribed by a professional transcriber (not without problems!) and checked by Will. The full transcript of the FG is available on the *companion website*; the research materials we developed for the FG (participant information sheet [PIS], consent form and demographic form) are presented later in the chapter as Material Examples 5.2–5.4. (There is also a transcript and audio file of another FG, on body art, and copies of all of the relevant research materials for that FG, on the *companion website*.)

> ## ILLUSTRATIVE RESEARCH EXAMPLE 5.1
>
> ### Boys' and men's 'body image' concerns
>
> Recent years have seen a significant increase in men's apparent concerns about their bodies. Identifying this as a social problem, British health and clinical psychologists Sarah Grogan and Helen Richards (2002) argued that understanding 'body image' in boys and men was imperative to avoid the significant health risks associated with poor body image (see Gleeson & Frith, 2006, for a deconstruction of the social cognitive concept of 'body image' and the reconceptualisation of 'body imaging' as a process and activity, more in keeping with the principles of contextualist and constructionist qualitative research).
>
> Although quantitative research had identified the proportions of men experiencing body dissatisfaction, and what body parts this was about, what had been missing were detailed understandings of *why* men were dissatisfied, and *how* this affected them, notably around issues like diet and exercise. Choosing a focus group methodology, Grogan and Richards aimed to 'explore how young men experience their bodies within a culture that is apparently placing more emphasis on the importance of body image for men' (p. 221). Focus groups were chosen for a number of reasons: to generate interactive data; to access 'natural' language; to increase disclosure (piloting had confirmed that group discussions facilitated disclosure on sensitive topics like this, for their sample); to create a non-hierarchical research context; and to reduce researcher influence. Participants were 20 white working- or middle-class boys and men, of 'average build for their heights' (p. 223), who took part in an age-matched focus group discussion of approximately 30 minutes. Each group contained only

WHEN AND WHY WOULD I USE FOCUS GROUPS?

FGs have the potential to access forms of knowledge other methods cannot (Wellings et al., 2000) and generate completely unexpected or novel knowledge (Wilkinson, 1998a), as Illustrative Research Example 5.1 shows. They can provide an open, supportive environment in which participants talk in-depth on often quite sensitive issues (Wilkinson, 1998c) and the interaction between participants can result in elaborated and detailed accounts (Wilkinson, 1998a, 1998c). Because FGs mimic 'real life', with people talking to each other rather than to a researcher, they encourage the use of participants' real vocabularies and ways of talking about the topic (Kitzinger, 1994b; Wilkinson, 1998a) – participants might not feel the need to use the 'correct' terms.

FGs are an excellent method if you want to elicit a wide range of views, perspectives, or understandings of an issue (Underhill & Olmsted, 2003; Wilkinson, 1998a). They can be a useful exploratory tool to start looking at under-researched areas, because they don't require any prior empirical knowledge about the issue (Frith, 2000). They can also be good for accessing the views of underrepresented or marginalised social groups (Wilkinson, 1999), not least because speaking with others 'like you' may be less intimidating than speaking just to a researcher (see Liamputtong, 2007).

four boys/men, to increase the *depth* of discussion, aged either 8, 13, 16 (two groups) or between 19 and 25. Piloting had confirmed men/boys would be more comfortable talking with a female moderator, so all were moderated by a woman, who was otherwise matched with participants in terms of regional accent, social class and ethnicity. Data were audio-recorded, transcribed and analysed using 'thematic decomposition' (Stenner, 1993) to identify patterns across men's accounts. Thematic decomposition combines discourse and thematic approaches; it identifies themes within a text, and interprets these within poststructuralist framework (Stenner, 1993), and resembles some forms of poststructuralist discourse analysis (see Chapter 8).

Their results were both expected *and* surprising. Muscularity was prized, but only a limited muscularity (bodybuilding was universally described negatively), and linked to a 'masculine' domain – fitness. Being 'overweight' was framed negatively, as the responsibility/fault of the individual (a lack of control), and as something (therefore) to legitimately tease (fat) people about. Exercise was framed as a domain for avoiding 'getting fat', but the participants' accounts were complex and contradictory around it: they could 'be bothered' to exercise to avoid getting fat, but would not put in effort to develop muscularity. The authors interpreted this finding as reflecting a tension between masculine (doing exercise for fitness) and feminine (caring about the appearance of the body) modes of engaging with the body. However, 'self-esteem' *was* related to the participants feeling good about their bodies. They summarised that the 'men and boys presented complex stories where they described pressure to look lean and muscular but felt that trying to get closer to their ideal through exercise was too trivial to justify the time and effort involved' (p. 230). The stories men told were complex, and not entirely predictable or consistent with what might have been anticipated from quantitative studies, showing the value of focus group methodology for gaining in-depth and unanticipated accounts.

If you have some kind of social change or activist intent to your research, then FGs also offer a potentially useful method. Taking part in a group discussion about a topic can have a 'consciousness-raising' effect on individuals, and lead to some kind of individual (and perhaps ultimately social or political) change (Morgan, 1997; Wilkinson, 1999). Being part of research, in a group context, thus potentially results in a different consciousness among participants, and so research can become a tool to foster social change. FGs can also be experienced as empowering – with the sharing of views meaning that people can realise they're not so isolated in their experience or perspective. For these reasons, among others, they have been noted as a particularly suitable method for conducting research with people from less privileged and more marginalised communities (Liamputtong, 2007; Wilkinson, 1999); they have been employed within participatory action research frameworks, to produce change (e.g. Chiu, 2003; Kamberelis & Dimitriadis, 2005).

Self-moderated FGs can be particularly useful for generating socially undesirable responses, as the absence of the researcher decreases concerns about social desirability. For example, we can compare Victoria's (Clarke, 2005) and British-based LGBTQ psychologist Sonja Ellis's (2001) results from their researcher-moderated FGs with

British university students talking about lesbian and gay rights, with US communication researchers Laura O'Hara and Marcy Meyer's (2004) self-moderated FGs. Whereas Victoria's and Sonja Ellis's participants' accounts were firmly underpinned by liberal discourse, O'Hara and Meyer's participants often articulated more overtly anti-gay views. Although context of data production must be considered (the US vs. the UK), it is worth considering using self-moderated groups for topics where social desirability may be of concern. Depending on the nature of your research topic, it may also be appropriate to consider some sort of participant–moderator matching, such as getting a man to run FGs with men if you are a female researcher.

Although you might imagine that sensitive topics – such as sex (Frith, 2000) or drug-addiction (Toner, 2009) – might not be suited to face-to-face FG research, because people would be uncomfortable talking about these things in a public forum, FGs can actually be *good* for collecting data on sensitive or personal topics, perhaps even better than methods like interviews (Frith, 2000; Kitzinger, 1994b; Liamputtong, 2007; Renzetti & Lee, 1993; Wellings et al., 2000). Some researchers have found them good for talking to children and young people about sensitive and personal topics (Fox, Morris, & Rumsey, 2007; Hoppe, Wells, Morrison, Gillmore, & Wilsdon, 1995). People can feel less uncomfortable discussing sensitive topics in a collective rather than individual context – though in larger studies, the opportunity to participate in either an FG or an individual interview may be appropriate (e.g. Braun & Kitzinger, 2001; Braun & Wilkinson, 2003, 2005).

Topics generally don't preclude the use of FGs, although in some cases they could – for instance, it would be hard to imagine that face-to-face FGs would be suitable for research about people's experiences of shyness; individual interviews might be better (Morgan, 1997). Topics where there are likely to be strongly (emotive) conflicting views might not suit FGs in any form (Hughes & Lang, 2004), for very different reasons – they could just descend into a bitter argument that leaves everyone upset. It's really important that you judge this latter possibility on the basis of topic and the context that your research is being conducted in. Take, for instance, the topic of abortion, which in some countries is not *particularly* controversial and in others, *highly* controversial. Say your research question was 'What are late adolescents' understandings of abortion?' Without taking the context into account, the question appears well suited to the FG method. But in many places, participants may have strong pro- or anti- views, and be very invested in those views. Given that, it might be unwise to run a group on the topic unless you are an experienced researcher with a lot of FG experience and think through the issues very carefully. For topics where there are conflicting views one solution could be to organise your groups around a particular viewpoint, which would eliminate the likelihood of (high-level) conflict.

However, FGs are not the ultimate method (see Table 5.1), and any method is only as 'good' as it is for the purpose and fit of the research project overall (see Tables 3.1–3.3 in Chapter 3). FGs are suitable to almost all types of qualitative research question, with the exception of representation and, generally, experience questions. FGs are not the *best* method if you want to elicit detailed personal narratives, due to the collective nature of the discussion and the fact that individual narratives can get lost in the cut and thrust of dialogue between participants, or for researching sensitive topics when you are asking in *detail* about personal experiences rather than broader socio-cultural or personal meanings (Liamputtong, 2011). And for getting data from busy professionals, they might prove logistically challenging. In such cases, individual interviews are likely better. The key is to choose your data collection tools to get the information you want, for the question and topic, from the particular sample.

Table 5.1   Advantages and disadvantages of focus groups

Advantages	Disadvantages
Flexibility in exploring unanticipated issues	Do not allow in depth follow-up of individuals' views or experiences
Good for gathering new knowledge about issues little is known about	Can be difficult to manage
Access to everyday ways of talking about topics (high ecological validity)	Can easily get 'off topic' and be hard to bring back on topic
Access to interaction and meaning-making processes	Logistically difficult – difficult to recruit for and organise
Can facilitate disclosure (even or especially around sensitive topics)	Not a good method to use with busy people
Can lead to some level of empowerment of participants, or social change	Not good for people who are geographically dispersed
Reduce the power and control of the researcher, data potentially less influenced by the moderator	More inconvenient for participants if they have to travel to you, at a particular time
	Focus groups are generally longer than interviews so more time consuming for participants
Good for groups for whom research participation might be daunting	May need an assistant to manage practical matters
	Transcription of FG data is very time-consuming

ISSUES TO THINK ABOUT IN RELATION TO PARTICIPANTS

Because of their collective nature, the composition of FGs – who is, and who is not, part of any particular group – is a really important issue. However, how much composition matters also depends in part on the topic and the context (consider the abortion example, above), so these sorts of choices should not be made in isolation. Two key dimensions to consider in relation to participants are how similar they are, and whether they know each other. In each case, there's no right or wrong position; you just need to explain what you did, and why.

HETEROGENEITY OR HOMOGENEITY?

Should participants in the groups be *different* or *similar*? Some people argue that heterogeneity is good; it brings different views, and produces a more diverse discussion. Others argue that homogeneity is good, as it creates an easy or familiar social environment, meaning participants feel comfortable and start from a similar place (Liamputtong, 2011). Mostly, homogeneity seems to be favoured as providing a shared basis for discussion (Liamputtong, 2011), but the obvious question is *how* similar and in what ways? We all carry multiple, and intersecting, personal, social and political identities, which hold salience for us at different times. For instance, on the surface, Virginia and Victoria appear very similar: we're both white, middle class, non-religious, highly educated women, who grew up as only children in the 1970s and 1980s and are currently academics in psychology departments. We also both have tattoos and share a fondness for cinema and good food. But we also differ, and some of these differences are not insignificant: Virginia is a Pākehā New Zealander who identifies as straight, has a conventionally acceptable body size, grew up very poor (yet 'middle class') in a non-conventional setting, was raised by just her mother, and, despite being rather accident prone, is not currently disabled. Victoria, in contrast, is English, identifies as non-heterosexual, comes from an intact heterosexual nuclear family and had a conventional upbringing that became increasingly middle class as she got older, but does not have a conventionally 'acceptable' body size, and is currently legally regarded as disabled by virtue of a chronic illness (see also Boxes 1.3 and 1.4 in Chapter 1). Furthermore, although we both identify as non-religious, Victoria's position is more active; she is a member of the campaigning organisation the British Humanist Association. So even apparent similarities can mask quite different practices and experiences. Even if your sample is students – a sample group often critiqued for their particularity and homogeneity (Henrich et al., 2010) – you shouldn't assume homogeneity, as noted above in relation to our FG sample.

One recommendation is that similarity be determined in relation to the topic of the research: if you wanted to explore the social problem of binge drinking, groups of (school-leaver) students of the same gender and social class background would be a homogeneity strategy; groups that are mixed in terms of gender, social class, age and occupation would be a heterogeneity strategy. Ultimately, which strategy you use depends on the specifics of the research itself (Morgan, 1997). But you need enough diversity in any group to ensure an interesting discussion (Barbour, 2005); you don't want the participants to just keep saying 'yeah' and 'I agree'.

FRIENDS, ACQUAINTANCES OR STRANGERS?

FGs can consist of friends, acquaintances or strangers. Being part of the same social network (e.g. as friends, as members of a support group, as work colleagues) can inhibit disclosure and open discussion, especially if people feel more vulnerable (e.g. Leask, Hawe, & Chapman, 2001). Confidentiality can also be more of a concern if participants are part of our networks (see Box 5.2 later in this chapter). With strangers, there's the comfort that you'll probably never see them again (Liamputtong, 2011). However, being with people you know can also create an easier context in which to discuss the issues. In our experience, FGs work best when made up of either friends or strangers. With acquaintances, there seems to be some uncertainty that inhibits free discussion and deep disclosure. But again, topic and research question (and indeed pragmatics around recruiting) might be a determining factor; some participants may not talk about some topics with strangers (or with friends) (Liamputtong, 2011). In our FG, the participants were *potentially* known to each other (studying the same degree), and this appeared *not* to inhibit disclosure.

There are two additional advantages to friendship groups: a) their history – when someone is expressing a particular point of view, those who know that person can challenge what they say, or elaborate on an account based on what they know (Kitzinger, 1994b), which can lead to really rich and complex data (Liamputtong, 2011); b) ready-made interactional familiarity – this means that FGs potentially run more *ideally*, with participants talking among themselves, discussing and (dis)agreeing with each other, rather than just responding to the moderator. However, both come with a downside – familiarity can mean much is left unstated, because of histories of shared knowledge and interactional patterns. Furthermore, we don't always share everything with friends, and group norms can suppress dissenting views among friends (Leask et al., 2001). Therefore, within the context of stranger groups, people might feel free to express a range of perspectives (Bloor, Frankhand, Thomas, & Robson, 2001). There are no hard-and-fast rules. Ultimately, it's a question of weighing these things up alongside your topic and pragmatic considerations (e.g. recruitment).

SAMPLE SIZE

When thinking about sample size, it's important to realise that the 'unit' of data collection is the FG, not the participant: if you run five FGs each with five participants, you've collected five units of data; if you'd done individual interviews with 25 participants, you'd have 25 units of data. FGs aren't a quick and dirty route to gaining a large sample (Liamputtong, 2011). But you do *generally* collect a smaller number of data units with FG research than with interviews.

One concept for determining when you cease data collection is saturation – the point where your data collection does not generate anything (substantially) new and the range of perspectives appears to have been completely covered (see Chapter 3) (Morgan, 1997). Other pragmatic concerns may (also) determine sample size, as will your research topic, questions and aims (see Bloor et al., 2001) – for example, if you want to compare different groups of participants (e.g. women/men; young/old), you'll need more groups (Liamputtong, 2011) – the diversity of the sample (more diverse, more groups), and the size of the individual groups (generally, smaller groups, more groups). See Tables 3.1–3.3 in Chapter 3 for further guidance.

Recommendations for FG *size* vary (Krueger & Casey, 2009; Liamputtong, 2011; Morgan, 1997); in our experience, we've found *smaller* groups (three–eight participants) work best in terms of generating a rich discussion, and are easier to manage. With smaller groups, however, there's a risk that you'll get less diverse viewpoints expressed, or if participants are not engaged, the conversation may stutter (Morgan, 1997). Larger groups can be much harder to manage, and it's not unusual to have at least one person silent throughout most of the group. Smaller group sizes can be better for more sensitive topics, where there is more risk of distress or intense responses (Smith, 1995b).

ETHICAL ISSUES IN FOCUS GROUP RESEARCH

Ethics is imperative in any research, and consent needs to be obtained before an FG begins (see Chapters 3 and 4). But certain ethical issues have particular resonances with FG research: 1) withdrawal during data collection; 2) withdrawal after data collection; and 3) confidentiality.

1   A participant changing their mind and deciding to leave during a group is possible, and is their right – before you worry unnecessarily, it's never happened to us. If it does happen, we advise temporarily stopping the group, taking the participant to somewhere private, and checking they're are okay. If they are visibly upset (discussed later), you will need to follow the protocol laid out in your ethics proposal. We suggest telling them that you'll be in touch with them again, after the group; they may wish to meet with you directly after the group.

2   In this instance, they may wish to also withdraw their data. The withdrawal of FG data is a complex but rarely discussed issue. Some ethics committees say it isn't possible, because of the interactive/interdependent nature of the data. If you do offer it, consistent with psychology ethics codes (e.g. The Ethics Committee of the British Psychological Society, 2009), no solution is satisfactory. The most likely possibility is that you simply 'lose' the whole group; another is that you try to avoid this by removing any of their substantive contributions (e.g. anything beyond a 'mm' or laughter) – but this requires identification with absolute certainty, and may not be satisfactory to the participant; if they contributed a lot, it also destroys much of the interactive nature, discussed above, potentially ruining the data. So withdrawal requires thought, and must be specified on the participant information sheet (see Chapter 3).

3   In FGs, there is an added ethical 'risk' around confidentiality and disclosure: others in the group may potentially break it (see Box 5.2) (Liamputtong, 2011; Smith, 1995b). It is imperative that you highlight that everyone needs to maintain confidentiality (Wilkinson, 1998a), before and *after* the group. We also feel it's important to explicitly have this in the consent form, so that participants 'sign up' to maintain confidentiality as a consent 'contract'. What does maintaining confidentiality actually mean in practice? Does it mean that they can't say anything about the group? No. It's okay to talk very generally about the topic of the group. What isn't okay is identifying individuals in any way, such as talking (to others) about *who* took part in the group, or attributing specific comments or behaviours to specific individuals (such as telling a mutual acquaintance: 'Did you know Mark has anorexia? I was in a focus group with him and other day, and he said ...'). It's useful to explain these parameters to participants. If something comes up in an FG that a participant really feels the need to discuss, the moderator (or researcher, if different) is the person to speak to.

BOX 5.2   A BREACH OF CONFIDENTIALITY

How often confidentiality is breached is unknown, but breaches of confidentiality can have serious implications for other participants. When we were doctoral students, we found out that a participant (A), who had taken part in one of our FGs made up of undergraduate students, had subsequently 'outed' another participant (B) as gay to the rest of their class – a clear breach of confidentiality. The breach of confidentiality was compounded by the fact participant B was *not* out to their classmates, but had come out during the FG. This outing and breach of confidentiality was only inadvertently discovered in a chance interaction with participant B, who had been upset by it (because participant B felt the outing was motivated by anti-gay feeling), but did not want us to follow it up in any formal manner (partly because participant B felt this would make the situation worse).

PREPARING FOR FOCUS GROUPS

The main drawback of the FG method is logistical. FGs are very time-consuming to plan, and run. But *don't let that put you off* – they're a fantastic method of data collection, but preparation is essential (Wilkinson, 2004).

TIMEFRAMES FOR FOCUS GROUPS

A basic ground-rule for FG research is that everything will take longer than you think. For running a FG, you need to allow lots of time. Participants need to be told how much time they're expected to give, and to allow at least half an hour *more* than the maximum time you think you'll need. Why? Because inevitably someone's late, so the group starts later than anticipated, and they can easily go over time, too. You don't want your participants to have to leave early. If your group was scheduled for 1 p.m., to take 1.5 hours, you don't want a participant to have made another appointment at 2.30, as they may have to rush off before the group finishes. This also allows time at the end of the group for discussion, which can be important if the dynamics or topic have been difficult.

DESIGNING A GUIDE; SELECTING STIMULUS MATERIALS

One of the first things you'll do in preparing for the FG is carefully design the question guide. The FG guide has been described as a '*map* to chart the course' (Vaughn, Schumm, & Sinagub, 1996: 41) of the FG. In many ways it is similar to an interview guide: it covers the range of issues that you want the participants to discuss, and the questions should be clear, succinct, precise and only ask about one issue (see guidelines in Chapter 4 for developing questions). However, in contrast to an interview guide, the questions in an FG guide act as *prompts* to elicit general discussion: you want questions which will stimulate participants to respond and to agree and disagree *with each other*, rather than just answering the moderator. Questions which 'open out' the conversation

MATERIAL EXAMPLE 5.1

Weight and obesity focus group guide

Set up by saying we're seeking *their* thoughts and opinions; that nothing is right or wrong, that they are welcome, but aren't required, to talk about personal experiences. Some of the questions will be about real issues, and some will be speculative.

Start by asking everyone to introduce themselves and briefly say what the last thing they ate was (you set a 'light-hearted' tone by going first).

Starting questions

- What's the first thing that comes to mind when I say the word 'weight'?
- What's the first thing you think about when I say the word 'obesity'?
- Who counts as obese? (How fat do people need to be for you to think they're obese?)

> These questions are broad, and aim to access the meanings most commonly available – the general discourse on the topic.

> Questions in parentheses are clarificatory and/or could work as probes.

> Questions are organised into 'themes' that cover the range of issues we want to discuss. Each theme addresses a particular issue.

Obesity and weight (individuals)

- Why do you think people get fat or obese?
  - Lack of exercise?
  - Eating? (healthy/unhealthy? junk food? Quantity?)
  - Compulsive (over)eating?
  - Modern lifestyles (sedentary lifestyles, driving, television, convenience foods [ready meals])
  - Advertising of junk foods?
  - Genetics (a 'fat gene')?
  - Lack of will power?

> Questions like this are very open questions, that should stimulate a diverse discussion among participants, but they also target a particular form of 'knowledge' – we wanted ideas or attributions about 'causation'.

> Questions listed under the main question (either as inset bullet points or in parentheses) act as prompts for discussion. They would only be used if they weren't first raised by the participants, or if participants didn't say anything in response to the question.

- Some people get fat (obese), while others do not – why do you think that is?
  - Genetics (a 'fat gene')?
- Do you think willpower is a useful idea for thinking about weight and obesity? (get them to discuss)
- Do you think people can be 'fat and fit'? (get them to discuss)
- What do you think/feel when you see an obese person?

Weight and society

- Do you think it's acceptable to be obese in society? (why/why not?)
  - How about fat? What about just 'chubby'?
  - Does this vary by age? (Class? Race?)
- What media messages have you encountered about people's weight?
  - Do you think the media depict fat/obese people in a negative way? If yes, how do you feel about these depictions?

> In the original guide, this question was worded: "How do you think the media depict fat/obese people? (What do you think about such depictions?)". However, piloting showed that it didn't work, and we changed it to this.

The obesity epidemic

- Do you think we're having an obesity epidemic? (If not, why not? Moral panic by the media?)
- Why do you think are we having an obesity epidemic?

Beyond the obesity epidemic

- What do you think could be done to resolve an obesity epidemic?
  - o Banning junk food?
  - o Food industry standards for food content?
  - o Having a 'fat tax' (taxing high fat and sugar foods more than healthy foods)?
  - o Banning advertising of junk and convenience food?
  - o More government healthy-eating campaigns (e.g. 5 a day)?
  - o More government exercise campaigns (to get people exercising at least 5 × a week)?
  - o Teaching children how to cook?
  - o More physical education in schools?
  - o Incentives for active commuters (e.g. walking, biking etc.)?
  - o Safe walking to school schemes for kids?
  - o Gastric band surgeries for individuals to help them lose weight?
- What levels of intervention do you think would be necessary to resolve an obesity epidemic? (Government? Local Government? Industry? Individuals?)

> As you will see, many of the main questions are very general, and seek views and perspectives, and should stimulate discussion among participants.

Weight and responsibility

- Do you think obese people are more of a 'burden' on society than thinner people?
  - o In what ways? Why/how is it a problem?
  - o If so, what could be done?
- What do you think about the idea that fat/obese people should be held responsible for their weight?
  - o Should they have to pay more tax (because they are more of a burden on health care systems)?
  - o Should they be required to pay more for things like seats in airplanes, trains, etc. – if they need more than one seat or a wider seat?
- Do you think *society* should be held responsible for individuals' weight? If so, what could society do?
  - o Should advertising of high sugar/high fat foods be banned?
  - o Should tax payers pay for surgery and weight loss programmes for obese individuals (e.g., gastric bands on the NHS, Weight Watchers and exercise programmes prescribed [paid for] by GPs)?
  - o Do you have any other ideas for societal-level interventions?

> On the original guide, this was worded "What other things might society be required to do?": In the pilot, it didn't work as a question, so we changed it to this.

Closing

- Do you have any other thoughts or views you'd like to share?
- Can you tell me why you decided to participate in this focus group?
- What has it felt like to participate in a focus group? Is it what you expected? (If not, what did you expect?)

> The first closing question is designed to allow for anything relevant that hasn't been covered to be addressed. Sometimes really important data appear at this point.
> The second and third questions bring the session back to the participants; they also provide the researcher with information about possible 'perspectives' on the topic that may inform analysis, and provide a back-up check that the group has been 'ok' for the participants.

are good ones (more specific questions work best as probes at particular points). For example, in our body art focus group guide, we had questions like 'Why do people get tattoos/piercings?' and 'Is it possible to have too many tattoos/piercings?', with probes like 'Is this different for men and women?' (see the ***companion website*** for the body art FG guide).

Material Example 5.1 shows our weight and obesity FG guide (it includes instructions about opening the session). We have annotated it to highlight some of our considerations and decisions as we designed and piloted it. Piloting is not always within the scope of a small project, but, depending on your topic, it may be appropriate for you to do what we did and try out the schedule more informally with a group of friends to ensure it 'works' and you get the data you need. At the very least, you should review the guide after conducting your first group. Ensuring that you know the guide really well is always important; it also frees to you manage group dynamics more fully (discussed below).

FGs often use some kind of stimulus material, such as exercises (Colucci, 2007; Kitzinger, 1994b), vignettes (Bailey, 2008), or print images or film clips (e.g. YouTube) for participants to reflect on (e.g. Finlay, 2001; Speer, 2002b), either as 'icebreakers' or to structure and stimulate the conversation. Stimulus materials and activities can be a great way to engage participants and foster discussion, generating rich data and making the FG experience particularly enjoyable for participants (Colucci, 2007). If using stimulus materials, it's important to consider why you are picking a particular stimulus. Do you want participants to discuss that particular instance, or talk more generally from it? If appropriate, try out the materials on friends to check that they work in the way that you want them to. Moreover, if you are using anything audiovisual, you need to check that it works, in the place you are going to use it, *directly* before each group.

RECRUITING FOR AND ORGANISING FOCUS GROUPS

Recruiting for and organising FGs can be some of the most time-consuming aspects of FG research. Recruitment is a challenge because it involves getting numerous individuals together in one place. It is vital to start recruiting *as early as you can*; for instance, as soon as you get ethical approval. Depending on what collection of participants you want (e.g. friends, strangers), recruitment will pose different challenges (see Box 5.3). If recruiting strangers, you need to recruit every member of each group. If you're recruiting *groups of friends*, you'll quite likely just need to recruit *one* member of each group – they recruit the rest. This isn't necessarily as painless as it sounds, but it can be a relatively easy way of accessing friendship groups. See Chapter 3 for further information on recruitment.

Choosing a location is an important aspect of planning an FG – you should balance your needs (safety and quiet) with those of the participants (ease of access and comfort); see Chapter 4 for advice. Just as with interviews, providing (quiet) refreshments is important in focus groups, as sharing food can facilitate communication (Krueger & Casey, 2009) and put people at ease.

BOX 5.3   STRATEGIES TO AID FOCUS GROUP ORGANISATION

When recruiting for FGs, certain strategies (sometimes combined) can ease group organisation:

- If you are organising groups around some participant feature (e.g. age, sex) make sure you 'screen' for this information at the point of signing people up because participants don't always take note of such information in advertisements and information sheets.
- When organising times, consider your participant group and try to think about times that might suit that group (e.g. if undergraduate students, when are they likely not to have classes? For stay-at-home parents, what times of the day – or weekend – might work best?).
- Have a range of pre-determined times that you will run groups (plus another 'free' category). As people volunteer to participate, sign them up for the session 'on the spot'. If they can't do any, put them into the free listing, and arrange them into a group later.
- If recruiting for more than a couple of groups, have fewer group times on offer than the number of groups you anticipate – for instance, if you think you'll run six groups, start with four time slots, try to fill those, and then add additional ones as needed. If you have *more* times than groups, you may end up with lots of half-full groups, and virtually no full groups, which means a whole lot of reorganisation.
- Another option is to have a list of potential times, and note down for each participant you recruit when they would *not* be available, and then organise once recruiting is done. This only really works if you recruit very quickly; otherwise people's schedules fill up, and you're back to square one.
- Free online meeting-arranging software (e.g. Doodle.com) can be used to set up potential times, and then you get participants to indicate availability. While an excellent tool, it requires confidence that all participants will respond, and quickly.
- It's often easier to organise groups with people you know or with pre-existing friendship groups (your contact participant may be able to organise a suitable time with the rest of the group).
- Always ensure you confirm with participants when their groups is, and remind them of the upcoming group the day before (this is especially important if the groups have been set up well in advance). One confirmation and one reminder should suffice. These can be done via text, email, social media or telephone, depending on their and your preferred mode of communication.

CONDUCTING FOCUS GROUPS

Okay, so the participants are about to arrive ... The arrival of participants is not without a few anxious moments (see Box 5.4). As they arrive, offer refreshments, and engage in small-talk. If they are to wear name-tags, give them these. Tell them

MATERIAL EXAMPLE 5.2

Participant Information Sheet

NB: This PIS is the one we used recruiting for the focus group for this book. A PIS outlines to potential participants the practical and ethical aspects of the research, and is designed to give them all the necessary information to make an informed decision as to whether or not they want to take part. It is usually given to participants who indicate interest, before they 'sign up' for a study. We use a 'question/answer' style because it highlights *different* elements of participation, and gives a very clear structure to the PIS – this format is preferred in both our institutions. But different ethics committees/codes require slightly different details in the PIS, so you need to make sure yours is accurate for your institution and country. The PIS would typically be required to be on institutional letterhead, too.

Participant Information Sheet – Focus Group on Weight & Obesity

Who are the researchers and what is the purpose of the research?

> Information on who the researchers are, and what the purpose of the project is, should appear right at the start of the PIS.

We are Dr Victoria Clarke (a lecturer in social psychology at UWE) and Dr Virginia Braun (a lecturer in psychology at Auckland University, New Zealand). We are collecting data for a textbook that we are writing on qualitative research in psychology for the publisher Sage (the book will be published in 2011). The data will be used for the analytic examples we provide in the book and a long anonymised extract will be reproduced in the book. A psychology postgraduate student (William Hanson) will moderate the focus group – we want the data we analyse in the book to replicate as closely as possible the typical student project (i.e. data collected by a student with students as participants).

> In some PISs, you might want a more detailed – and separate – section on how the data will be used.

What type of data are being collected?

> This section outlines how data will be collected and some practicalities of taking part.

We are collecting data using a focus group discussion. A focus group is simply a group discussion 'focused' on a particular topic or theme – in this instance, weight and obesity. One of the purposes of focus groups is to closely replicate how we express views and form opinions in real life. This means that you will be expected to talk to each other, as well as to the moderator, and to indicate when you agree and disagree with each other. We are interested in your views and opinions on the topic of weight and obesity, and we'd like the focus group to be a lively discussion; there are no right or wrong answers to the questions you will be asked to discuss!

What will participation in the focus group involve?

> Further details about participation are set out in this section, including outlining the scope of the research question.

This particular focus group will involve around six participants and one moderator, and will be audio-recorded. It should last around an hour and a half, but please allow for the group to last for up to two hours. In the group, you will be asked to talk about issues relating to weight and obesity, and to the much discussed 'obesity epidemic' (such as possible solutions to the epidemic). The questions will relate to your perspectives and views on these topics, rather than to your own individual practices related to weight or body management. However, you are more than welcome to draw on personal experiences in the group, if you wish.

> This sort of information may not be specified in advance. However, you should let people know how the FGs will be set up and when they are likely to happen.

When is the focus group scheduled for?

> It's not always wise to give out personal numbers (for safety reasons), so you may wish to leave out the telephone number, if you do not have an office one. We recommend never giving out home telephone numbers.

One of difficulties of organising focus groups is getting a group of people together in the same place at the same time! The group is provisionally scheduled for 25 February, 2.30pm.

Given the difficulties of getting people together, please contact Victoria via email (victoria. clarke@uwe.ac.uk) or phone (0123 4567 890) if you can't attend the group for any reason (we will have a list of reserve participants and we will ask one of them to step into your place). Please also be prompt (and let us know if you are delayed)!

This sets everything out so the participants know what to expect. Note that in various places, the opportunity to ask questions is emphasised.

What will happen on the day?

Once everyone has arrived, the **focus group moderator** will give everyone a name badge (to help them remember your names, and in case you don't know the other participants) and ask you to read and sign the consent form. You will be given a copy of the consent form signed by the moderator. You will also be asked to complete a short demographic questionnaire. The moderator will discuss what is going to happen in the group and you will be given an opportunity to ask any questions that you might have. Refreshments (soft-drinks and quiet snacks!) will be provided. The moderator will then ask everyone to agree on some ground rules for the group (e.g., avoiding speaking over other people, being considerate of other people's feelings). Once everyone is happy for the group to begin, the moderator will switch on the recording devices and ask the first question. You will be given another opportunity to ask questions at the end of the group.

Focus group moderators often have an assistant who observes and takes notes during the focus group but doesn't participate in any way. The assistant's notes help the transcriber to distinguish between all the different voices (this can be a rather tricky task!) and produce a more accurate transcript. On the day, Victoria or another postgraduate psychology student may take the role of observer. They will sit quietly in the room (or in an adjoining observation room) and observe and take notes during the focus group.

This is an unusually big 'thank you' gift for participation. The scale recognises the participants' 'gift' in allowing the data to be publicly used in this book. It also potentially assisted recruitment in a context where students mostly participate for course credit - as you can see, we did 'advertise' this. However, participants indicated reasons other than this as the main reason they took part: interest, relevance of topic, wanting to learn about the focus group method.

It's a good idea to specify the benefits of taking part, which potential participants might not necessarily appreciate. For student participants, learning about the research process is a benefit.

What are the benefits of taking part?

You will get the opportunity to participate in a research project and experience the research process from 'the inside'. We think that participating in research is one of the most valuable ways to learn about research (between us, we have participated in more than a dozen different research projects), and it can help us to be better researchers because we have a genuine sense of what it feels like to be a research participant. You will also get the opportunity to participate in a (hopefully) lively and interesting discussion on weight and obesity, and to share and develop your views on an important social issue. As a thank you for participating in the group, the publisher Sage will give each participant a £50 book voucher to spend on Sage books or journals (see *www.sagepub.co.uk*).

Are there any risks involved?

There are no particular risks involved in this project, and there is also no deception. The *general* 'risks' of participating in focus groups centre on the potential to become upset by a particular question or topic (e.g., if a question reminds you of a distressing personal experience), or by another participant's comments or behaviour. If you feel distressed as a result of participating in the focus group, the UWE Counselling and Psychological Service provides support to people studying at UWE. (*We provided web, telephone, email and physical contact details here.*)

Specifying the risks – actual and potential – is a key ethical requirement in the PIS. We recommend always including information on relevant support services, should participants become upset during or after the data collection. As they retain the PIS, such information is on hand if needed.

This section in this PIS is relatively brief. You typically would include information about the possible limits that would affect confidentiality or anonymity, and also more detail about how you would anonymise data – and any possible limitations (e.g., if participants are members of a very small community, others in that might suspect they recognise them).

Will I be identifiable?

No. The focus group will be transcribed by a professional transcriber, and Victoria and Virginia will make sure the transcript is anonymised so that any personally identifying information has been changed or removed.

Can I withdraw from the research?

Once you have agreed to be part of the research, you can still withdraw. If you wish to withdraw, please email Victoria as soon as you can.

Right to withdraw is a key ethical requirement. In some research you might want to specify a time-frame (e.g., one month after data collection is one we commonly use), as there are practical considerations – for instance, if you have already published your analyses, it is impossible to then withdraw. Key is to be specific and clear about this.

If you have any questions, please contact:

Dr Victoria Clarke, Department of Psychology, Faculty of Health and Life Sciences, Frenchay Campus, Coldharbour Lane, Bristol BS16 1QY. Email: Victoria.Clarke@uwe.ac.uk.

This research has been approved by the School of Life Sciences Ethics Committee.

Most PIS sheets (and other document like consent forms) will need a statement of ethical approval like this. Requirements vary (e.g., if you need to include date, approval number, etc) so check.

where the bathrooms are; check if they wish to go before the group. Allow them to choose a place to sit (unless you are deliberately placing people; see Krueger & Casey, 2009); once seated, give them the PIS to read again (see Material Example 5.2). Introduce participants to each other as they arrive. A *moderator's assistant* can offer excellent support through getting participants settled and distributing and collecting documentation before the group. They are also helpful for managing the recording equipment and taking notes/observing during the group; later they can be useful for checking the FG transcript or identifying speakers. It's worth considering an assistant, especially for larger groups (Krueger & Casey, 2009; Liamputtong, 2011); the use of an assistant needs to be included in your ethics application.

BOX 5.4   ANXIOUS MOMENTS BEFORE THE FOCUS GROUP

Despite doing everything you can, sometimes people just don't show up, or get ill at the last minute, and you're left with only a few participants ready and willing to discuss your topic. This is one of the reasons some (e.g. Morgan, 1997) advise over-recruiting. But if people just don't show, you have to make a decision on whether to proceed with a small group (or an individual interview, if there is only one participant). The most important thing is that you have anticipated this so that you can make a methodologically sound (rather than panicked) decision, and not waste the time of those who did show up. How crucial is it to your methodology and topic that you have a certain number of participants taking part in an FG? Small groups can generate rich data and have many of the key characteristics of FGs (Toner, 2009). If a larger group is essential (e.g. because you want to explore the negotiation of collective meaning making around a topic), you need to have considered what you will offer those who did show (a thank you, a reschedule, any compensation?), and *how* you will reschedule, if relevant.

A second dilemma occurs when starting an FG that should be made up of *strangers*, but two or more of the participants discover that they know each other to some degree. This may or may not be a problem (e.g. see Farnsworth & Boon, 2010), but when doing your recruitment, you need to be clear that participants may end up in a group where they *may* know someone else, coincidentally, and that they can usually change to a different group, or withdraw, if this is a problem. Forewarning them both prepares them for the possibility, and allows them to legitimately change groups (or withdraw) at that point, should they want to. In such an event, discuss the matter privately with each participant before going ahead with the group.

Once everyone is ready, it's time to start the group. After generally welcoming people, you want to make sure you explain carefully what will happen, gain consent (see Material Example 5.3), collect demographic information (see Material Example 5.4) and set up ground-rules for the group (see Material Example 5.2). This should all happen before the recording equipment is turned on.

MATERIAL EXAMPLE 5.3

Research consent form

NB: this consent form was the one we used for the focus group on weight and obesity for this book, so it has some elements specifically related to that. This is the typical level of detail needed in the UK. Compare it to the New Zealand example on the **companion website**, which is more specific. Always check the specific requirements of your local/institutional ethics codes and develop your consent form accordingly. It would typically be required to be on institutional letterhead.

Participant Consent Form – Focus Group on Weight & Obesity

I give my consent to participate in the focus group on weight and obesity. I understand that I am participating in the group on a voluntary basis and I am free to decline to answer any question or to leave the focus group at any time, without giving a reason. I also understand that I can withdraw from the research at any time before (*insert data one month after date of focus group*), without giving a reason.

I understand that all information provided is anonymous and confidential and that I cannot discuss the things that other participants say in the group with other people outside of the group.

I understand that the focus group will be audio-recorded and transcribed by a professional transcriber. Only the researchers (Victoria Clarke and Virginia Braun) and the transcriber will hear the audio-recording of the focus group in full.

> Different ethics bodies view retrospective withdrawal differently, so check your local requirements. We recommend a date of one month after data collection. This gives participants time to reflect and change their mind, but it also does not mean you need to delay your analysis too long, for fear of participant withdrawal of data.
> In our experience, no participant has ever retrospectively withdrawn any data, and we research some of the most sensitive topics possible.

I understand that the focus group will be reproduced and analysed in *Qualitative Research in Psychology: A Practical Guide* (working title) by Virginia Braun and Victoria Clarke (Sage). Extracts from the focus group may be quoted in other publications and presentations.

Name: ....

Signature: ....

Date: ....

> In some places like the UK, the researcher may be expected to sign a consent form. As best practice, you may also need or want to give a signed copy of the consent form to the participant.

Signature of researcher:..

If you have any questions about this research, please contact:

Dr Victoria Clarke, Department of Psychology, Faculty of Health and Life Sciences, Frenchay Campus, Coldharbour Lane, Bristol BS16 1QY. Email: Victoria.Clarke@uwe.ac.uk.

This research has been approved by the School of Life Sciences Ethics Committee.

Questions 1-8 are the very basic questions you should include to capture how your participants are positioned in relation to key social categories. You might also want to add additional questions related to your research topic (here, questions 9-12 are topic-specific ones).

MATERIAL EXAMPLE 5.4

Participant demographic form – Focus Group on Weight & Obesity

In order to learn about the range of people taking part in this focus group, we'd be very grateful if you could answer the following questions. All information provided is anonymous and confidential.

Please either write your answer in space provided, or circle the answer that best applies to you.

Although the categories 'male' and 'female' are the most common, not everyone identifies as male or female. The addition of a third open category 'Other' can go a long way to avoiding *genderism* in research (see Chapter 3).

1	How old are you?			
2	I am:	Male	Female	Other _____
3	I am a:	Full-time student	Part-time student	
4	Do you work?	Yes, full-time	Yes, part-time	No
4a	If you work, what is your occupation?			
5	How would you describe your sexuality?		Heterosexual Bisexual Lesbian Gay Other:_____	
6	How would you describe your racial/ethnic background? (e.g. White; Black; White Jewish; Asian Muslim)			
7	How would you describe your social class? (e.g. working class; middle class; no class category)			
8	Do you consider yourself to be disabled?		Yes	No
9	I consider myself to be:	Below the normal range for body weight	Within the normal range for body weight	Above the normal range for body weight
10	I consider myself to be:	Below the normal range for fitness	Within the normal range for fitness	Above the normal range for fitness
11	I consider myself to have:	Below an averagely healthy diet	An averagely healthy diet	Above an averagely healthy diet
12	Have you ever tried to lose weight?		Yes	No

These response options combine the most common categories, and include an option for people who don't feel they fit in any of them.

It is difficult to capture social class – you might also want to ask people for information about their income (although this can be sensitive).

Here we chose to use an open answer format (although providing examples of what we meant) to capture information as close to people's lived experience as possible. In the past we have provided participants with a list of options, but many participants complained that the options provided did not capture their identity/experiences.
If you do use a list, the racial/ethnic listings will need to be determined by the study's cultural location.

INTRODUCING GROUND-RULES

It can be helpful to have basic ground-rules specified at the top of your FG guide, to ensure you cover everything you need to. With our weight and obesity FG, we included the following instructions:

- The discussion should take approximately one hour, but may go a little longer.
- Mobile phones should be switched off or silent, *not* on vibrate.
- If you need to go to the bathroom, please just leave and return quietly.
- Try to talk to each other, rather than (just) answer the moderator.
- There are no right and wrong answers. Feel free to disagree with each other and offer alternative viewpoints. However, if you do disagree, please do so in a respectful manner.
- Please try not to talk over the top of each other, as this makes transcription of the group almost impossible, and we want to hear your viewpoints.
- The moderator may interrupt the group if these ground-rules are not being followed.

In addition to the ground-rules, we also give participants information about the scope of discussion (see Material Example 5.1). Why is this all important? For a start, ground-rules ensure participants understand what is expected of them, and they set the tone for the interaction; second, they provide a 'rationale' the moderator can use to intervene if, for example, a participant is being disrespectful; third, they set the stage for data which are likely to facilitate easier transcription. With FG data, transcription (see Chapter 7) is complicated by multiple speakers and overlapping talk. Transcription of FG data can be facilitated by getting all participants to give a brief introduction to themselves at the start that is more than just their name; something that requires them to say a few sentences, something easy and non-threatening (and the moderator can go first to break the ice). In our weight and obesity FG, Will asked the participants to talk about the last thing they ate. The idea is to help the transcriber gain familiarity with different speakers' voices. In our weight and obesity FG, the responses were a bit too short (see the FG transcript on the *companion website*); something slightly longer might give a clearer distinction between speakers (see the body art FG transcript and audio file on the *companion website*).

RUNNING FOCUS GROUPS

Running an FG involves both interviewing skills (see Chapter 4) and group management/ moderation skills (Krueger & Casey, 2009; Liamputtong, 2011; Stewart, Shamdasani, & Rook, 2007). It involves being acutely attuned to the dynamics of groups, and the unstated processes that can go on in groups (such as power and silencing). It is a skill that takes time to learn. It can be helpful to observe an experienced moderator before you do your first one. For self-moderated groups, it's important to think about how much instruction around these aspects you will provide.

Moderating involves a range of tasks, and your main one is to get people talking, and to (gently) steer the conversation to cover the sorts of issues you want to hear about; the job is *facilitation*, not control (Bloor et al., 2001). Ideally, your involvement is quite organic, where you interject at certain points to follow up on or seek clarification about something that's been said, or raise a new issue for consideration (this is a fairly non-controlled style of moderating, there are others; see Stewart et al., 2007). There's no 'correct' moderation style to aim for. Some moderators are somewhat 'passive', making the minimal interventions possible to keep the discussion flowing and on target; others have a more 'active' style, encouraging shyer/quieter participants to express their views and even participating in the discussion to some extent (taking a role of a participant-moderator; as in many self-moderated groups).

If a group is working well, and you know the guide well, topics can be covered in a seemingly unplanned or unforced manner. Don't, however, be afraid of making transitions to quite different topic areas explicit – and you can mark these *as* transitions by using 'structuring' questions (Kvale & Brinkman, 2009; see Chapter 4). In the weight and obesity FG, for example, the moderator did this in a few places, such as: 'Just to move you on a bit I think Carla you touched on advertising slightly (?: mm) So I was wondering what the group thinks about advertising of junk foods […]' (lines 211–213 in the transcript; see the ***companion website***). The moderator is part of the FG, and you need to be aware of yourself, not just what you say (the questions you ask, the things you do and don't follow up, Braun, 2000), but also your body language, your facial expressions, your gaze and indeed your silence. These help create the atmosphere of the FG; they help generate the interactive data produced. All can be used to encourage, and discourage, contributions (see Box 5.5).

As you may have already gleaned, FGs are hard work. They are also fascinating, rewarding and generate great data. But in running FGs, do not underestimate the time and energy needed. As with interviews, we do not recommend doing more than one on any one day.

When the group has covered the issues on the guide, it's important you give participants the opportunity to add anything you haven't asked about. In the weight and obesity FG, the moderator did this by saying, 'Is there anything specific anyone would like to share that we haven't covered already that you particularly wanted to?' (lines 1206–1207; see the ***companion website***). Be prepared for quite a lot of further discussion following such a question. Finally, close the group by thanking all participants and reiterating the points about confidentiality mentioned at the start. Then it's time to turn off the audio-recorder, give people another opportunity to ask you questions about the research and pack up. It's a really good idea to make detailed notes about the group, as soon as you can, in a research diary – this could include reflections on how it went, perceptions about comfort/discomfort among participants, analytic 'insights' or ideas you had as people were speaking (see Box 3.8 in Chapter 3).

BOX 5.5   PARTICIPANTS WHO MAKE FOCUS GROUPS MORE CHALLENGING

As we know from real life, interaction with others – as individuals *and* in groups – can sometimes be challenging: different viewpoints, 'personalities' and interactional styles can produce tension. These create challenges for FG data collection. Various types of 'difficult' participant have been identified (see Krueger & Casey, 2009), including:

An *(self-appointed) expert* – someone who presents themselves as *the* expert on a topic, which can be a problem because people might defer to their 'knowledge'. This can be managed by emphasising within the group that everyone has worthwhile opinions, and seeking views from different participants.

A *dominant talker* – someone who dominates the conversation and prevents others from contributing. This can be managed through non-verbal indications of disinterest (e.g. lack of eye contact, turned-away posture and not using guggles) and through explicitly asking others for their views.

A *shy* or *quiet* participant – tends to say little, or speak quietly. The moderator needs to put extra effort into encouraging participation, which they can do though non-verbal indications of interest which reinforce participation (such as making eye contact, nodding, use of guggles), and through verbal reinforcements when they do contribute. Gently asking them for their views might also help (e.g. 'Amy, we haven't heard from you on this; do you have any thoughts to share?').

A *bored* or *restless* participant – someone who engages in a range of behaviours that signal disinterest – such as looking around, tapping a pen, doodling. They may provide a distraction to other participants. The moderator needs to try to engage their interest. In addition to strategies for shy or quiet participants, a direct approach of using their name and asking for views may be useful.

Concerns about getting everyone to contribute (a lot) do reflect an implicitly realist and **essentialist** view of participants and data collection, where participants are vessels of information, and come to the FG more or less willing to spill that content. If we take a constructionist view, and see FG data produced within the immediate context (Wilkinson, 1998a), then the ways FG participants behave is *part of the context* of data-generation (Hollander, 2004). Indeed, the emphasis on the need to focus on, and analyse, interaction (Kitzinger, 1994b) partly reflects this concern. However, as much as this is a theoretical concern, it's also important to keep in mind the experience of participants; a dominating or silencing group member may make taking part unpleasant for other participants.

WHAT TO DO WHEN FOCUS GROUPS GO BADLY

Despite the potential of FGs to generate wonderful data, and provide very positive experiences for participants, there are things that can, and do, go badly. Being aware of what can go badly helps you reduce the likelihood that it will occur, and deal with it successfully if it does. Some concerns relate to poor moderation, others to the ways participants behave.

Ideally, you'd like all participants to contribute to the discussion; in practice some participants don't appear to want to talk at all. Others hog the conversation and really dominate the group. Both of these extremes can be problematic (see Box 5.5); participants who just won't talk can be one of the most frustrating experiences as a moderator. When a whole group is like this, it becomes very challenging. Virginia had one group for her project on sexual health where *none* of the five young women really had anything to say in it; getting any response to any question was like trying to get the proverbial blood out of a stone. When she looked at the transcript, she contributed about 50 per cent of the (mostly useless) data.

As noted, one of the benefits of the group setting is that it can facilitate disclosure (Wilkinson, 1998c); however, there is also a risk that participants *might* get 'carried away' and disclose too much information, which they later feel unhappy about (Smith, 1995b). This might not become apparent until after the group; this is one reason we feel that retrospective withdrawal remains an important issue for FG research – and we tend to include it (see Material Example 5.2).

Another risk is participant distress during the FG (see Chapter 3); this should be considered *before* any research is approved. In FG research, it can occur because of a participant's own feelings about the topic (Liamputtong, 2011), or through the behaviours or comments of other participants, who can and do sometimes make comments offensive to the researcher or other participants (Farnsworth & Boon, 2010; Kitzinger, 1994a; Wilkinson, 1998b). Offensive comments or behaviour can be challenged either subtly or directly, by reference to the ground rules around respect. Potential participant distress should be monitored (Smith, 1995b). How it is managed to some extent depends on the situation. It may be a case of simply checking with the participant that they want to continue, or pausing the group to give them a chance to compose themselves (see also Chapter 4).

A final issue relates to what we might call *silencing* and issues of power in FGs. Participants might effectively collude with each other to exclude particular participants or particular perspectives from discussion (Wilkinson, 1998b). This process can be overt, but it is more often subtle, and quite unintentional. These issues are possibly more likely in friendship groups, but they can also happen among strangers. Being alert to this possibility is the best advice we can give. And realise that moderators can themselves (unwittingly) 'silence' particular topics, both in prepared questions and in their actions in the group – for instance see Virginia's (Braun, 2000) discussion of heterosexist omission of lesbian accounts in her research on female genitalia.

CHAPTER SUMMARY

This chapter:
- identified what FGs are and highlighted advantages and disadvantages of the method;
- introduced our FG data;
- discussed when and why to use FGs;
- raised particular issues to think about in relation to participants, such as group composition and recruitment;
- explained the different elements of preparation for FG research;
- discussed running FGs;
- briefly outlined some potential difficulties in FG research;
- presented material examples of FG research documents.

? QUESTIONS FOR DISCUSSION AND CLASSROOM EXERCISES

1   A sensitive topic like eating disorders might not at first appear suited to FG research. Try to think about a research question for this topic that *would* suit FGs. What sorts of research questions would make this topic suitable? What sorts of choices would you need to make in terms of group composition to increase the likelihood that FGs will be a successful method of data collection for this topic?

2   In small groups, design an FG guide for a short (20 minute) FG on student experiences of university life. If you have designed an interview guide on this topic (see Chapter 4), consider the similarities and differences between the two. Now run an FG using this guide. One person should take the role of moderator, and at least once person should observe and provide feedback on the FG. After you have run the group, discuss what it was like to moderate and participate in an FG. What worked well and what worked less well? What changes would you make to the FG guide if this was a pilot FG for a real study?

3   Using our FG guide on weight and obesity or body art (see Material Example 5.1 or the *companion website*), or your own, role-play an FG in which two–three of the participants are 'problem' participants (see Box 5.5) who the moderator

has to manage. Have everyone else in the class observe the group. After 15–20 minutes, regroup and discuss ways that the management of these participants was successful and the ways it was unsuccessful. Consider how it could be done differently.

4   You are the moderator of an FG on interracial adoption, and all participants have been very agreeable with each other, except one, Michelle, who hasn't said much. When you try to bring Michelle into the group, by asking her opinion, her response is highly judgemental about interracial adoption, and critical of the views of other participants. One, Saha, gets very angry and starts shouting at Michelle; another, Dana, starts crying. How might you manage this situation?

5   FG moderation styles vary considerably, from passive and removed to engaged and interactive. Will, the (inexperienced) moderator of the weight and obesity FG, and Victoria, the (experienced) moderator of the body art FG have quite different moderating styles. Look at the transcripts for each group (on the *companion website*) and identify differences in their moderating styles. Who asks more questions/makes more comments? How do they formulate their questions? (How) do they manage/ steer the discussion?

FURTHER RESOURCES

Further reading:

For a comprehensive and very practical guide to FG research (which includes discussion of telephone and online FGs), see: Krueger, R. A., & Casey, M. A. (2009). *Focus groups: A practical guide for applied research* (4th ed.). Los Angeles: Sage.

For detailed discussion and guidance on FG practice from a more academic angle, see: Liamputtong, P. (2011). *Focus group methodology: Principles and practice*. London: Sage. Issues related to doing FG research with sensitive topics or participants are well-covered in Chapter 7 of this book (Focus group methodology and sensitive topics and vulnerable groups).

For a detailed discussion around interaction and FG data, see: Kitzinger, J. (1994b). The methodology of focus groups: the importance of interaction between research participants. *Sociology of Health and Illness*, *16*, 103–121.

Wilkinson, S. (1998). Focus Groups in feminist research: power, interaction and the co-construction of meaning. *Women's Studies International Forum*, *21*, 111–125.

Online resources:

See the *companion website* (**www.sagepub.co.uk/braunandclarke**) for:

- self-test multiple choice questions relating to Section 2;
- the flashcard glossary – test yourself on the definitions of key terms used in this chapter;
- the weight and obesity FG transcript;
- an audio file and transcript of the body art focus group, plus all the research materials for that FG;
- further readings (articles from Sage journals).

6

Textual data collection: surveys, stories, diaries and secondary sources

OVERVIEW

Collecting participant-generated textual data
Qualitative surveys
Story-completion tasks
Researcher-directed diaries
Collecting pre-existing textual data

Words as directly articulated by people (in all their messy and often contradictory glory) are the typical form of data for qualitative research, certainly in psychology: the common methods of interviews and focus groups (FGs) collect words as people speak them as data. We then typically translate them into a *written* form to analyse them (see Chapter 7). However, there are lots of other methods for collecting qualitative data where the data themselves are primarily produced in a written form. Such *textual* data can be anything from researcher-directed diaries in which participants record their thoughts and feelings about their bodies over a fortnight, to a year's worth of newspaper articles about binge drinking. This chapter tells you all you need to know to start collecting textual data. We divide textual data into two main types: (a) *participant-generated textual data* covers methods in which participants record (primarily by writing or typing, but potentially also by audio or video recording) their experiences or views in relation to a series of questions or prompts; and (b) *pre-existing textual data* involves the selection and use of words which already exist in a written (or audio) form. Such **'secondary' sources** can include official documents, online forums and transcripts of television programmes.

COLLECTING PARTICIPANT-GENERATED TEXTUAL DATA

We discuss three distinct methods of generating data from participants: qualitative surveys; **story-completion tasks**; and researcher-directed diaries (see the *companion website* for a discussion of a fourth method: vignettes). Each of these is far more widely used as a *quantitative* data collection method than a qualitative one, yet all offer a lot to the qualitative researcher.

QUALITATIVE SURVEYS

Qualitative surveys, at their most basic, consist of a series of open-ended questions about a topic, and participants type or hand-write their responses to each question. They are self-administered; a researcher-administered qualitative survey would basically be an interview. There are three main formats for qualitative surveys: hard copy (paper and pen), email and online (see Table 6.1 for an overview of the pros and cons of each format):

- *Hard copy* surveys are distributed and returned by hand or post; participants hand-write their responses and the researcher usually types these up into a Microsoft Word document for analysis (often collating responses to each question).
- *Email* surveys are usually Microsoft Word documents which are emailed to participants as an attachment; participants usually complete the survey electronically and return it by email and the researcher cut and pastes the data into a Microsoft Word document. The second option is for participants to print the survey – either to complete by hand, or after typing in responses – and return by post.
- *Online* surveys require the use of specialist software (such as *SurveyMonkey* or *Qualtrics*) to publish the survey on the internet; participants are given a link to the survey, and complete it online. The software collates the responses; some software also allows for data **coding** (see Chapter 9) of some kind, and collation of data by codes. Some versions of the software are free to use.

Qualitative surveys don't just have to be limited to questions and answers. All types of qualitative survey can include images that participants respond to (see the drawing task in our 'Views on pubic hair survey' on the *companion website*); online qualitative surveys can also include video and audio clips as question prompts. So there's potential to be quite creative in what you ask about. All types of qualitative survey need to be accompanied by the collection of demographic information to ensure you have a sense of who took part (see Chapter 3). Demographic data are generally best gathered *after* the topic data have been collected (e.g. Bradburn, Sudman, & Wanskin, 2004). Asking about personal details can appear threatening at the start, and people are more likely to answer these questions once they have finished answering the topic questions.

Table 6.1   The pros and cons of different qualitative survey formats

	Pros	Cons
Hard copy	Data can be collected in a structured way (e.g. student participants complete surveys during a teaching session), which can increase sample size Easiest for participants to do drawing tasks If using postal distribution, can send reminders to increase participation	*Potentially* limited anonymity Data entry required Costs associated with postal distribution (e.g. to post 60 surveys in the UK, and include SAEs for returning the survey, would cost around £90 based on 2012 prices; further costs associated with sending reminders) Excludes participants with limited literacy skills
Email	Hand-writing or electronic completion options Good for geographically dispersed participants Potential for follow-up data collection (depending on research design) Can send reminders to increase participation	Potentially limited anonymity Participants need computer access and skills Risks excluding marginalised groups (those not online or with limited literacy skills) Data collation required If electronic completion, difficult for anything other than textual responses
Online	Quick and easy distribution Highest level of anonymity Good for geographically dispersed participants Great for using with (colour) images and audio and video clips Potentially very quick data collection No need for data entry or collation Potential to start data coding in the programme	Needs computer access and skills Risks excluding marginalised groups Follow-up data collection and sending reminders less possible Difficult for anything other than textual responses Data output formats may be restrictive, especially if working with large samples

WHEN AND WHY WOULD I USE QUALITATIVE SURVEYS?

Qualitative surveys are not as widely used as quantitative ones, and are often excluded from discussions of qualitative methods (Toerien & Wilkinson, 2004), although a mixture of closed and open-ended questions is relatively common in survey research (for a good example, see Fish, 2006; Fish & Wilkinson, 2003a, 2003b). We have included them here because they can generate great data, can be less daunting than doing interviews or FGs, and can be a very quick and cheap way to collect (lots of) data. Surveys are also ideally suited to *sensitive* topics, partly because they offer privacy and anonymity to the participants, and partly because they require less 'skill' and experience on the part of the researcher to collect good data. They also raise fewer ethical concerns related to inexperienced researchers researching sensitive topics (see Chapter 3). This all means they're *ideally* suited to student and other resource-lite projects. Qualitative surveys can be used across a range of types of research questions, but they are particularly well suited to experience, understandings and perceptions, and practice type questions (see Table 3.1 in Chapter 3; see the **companion website** for examples of surveys addressing these types of questions).

Because qualitative surveys are a quick and inexpensive way to collect data from lots of people in a short period of time, you can access a wider range of views than is typical or practical using interactive qualitative methods. For example, British feminist psychologists Merran Toerien and Sue Wilkinson (2004) used qualitative surveys to research women's body hair removal in order to obtain a 'wide-angle' picture of women's experiences, perspectives and practices. Using surveys allowed them to collect a very large sample: 678 women completed a hard copy survey (it could take two researchers *years* to interview that many people!). In addition, compared to interactive data, survey data tends to be more focused on the topic, and the method produces greater standardisation of responses, as all participants are asked the same questions in the same way. This can be useful for pattern-based analysis. However, participants still provide their own answers, in their own words, so their frameworks are still prioritised, which is important for qualitative research.

DESIGNING AND PILOTING QUALITATIVE SURVEYS

The first thing you need to decide is the format(s) for survey delivery, considering the pros and cons of each (see Table 6.1). Regardless of format, a qualitative survey generally contains the following elements:

- a clear and informative title (e.g. 'Views on pubic hair: a qualitative survey' or 'Qualitative survey on lesbian and bisexual women's dress and appearance');
- pre-participation information (this information should also appear on the participant information sheet [PIS]):
  - guidance on who is eligible to complete the survey;
  - information about how the data from the survey will be used and about participants' rights to anonymity, confidentially and retrospective withdrawal;
  - information about consent (e.g. a separate consent form or a declaration that completion/return indicates consent – the consent process needs ethical approval);
  - a deadline for completing/returning the survey – make this as generous as possible but be realistic about your time scale.

- instructions on how to complete the survey and how to answer questions: should participants spend some time reflecting on their responses or write what first comes to mind? Should they provide examples? Completion instructions might usefully be repeated on individual questions (see the 'please explain your views' instructions for some questions in the example surveys on the ***companion website***);

- the main body of the survey, in which you ask a series of (predominantly) open-ended questions. The total number of questions depends on your research question and the depth and detail of response required for each. Ideally you should keep a survey as short as possible to avoid 'question fatigue' from participants, and diminishing detail in the answers. The minimum number of questions is about three (see Illustrative Research Example 6.1), the maximum about 30 (e.g. our 'Views on pubic hair' survey has 25). For longer surveys (e.g. more than about ten questions) grouping questions into two or three distinct and coherent sections can be good (as the 'Views on pubic hair' survey does);
- a final 'clean-up' question providing the participant with an opportunity to add any other information they think is important that you haven't anticipated (e.g. 'Is there anything else you would like to add about …?');
- a demographic section (see Chapter 3);
- a completion page that participants see after finishing the survey. It should contain:
  o   a thank-you;
  o   your, and/or your supervisor's, contact details in case participants have any questions or comments;
  o   details of sources of support and further information, if relevant (this will depend on your topic). For example Victoria's student Eleni Demetriou finished her online qualitative survey about the experiences of adults who had grown up with a lesbian, gay, bisexual and/or trans (LGBT) parent with: a) a short reading list of books written by, for and about the children of LGBT parents; and b) links to documents on the American Psychological Association website summarising the findings of psychological research on the children of LGBT parents (for the general public).

Hard copy surveys also need:
- space to write a participant code on every page;
- a page header with survey title and page number;
- a PIS and, if needed, a consent form (see Chapter 5 and the ***companion website*** for examples);
- clear instructions on where and how to return the survey;
- if relevant, an addressed (stamped) envelope for survey return – depending on your design, consent forms may need to be returned separately;
- additional space at the end of the questions in case participants want to expand on answers (see the surveys on the ***companion website***).

ILLUSTRATIVE RESEARCH EXAMPLE 6.1

Qualitative surveys: men managing 'body image' and appearance through clothing

Changes in the advertising of men's clothing and in the representation of the male body in popular culture in the preceding decade, among other things, created an interest in men's clothing practices for British social psychologists Hannah Frith and Kate Gleeson (2004). Their research aimed to explore men's perceptions of whether and how their feelings about their bodies guided their clothing practices, and whether men used clothing to alter their appearance.

They collected survey data from an opportunistic, snowball sample of 75 mostly white men, aged between 17 and 67 (mean age: 25.79). The participants received a pack containing a hard copy PIS, consent form, demographic form and the *Clothing and the Body Questionnaire*, which contained three main questions and one 'clean-up' question:

1 How much does the way you feel about your body influence the kinds of clothing you buy or wear?
2 Do you dress in a way that hides aspects of your body?
3 Do you dress in a way that emphasises aspects of your body?
4 Is there anything else you think we should know, or are there any questions we should have asked but didn't?

Men were instructed to: spend time thinking about their answers before they started to write, answer questions fully and give specific examples. Some men wrote at length; others wrote very little. The longest answers were provided in response to question one. The researchers used thematic analysis (see Chapter 8), which generated 50 codes, organised into five themes. Four key themes were discussed:

1 Men valued the practical rather than the aesthetic aspects of clothing; they emphasised the importance of clothes being fit for purpose.
2 Men portrayed themselves as unconcerned with appearance and most argued that their body shape did not influence their choice of clothing; however, many men described in detail how particular types of clothing complement their body shape.
3 Men reported using clothing both to hide and to display their body and to emphasise particular body parts; men's perceptions of their bodies were not static and shifts in perception and in the use of clothing to conceal or reveal occurred daily.
4 Men felt pressure to conform to an ideal body type and reported using clothing to manage the appearance of their bodies, depending on the extent to which they perceived their bodies to fit the slim and muscular ideal.

Frith and Gleeson concluded that their male participants actively used clothing to 'manipulate their appearance to meet cultural ideals of masculinity' (p.45), but felt they should *display* a lack of concern with appearance.

Good questions are essential to getting good survey data, so how do you write good survey questions? First, you should only ask questions that you can reasonably expect participants to be able to answer. Think carefully about wording and language – the hints and tips for designing interview guides outlined in Chapter 4 are relevant here, so (re)visit that section. Good survey questions are generally: a) as short as possible (e.g. '*Why* do you think *women* remove pubic hair?'); b) expressed clearly and unambiguously (you cannot clarify your meaning during data collection); and c) use simple and appropriate language (avoid jargon). It may be important to define key terms, especially if ambiguous (see Box 6.1). You need to *avoid* leading, judgmental, closed or multiple questions. There is an important exception to the 'avoid closed questions' rule: a closed question, if followed by instructions for explanation or clarification (see the example surveys on the *companion website*), can sometimes be the best way to ask a short, clear question. There is also an exception to the 'avoid multiple questions' rule: sometimes, additional prompt or explanatory questions (in brackets) can help to clarify the meaning of a main question. For example, in our 'Experiences of orgasm and sexual pleasure' survey (see the *companion website*), a main question – 'Please can you describe in detail your last (or typical) experience of orgasm during sexual activity with a partner?' – was followed by a prompt question – 'What physical and emotional sensations did you experience?' – to clarify the type of information we wanted participants to write about.

BOX 6.1   DEFINING 'SEX'

Sex is an ambiguous term, is notoriously difficult to define and meaning is not necessarily shared: one person's sex is another person's foreplay (Sanders & Reinisch, 1999). In their survey on orgasm and sexual pleasure, Victoria and Cassie Rogers told participants exactly what they meant by the term: *The questions focus on experiences of orgasm and sexual pleasure during sexual activity (or sex) with a partner (rather than during solo masturbation). We use the term sex in its broadest sense to include any kind of sexual activity with a partner (including, for example, oral sex, penis-in-vagina intercourse/coitus, anal sex and mutual masturbation).* By providing a clear definition, participants knew what practices were covered by the questions asked. However, *even* so, participants often resorted to a very narrow definition of sex (Opperman, Braun, Clarke, & Rogers, 2013).

The next thing to think about is survey organisation and layout. The order and flow of questions is very important: as in interviews, start with general and 'gentle' questions; ask specific and 'difficult' questions later. This eases the participant into the topic. Imagine a survey on university students' perspectives on binge drinking which started with 'Have you ever been hospitalised as a result of excessive alcohol consumption? *Please explain*', compared to one that started with 'What does binge drinking mean to you?' They should also flow logically; as noted above, cluster together questions on a similar aspect of the issue being researched. With hard copy/email surveys, you generally want to avoid a complex format with 'if yes, then go to question 8a ..., if no, then go to question 11b ...,' type instructions (this kind of question filtering is easy to do online). Overall, a survey should be pleasant to look at, with an easily readable font (the humanist sans serif font Calibri, the current default font in Microsoft Word, is ideal) and *clear* instructions. A key design issue for *hard copy* surveys is how much *space* you give for answers: it will be seen as an indication of how long you want answers to be. We suggest four questions *maximum* for each A4 page (see the examples on the ***companion website***).

The only way to discover if a survey 'works' is to pilot it. There are two ways to pilot: 1) invite people to complete the survey and use their responses to establish whether you are getting the data you want; 2) invite people to complete the survey *and* ask them to comment on the clarity of the instructions, the wording and ordering of questions, and the design and layout. For a small project, using five–ten members of your population should be sufficient. Piloting may result in tweaks to your survey: by piloting the 'Views on pubic hair' survey, we noticed that participants often gave subjective evaluations of amounts of pubic hair (e.g, 'a lot'); we realised we had no way of knowing *what* that actually meant to participants. Therefore, two questions were added which required participants to draw pubic hair on images of a male and female groin (see the ***companion website***), to identify their norms and preferences, allowing better interpretation of the data.

COLLECTING AND MANAGING SURVEY DATA

In general, survey data tends to be *thinner* than interview data (although the depth and detail of responses can vary massively): the ***companion website*** has data examples from our 'Views on pubic hair' and 'Experiences of orgasm and sexual pleasure' surveys. Larger sample sizes (for surveys and other participant-generated textual data methods) can partly compensate for (some) thinner responses, but you still want your survey to produce the richest data it can. The depth and detail of responses partly depends on participants' motivation to participate in the study and their interest in the topic, but it's also triggered by well-designed questions which stimulate them to respond and engage, as well as practical issues, such as how much time they are able and willing to commit. Survey data will only be suitable for certain forms of qualitative analysis (see Table 3.2 in Chapter 3).

When typing up or collating data for analysis, anonymise if necessary (see Chapter 7), but the record should be otherwise verbatim: do not correct participants' spelling and grammar (for now; you can do this later when presenting extracts in your report, to aid the readability). And make sure each answer is clearly marked with a participant number/code. A spreadsheet (e.g. Microsoft Excel) is often the best way to compile demographic responses, especially if some are quantitative.

WHAT CAN GO WRONG WITH SURVEYS?

A major limitation of surveys is lack of flexibility. Because questions are set in advance, responses are constrained: they cannot be probed and extended (Frith &

Gleeson, 2008). When Victoria was learning to drive her instructor told her to 'assume that everyone's an idiot'. This (somewhat uncharitable) maxim is a good one to apply to survey design. If there is any scope for people to misunderstand an instruction or a question, it will happen; if there is an obvious misunderstanding, your data may be useless. This cannot be completely eliminated by piloting. The other major limitation is that, unless you hand participants a survey and wait to collect them, people who promised to participate may forget, or get too busy, meaning you get very few responses. Sending one or two polite reminders can increase responses, but may not be possible with your sampling strategy (e.g. with an online survey distributed through listservs).

STORY-COMPLETION TASKS

Story-completion tasks are a completely different method. They require participants to either complete, or write, a story. In the 'complete a story' approach, participants are provided with a **story stem**: the start of a story involving a hypothetical scenario and characters. They are then typically asked to write 'what happens next' (Material Example 6.1 provides an example of a story stem from our research on people's perceptions of trans parenting). In the 'write a story' approach, participants are provided with a **story cue**, a 'bare bones' scenario for a story, and asked to write a story about that scenario (e.g. 'a white couple adopt a black child – tell the story of how people react'). While a story stem can provide more 'direction' than a story cue, it's important to leave some ambiguity, as getting at participants' assumptions is one of the key elements of this method. In British feminist psychologists Celia Kitzinger and Debra Powell's (1995) research on infidelity in heterosexual relationships (see Illustrative Research Example 6.2), for example, their story stem described the main characters as 'going out', and one character realising the other is 'seeing someone else'. As '"seeing" leaves the precise nature of the relationship ambiguous and "someone else" leaves the sex of the other person unspecified' (p. 352), Kitzinger and Powell could explore participants' assumptions about what 'seeing someone else' meant, as well as about the gender of the 'someone else'.

WHEN AND WHY WOULD I USE STORY-COMPLETION TASKS?

Quantitative researchers typically treat story completion as a 'projective technique' (like the Rorschach inkblot test and the Thematic Apperception Test) through which to *indirectly* access people's psychological worlds. Participants' (unconscious) thoughts and feelings are assumed to shape what they write in response to the ambiguous stimulus material provided; the researcher 'reads off' the participant's underlying anxieties and motivations from their story (Kitzinger & Powell, 1995). Qualitative story-completion research typically has a quite different aim: to understand something about the

---

MATERIAL EXAMPLE 6.1

Trans parent story-completion task and instructions to participants

Participants were presented with the following story and instructions (bold in original).

Please read and complete the following story:

Before he leaves for work, Brian tells his children that he has something important to discuss and he wants to have a family meeting that evening. When the children get home from school, Brian is already home. He is pacing around the kitchen looking nervous. When everyone is seated around the kitchen table, Brian tells the children that he feels uncomfortable living as a man, and has done so for a very long time, and wants to begin the process of changing sex to become a woman ...

What happens next? (Please spend at least ten minutes writing your story; continue on the back of the 'questions about you' sheet if necessary).

On the participant information sheet, participants were given these additional instructions:

You are invited to complete a story-completion task – this means that you read the opening sentences of a story and then write what happens next. There is **no right or wrong way to complete the story**, and you can be as creative as you like in completing the story! We are interested in the range of different stories that people tell. Don't spend too long thinking about what might happen next – just write about whatever first comes to mind. You should **spend at least ten minutes completing the story**. Your story can unfold over the following hours, days, weeks, months or years – you can choose the timescale of the story. Some details of the opening sentences of the story are deliberately vague; it's up to you to be creative and 'fill in the blanks'!

---

meanings participants draw on in writing their stories. A few groundbreaking qualitative researchers have used story-completion tasks in this way (e.g. Livingston & Testa, 2000; Walsh & Malson, 2010; Whitty, 2005) to great effect.

Story-completion tasks are best suited to understandings and perceptions, and constructions-type research questions (see Table 3.1 in Chapter 3). Instead of asking participants to report their own experiences, understandings or perceptions, story-completion tasks ask participants to provide their imagined outcome from a plausible but hypothetical scenario. This means they are particularly useful for exploring participants' assumptions about a topic, because the topic is addressed indirectly and because stories stems are deliberately ambiguous and require participants to 'fill in' the detail. For the same reason, they provide an ideal tool for researching topics

ILLUSTRATIVE RESEARCH EXAMPLE 6.2

Story-completion tasks: perceptions of infidelity in heterosexual relationships

British psychologists Celia Kitzinger and Debra Powell (1995) explored perceptions of infidelity in heterosexual relationships, something both common and 'abnormal', using the story-completion-task method. Participants (116 undergraduate students – 72 women, 44 men) were given one of two versions of a story-completion task featuring a presumably unfaithful heterosexual partner. In version A the story stem read 'John and Claire have been going out for over a year. Then John realises that Claire is seeing someone else ...'; version B reversed the character's names. The researchers were interested in similarities and differences between the two versions of the stories, and between stories written by male and female participants. They used thematic analysis (see Chapter 8), which they reported under the following headings:

Depictions of the cue relationship: The vast majority of stories were about an unfaithful partner. 'Going out for over a year' was interpreted by everyone as implying a sexual relationship. The word 'seeing' was more ambiguous, with 10 per cent of the version A stories (but just one of version B stories) rejecting the implications of infidelity (e.g. the man John suspects Claire is having an affair with turns out to be a relative or friend). Male and female participants depicted the relationship between John and Claire quite differently: women wrote about a deeply loving and trusting couple; men about a relatively uncommitted and sexually focused relationship.

Accounting for infidelity: Men and women explained infidelity in different ways. In explaining Claire's infidelity, men often portrayed John as questioning his sexual technique or performance; women gave more complex reasons that often revolved around emotional difficulties in the relationship. Men offered little by way of explanation for John's infidelity; women again focused on the emotional quality of the relationship. In 15 per cent of the stories written by men (and two by women), Claire's new partner was a woman; only one story (written by a man) depicted John as gay.

Responses to infidelity: Perceived responses were gendered. Both men and women described Claire's reaction to John's infidelity in terms of how hurt and miserable she was (women often emphasised John's regret about his infidelity). Women tended to depict John as suffering extreme emotional turmoil over Claire's infidelity; men portrayed John's reaction as often indifferent or unemotional (about a quarter of the stories written by men contained no emotion words); the most common emotion men attributed to John was anger. Overall, men's stories were more violent than women's stories.

Kitzinger and Powell provided both essentialist and social constructionist interpretations of their analysis (see Chapter 2): from an essentialist perspective, the analysis demonstrated psychological differences between women and men; from a social constructionist perspective it highlighted the different narrative genres (e.g. pornography, romantic fiction) women and men drew on in writing their stories and making meaning of heterosexual relationships and infidelity.

where clear norms dictate socially desirable viewpoints. For example, the use of homophobia scales in cultures where there is a pro-equality climate tends to produce a 'floor effect' (with most participants scoring as 'not homophobic'), because participants can relatively easily deduce from items like 'lesbians are sick' and 'male homosexuality is a perversion' (Herek, 1984) the socially desirable (pro-equality) response to each item (Clarke, Ellis, Peel, & Riggs, 2010). Story-completion tasks, by contrast, can permit access to a range of meanings surrounding a topic, not just socially desirable ones, because they provide participants with less overt cues about socially desirable responses and because participants are not asked directly for *their* view. This is one reason we chose story-completion tasks for examining people's perceptions of trans parenting (see the versions on the ***companion website***). However, whether you then see this as a way of getting at the 'real truth' from participants, or something else, depends on your theoretical framework (see Chapter 2). Because the topic is addressed *indirectly* through storytelling, story-completion tasks are also useful for sensitive topics, and they avoid some of the ethical concerns associated with (inexperienced) use of interactive methods, such as managing participant distress.

DESIGNING AND PILOTING STORY-COMPLETION TASKS

Good story-completion design centres on striking a balance between providing enough context and information so the scenario is meaningful to, and easily understood by, participants, but ambiguous enough for participants to 'fill in' the details. When designing story stems (and cues), you need to think about six issues:

1   How much of the start of the story you will write. A story stem can be as short as a sentence or as long as a paragraph (compare the Kitzinger & Powell, 1995, story stem with our trans parenting one). Length should be guided by how much, and what, information participants will need to write a *meaningful* story. If your topic is not familiar to your participant group, you will probably need to provide a longer story stem with more information.

2   Whether the scenario and characters will be plausible and meaningful to your participant group. Providing some detail, and using character names (where appropriate) and authentic language can make a story vivid and engaging. Overly complex stories with lots of characters don't work well.

3   Whether the depicted scenario is broad enough to stimulate a range of rich and complex stories. Avoid scenarios with an obvious or clear ending (such as a student feeling nervous about giving a presentation in class); these are likely to result in most or all participants writing relatively short, 'thin' and dull stories with limited variation across the data.

4   Whether any aspects of the story should be deliberately ambiguous, so that you can explore assumptions across a range of different elements of the story (e.g. different aspects of the characters, such as sex, race, sexuality and age, or the scenario – e.g. interracial adoption in conservative versus liberal communities).

5   How much direction you will provide to participants for writing their story. If some information is vital (e.g. what a certain character does in the next hour) participants need to be directed that this is a requirement for their story.

6   Whether you want the participants to empathise with, or adopt the point of view of, a particular character in the scenario. If so, you need to focus their attention (and sympathies) on that person, whether explicitly or implicitly. Writing a story in the first person – from the point of view of a particular character – can be one way to encourage participants to view the scenario from the standpoint of that particular character (e.g. our scenario about Brian could have been written from his point of view – 'There's something I really need to tell my kids ...'). Writing a story in the third person – from the point of view of an omniscient narrator – may produce a wider range of responses, and prompt participants to include more socially *un*desirable information in their stories (Kitzinger & Powell, 1995).

When putting together a story-completion study, you need to include the same materials and information discussed in relation to qualitative surveys. You also need to pilot your story-completion task, and compile your data for analysis, in a similar fashion.

Story-completion tasks are one of the few qualitative data collection methods that are ideally suited to comparative research designs: you can compare the responses of different groups to the same story and/or see whether varying a key feature of the story (e.g. character gender or whether or not a character is disabled or able-bodied) produces different responses. We used a comparative design for our trans parenting research: female and male participants' responded to a story involving either a *male* parent (Brian) or a *female* parent (Mary). Both versions were identical apart from parent name and gender pronouns. Why was this of interest? Existing research shows that men tend to hold more negative attitudes toward trans people than women (e.g. Tee & Hegarty, 2006), and mothers and fathers are viewed very differently in western society (Sheriff & Weatherall, 2009). This design allowed us to explore differences between female and male participants' stories (overall) and between stories about a male/female parent.

Story-completion tasks generate very interesting and often completely unanticipated data, but the data can be tricky to analyse for two main reasons: 1) the data are stories, rather than direct reports of experience or opinion, which tap participants' assumptions; 2) there can be huge differences in how participants complete stories. Some participants take the task very seriously, while others clearly don't; most participants usually 'accept' the scenario, but some may 'refuse' it (Kitzinger & Powell, 1995). Some write very long and complicated endings; others write brief and relatively straightforward endings. Some are really creative, others fairly perfunctory. Most participants usually write relatively realistic stories, but some stories can involve fantasy or humour (which may be a way of resisting the task) (see the ***companion website*** for examples of story-completion data from our trans parent study). Chapter 10 provides guidance on analysing story-completion data.

Another participant-generated textual data collection method similar to the story-completion task is the vignette. Vignettes involve presenting participants with *completed* stories, and then asking them to respond to a series of open-ended questions about the stories. We provide information and guidelines for using the vignette technique on the *companion website*.

RESEARCHER-DIRECTED DIARIES

Researcher-directed (or solicited) diaries are diaries produced for the purpose of research. They require participants to record their thoughts, feelings, experiences and/or practices over a specified period of time. They differ from *personal* diaries, which are generated for purposes other than research (personal diaries are a type of secondary source). Researcher-directed diaries can take many formats: hard copy, handwritten diary; typed online or emailed electronic diary; audio-recoded diary; 'performed' video diary; or a (creative) 'scrapbook' diary in which participants write, draw, and cut and paste in mementos, pictures from magazines, postcards, etc. (Thompson & Holland, 2005). Video (and email, online and audio) diaries are thought to be particularly 'empowering' for participants because they can edit their entries before submitting their diaries, giving them control over what they submit as data (Holliday, 1999).

Diaries require regular entries over a period of time. Participants can be asked to make entries once (or more) a day, a week or a month, for periods as short as a week and as long as several months. Diaries range from very structured, which specify exactly what information participants should record, and when, to very unstructured, which specify little more than the topic (e.g. Holliday, 1999). The *companion website* provides an example of a relatively structured diary (hard copy or email) from our research on how people define and experience prejudice and social privilege on a day-to-day basis (our design was strongly influenced by Meth's, 2003, diary research on black women's fear and experiences of crime and violence in South Africa). We structured our prejudice and privilege diary to encourage participants to make an entry (related to 'prejudice' and to 'privilege', separately) on each of 14 consecutive days. We suggested *when* participants should make their daily entry, and provided detailed guidance on *what* information they should record. We provided some sample diary entries to guide and help sensitise participants to the sorts of issues they should consider in their entries.

WHEN AND WHY WOULD I USE RESEARCHER-DIRECTED DIARIES?

Diaries can be used to answer a wide range of qualitative research questions: about experiences, understandings and perceptions, accounts of practice, influencing factors and construction (see Table 3.1 in Chapter 3). They are generally used to access the details of mundane, everyday, routine, taken-for-granted phenomena that other methods cannot reach. This is partly because diaries require participants to record the details of their experiences and perspectives 'in situ', temporally (and even spatially) close to when they happen. British sociologist Jenny Hislop and colleagues (2005), for instance, used audio diaries to research sleep, collecting daily records of how participants had slept the night before (participants had to record their diaries within 20 minutes of waking). Such information would be more difficult to access using methods that rely on (distant) recall (e.g. interviews, surveys) because micro-detail is likely to be forgotten over time. So a particular strength of diaries is that they are 'less subject to the vagaries of memory, retrospective censorship or reframing' (Milligan et al., 2005: 1883) than other experiential methods. However, this view of diaries (as a more accurate way of recording the micro detail of the mundane) only makes sense within a realist framework; within a more constructionist framework, diaries provide a *different*, rather than a (necessarily) more accurate, view. Diaries have been widely used as a mostly quantitative method in health (Elliott, 1997) and sex (Coxon, 1994) research to log people's practices, but are now increasingly used as a *qualitative* method to explore a wide-range of topics, such as stress in trampolinists over a competitive season (Day & Thatcher, 2009), the health and well-being of older people (Milligan et al., 2005), and the transition to adulthood of young people with visual impairments (Worth, 2009).

Diaries are also a longitudinal method, meaning we can track experiences and events over continuous time and space (Milligan et al., 2005), and explore how practices evolve over time (such as patterns in intravenous drug use; Stopka, Springer, Khoshnood, Shaw, & Singer, 2004). Furthermore, because diaries consist of multiple entries over time (e.g. describing 'how I slept last night' every morning for a fortnight), they can help us to understand the *contexts* surrounding particular experiences and activities. For example, by collecting sleep diaries from both partners in heterosexual couples, Hislop et al. (2005) could identify the social environment that shaped sleeping experiences, as well as differences in men's and women's sleep.

As well as a stand-alone tool, diaries can be used with other methods. US ethnographers Zimmerman and Wieder (1977) pioneered the 'diary-interview method', where participants keep a diary for a particular period of time and then discuss and elaborate on their entries in an interview. Diaries are used either to stimulate and/or enrich the interview method (they work as an elicitation tool; the words from the interviews form the data analysed), or as an additional form of data.

It's important to recognise the time and energy commitment diaries require from participants. For instance, in our diary study, participants had to find the time (and remember) to complete an entry every day for a fortnight – that may have been 20 minutes a day, or more. Completing the diary required participants to focus on a particular aspect of their daily experience that they might not have otherwise paid much attention to, which can itself be demanding. These reasons mean that compared to other qualitative data collection methods, participant recruitment can be difficult, and there can be a high drop-out rate, especially when diary data collection spans several months (Breakwell

& Wood, 1995). Experienced diary researchers have developed techniques to engage participants in diary research and maintain interest, including:

- Having an initial meeting with participants (individually or as a group) to explain the task of diary-keeping and hand over the diary and/or any necessary materials (e.g. audio recorders). We met our participants as a group for an initial briefing, to collect demographic data and complete consent forms, and to hand out hard copies of the diary.
- If participants are asked to keep a diary for several weeks, arranging to meet the participants to collect their diaries at the end of every week (we did this with our diary study). This can help maintain motivation and provide participants with an opportunity to ask questions and clarify any areas of confusion. Some researchers require diaries to be returned at regular intervals, because they engage in on-going analysis of the diary entries in preparation for an eventual 'diary interview'.
- Regularly contacting participants via email, telephone, text message or post to aid memory and motivation (e.g. Thompson & Holland, 2005).

DESIGNING AND PILOTING RESEARCHER-DIRECTED DIARIES

The first thing to decide in a diary study design is diary format (e.g. written, audio, visual). This decision needs to be informed by both your research question and your participant group. For instance, if researching something like *visual* identity, as British sociologist Ruth Holliday (2004) did, video diaries are an ideal method. Recognising that different groups may favour different diary formats (see Hislop et al., 2005), the mode of diary keeping you use has to 'work' for participants (and work to keep them engaged). Other important factors to determine are:

- How frequently do you want participants to make diary entries? Over what time-span? If participants are required to make *daily* entries, diaries are typically kept for no more than a few weeks (short enough to maintain data quality and keep participants engaged, long enough to avoid only capturing unusual experiences; Milligan et al., 2005). If entries are less frequent, diary-duration can be (quite a bit) longer. Choice of frequency and duration relates to what events or issues you are aiming to capture in the diary: are these things that happen routinely every day (e.g. sleeping), once or twice a week (e.g. a gardening group for older people), or on a more ad hoc basis (e.g. the transition to adulthood)? The more regular the event, the more useful routine *daily* entries are likely to be. Diaries which are less explicitly 'event' oriented are likely to involve less frequent entries. For instance, Thompson and Holland's (2005) research on young people's transitions to adulthood asked participants to keep 'memory books' (scrapbook diaries) over several months, making entries whenever they liked.
- How structured should the diary be? A structured diary provides many clear (limiting) guidelines; an unstructured diary gives participants more scope to write about what is important to them. How much structure is suitable depends on your

topic, research question and approach. Structure applies both to frequency and time-frame of completion, and to diary content. Important considerations related to structure are:

- o Deciding how prescriptive your instructions need to be. It may be important to provide clear instructions related to when (and what) participants record. For instance, we did this in our prejudice and privilege diaries, asking for daily entries related to specific events (see our prejudice and privilege diary on the **companion website**). In other research questions, it may not be important or productive to provide such detailed instructions. For instance, simply giving participants a video recorder and instructing them to document how they express their identity through their clothing and appearance practices over a month, as Holliday (1999) did, allows participants freedom to determine what is important.
- o Deciding whether to include a sample completed entry, which may be useful for more structured diaries (but can be problematic if it inhibits how participants complete the diary); we did this in our diary study.
- o Deciding how important it is that participants complete their diaries at a certain point in time (e.g. every morning, Sunday evenings), and/or record events as close as possible to when they happen. Such considerations need to be balanced by the fact that participants are more likely to be effective diary keepers if it causes minimum disruption to their routine (Day & Thatcher, 2009).

- When should participants return diary entries? This can range from daily returns to a single return at the end of data collection. As noted above, returns during an extended data collection period may help with maintaining participant interest (and assist you if you need to start analysing the data quickly – for instance, if using an interview-diary method). Organising the diary into weekly or monthly diaries, where participants return them at the end of each period, can be one way to do this.
- Will you have contact with the participants while they're keeping the diary? Is an initial meeting to explain the diary and/or hand-over equipment necessary? Is a final meeting/equipment return necessary?
- Finally, what materials, if any, will you need to give participants to keep their diary? It may be as simple as a pen and a printed paper diary; it may be audio- or video-recording equipment; scrapbook diaries can require a notebook, folders, stickers, glue and disposable cameras (Thompson & Holland, 2005).

In general, diaries should include all materials needed to complete the diary, and clear, comprehensive instructions (as relevant) on:

- how frequently participants should make entries;
- when and where they should make them;
- what *kind* of information they should record;
- for diaries requiring regular entries, what they should do if they miss an entry (can they complete it the following day, or not; do you want to know that it was missed and why?);

- how (and when) to return entries.

Alongside this you will need relevant participant information, consent and demographic forms (as discussed in relation to surveys). For written or electronic diaries, formatting is important (see our diary on the ***companion website***). Hard copy written diaries also need:

- a cover page that includes: a) the diary title; b) space for a participate code; c) researcher contact details;
- for a more structured diary, you should provide space for each entry, either already dated, or with a space for participants to record the date (and time) of their entry.

As with other methods, diaries need to be piloted. Once data are collected, written diary data should be compiled electronically. In general, all entries for each participant should be kept together (in contrast, compilation by question can be better for surveys). Audio/video diaries should be transcribed in the same way as interview or FG data (see Chapter 7).

Some participants may take to diary-keeping like a proverbial duck to water; others may struggle with it – although participants tend to become more confident diarists over time (Elliott, 1997). Some may record intimate details and provide rich narrative accounts of their everyday lives; others may descriptively report (assumed-to-be) relevant events, with little affective commentary (Hislop et al., 2005). Some may experience diary-keeping as a boring, repetitive chore (Milligan et al., 2005); others may value the opportunity to reflect on their everyday lives, including reflecting back on earlier entries (Elliott, 1997). Diary keeping may encourage participants to identify patterns in their experiences and enhance their ability to reflect on their lives, which fits with the claim that diaries are potentially empowering for participants (e.g. Meth, 2003). These mean that the quality and quantity of data generated using diaries can vary hugely. Table 3.2 in Chapter 3 overviews appropriate analytic approaches for analysing diary data.

PARTICIPANT-GENERATED TEXTUAL DATA: A BRIEF SUMMARY

Diaries, qualitative surveys, story-completion tasks (and vignettes) are far less common in qualitative research than interactive methods such as interviews and FGs, and yet, as we hope we have conveyed, they hold exciting possibilities for qualitative research. Table 6.2 provides an overview of the pros and cons of participant-generated textual data.

COLLECTING PRE-EXISTING TEXTUAL DATA

Using pre-existing textual data involves selecting as data something that is already (generally) publicly available in written or audiovisual form. The researcher has no

Table 6.2   Pros and cons of participant-generated textual data

Pros of participant-generated textual data collection	Cons of participant-generated textual data collection
Can be a relatively quick way to generate data (from large samples)	Some forms have less depth than interactive data
Can be an easy way to access samples of geographically dispersed participants	There is limited scope for flexibility with data collection – you can't probe participants or ask unanticipated questions
Quick to get from data collection to analysis, with often no need for transcription. If data are collected online, no need to type up and/or compile responses	Some groups (e.g. people with limited literacy skills, learning disabilities or visual impairments) may find participation difficult
Can be a quick and easy experience for participants: 'harder to engage' participants might be more willing to participate	Some forms (e.g. diaries) can require a big commitment of time/energy from participants
People with concerns about anonymity may be more willing to complete an anonymous online survey than a face-to-face interview. If you are researching a sensitive topic, some people might be more willing to write about it in a survey than discuss it face-to-face	A skilled interviewer can get people to talk and some people might feel more comfortable discussing a sensitive issue with a stranger or in a group with other people who have similar experiences
It can avoid some of the ethical issues associated with interactive data collection – so is a suitable way for less experienced researchers to explore more sensitive topics	Arguably, participants have to be highly motivated to complete a survey or, especially, a diary in their own time and space without the structure of a planned time for collecting data as with interactive data collection
People can participate in their own time and space	
Some types (e.g. surveys, more structured diaries) are more standardised and therefore can be easier to analyse for patterns than interactive data	Some data are more variable and less transparent (e.g. stories) than interactive data, and therefore can be harder to analyse
The participants have more control over the data produced	The researcher has less control over the data produced

role in the production of the data; so-called *secondary* sources of data cover materials sourced in printed copy, electronic, and broadcast media formats. Examples include newspapers (Shaw & Giles, 2009), magazines (Toerien & Durrheim, 2001), public health information leaflets (Rúdólfsdóttir, 2000), textbooks (Myerson, Crawley, Anstey, Kessler, & Okopny, 2007), billboard advertisements (Adams, McCreanor, & Braun, 2007), websites (Braun, 2009), blogs (Potts & Parry, 2010), bulletin boards (Malik & Coulson, 2008), political speeches (Capdevila & Callaghan,

2008), *Hansard* – the official report of parliamentary proceedings (Summers, 2007), television talk shows (Clarke & Kitzinger, 2004), adverts (Gill, 2008), comics (Walkerdine, 1987) and documentaries (Clarke et al., 2004). Some sources are available in more than one format – for instance, many newspapers and *Hansard* are both online and printed (and newspaper articles are archived in the LexisNexis electronic database). Researchers may collect data from *one* type of secondary source (e.g. women's magazines; see Illustrative Research Example 6.3) or from a range (e.g. British LGBTQ psychologists Sonja Ellis and Celia Kitzinger, 2002, used national newspaper, gay media and *Hansard* reports to explore arguments used to oppose lowering the age of consent for sex between men in Britain). Or they may combine primary and secondary sources. For example, Victoria (Clarke, 2001) collected interview and FG data, television talk shows and documentaries, and newspaper and magazine articles for her analysis of the social construction of lesbian and gay parenting.

Secondary sources are ideal for answering representation and construction-type research questions (see Table 3.1 in Chapter 3). Secondary sources like magazines and television shows can be viewed as fragments of (popular) culture, things that influence our views of the world and other people, and how we think, feel and act (Lyons, 2000; Silverman, 2006). Researchers study these 'fragments of culture' in order to understand the 'meanings that make up the social reality shared by members of a society' (Altheide, 1996: 2). Some secondary sources (e.g. online forums where people write about their experiences or perspectives) may be useful to answer experience, understandings and perceptions, accounts of practice, and influencing factors type-research questions. Such secondary sources are valuable because we can access people's experiences and perspectives without shaping their responses through our data collection questions and methods. In summary, secondary source data can be used to:

- explore people's experiences, understandings and practices (e.g. Malik & Coulson, 2008), much like you would use interview, survey or diary data (see Hookway, 2008, on blogs as an accessible alternative to diary data);
- explore the socio-cultural meanings surrounding a particular topic, either generally (e.g. Clarke, 2001) or in relation to *a particular context* (such as women's magazines; see Illustrative Research Example 6.3);
- exploring how particular 'cultural fragments' work, the effects they have and the socio-cultural ideas they incorporate, rework or resist (Silverman, 2006) (e.g. Clarke & Kitzinger, 2004).

These latter two can either focus on a particular cultural/historical moment, or look at change over time.

ILLUSTRATIVE RESEARCH EXAMPLE 6.3

Secondary sources: representations of male and female sexuality in women's magazines

Women's magazines convey popular socio-cultural messages about gender, sex and sexuality. New Zealand psychologists Panteá Farvid and Virginia Braun (2006) analysed six consecutive issues of *Cosmopolitan* and *Cleo* (to focus on constructions prevalent in a particular cultural moment), two popular lifestyle magazines targeted at young women, to identify the ways they constructed and represented men's and women's sexuality. Any part of the magazine (except advertisements) that made any reference to *male* sexuality was selected as data; this resulted in 200 pages from *Cosmo*, and 199 pages from *Cleo*. Analysis used a constructionist version of thematic analysis (see Chapter 8).

Although the magazines' representation of sex and sexuality was resolutely heterosexual, the data were 'characterised by multiple, competing, and contradictory accounts of male and female sexuality' (p. 299). As might be expected in contemporary women's magazines, women were represented as sexually active and independent, with the right to desire sex and experience sexual pleasure. However, the magazines could be described as 'obsessed' with men and male sexuality; male sexuality was a central concern in discussions of *women's* sexuality, which often centred on producing men's sexual pleasure. Sex was represented as 'very important to men, as something that men are willing and able to engage in "anytime", something that men (always) want' (p. 301). Strong gender differences were present in the depiction of sexuality. For example, 'cheating' was presented as normative for men, but women were rarely represented as 'cheating' (but they were implicitly represented as responsible for *his* cheating); when women's infidelity was portrayed, it was presented as 'more condemnable and less forgivable than men's cheating behaviour' (p. 303). As a result of the contradictory and gendered representations present, Farvid and Braun concluded that the autonomy and sexual agency promoted to women in the magazines was more accurately '*pseudo* liberation and sexual empowerment' (p. 306, emphasis in original), and the magazines tell a familiar and traditional story about (hetero)sexuality and relationships. Men's sexuality was privileged in the magazines; women were expected to take responsibility for 'making things work' in (monogamous) heterosexual relationships, which men were depicted as reluctant (and 'unnatural') participants in.

ACCESSING AND SAMPLING SECONDARY SOURCES

Secondary sources may sound appealing as a way of getting data *easily*. And indeed, one advantage is that they do tend to be easy, as well as relatively quick, and inexpensive to access. University libraries provide access to a wide range of electronic databases (e.g.

LexisNexis), textbooks, *Hansard*, the internet, etc. Another advantage is that secondary sources sidestep *some* ethical concerns because you do not directly interact with participants to generate data (see Chapter 3). However, the use of secondary sources still requires us to think about ethics, and some sources raise particular concerns (see Box 6.2). But these alone are not *adequate* reasons to use secondary sources; you need a research-based reason as well. Beyond this, it's also vital to have a clear rationale for your sample – which may consist of all relevant items relating to your topic/research question, or a selection of available items. Imagine you are researching how non-white people are represented in contemporary psychology textbooks. You are interested in this topic because of the influence psychology textbooks have on students, and because western psychology has a notably racist past (Howitt & Owusu-Bempah, 1994). If you just popped to the library and grabbed the first ten psychology textbooks you found, your sampling strategy would not withstand much scrutiny: your chosen books may be arcane textbooks that no-on used; they may not cover relevant psychology curriculum. Instead, you need a plan and a rationale for sampling secondary data. British psychologist Meg Barker (2007) provided an excellent description of a robust sampling strategy for her research on representations of non-heterosexual sexualities in psychology textbooks. Her study was based on a sample of 22 undergraduate textbooks:

> including seven in the area of introductory psychology, and five in each of the following areas: biological psychology, developmental psychology and social psychology ... The aim was to cover key areas of the psychology curriculum that all students study internationally ... and where issues of sexual identity and relationships are relevant. All were published between 2000 and 2005 ... Textbooks were selected from the lists of bestsellers on the US and UK Amazon websites ... in an attempt to focus on the most popular and widely used books. I chose texts from the top 10 in each category including the number one bestseller plus a range of others from a variety of publishers and authors. The market is dominated by US published texts, but I attempted to include at least one European book in each category as a point of comparison. (Barker, 2007: 98–100)

Some types of secondary sources are relatively easy to access in a systematic fashion (e.g. you could search Nexis.com for all the articles published on men and diet in British national newspapers in the last year), meaning a robust sampling plan can be developed. Other secondary sources may be harder to access, and to access systematically. One reason could be that data instances are rare and dispersed. When Victoria analysed television talk shows and documentaries about same-sex parenting, it took a huge amount of energy and time (four years!) to generate a sample of 27 talk shows and 11 documentaries. Her strategy was to collect all instances of data she could identify by monitoring the TV guide and recording all relevant and potentially relevant shows; by contacting producers; by purchasing copies of documentaries and transcripts of talk shows; and by friends and family notifying her of things they'd noticed.

With secondary sources, it is important to collate **data items** systematically as you collect them, and to give each data item an ID code. You should keep a separate record that lists, for each item, the ID code, when, how and from where you collected the item (e.g. the magazine name, date of the issue and page number of the data item; or the television programme title, broadcast channel, date and time, and production details). Any broadcast audio or video data will need to be transcribed into written text for analysis (see Chapter 7). See Table 3.2 for an overview of appropriate analytic approaches to use with secondary sources.

BOX 6.2   ETHICAL CONSIDERATIONS WITH ONLINE SECONDARY SOURCES

The emergence of online secondary sources as a viable data source for qualitative research has created new ethical challenges for qualitative researchers. Discussion of the ethics of online research has centred on notions of public and private: Hookway (2008: 105) asked, for example, 'is blog material academic fair game or is informed consent needed?' There are a range of different perspectives on this issue, with some researchers arguing that online material is public (in the same way that newspaper articles or television shows are) and therefore consent is not needed; others argue that some online material is written with an expectation of privacy and therefore consent *is* required (in the same way that it would for an interview or a survey) (Hookway, 2008). The latter view reflects the position of the British Psychological Society (The Working Party on Conducting Research on the Internet, 2007), which also highlights the potential to breach people's anonymity if researchers use quotes 'that are traceable to an individual's posting via a search engine' (The Working Party on Conducting Research on the Internet, 2007: 4; see also Wishart & Kostanski, 2009). The Association of Internet Researchers (AIR) (2002) argues that it is not always clear whether materials are public or private, but suggests that the greater the acknowledgement of the public nature of the materials, the less obligation there is to protect the privacy and confidentiality of the people who have created the materials. They also argue that caution is needed when accessing both materials that may not be intended for public consumption and those created or written by children and members of other vulnerable groups (who may not understand the dangers and implications of posting personal information on the Internet). As well as considering issues around privacy, consent, confidentiality, anonymity and vulnerability, Eysenbach and Till (2001) recommend that researchers consider whether their research has the potential to cause harm to the authors of online materials and the broader groups or communities to which they belong.

CHAPTER SUMMARY

This chapter:
- outlined three main types of participant-generated textual data (qualitative surveys, story-completion tasks and researcher-directed diaries) and discussed how and when to use each of these methods;
- discussed the collection and use of secondary sources of data.

? QUESTIONS FOR DISCUSSION AND CLASSROOM EXERCISES

1   Read the Brian-version story-completion task in Material Example 6.1 and identify which features of the story are deliberately ambiguous. What are some of the different ways in which these aspects of the story could be interpreted by participants? From whose point of view is the story written? We attempted to avoid cueing participants into viewing Brian negatively *in his parental role* (to avoid prompting obvious allegations of 'selfishness') – can you identify how we did this? Do you think we were successful?

2   Identify some of the pros and cons of using 30 qualitative surveys or ten interviews to explore people's experiences of shyness and social anxiety? Which method would you choose if you wished to research this topic? Look at Swedish psychologists Charlotte Alm and Ann Frodi's (2008) interview study of shyness, and think about whether and how you could improve on it.

3   Imagine you are conducting a research project on the meanings of teenage parenting in contemporary society. What types of secondary sources could you collect? What would be some of the strengths and weaknesses of using secondary sources to examine this issue?

4   In small groups, develop a research question on any topic that suits the story-completion method, and design an appropriate story stem or cue. Join with another group, swap stories, and attempt (individually) to complete their story. Once done, collectively discuss your experiences of designing and responding to the different stories. What were some of the challenges you faced in designing a story-completion task? What was it like to complete one?

5   In Illustrative Research Example 6.1, Frith and Gleeson (2004) reported that male participants' feelings about their bodies, and the impact this had on their dress and appearance, changed on a daily basis. How could you use diaries to investigate this further with young men in their late teens and early twenties? What type of diary would be most fruitful? How often would you ask the participants to make entries, and over what timeframe? What information would you ask participants to record in the diaries, and why?

FURTHER RESOURCES

Further reading:

Most of the reading we suggest discusses these methods in the context of reporting on research. This allows you not only to learn more about the method, but also to see what sort of analysis can come from it.

For a detailed discussion of why the authors chose to use a qualitative survey – to understand body hair removal – see: Toerien, M. & Wilkinson, S. (2004) Exploring the depilation norm: a qualitative questionnaire study of women's body hair removal. *Qualitative Research in Psychology*, *1*, 69–92.

For a succinct discussion of the use of story-completion tasks – in relation to research on anorexia and bulimia – see: Walsh, E. & Malson, H. (2010) Discursive constructions of eating disorders: a story-completion task. *Feminism & Psychology, 20*, 529–537.

For an excellent account of the use of audio diaries – to examine a very mundane activity, sleeping – see: Hislop, J., Arber, S., Meadows, R. & Venn, S. (2005) Narratives of the night: the use of audio-diaries in researching sleep. *Sociological Research Online, 10*. [Online: www.socresonline.org.uk/10/4/hislop.html].

For an informative example of a study based on the analysis of secondary sources, in this case human sexuality textbooks, see: Myerson, M., Crawley, S. L., Anstey, E. H., Kessler, J. & Okopny, C. (2007) Who's zoomin' who? A feminist, queer content analysis of 'interdisciplinary' human sexuality textbooks. *Hypatia, 22*, 92–113.

Online resources:

Both SurveyMonkey and Qualtrics offer free (limited scope) or paid (full-version) software for online surveys:
- www.surveymonkey.com/
- www.qualtrics.com/

Among other things LexisNexis provides an online database of national and regional newspaper articles for many different countries. http://www.lexisnexis.co.uk/our-solutions/academic/

See the ***companion website*** (**www.sagepub.co.uk/braunandclarke**) for:
- self-test multiple choice questions relating to Section 2;
- the flashcard glossary – test yourself on the definitions of key terms used in this chapter;
- an introduction to the vignette technique, including example materials from a vignette study;
- copies of the data collection tools discussed in this chapter (the 'views on pubic hair' survey, the 'privilege and prejudice' diary, the trans parent story-completion task, and others) and related research materials;
- further readings (articles from Sage journals).

SECTION
3

Successfully analysing
qualitative data

7

Preparing audio data for analysis: transcription

OVERVIEW

Orthographic transcription and the messiness of language use
Understanding what a transcript is, and what it is not
What makes a (quality) transcript?
Producing the transcript
Giving yourself enough time to transcribe

With your data collected (hoorah!), you're sitting at the edge of analysis. But before you jump in and get started you may need to *prepare* your data ready for analysis. This chapter outlines and discusses the main way audio (and audio-visual) data are made ready for analysis – through transcription. Transcription is an important part of qualitative research using audio data and, at first sight, it might seem like a straightforward process: you play a recording in *very* short bursts and type up what you hear. Indeed, transcription is often (implicitly) treated as a 'minor or merely technical concern' (Nelson, 1996: 12) and given little, if any, coverage in qualitative textbooks. But it's not just a technical concern. When transcribing, we have to *choose* how – and what – we translate from speech and sounds into written text, making transcription a theoretically influenced practice (Ochs, 1979). And you soon discover that transcription's not simple when you try to do it. Before reading any further, we recommend trying the first transcription exercise at the end of this chapter; our discussion of transcription will be much more meaningful if you've already had a go.

ORTHOGRAPHIC TRANSCRIPTION AND THE MESSINESS OF LANGUAGE USE

There are many different styles of transcription, which suit different analytic methods. We outline a style of audio transcription often called **orthographic** or verbatim. This style, which focuses on transcribing spoken words (and other sounds) in recorded data, can be contrasted with audio transcription styles that include more *phonetic* or **paralinguistic** features, where the transcript aims to record not only *what* was said, but also *how* it was said (that form of transcript – Jeffersonian – is used in **discursive psychology** [DP] and **conversation analysis** [CA]; see Boxes 8.1 and 8.2 in Chapter 8), or visual elements (e.g. Heath & Hindmarsh, 2002; Norris, S., 2002; Peräkylä, 2002, 2006).

Orthographic transcription records what was said. Even doing this form of transcription isn't simple, as spoken language and written language are very different. When we speak, we don't use punctuation to make ourselves understood. We use pauses and intonation; we vary our speech in pace (faster, slower), volume (louder, quieter) and many other ways. Spoken (natural) language is 'messier' than written language: we hesitate when we speak, we stumble over our words, start a word or phrase and don't finish it, and say the same word or phrase a number of times. One of the most startling research experiences we've had was hearing how we *actually* speak, how inarticulate we actually are, in real life; transcribing your first interview can be a horrifying yet eye-opening experience! The orthographic transcripts from the weight and obesity and body art focus groups (FGs) on the ***companion website*** show how *messy* real speech is.

UNDERSTANDING WHAT A TRANSCRIPT IS, AND WHAT IT IS NOT

Most qualitative analysis uses transcripts, rather than the original audio(visual) recording, so it's important that your transcripts are *thorough* and of high quality. We avoid using the term 'accurate' in relation to transcripts because there is considerable debate among qualitative researchers about what constitutes an *accurate* transcript and whether such a thing is possible (see Potter, 1996; Sandelowski, 1994a). You can avoid these debates, and still produce a good transcript, or rather, a 'good enough' transcript, as it's important to know when to stop. You need to be aware that a transcript of audio(visual) data is not a facsimile; it's a *representation*. Just as an audio recording of an interview is not the same as the actual interview experience, a transcript of an audio recording is not the same as the audio recording, making a transcript two-steps removed from the actual interview experience. With each step, information is lost or changed in some way. Rather than seeing a transcript as raw data, it can be seen as 'partially cooked' (Sandelowski, 1994a: 312) data, already prepared and slightly altered from its original stage. So far from being 'a neutral, simple rendition of words' from audio to written form (Potter, 1996: 136), a transcript is a 'selective arrangement' (Sandelowski, 1994a: 311), produced for the purposes of analysis. The transcript is the product of an interaction between the recording and the transcriber, who listens to the recording, and makes choices about what to preserve, and how to represent what they hear.

A transcription notation system allows you to clearly and *consistently* translate spoken language into written language, meaning your approach to transcription is thorough and meticulous. With no definitive notation system for orthographic transcription (unlike CA transcription, e.g. Atkinson & Heritage, 1984; Jefferson, 2004), qualitative researchers most often construct their own notation systems (we provide ours, with instructions, in Table 7.1; we show a section of annotated transcript in Box 7.1, explaining the features in situ). Idiosyncrasy can create confusion if authors don't include a notation *key* so the reader can decode their transcription system. For example, researchers often use three full-stops '…' in transcripts. Some common uses of '…' are to signal a pause, hesitation, or trailing off, or that a section of data has been deleted. The reader needs to know which it is. If you're not doing your own transcribing, you need to make sure the person doing it follows your transcription notation system, as well as all other instructions (including confidentiality; see the transcriber confidentiality agreement on the *companion website*).

WHAT MAKES A (QUALITY) TRANSCRIPT?

Vitally, a transcript needs to both signal *what* is said and *who* is speaking. A good orthographic transcript records in written form *all* verbal utterances from all speakers, both actual words and non-semantic sounds – such as 'erm', 'er', 'uhuh', 'mm' and 'mm-hm'. Your aim is to create as clear and complete a rendering of *what* was uttered as possible. Nothing should be 'corrected' or changed – for example, don't translate slang or vernacular terms into 'standard' English (if a participant says 'dunno,' it should *not* be transcribed as 'don't know'). If you 'clean up' or edit your data, your participants will sound more fluent and more like they are using written language (DeVault, 1990), but the whole point of collecting spoken data is that we capture how people express themselves. Some researchers signal some more significant paralinguistic features of the data (e.g. laughter, crying, long pauses, or strong emphasis – see Table 7.1).

Very simple errors or mishearings in transcription can radically change the meaning of data. For instance, in the weight and obesity FG, the line 'Oh god it's home ec [home economics] again' (Line 887; see the *companion website*) was originally transcribed by a professional transcriber as 'Oh god it's homework again'. In the context of a discussion about schools teaching students how to cook, the meaning is quite different (home economics traditionally teaches skills relevant to domestic life, such as cooking). Canadian public health researcher Blake Poland (2002) identified four common types of transcription error:

1 *Sentence structure errors*: as noted, people don't talk in sentences – indeed, the concept of a 'sentence' doesn't translate well into *spoken* language – yet some people use punctuation in a transcript, as if it were written language. But in so doing, they make decisions about punctuation use, such as where to begin and end sentences, that can alter the interpretation of the text. For example, 'I hate it, you know. I do' carries a different meaning from 'I hate it. You know I do'. For this reason, we tend to include little or no punctuation in our orthographic transcripts. If you want to add punctuation to extracts of data included in written reports and presentations, to aid 'readability', always check the audio, so you can get a sense

from intonation and language use where 'sentences' stop and start, and where the pauses really are.

2   *Quotation mark errors*: these errors fail to capture a feature of talk called reported speech. Reported speech is where a person reports what someone else said (or thought), or indeed what they themselves said at another point in time. Our example of 'oh God, it's home ec again' is reported speech, because Anna is reporting on what her parents used to think or say:

Anna: My parents used to dread that day

?:   Yeah

((General laughter))

Anna: 'Oh god it's home ec again'

Whether or not someone uses reported speech is meaningful (e.g. Buttny, 1997), especially for some forms of qualitative analysis such as conversation analysis (CA; see Box 8.2 in Chapter 8) and discursive psychology (DP; see Box 8.1 in Chapter 8); in transcripts, it should be signalled with inverted commas or quotation marks.

3   *Omission errors*: these errors are ones where words (or vocalised sounds) are not included. Sometimes they can be inconsequential; at other times, crucial. Poland gives an example from his research on smoking cessation of a transcriber who missed the vital word *lung* from 'I lost a very close friend to [lung] cancer', an obviously a significant omission given the focus of the research.

4   *Mistaken word/phrase errors*: these errors are ones where an incorrect word or phrase is used – our homework/home ec error is a good example of this. Although these words sound somewhat similar, their meaning is different, and in our data, important analytically.

Omissions and mistaken words can occur because you're tired (transcription requires intense concentration and focus; it's important to break at regular intervals), or because you've left too long between collecting the data and transcribing it. As noted in Chapter 4, if collecting interview (or FG) data, we strongly recommend scheduling time to transcribe it as soon as possible (ideally the following day). A surprising amount of detail from an interview or FG remains clear for a few days; this memory rapidly fades. The quality of the recording and the nature of participants' speech (volume and speed, accents and overlap) can also lead to errors (see below); if you can't understand what was said, your transcript might not only contain errors; it will also contain lots of blanks, making it far less viable as data.

In the actual transcript itself, each speaker needs to be identified by a name (a pseudonym rather than their real name) or role (e.g. interviewer/moderator); each time a new speaker says something (technically called a turn of talk), it's presented on a new line. Using a hanging indent style, with each speaker's name or role followed by a colon and a tab, before what they said, makes the transcript visually clear and easy to analyse (see Box 7.1).

Table 7.1   Our transcription notation system for orthographic transcription (adapted from Jefferson, 2004)

Feature	Notation and explanation of use
The identity of the speaker; turn-taking in talk	The speaker's name, followed by a colon (e.g. Anna:) signals the identity of a speaker (use Moderator/Mod: or Interviewer/Int: for when the moderator/interviewer is speaking; or the moderator/interviewer's first name); start a new line every time a new speaker enters the conversation, and start the first word of each new turn of talk with a capital letter
Laughing, coughing, etc.	((laughs)) and ((coughs)) signals a speaker laughing or coughing during a turn of talk; ((General laughter)) signals multiple speakers laughing at once and should be appear on a separate line (to signal that no one speaker 'owns' the laughter)
Pausing	((pause)) signals a significant pause (i.e. a few seconds or more; precise timing of pauses is not necessary); can also use (.) to signal a short pause (a second or less) or ((long pause)) to signal a much longer pause
Spoken abbreviations	If someone speaks an abbreviation, then use that abbreviation (e.g. TV for television; WHO for World Health Organization), but do not abbreviate unless a speaker does so
Overlapping speech	Type ((in overlap)) before the start of the overlapping speech
Inaudible speech	Use ((inaudible)) for speech and sounds that are completely inaudible; when you can hear something but you're not sure if it's correct, use single parentheses to signal your best guess or guesses as to what was said – for example (ways of life) or (ways of life/married wife)
Uncertainty about who is speaking	Use ? to signal uncertainty about the speaker – just ? for total uncertainty, F? or M? if you can identify sex of the speaker, or a name followed by a question mark (e.g. Judy?) if you think you might know who it is
Non-verbal utterances	Render phonetically and consistently common non-verbal sounds uttered by your participants. For English-as-a-first-language speakers, these include 'erm', 'er', 'mm', 'mm-hm', but note that how these are written is context-dependent. In Aotearoa/New Zealand, the first two would be written 'um' and 'ah'
Spoken numbers	Spell out all numbers (and be mindful of the difference between 'a hundred' and 'one hundred')
Use of punctuation	It is common to use punctuation to signal some features of spoken language (such as using a question mark to signal the rising intonation of a question or a comma to signal a slight pause but with the intonation of continuing speech). However, adding punctuation to a transcript is not straightforward and it is important to be mindful of the ways in which adding punctuation can change the meaning of an extract of data. Equally, punctuation enhances the readability of spoken data, especially extracts quoted in written reports (see Box 11.5 in Chapter 11)

(Continued)

Table 7.1   (Continued)

Feature	Notation and explanation of use
Cut-off speech and speech-sounds	This level of detail is not necessary for most experiential forms of analysis, although it can be useful to signal moments when participants are struggling to articulate their thoughts, feelings etc.; to signal cut-off speech, type out the sounds you can hear, then add a dash (e.g. wa-, wor-, worl-); try to capture this at the level of phonetic sound
Emphasis on particular words	Again, this level of detail is not necessary for most experiential forms of analysis, although it can be useful to indicate words or sounds that are particularly emphasised by underlining (e.g. <u>word</u>)
Reported speech	Reported speech is when a person provides an apparent verbatim account of the speech (or thoughts) of another person (or reports their own speech in the past). Signal this with the use of inverted commas around the reported speech (e.g. ... and she said 'I think your bum does look big in that dress' and I said 'thanks a bunch'...)
Accents and abbreviations/ vernacular usage/ mispronunciation	It's important not to transform participants' speech into 'standard' English; however, fully representing a strong regional accent can be a complex and time consuming process. A good compromise is to signal only the very obvious or common (and easy to translate into written text) abbreviations and vernacular usage, such as 'cos' instead of 'because' or a Welsh speaker saying 'me Mam' (instead of the English 'my Mum'), unless it is absolutely critical for your analysis to fully represent exactly how a speaker pronounces words and sounds. Don't 'correct' mispronunciation or misspeaking of works, such as 'compostle' instead of 'compostable'
Names of media (e.g. television programmes, books, magazines)	Should be presented in italics (e.g. *The Wire*, *Men's Health*)
Identifying information	You can change identifying information such as people's names and occupations, places, events, etc. in one of two ways (see also Box 7.2):
	By changing details and providing unmarked, appropriate alternatives (e.g. 'Bristol' to 'Manchester'; 'my sister is 14' to 'my sister is 12'; 'I'm a really keen knitter' to 'I'm a really keen sewer')
	By replacing specific information with marked generic descriptions (indicated by square brackets, so 'London' might be replaced with [large city]; 'Michael' with [oldest brother]; 'running' with [form of exercise])

PRODUCING THE TRANSCRIPT

Transcription is often thought of as a chore, and boring; but although it can be hard to do, it's a *really* good skill to develop and essential for any qualitative researcher working with audio data. We're going to talk about transcribing *digital* data, as most data are digital these days (previously, most were recorded on audio tape). To transcribe digital data, the minimum you need is computer software to play it. Transcription software (rather than Media Player or iTunes) has features that allow you to speed up or slow down the playback pace. This can be really useful for deciphering what is being

BOX 7.1   ANNOTATED EXAMPLE OF ORTHOGRAPHIC TRANSCRIPTION

Start the first word of a new turn of talk with a capital letter.

You can use the interviewer/ moderato's name, but it is often clearer to use their role (often abbreviated to 'Int' or 'Mod').

You can use this symbol to indicate very short pauses if you are doing pattern-based DA.

Give each new speaker/new turn of talk a new line.

Cut-off speech or sounds.

Best guess.

Underlining used to indicate emphasis.

UK English speakers tend to say 'erm' whereas people speaking US or New Zealand English tend to say 'um'.

A longer pause.

Moderator:	Okay so (.) I want to focus on (.) obesity rates (.) within individuals (.) so why do you think people become fat or obese
Sally:	I think there are a number of reasons erm. I think one o-erm one of the main reasons I became obese was because ((pause)) erm I had to go through a number of various orthopaedic surgeries which actually meant that I was in a wheelchair for quite a few months at a time and unfortunately (.) part of when you're stuck in a wheelchair you suddenly feel like a little bit depressed as well so (well) you tend to have the knock-on effect of eating so you're eating more than you should do cos really when you're very immobile you shouldn't eat very much at all because hence you do gain weight and you get there and that's one of the reasons a lot of people erm who were generally quite fit people who I've spoken to have gained weight through ((pause)) mainly things like surgery and various life impacts like that life events
Moderator:	What does everyone else think
Rebecca:	I think that I think you're right about life events even if you know nothing to do with surgery I think
Sally?:	Oh

A question mark after a name signals your best guess as to who is speaking – unless you know participants' voices very well, it can be hard to identify the speaker of very short bursts of speech and sound, especially when there are multiple speakers as in a focus group.

said. The basic software Express Scribe, free to download, is more than adequate. More advanced programmes can include features like tone adjustment, and an auto-reverse option. Other useful equipment includes:

- decent quality headphones – vital if you're transcribing on a public computer, for confidentiality reasons, but important for potentially increasing clarity and volume of the playback;
- a specially designed transcription foot pedal, which allows you to control play, pause, rewind and fast forward with your foot – this can speed up transcription considerably, as you don't have to use your hands to press play, pause and rewind, and they can stay dedicated to typing the transcript; you also don't need to switch between different active windows on your computer to play/pause the recording, and type up the transcript.

To actually transcribe the data, you play a *very* short segment of the recording (a few seconds) and type what you hear, using your notation system to guide you. You need to rewind the recording a little, to avoid missing anything, then play another short segment, transcribe it, etc. It's not this straightforward though. You may need to play each snippet of the recording a number of times to make out what has been said (slowing down or speeding up the recording can help here), and you should always go back and double check what you've transcribed. We have a natural tendency to 'correct' what we hear, and this creeps into transcription all over the place. One of the key bits of advice we give our students who are learning to transcribe is to try *not* to listen to the *meaning* of the words, just to the sounds of the words. But it is tricky to learn this skill.

There is no right way to manage the process of producing a transcript. When and how frequently you go back and check the 'accuracy' of your transcribing is up to you. You'll soon learn how many errors you are making, and how much checking you need to do. Even if you thoroughly check your transcribing as you go, we recommend checking (and if necessary editing) each transcript in full at least once, after it has been completed (it's very easy to miss tiny details in the gaps between stopping and starting the recording). Leaving a bit of time between producing the transcript and checking it can be helpful, particularly for hearing things that you couldn't make out the first (or tenth!) time you listened to the recording. If you're missing something you think is important, you can also get your supervisor or a co-researcher to listen; it's amazing how another person can *instantly* and clearly hear something you think is completely incomprehensible. Once you're done, it's generally a good idea to password-protect or encrypt transcript files, even if anonymised, for confidentiality reasons. Just don't forget the password!

The main aim of doing an orthographic transcription is to produce a thorough record of the words spoken. Non-semantic sounds, hesitation, repetition, false-starts, pauses, laughter and so on are less important (they can be really time-consuming to transcribe). How much of such detail you need relates to your analytic, methodological and theoretical positions. An orthographic transcript is going to provide enough information to analyse data using the methods we discuss in depth in this book. Experiential analytic methods, like interpretative phenomenological analysis, and some versions of thematic analysis (TA) and grounded theory (GT), focus on the words spoken by the participants – *what* was said rather than *how* it was said. At most, the analysis might discuss moments when a participant cried, struggled to articulate themselves or was hesitant. Critical analytic methods, like constructionist TA and GT, and pattern-based discourse approaches, are also interested in *how* things are said. However, a very *thorough* orthographic transcription, such as the one we've outlined, generally captures enough detail for these forms of analysis.

Finally, another exception to the rule of 'recording everything that was said' relates to anonymising data as you transcribe it (see Box 7.2). Anonymity of participants is an important ethical issue (see Chapter 3) and participants are typically informed that their data will be anonymised (see the participant information sheet in Chapter 5, and the others on the ***companion website***).

BOX 7.2   ANONYMISING TRANSCRIPTS

Anonymising data means removing or changing any information that could identify the participant. You should *always* change participants' names, and the names of other people mentioned in the data, by giving them a pseudonym (fake name) (unless you have people's express permission to use their real names and this doesn't compromise the anonymity of other participants). As a basic rule beyond this, consider what information may potentially make the participant identifiable – such as their occupation, their age, the fact that they have three sisters. It's important to consider what information may be potentially identifying not in isolation, but as a *cumulative* effect. For instance, information that a participant is a teacher might not be identifying; information that a participant is a disabled 50-year-old Chinese male teacher who lives in East Grinstead is far more potentially identifying. Whether you remove or change such information, and the degree to which you change it, depends on a number of factors including the extent to which a participant is identifiable by others who may read your research, the importance of *complete* anonymity to individual participants, and the importance of such information to your analysis. For instance, if you are interested in understanding experiences of eating difficulties in the context of family relationships, preserving information about the age and gender of participants' siblings may be important.

As shown in Table 7.1, there are two main ways of anonymising data – a marked, generic description, or an unmarked equivalent description. In either case, but especially when anonymising via unmarked changes, it's important to keep a *separate* (password-protected) document that contains the non-anonymised data, and/or a record of all changes (so you can check what has been changed if necessary).

GIVING YOURSELF ENOUGH TIME TO TRANSCRIBE

It does take *time* to transcribe data well. Some suggest it takes about an hour to transcribe ten minutes of data from an interview (Arksey & Knight, 1999), and an hour to transcribe four–five minutes of data from an FG. In our experience, it often takes quite a bit longer, especially if you're not experienced. Many factors influence this, including:

- the quality of the recording and playback – the clearer, the quicker;
- how much people talk over the top of each other – every overlap adds transcription time;
- speech characteristics (such as accent, speed and volume of speech) – some may be harder to understand; in FGs differences in accent and gender can *aid* transcription by making speaker-identification easier;
- the number of people involved – the more, the longer it takes;
- what sort of transcript you're producing – the less detail, the quicker;
- what transcribing equipment you're using – if you have to interrupt your typing to stop and start the recording over and over again, or switch between different software programs, it will take longer;
- how fast you are as a typist – fast touch typists have the edge here.

As a starting guide, we suggest allowing *at least* eight hours per one-hour interview; you will, however, become quicker at transcribing with practice.

CHAPTER SUMMARY

This chapter:

- introduced orthographic transcription of audio data;
- outlined what a transcript represents, and what it does not;
- discussed issues related to transcription quality;
- described how to transcribe audio(visual) data;
- provided notation guidelines for orthographic transcription.

? QUESTIONS FOR DISCUSSION AND CLASSROOM EXERCISES

1   In a small group, select a short (two–five minutes) audio or video clip that features people speaking (ideally with more than one speaker), to practise transcription – we recommend an extract from the body art FG on the *companion website*, but something else would be fine. First, working alone, attempt to transcribe the clip (you will need to play it a number of times, ideally playing the clip in very

short bursts and rewinding slightly before playing again, so you don't miss any-thing). Once you are reasonably confident you have a 'good enough' rendition of the clip, compare your transcript with that of the other people in the group. Did you all hear the clip in exactly the same way? What exactly did everyone transcribe? If there was laughing, coughing, sneezing or any other non-semantic sounds (such as expressions of hesitation or agreement – 'erm', 'mm', 'ah-ha') in the clip, did everyone transcribe these? Did anyone use punctuation in their transcript? If so, what punctuation symbols did they use, and what features of speech were they trying to capture in using punctuation? Did anyone indicate pauses or emphasis on particular words? Now, working together try to produce a 'definitive' transcript of the clip. How different is this 'definitive' collectively produced transcript from your initial individually produced transcripts?

2   Working in small groups, read the following (fictional) extract from an inter-view (designed to include lots of identifying information) and decide which information could identify the participant. Then decide how to best anonymise the extract. Afterwards, compare yours to the different anonymised versions on the *companion website*.

Jane:	...I grew up in Brighton and you see men holding hands all the time in Brighton, and Tim came out when I was about 12 or 13 ((pause)) I think he was 16 or maybe 15, he was definitely still at Michael Hall because I used to get teased about being gay myself...
Interviewer:	And, when did you come out?
Jane:	I came out in the first year of university so I must have been 19 or 20, I had a gap year before going to Durham...my mum freaked a bit, she was totally okay, but I think even for her – someone who lives in Brighton and writes for the *Guardian* newspaper – two gay kids was a bit much...my Aunty Julie, my mum's sister, was absolutely wonderful though, and she's a lesbian...

FURTHER RESOURCES

Further reading:

For a comprehensive discussion of the processes involved in producing a high-quality tran-script, which includes potential pitfalls to avoid, see: Poland, B. D. (2002). Transcription quality. In J. F. Gubrium and J. A. Holstein (Eds), *Handbook of interview research: Context and method* (pp. 629–650). Thousand Oaks, CA: Sage.

For a short discussion of the theoretical underpinnings of transcription, see: Sandelowski, M. (1994). Notes on transcription. *Research in Nursing & Health, 17,* 311–314.

Online resources:

For information and resources on a more detailed, discursive form of transcription (Jefferson style): www-staff.lboro.ac.uk/~ssjap/transcription/transcription.htm

Express Scribe offers excellent free transcription software: www.nch.com.au/scribe/index.html

Audacity provides free digital sound-editing software: http://audacity.sourceforge.net/

See the *companion website* (**www.sagepub.co.uk/braunandclarke**) for:

- self-test multiple choice questions relating to Section 3;
- the flashcard glossary – test yourself on the definitions of key terms used in this chapter;
- the weigh and obesity and body art FG transcripts, the body art audio file and the transcriber confidentiality agreement;
- answers to the anonymising exercise;
- further readings (articles from Sage journals).

8 Moving towards analysis

OVERVIEW

The scope of qualitative analysis
Introducing qualitative analytic methods suitable for beginners
A flexible foundational method: thematic analysis
An experiential and interpretative approach: interpretative phenomenological
   analysis
An inductive yet theorised approach: grounded theory
An approach for looking at what language does: discourse analysis

By the time you have finished transcribing your data, you'll be very familiar with it and may have started to note down some initial analytic ideas – this is one reason transcription is often described as *part* of the analytic process, part of the process of familiarising yourself with your data. But once you're done transcribing, the analysis *really* begins. Before you jump in and get started with the exciting task of data analysis, you need to decide what method you're going to use to analyse them (though you should already have a sense of that when designing a project, before collecting data). This chapter introduces seven key methods of analysis, four of which (the pattern-based methods – thematic analysis [TA], interpretative phenomenological analysis [IPA], grounded theory [GT] and **pattern-based discourse analysis** [DA]) we discuss further in this book.

THE SCOPE OF QUALITATIVE ANALYSIS

Qualitative analysis covers a spectrum from *descriptive* (and exploratory) through to more interrogative, theorised, *interpretative* analysis; this spectrum closely aligns with the experiential/critical orientation outlined in Chapter 2. *Descriptive* work aims to 'give voice' to a topic or a group of people, particularly those we know little about. For instance, US psychologists Marianna Litovich and Regina Langhout (2004) explored experiences of heterosexism in an interview study with five lesbian families. They reported that the parents often claimed that their families had not been victims of heterosexism, but nonetheless discussed multiple incidents of heterosexism and prepared children for heterosexism in a number of ways. The authors make sense of this discrepancy in their data by suggesting that lesbian parents deal with heterosexist incidents in ways that minimise the negative repercussions for their children. Qualitative analysis which is *interpretative* aims to go further than **descriptive analysis**, unpicking the accounts that are given, and asking questions like 'What's going on here?' and 'How can we make sense of these accounts'? It tries to gain a *deeper* understanding of the data that have been gathered, and often looks 'beneath the surface' of the data, as it were, to try to understand how and why the particular accounts were generated and to provide a *conceptual* account of the data, and/or some sort of theorising around this. For example, Victoria took this approach when analysing data from interviews with lesbian and gay (LG) parents about their children's experiences of homophobic bullying (Clarke et al., 2004). Just as in the Litovich and Langhout (2004) study, parents either reported that their children hadn't been bullied or they minimised the extent and impact of any bullying their children had experienced. Instead of treating these as factual accounts of children's realities, she asked what effects these types of accounts have, in talk about LG parenting. Taking a *language practice* approach to qualitative data, Victoria made sense of this talk within a socio-political context relatively hostile to LG parents, where the possibility of homophobic bullying is used to support arguments *against* LG parenting. The analysis showed that parents' accounts were designed to protect LG parents from outside critique. Such *interpretative* accounts go well beyond what is obvious in the data, to explore meaning at a much deeper lever.

INTRODUCING QUALITATIVE ANALYTIC METHODS SUITABLE FOR BEGINNERS

There are many different methods of qualitative data analysis, but some are more common in qualitative psychology than others, and some are easier to learn and do than others. We focus on describing and demonstrating those that are both common within psychology *and* relatively accessible to those new to qualitative research – TA, IPA, GT and pattern-based DA. Table 8.1 provides a quick overview for comparison of these pattern-based methods. Three other methods that require more advanced skills – discursive psychology (DP), conversation analysis (CA), **narrative analysis** – are briefly described by expert practitioners of these methods, to give you a sense of the wider scope and diversity of qualitative analysis (see Boxes 8.1–8.3).

A FLEXIBLE FOUNDATIONAL METHOD: THEMATIC ANALYSIS

Some sort of 'thematic' coding is common across many qualitative methods within the social sciences. TA as a named approach was first developed by Gerald Holton, a

Table 8.1 Overview of pattern-based analytic methods

Basic method	What is it?	Varieties?	What is it?
Thematic Analysis (TA)	A method for identifying themes and patterns of meaning across a dataset in relation to a research question; possibly the most widely used qualitative method of data analysis, but not 'branded' as a specific method until recently (see Braun & Clarke, 2006)	Inductive TA	Aims to generate an analysis from the bottom (the data) up; analysis is not shaped by existing theory (but analysis is always shaped to some extent by the researcher's standpoint, disciplinary knowledge and epistemology)
		Theoretical TA	Analysis is guided by an existing theory and theoretical concepts (as well as by the researcher's standpoint, disciplinary knowledge and epistemology)
		Experiential TA	Focuses on the participants' standpoint – how they experience and make sense of the world
		Constructionist TA	Focuses on how topics are constructed and also how accounts construct the world
Interpretative Phenomenological Analysis (IPA)	Developed by British health psychologist Jonathan Smith and colleagues; focuses on how people make sense of their lived experience; can be used to analyse individual cases or to generate themes across a small group of participants (see Smith et al., 2009)	IPA	IPA is phenomenological because it is concerned with how people make sense of their lived experiences (phenomenology is focused on how people perceive and talk about objects and events); it is interpretative because understanding how people make sense of experience is achieved through interpretative activity on the part of the researcher

(Continued)

Table 8.1 (Continued)

Basic method	What is it?	Varieties?	What is it?
Grounded Theory (GT)	Developed by the US sociologists Glaser and Strauss in the 1960s (Glaser & Strauss, 1967) and has evolved considerably since then, with many different varieties of GT on offer; focuses on building theory from data and, because of its sociological origins, there is an emphasis on understanding social processes; analysis is organised around key categories (similar to themes) (see Pidgeon & Henwood, 1997; Charmaz, 2006)	GT-lite	Aims to generate a taxonomy of categories (clusters of related codes; similar to themes in GT and IPA) from data, with some indication of the relationships between concepts and the relative importance of concepts to the research question (see Pidgeon & Henwood, 1997); leaving aside questions of epistemology, the outcome of GT-lite is very similar to that of thematic analysis and IPA (a set of themes or categories that fit together in various ways)
		(Full) GT	There is some debate as to what constitutes a 'full' GT, but generally it aims to build a theory from the data (Glaser & Strauss, 1967; theoretical sampling is used, saturation is achieved and similar concepts are grouped together into categories and used to generate a theory
		Positivist GT	Aims to represent reality (see Glaser, 1978, 1992)
		Contextualist (constructivist) GT	Acknowledges the role of the researcher in shaping the analysis, views meaning as contextual, and argues that it is not possible to generate one 'true' reading of data (see Charmaz, 2006)
		(Radical) constructionist GT	Similar to DA-lite and constructionist TA; pays closer attention to language use; emphasis on the discourses that shape accounts the discursive devices through which participants construct and give meaning to their lives; and acknowledges ambiguity and inconsistency (see Madill et al., 2000)

Basic method	What is it?	Varieties?	What is it?
Pattern-based Discourse Analysis (DA)	Broadly speaking analysis is concerned with patterns in language use connected to the social production of reality, and with understanding how accounts of objects and events are constructed in particular ways (see Coyle, 2006, 2007; Potter & Wetherell, 1987)	Thematic discourse analysis (DA-lite)	Largely the same as constructionist TA; identifies discursive themes and patterns in data and applies the tools of DA 'lightly' to explore how themes construct reality in particular ways; a more detailed focus on discursive features of language than other forms of TA (for an example, see Taylor & Ussher, 2001)
		Poststructuralist DA	Heavily influenced by poststructuralist theory and the work of Michael Foucault; is concerned with the ways in which discourses constitute objects and make available particular subject positions. Has an explicit concern for the operation of power in and through discourse (for an example, see Gavey, 1989)
		Interpretative repertoires	Interested in both the patterned resources that participants use in their talk *about* an object, such as race relations (Wetherell & Potter, 1992), and the functions of the *use* to which such repertoires are put (Potter & Wetherell, 1987)
		Critical discursive psychology	Offers a 'synthetic' approach that cuts across different traditions, retaining an interest in both patterned socially available linguistic resources and language practices (Wetherell, 2007)

physicist and historian of science, in the 1970s (Merton, 1975), but has only recently been recognised as a distinctive method with a clearly outlined set of procedures for the social sciences (Braun & Clarke, 2006). Prior to 2006, some qualitative researchers had written about 'thematic analysis' (e.g. Aronson, 1994; Boyatzis, 1998; Joffe & Yardley, 2004), thematic coding (e.g. Patton, 1990) or 'template analysis' (King, 1998, 2004), and numerous authors were essentially doing TA – but often calling it something else, like 'grounded theory' or 'discourse analysis' or a combination of the two (even though they are often incompatible in their theoretical bases). Frustrated by this situation, and by the lack of a 'named' method for providing a systematic approach for identifying, analysing and reporting patterns – themes – across a dataset, which was not tied to a particular theory, we 'named and claimed' TA within psychology. Since then, it has grown in popularity and is now a recognised, accepted and more widely discussed method (e.g. Howitt, 2010; Howitt & Cramer, 2008; Joffe, 2011; Stainton Rogers, 2011; Whittaker, 2009), and has been used to research a wide range of topics from experiences of online gaming (Hussain & Griffiths, 2009) to women's clothing practices (Frith & Gleeson, 2004, 2008) to living with multiple sclerosis (Malcomson, Lowe-Strong, & Dunwoody, 2008). For an example of a study using TA, see Illustrative Research Example 8.1. We base our description of 'how to do' TA (Chapters 8–10) on the method we developed (Braun & Clarke, 2006, 2012), which involves a systematic, six-phase process; versions of TA described elsewhere do differ, for instance by being treated as a realist method rather than a theoretically flexible one, or through treating 'themes' in a somewhat different way (e.g. Bernard & Ryan, 2010; Guest, MacQueen, & Namey, 2012; Joffe, 2011).

TA is relatively unique among qualitative analytic methods in that it *only* provides a method for data *analysis*; it does not prescribe methods of data collection, theoretical positions, epistemological or ontological frameworks. It really is 'just a method'. One of the main strengths of TA is this flexibility. It can be used to answer almost any type of research question (with the exception of questions about language practice) and used to analyse almost any kind of data, including all those discussed in Chapters 4–6, with larger or smaller datasets (see Table 3.3 in Chapter 3). Themes can be identified in a data-driven, 'bottom-up' way, on the basis of what is in the data; alternatively, they can be identified in a more 'top-down' fashion, where the researcher uses the data to explore particular theoretical ideas, or brings those to bear on the analysis being conducted (bottom-up and top-down approaches are often combined in one analysis). TA can be applied to data in different ways, from experiential to critical. It can be used to develop a detailed descriptive account of a phenomenon (e.g. the reasons boys give for dieting), or some aspect of a phenomenon (e.g. one particular explanation for dieting); it can also be used to develop a critical, constructionist analysis which can identify the concepts and ideas that underpin the explicit data content, or the assumptions and meanings in the data (e.g. that food is a 'friend' or food is a 'foe'). TA offers the chance to learn basic data-handling and coding skills, without having to delve deep into theoretical constructs; many of these will serve you well in using other analytic approaches. For this reason, it's an excellent method for those new to qualitative research, and particularly suitable to student projects; this is why it is the main approach discussed and demonstrated in this book. For an evaluation of the strengths and weaknesses of TA see Table 8.2.

ILLUSTRATIVE RESEARCH EXAMPLE 8.1

Thematic analysis: Men's experiences of infertility

British health psychologists Sumaira Malik and Neil Coulson (2008) examined men's experience of infertility via an online support group bulletin board. They noted that previous research suggested that men and women differ in their response to infertility but there was very little research specifically examining men's experiences and perspectives. They also noted that infertile couples are increasingly turning to online sources for advice and support, and so chose to analyse the messages posted to the 'Men's Room' bulletin board of an online fertility support group over a period of 18 months (53 threads consisting of 728 messages from 166 senders; messages from women were excluded from the analysis). Inductive TA, conducted within an essentialist/realist framework and emphasising semantic themes, generated five key themes, with analytic claims illustrated by data extracts:

Supporting dearest partner is our key role: Many men felt that their role in the fertility treatment process was to support their (female) partner, and they used the support group to gain advice on fulfilling their role. This lead some men to stifle their emotions, and use the message board as an outlet for expressing them.

Is this a good or bad pain? The men used the message boards to discuss their, and their female partner's, fertility treatment and many perceived a lack of information from health professionals, which created feelings of anxiety. Many experienced a lack of control and helplessness in relation to fertility treatment and the often unexplained symptoms of the treatment.

Us blokes are mere spectators in most people's eyes: Many men reported feeling unimportant and lonely in relation to the treatment process, which for some was compounded by the fact that many health professionals did not appreciate the emotional impact of infertility on men and the distress they can feel.

Sometimes a male perspective is needed: Many men appreciated the emotional support and practical advice of other men going through a similar process.

I don't want to get my hopes up, but I can't help it: Some men used the message board to articulate their hopes and fears with regard to the treatment. Many of these men reported conflicting and multiple emotions (hope and optimism and fear of failure), and often an effort was made to suppress positive emotions in order to protect themselves from disappointment.

Malik and Coulson argued that their findings challenged the view that men experience low levels of emotional distress in response to infertility and showed that men used the online support group to openly express their feelings and gain support from other men.

Table 8.2   Evaluating thematic analysis

Strengths	Weaknesses
Flexibility in terms of theoretical framework, research questions, methods of data collection and sample size	Is perceived by some qualitative researchers as 'something and nothing', as lacking the substance of other 'branded' and theoretically driven approaches like IPA and GT
Accessible to researchers with little or no (qualitative) research experience; a great 'starter' qualitative method	Has limited interpretative power if not used within an existing theoretical framework; in practice analyses often consist simply of (realist) *descriptions* of participants' concerns
Relatively easy and quick to learn, and to do, compared to other more labour-intensive qualitative analytic methods	Lack of concrete guidance for higher level, more interpretative analysis
The results of TA can be accessible to an educated wider audience (for this reason, TA can be an appropriate method for participatory approaches, where the participants have a role in the analysis of the data they help to generate, and is a useful method for applied research)	Because of the focus on patterns across datasets, it cannot provide any sense of the continuity and contradictions within individual accounts; also the 'voices' of individual participants can get lost (especially when working with larger datasets)
	Cannot make claims about the effects of language use (unlike DA, DP or CA)

AN EXPERIENTIAL AND INTERPRETATIVE APPROACH: INTERPRETATIVE PHENOMENOLOGICAL ANALYSIS

IPA is a fairly new addition to the established qualitative analytic methods. Developed by British psychologist Jonathan Smith and colleagues in the 1990s (see Smith, 1996), it is an increasingly popular approach to qualitative research, particularly within applied areas like health, clinical and counselling psychology. IPA is also particularly popular with those new to qualitative research, because its proponents have produced highly accessible and detailed guidance on doing IPA (Smith et al., 2009). It is one of a number of phenomenological approaches to qualitative research (Langdridge, 2007), which are generally concerned with 'persons-in-context' or 'being in the world' (Larkin, Watts, & Clifton, 2006), phrases which evoke the idea that 'the individual' and 'the social' are 'mutually constitutive' (Larkin, Eatough, & Osborn, 2011: 321), so you cannot meaningfully take a person out of context. Like most other qualitative analytic approaches, it is a wholesale *approach* to qualitative research (a methodology), rather than just an analytic method, specifying guiding theoretical principles, appropriate research questions and study designs, ideal methods of data collection, as well as analytic procedures (see Chapters 9 to 11). Larkin et al. (2006) described IPA as a broadly 'contextualist' approach (see Chapter 2) because of its focus on persons-in-context.

IPA's overriding concern is with exploring people's lived experiences and the meanings people attach to those experiences (it is thus best suited to experience-type questions; see Table 3.1 in Chapter 3). This is the phenomenological aspect; phenomenology is about the study of experience. IPA is based on a model of the person as a self-reflective, self-interpretative being; that is, we have experiences – we fall in love, become ill, become parents, etc. – and we *reflect* on those experiences and attempt to make sense of them; we interpret them. IPA acknowledges, however, that researchers cannot access a participant's world *directly*; researchers also make sense of the participant's world using their *own* interpretative resources. This is the interpretative part. IPA therefore involves a *dual* interpretative process, referred to as a 'double hermeneutic' (hermeneutics refers to a theory of interpretation): the researcher is trying to make sense of the participant trying to make sense of their world (Smith et al., 2009; Smith & Osborn, 2003). Making sense of a participant's concerns involves another dual analytic process: first, staying close to the participant's account of their experiences, and representing their experiences in a way which is 'true' to the participant's understandings. This 'insider' stance has been described as a hermeneutics of empathy. Second, stepping back from participant's accounts, viewing the data through a *critical* lens and asking questions like 'What assumptions underpin this account?' and 'Why are they making sense of their experiences in this way (and not that way)?' This 'outsider' stance has been described as a hermeneutics of suspicion (Smith et al., 2009).

The core (prescriptive) features of IPA have been described as '**idiographic** analysis balancing experiential claims against more overtly interpretative analyses; drawing from small samples; and focusing on verbatim accounts' (Larkin et al., 2006: 118). IPA is both a thematic approach and concerned with the specifics of individual experiences; as such, it can be used to analyse single cases (e.g. Eatough & Smith, 2006) or, more commonly, small samples. Samples of four (Smith, 1999a), five (Eatough, Smith, & Shaw, 2008) or six (Smith & Osborn, 2007) 'homogeneous' participants are typical. Homogeneity can be defined in different ways depending on the requirements of the study, from obvious socio-demographic factors such as sex and age, or factors related to key elements of experience – such as the length and severity of experiencing chronic pain. Semi-structured face-to-face in-depth interviews (see Smith, J.A., 1995) are viewed as the ideal method for collecting verbatim accounts; other types of data sometimes used in IPA studies include surveys, diaries and focus groups (FGs) (Palmer, Larkin, de Visser, & Fadden, 2010). Comparative designs are possible in IPA, comparing the experiences of different groups, as are longitudinal 'before and after' designs (Smith et al., 2009). In practice, IPA studies tend to focus on significant life experiences that often have implications for our identities, as they unfold in particular contexts. For example, IPA researchers have explored the transition to motherhood and how women make sense of changes to their identity (Smith, 1999a, 1999b), women's experiences of anger and aggression (see Illustrative Research Example 8.2), and the impact of chronic pain on sufferer's sense of self (Smith & Osborn, 2007).

ILLUSTRATIVE RESEARCH EXAMPLE 8.2

IPA: Women's experiences of anger and aggression

British psychologists Virginia Eatough, Jonathan Smith & Rachel Shaw (2008) reported a phenomenological study of five women's lived experience of anger and aggression. They argued that 'human beings are intrinsically embedded in the world and that we come to make sense of ourselves and others through our world dealings' (p. 1767), and so aimed to understand the women's subjective experience of anger and aggression to reveal the 'relational and being-in-the-world' (p. 1767) nature of anger. Eatough et al. situated their study in relation to wider literature on women's anger and aggression, noting the existence of only a small number of qualitative studies. A purposive sample of five women, all residing in the same area, of similar ages, all married or cohabiting and all but one having at least one child, were each interviewed twice over a period of three weeks. The women were asked to describe episodes of anger and how they made sense of them and the strategies they used to resolve conflict. When analysing the data, the two interviews for each participant were treated as one transcript. Eatough et al. identified three superordinate (or higher order) themes generated from their analysis of the data (with two–four **subthemes** nested within each **superordinate theme**): *the subjective experience of anger; forms and contexts of aggression;* and *anger as moral judgement*. Each superordinate theme was discussed separately, with subthemes discussed sequentially, and data extracts presented to illustrate the analytic claims.

To give an example of their analysis, the first theme, *the subjective experience of anger,* incorporated four subthemes (bodily experience of anger, escalation of anger, crying/frustration accompanying anger, and anger and other emotions/feelings). Under the heading 'what anger feels like' the authors described the key features of the individual women's experiences of anger from 'seeing red' to a loss of bodily control, which eventually peak and run their course. The women cried for many different reasons including feelings of powerlessness and frustration. The women also described experiencing multiple and fluid emotions – anger turning into guilt, transitory feelings of elation and power and unbearable feelings of guilt and loss.

In their discussion, they related their results to existing psychological theory of the body, emotion and the subject. Eatough et al. concluded by noting the 'complex meaning making that lies behind the anger experience' (p. 1795).

There is currently only one version of IPA, and there has been no public 'in-fighting' between IPA practitioners (unlike among discourse analysts and grounded theorists, as discussed later). However, there are in practice different 'flavours' of IPA: some IPA researchers emphasise psychological interpretations of data, seek to dialogue with mainstream psychology and relate their findings to (mainstream) psychological theory and concepts (e.g. Wyer, Earll, Joseph, & Harrison, 2001); others (e.g. Eatough & Smith, 2006) make reference to 'dominant discourses' and findings are interpreted in relation to the wider social and cultural context. (However such interpretations are often rather 'thin' compared to other approaches; contrast Lavie and Willig's, 2005, IPA of women's experiences of 'inorgasmia' with Nicolson and Burr's, 2003, [unclaimed] TA of women's experiences of orgasm.) In general, however, despite the interests in 'persons-in-context', IPA does not seem to share the agenda(s) of critical (qualitative) psychologists (Fox, Prilleltensky, & Austin, 2009), and tends to emphasise *psychological* rather than critical *socio-cultural* interpretation. This may result from IPA's desire to not over-write the subjectivities of participants with the analyst's theoretical commitments and/or political frameworks.

There has also been very little critique of IPA; one of the few qualitative researchers to do so is the critical psychologist Ian Parker (2005b), who urged qualitative researchers to 'beware IPA' because of its compatibility with mainstream psychology and its failure to fully acknowledge that 'what is "inside" is dependent on what is "outside"'. Some proponents of IPA have been critical of the use of IPA as a 'simply descriptive' method (Larkin et al., 2006) and have urged IPA practitioners to place greater emphasis on interpretation in their analyses (Brocki & Wearden, 2006). Table 8.3 provides an evaluation of IPA's strengths and weaknesses.

Table 8.3 Evaluating IPA

Strengths	Weaknesses
Accessible for novice qualitative researchers; like TA, a great 'starter' qualitative method	Because of the dual focus on individual cases and themes across cases, it can lack the depth and richness of narrative analysis and the substance of TA and GT
Clear and precise procedures specified for the entirety of a project	
A model of the person that resonates strongly with common-sense understandings of what it means to be human and how we experience ourselves, and with models of the person in many areas of applied psychology (e.g. counselling, clinical, health psychology)	Because of small sample sizes, a willingness to dialogue with mainstream psychology and the experiential focus, IPA is viewed by some as lacking substance and sophistication (Parker, 2005b)
An approach developed within psychology that specifically orients to psychological concerns	Clear and precise guidance may be viewed as a recipe that *must* be followed
Some flavours of IPA seek to dialogue with mainstream psychology and are inclusive of mainstream psychological theories and concepts	Can only be used to answer research questions about experiences, and understandings and perceptions, and to analyse self-report experiential data
Allows a focus on *individual* experience and the detail of individual experience	Lacks the theoretical flexibility of TA
Suitable for use in time- and resource-limited research	The role of the social-cultural context in IPA is often unclear
	Lack of concrete guidance about higher-level (interpretative) analysis; analyses are often limited to simply describing participants' concerns

AN INDUCTIVE YET THEORISED APPROACH: GROUNDED THEORY

GT is a very popular qualitative method, particularly in the US, and has the longest history of the methods we discuss. Developed in the 1960s by the US sociologists Barney G. Glaser and Anselm L. Strauss in a ground-breaking study on dying in hospital (Glaser & Strauss, 1965), the principles of grounded theory were first outlined in their classic book *The Discovery of Grounded Theory* (Glaser & Strauss, 1967). Glaser and Strauss came from different theoretical backgrounds: Glaser was interested in the standard hypothetical-deductive method, Strauss in the work of symbolic interactionists, who were concerned with the role of interpretation and meaning in the social world – they argued that meaning derives from social interaction (Blumer, 1969). What united them was a critique of sociologists' preoccupation with testing 'grand' theories, rather than generating more contextually situated theories that were relevant to the lives of the people being studied. Glaser and Strauss chose the term *grounded* theory to capture the idea of a theory that is grounded in a close inspection of qualitative data gathered from concrete, local settings (Pidgeon & Henwood, 1997a). In essence, GT is an *approach* to qualitative research (not *just* an analysis method), concerned with constructing theory from data (Charmaz & Henwood, 2008). GT has been used to research a wide range of topics, such as chronic illness (see Illustrative Research Example 8.3), the phenomenon of 'pro-anorexia' (Williams & Reid, 2007) and the impact of wind turbines on people living in their locality (Pedersen, Hallberg, & Waye, 2007).

GT has become hugely popular across the social sciences. Many different versions have been developed, with no one predominating. The original proponents publically split and developed their own versions of GT: Glaser's version is more positivist (Glaser, 1992, 1978); Strauss's, particularly that developed with Juliet Corbin (e.g. in the hugely influential text *Basics of Qualitative Research*, Corbin & Strauss, 1990), is more contextualist (**constructivist**) in theoretical orientation. There are now versions of grounded theory situated across the epistemological spectrum: positivist (Glaser, 1992; Glaser, 1978); contextualist (Charmaz & Henwood, 2008; Pidgeon & Henwood, 1997a); and constructionist (Madill et al., 2000). We primarily draw on the version developed by British social psychologists Karen Henwood and Nick Pidgeon (Henwood & Pidgeon, 1994, 2003, 2006; Pidgeon, 1996; Pidgeon & Henwood, 1996, 1997a, 2004), whose work is heavily influenced by US sociologist Kathy Charmaz (2006), former PhD student of Strauss, and one of the world's foremost proponents of GT, and Birks and Mills's (2011) very practical and accessible book – which synthesises the work of the original proponents as well as 'second generation' grounded theorists like Charmaz.

Henwood and Pidgeon situate their approach within a, broadly speaking, contextualist framework; Charmaz (2006) locates hers within the symbolic interactionist tradition in sociology, and writes about 'constructing grounded theory', rather than *discovering* theory in data (as per Glaser and Strauss's, 1967, original model). She argues that researchers are part of the things we explore and the data we generate: 'we *construct* our grounded

ILLUSTRATIVE RESEARCH EXAMPLE 8.3

Grounded theory: Chronic illness

US sociologist Kathy Charmaz (1983) examined the loss of self experienced by chronically ill adults using a symbolic interactionist-informed version of GT, and drawing on 73 in-depth interviews with 57 chronically ill people living in Northern California who had various diagnoses including cancer, diabetes and multiple sclerosis. Symbolic interactionism views the self as fundamentally social – the self is developed and maintained through social relationships – so that changes in the self-concept occur across the lifespan. Applied to the study of chronic illness, this perspective highlights how the illness experience creates situations in which people learn new understandings of self and relinquish old ones. The participants ranged in age from 20 to 86 years (most were aged 40–60); two-thirds were women. The data analysed in the paper were limited to participants who were housebound or severely debilitated by their illnesses. Charmaz identified four types of suffering experienced by these participants: *leading restricted lives*, *experiencing social isolation*, *being discredited* and *burdening others*, each of which led to a loss of self. Each type of suffering was discussed in turn; analytic claims were illustrated with interview extracts.

For example, *living a restricted life* demonstrated that unlike 'healthy' adults, these chronically ill people lived narrow, restricted lives, which focused on their illness and offered few possibilities for creating valued selves. Charmaz argued that 'values of independence and individualism' (p. 172) intensified the experience of restriction: chronically ill people could not do the things (to the same extent) they enjoyed and valued before they became ill. If participants felt they had the choice and some freedom to pursue valued activities (even if they could not always exercise that freedom), they felt less restricted and maintained a valued self-concept. For others, the restrictions imposed by treatment regimes became 'daily reminders of the lessened freedom, and often, diminished self, that these patients experience[d]' (p. 173). Participants experienced a loss of control over themselves and their lives, which led to losses of self, with their past lives and selves seeming increasingly distant. Charmaz argued that the practices of health professionals sometimes reinforced restricted lives when patients were not supported in reducing their suffering (and consequent loss of self), and that a world designed for the healthy and able often led to unnecessary restriction (partly through the failure of the chronically ill to question social norms and through using the lives of the 'healthy' as the yardstick by which they judge themselves). The unpredictability of some forms of chronic illness also led some participants to voluntarily restrict their lives more than was perhaps necessary. For the chronically ill who were increasingly socially isolated, their restricted life 'foster[ed] an all-consuming retreat into illness' (p. 175). However, for participants whose health had improved, their past illness became a path to self-discovery and self-development – the freedom from ordinary existence led them to reflect on who they were and who they wanted to be. Charmaz concluded by noting that the language of suffering was a language of loss – the loss of self and a meaningful life (see Chapter 11 for a comparison with an IPA study on a similar topic).

theories through our past and present involvements and interactions with people, perspectives, and research practices' (Charmaz, 2006: 10, emphasis in original). In this respect, Charmaz's version of GT is rather similar to the emphasis on the researcher's *interpretative* activity in IPA (which also draws on symbolic interactionism; see Smith, 1999b).

Although GT is used to address a number of different types of research questions, because of its concerns with social and social psychological processes within particular social settings (Charmaz, 2006), it is probably best suited to questions about *influencing factors* and the (social) processes that underpin a particular phenomenon. The interview is a key method of data collection (as it is for IPA). Other possible methods include participant-generated texts and secondary sources (Charmaz, 2006) (see Table 3.3 in Chapter 3). The production of a 'full' GT is a demanding process, and only possible in larger research projects (not constrained by time and resource pressures); there is also some debate among grounded theorists as to what constitutes a 'grounded theory' (Pidgeon & Henwood, 1997a). In practice, many researchers only complete the earlier stages of GT (initial coding and concept development), which we refer to as 'GT-lite'. This 'lite' version of GT is ideally suited to smaller qualitative projects, and so this is the version we focus on in this book. Table 8.4 provides an evaluation of GT's strengths and weaknesses.

GT is famous for distinctive procedures such as 'line-by-line coding', 'constant comparative analysis', 'memo writing', '**theoretical sampling**', 'saturation', and for not engaging with the relevant literature prior to beginning the analysis (to avoid it being shaped by preconceptions from existing research, rather than being truly *grounded* in the data). Some of these, such as theoretical sampling (see Box 3.3 in Chapter 3), are specific to *full* (rather than lite) GT; those relevant to GT-lite are discussed through

Table 8.4   Evaluating grounded theory

Strengths	Weaknesses
Different versions of GT to suit different theoretical and epistemological frameworks	There are so many versions of GT, and so many different sets of guidance for doing GT, not to mention different terminology, that it can be difficult to know where to start (Birks & Mills, 2011)
A useful method for researchers interested in social and social psychological processes (rather than individual experience)	Some versions of GT procedures are bafflingly complex
	GT was developed in sociology and so emphasises sociological concerns, such as social structures and processes, rather than psychological ones
Some clear and comprehensive accounts of analytic procedures (some are less clear – see weaknesses)	Completing a full GT is highly demanding and time consuming; in practice, many grounded theorists use GT-lite
Many GT procedures such as line-by-line coding and memo writing are useful in almost any kind of qualitative analysis	Difficult or impossible to complete a 'full' GT in a small project

Chapters 9–11. Some of these procedures have assumed a status akin to Christianity's ten commandments: 'you *must* generate a code for every line of data'; 'you *mustn't* read any literature until after you have completed your analysis'. Such prescriptive and purist ideas are problematic, and set you up for a sense of 'failure'. In practice, it's virtually impossible not to have engaged with some of the relevant literature prior to beginning your research – research proposals, funding and ethics applications all *require* that we situate our proposed research in relation to the relevant literature; and you certainly can't do research without at least one of these (ethics). Moreover, as scholars we continually accumulate a wide variety of disciplinary knowledge, which is impossible to 'un-know'. *And* to do research that isn't a waste of time, we need to have some sense of whether our question hasn't already been answered. A good maxim to apply is that 'there is a difference between an open mind and an empty head' (Dey, 1999: 251); we can still strive to approach our (GT, or indeed any) research with an open-mind, even though we have some prior knowledge about our topic.

AN APPROACH FOR LOOKING AT WHAT LANGUAGE DOES: DISCOURSE ANALYSIS

DA is another immensely popular method, but 'discourse analysis' is also one of the most confusing terms in qualitative research. It's used in so many different ways, just *within* psychology, that one 'DA' can bear little correspondence *at all* to another 'DA'. If you look outside the discipline, such as into English, linguistics or media studies, it can get even *less* familiar. British psychologist Nigel Edley described DA as 'an ever-broadening church, an umbrella term for a wide variety of different analytic principles and practices' (Edley, 2001a: 189). We're going to try to narrow this down a bit, and explain some core concepts, but our main focus is on versions of DA that look at *patterns* (of meaning or language practice) across linguistic datasets (see Parker & the Bolton Discourse Network, 1999, on non-linguistic data).

DA is not a method (like TA); it is not even an approach to qualitative research (like IPA or GT). Rather, it is a whole *approach* to psychology and knowledge. It emerged in (British) social psychology in the 1980s, which was in a state of epistemological and ontological upheaval, following the 'crisis in social psychology'. This 'crisis' saw diverse paradigmatic, political and conceptual challenges to what had become the dominant framework and form of social psychology: a positivist cognitivist science using laboratory-based experimentation as its primary method of inquiry, married to an impoverished and diminished vision of 'the social' (see Parker, 1989). Now-classic texts, *Changing the Subject: Psychology, Social Regulation and Subjectivity* (Henriques, Hollway, Urwin, Venn, & Walkerdine, 1984), *Discourse and Social Psychology: Beyond Attitudes and Behaviour* (Potter & Wetherell, 1987) and *Arguing and Thinking: A Rhetorical Approach to Social Psychology* (Billig, 1987), took a knife to the foundations of (social) psychology, offering up a whole different way of seeing and doing psychology: different theoretical frameworks, methodologies and analytic concepts. Rather than locating psychology as produced and happening *inside peoples' heads,* as cognitively based approaches to psychology do, it shifted to psychology as produced and happening *outside the person* – in the social world, in social interaction (Potter & Wetherell, 1987). This is a radically different level of explanation – an external, rather than internal, to the person one (one which, from a *very different* perspective, shares some commonalities with behaviourism).

To understand the significance of this difference, imagine you're at a student bar (in a British university; in Britain anyone over the age of 18 can legally consume alcohol) with a group of friends and someone asks you why your (mutual) friend Toby is drunk. If you took an *internal, inside the head* approach to answering this question, you could tell them that Toby is feeling sad because his relationship ended, and he failed his exam; he is drowning his sorrows. That answer is a perfectly good one for the question. However, there are many other ways you could answer it. If you took an *external, outside the person* approach to answering the question, you might say that binge drinking is a socially normative way for British men to manage their emotions, or that commercial imperatives result in the promotion of a binge-drinking culture in British universities. These again are perfectly good answers to the question, but quite different ones. Discourse analysts aren't interested in explaining *why* people get drunk, but they may be interested in the socially patterned meanings that we make sense of drunkenness with, and/or the implications of different explanations for drunkenness.

The DA approach is an external approach. It suggests that things that (social) psychologists are interested in – like self, subjectivity, identity, memory, categorisation, emotion, prejudice, gender, sexuality – shouldn't be seen as private or individual, interior things, but rather as *social* processes or activities, which can be understood by looking at the level of language and discourse. It's part of a wider 'turn to language' across the social sciences and humanities, which started to see language use as important for understanding psychological and social issues (see also Box 8.1). DA is typically constructionist (Burr, 1995, 2003) and anti-essentialist (relativist), but may also be conducted within a critical realist framework (Sims-Schouten, Riley, & Willig, 2007) – see Chapter 2. Within DA there is no assumed 'real' version of an event or an object that we 'distort' through the language we use; rather, the meaning we produce through language is treated as 'real' and as the end-point of explanation.

Within this new framework for thinking *about* psychology, two broad 'schools' can be identified: one, often associated with psychologists Ian Parker and Erica Burman (e.g. Burman & Parker, 1993; Parker, 1992), as well as the authors of *Changing the Subject*, focused more on how shared social realities and psychological subjectivities are produced, and employed analytic constructs like discourses, subjectivity, **subject positions**, **positioning** and **power**. These versions of DA have been designated *Foucauldian* or *poststructuralist* (see below). The other, often associated with psychologists Margaret Wetherell, Jonathan Potter, Michael Billig and Derek Edwards, focused more closely on the specifics of talk, and employed analytic constructs like ideological dilemmas, identities, rhetoric, and action orientation. For these approaches to discourse analysis, terms like **interpretative repertoires**, rhetorical analysis and later DP (see Box 8.1) signal the particular version of DA used. But DA is a vast and evolving field: numerous other variations of DA – and labels for it – exist just in psychology, such as critical discourse analysis (Fairclough, 2010; van Dijk, 1993;

Wodak & Meyer, 2001) and *critical* discursive psychology (Edley, 2001a; Parker, 2002). We now outline two foundational approaches associated with the key early texts.

VARIATION 1: POSTSTRUCTURALIST OR FOUCAULDIAN DISCOURSE ANALYSIS

Poststructuralist DA is the most 'macro' form of DA: it has the widest scope and focus, and pays the least attention to the fine-grained detail of the texts it analyses. Emerging out of poststructuralism (e.g. Weedon, 1987), and especially the work of French scholar Michel Foucault (e.g. 1977, 1978), it theorises language and discourse as constitutive of our social and psychological realities. Language and discourse are also theorised as key to the operation of power, which is seen as a *productive* force – as *producing* meanings, categories and practices in society, or enabling them to flourish, rather than *repressing* pre-existing ('natural') meanings, categories or practices. Foucault treated power as *productive* (power produces knowledge rather than simply repressing it) and *relational* (as operating between people and institutions), rather than as a 'thing' that some people possess and others don't (a top-down or 'sovereign' model of power).

Poststructuralist discourse analysts tend to have a strong interest in power, and in contesting and challenging dominant – powerful – knowledges. This approach also understands the self and subjectivity as not unitary or coherent, but fragmented and contradictory, and produced through discourse (see Gavey, 1989, for an accessible overview of poststructuralist theory and DA). Poststructuralist DA therefore aims to understand the 'discursive worlds' that people inhabit, and interrogate and theorise these in relation to the possibilities for subjectivity and practice(s) they enable or constrain. This approach theorises that the ways we think, feel, experience and act as people are produced by discourse(s) that are available to us in our social contexts (Wendy Hollway's, 1989, identification of three dominant gendered discourses of heterosexuality is a classic example of such research). The idea is that discourses make available certain ideas and ways of seeing and understanding the word, and ourselves in relation to it, and precludes others.

A key element of this approach has been identifying discourses that shape people's realities. A discourse has been (basically) defined as 'a system of statements which constructs an object' (Parker, 1992: 5) in a coherent and particular way – an object might be something abstract, like 'the self' (e.g. Rose, 1996), or more concrete, like condoms (e.g. Lupton, 1994). An object is the target or focus of the discourse; a discourse provides culturally available and shared, *patterned* ways for talking and thinking about that object. The language we use is situated within these meaning-systems. Every time we talk about or describe something, we 'draw on' a discourse that gives a particular meaning or shape to what we describe. Typically, more than one discourse will exist for any object, offering different, and often contested, constructions of it (part of the interest in analysis can be exploring these contestations). For example, if 'fatness' were the object of discourse, you could identify a number of discourses around it: a 'medical' discourse, which constructs fatness in pathological and risk terms; a 'moral' discourse, which constructs fatness in terms of gluttony and poor self-control; a 'structural' discourse, which constructs fatness as resulting from commercial imperatives, lack of restrictions around food advertising, lack of education and socioeconomic deprivation; and a 'pride' discourse, which constructs fatness as a positive identity. One or two discourses will tend to dominate, and form the 'taken for granted' truth within society – currently, medical and moral discourses of obesity prevail. It is here that poststructuralist discourse analysts' interest in power is relevant.

However, discourses do more than just tell us how to think about an object; they offer positions that individuals (can) take up in relation to their object, known as subject positions (Davies & Harré, 1990). These simultaneously enable and constrain the ways individuals can understand themselves – their subjectivity – and the things individuals can see as possible, want to do, and indeed do – their desires and practices. In the examples of discourses around obesity, for instance, what subject position might be offered for a 'fat' individual? Only the pride discourse offers any positive subjectivity, where the individual can be 'fat and proud' or even just 'fat and okay with it', and where weight loss isn't the holy grail. The other three all situate fatness as an undesirable state the individual has (unwittingly) ended up in, through their own actions or social circumstances, but each offers different levels of individual culpability for fatness – the moral discourse is the only one to firmly 'blame' the individual. Both the moral and medical discourses also prioritise weight-loss as the *only* valid desire, and practice, with fatness framed as something a person *should* want to change.

Poststructuralist versions of DA most obviously suit construction type questions, but also representation questions (see Table 3.1 in Chapter 3), and have been used across a wide range of topics, such as weight and eating 'disorders' (Burns & Gavey, 2004; Malson, 1998), heterosexuality (Hollway, 1989) and heterosexual coercion (Gavey, 1989), masculinity (Willott & Griffin, 1997) and discourse in educational settings (Baxter, 2002). This version has no ideal data type, and can be used with textual data generated in a wide range of ways (interviews are common, probably partly because of the depth of data they generate, and because of their general popularity in qualitative research overall).

VARIATION 2: INTERPRETATIVE REPERTOIRES

DA which explores interpretative repertoires also looks at patterned meanings, but it draws on an intellectual tradition far wider than, but including, poststructuralism, such as ethnomethodology (Garfinkel, 1967), conversation analysis (Sacks, 1992) and the sociology of scientific knowledge (and more; see Potter & Wetherell, 1987). The idea of an *interpretative repertoire* was first articulated by the British sociologists Nigel Gilbert and Michael Mulkay in a book examining the way scientists talked about science (Gilbert & Mulkay, 1984). It became a cornerstone concept for the version of DA introduced by British/New Zealand psychologists Jonathan Potter and Margaret Wetherell (1987) in *Discourse and Social Psychology*. Interpretative repertoires have been defined as 'relatively coherent ways of talking about objects and events in the world' (Edley, 2001a: 198). This definition bears similarity to the idea of a 'discourse' discussed above (but see Burr, 1995), and was indeed developed to capture the systems of meaning that people live within, and draw on as collectively available resources in their use of language (Potter & Wetherell, 1995; Potter, Wetherell, Gill, & Edwards, 1990). British psychologist Nigel Edley describes repertoires as like books in a library, endlessly available for borrowing.

Repertoires can be seen as smaller and 'less monolithic' than discourses, more specific and fragmented, and potentially diverse (Edley, 2001a). Discourses could be seen as akin to an edge-of-town mega-store, like an IKEA, and repertoires more like smaller high-street stores. The difference between repertoires and discourses is, however, also theoretical, and Edley describes it as *signalling* the broader 'conceptual and methodological positions' (Edley, 2001a: 202) of DA work: talking about 'repertoires' or 'discourses' is a shorthand for your theoretical positions and your analytic take on the data.

Analysis within this tradition is not just interested in looking at talk to identify what resources – repertoires – are used; like poststructuralist discourse analysis, it goes further, but in almost the *opposite* direction. Although they share an agenda in considering what identified repertoires (discourses) tell us about the world, this approach is interested in *how* repertoires are put together and deployed in specific ('local') contexts, and in the effects they have at that level, in terms of the versions of realities and identities (among other things) that they construct. But where poststructuralist DA includes an interior orientation (through being interested in how the person can experience themselves, their desires, etc.), this DA approach keeps it fully exterior (e.g. looks at how identities are constructed and produced 'for others', and for contexts). Poststructuralist DA can be seen as interested (in part) in a 'person who is spoken into being' through discourse (a person conceptualised as 'used' by discourse; Potter et al., 1990); repertoire analysis is interested in the reality a speaking person *creates* (a person conceptualised as a user of discourse; Potter et al., 1990). So the person is theorised as a more *agentic* user of language and discourse than in poststructuralist approaches (this aspect has been emphasised in the development of this approach into DP – see Box 8.1 – but it does not invoke a consciously choosing *intentional* agent). And because of this, repertoire-based discourse analysis has a more 'micro' focus than poststructuralist DA; there is not necessarily the same interest in power, for instance. This dual focus is captured by the idea that language is studied as both *resource* (repertoires) and as *practice* (the way it is put to use; the effects – social, psychological, political, etc. – that it has), and that there is an interest in how descriptions in talk construct particular versions of reality (Potter & Wetherell, 1995).

This approach to DA suits questions of both the construction and language practice types (see Table 3.1 in Chapter 3), and has been useful, in various forms, to explore topics such as racist discourse and race relations (e.g. Wetherell & Potter, 1992), community conflict (e.g. Potter & Reicher, 1987), and sexism and justifications around gender inequalities (e.g. Gill, 1993; Peace, 2003). Again, there is no 'ideal' data type for this analysis (see Table 3.3 in Chapter 3) – the examples just cited used interviews, group discussions or media texts. (As the approach has evolved more towards DP, however, there has been a shift towards a preference for *interactive* and, particularly, 'naturalistic' datasets; see Box 8.1.)

SIMILARITIES, DIFFERENCES AND DEVELOPMENTS

What the various approaches to DA share, and what distinguishes them from most other methods for qualitative analysis, is a critical epistemology, and a view of language as productive rather than reflective (see Chapter 2). The analytic focus is on understanding, in different ways, *what language does*, what (big or small) realities are created through language, and *how* this occurs. Researchers within this tradition could be characterised as having a 'discursive sensibility' which orients them, when looking at data, to thinking of language in this way. Illustrative Research Example 8.4 provides an example of the sort of analysis pattern-based approaches to discourse analysis can produce. Differences between the different 'schools' of DA are mainly around whether or not it is the *content* of language (language as a resource) or the *process* of language use (language practice) which is seen as important; discourse analysts tend to be interested in either one (but sometimes both) of these (Potter & Wetherell, 1995). Poststructuralist DA focuses on the content of language, and treats language primarily as a *resource* for the constitution of realities and subjectivities, and the maintenance and disruption of power relations. It takes an outsider position, where it is the analyst's concerns in relation to language and language use that are prioritised. In contrast, repertoire analysis (and DP) takes more of an insider position, keeping closer to the data, with less extrapolation beyond them. It has an interest in both the *content* and *use* of language, but the use of language to construct certain social realities or psychological states is key. The different approaches have critiqued each other (e.g. Potter et al., 1990; Widdicombe, 1995), sometimes bitterly, and some see the differences as largely irreconcilable; others (Edley, 2001a; Peace, 2003; Wetherell, 1998) have explored ways to combine the insights different approaches offer. Table 8.5 provides an evaluation of pattern-based DA's strengths and weaknesses.

Table 8.5   Evaluating pattern-based forms of discourse analysis

Strengths	Weaknesses
Many different versions to suit a variety of topics and research questions	Require a constructionist (or critical realist) view of language and social life; this can require a relearning of what psychology is, and how you talk about psychological concepts, and so can be a challenging task
They take language seriously, treating it as more than information-transfer	
They offer exciting possibilities for understanding the social contexts in and through which individual psychological life is produced	Need to fully understand the (theoretical) frameworks that DA relies on; these can be complex and take time to really 'get'
They provide methods for accessing and understanding the subtle uses and effects of broader language patterns	Has been a lack of concrete or clear guidelines on how to actually do it; can leave new researchers confused and uncertain. If analysis is not a series of rules to follow, but a 'craft skill' that includes 'following hunches' (Potter & Wetherell, 1987), how do you know if you're on the right track?
They give credence to, and thus implicitly value, intuitive aspects of analysis; analysis is a skilled interpretative engagement, rather than the systematic application of a set of rules	
	Certain versions can lose a focus on *topics* or *issues*, which are often the things that researchers are interested in
Practical guidance for discursively engaging with data *is* available (e.g. see Howitt, 2010; Parker, 1992; Potter, 2003; Potter & Wetherell, 1987; Willig, 2008)	Can be too complex and difficult to learn for a small student project
	Doesn't produce analyses that easily translate for 'giving back' to participants, or for use in applied research and research with an explicit social change agenda

ILLUSTRATIVE RESEARCH EXAMPLE 8.4

Pattern-based discourse analysis: Broadcaster's accounts of inequality in radio

British feminist researcher Rosalind Gill (1993) used Potter and Wetherell's (1987) DA approach to analyse the ways in which male radio broadcasters account for the lack of women disc jockeys (DJs) at their radio stations. Gill interviewed five DJs and programme controllers (PCs) at two independent local radio stations (one had no women DJs at the time of data collection; the other had one who presented a late-night phone-in show twice a week). She was interested in the 'practical ideologies' used by the participants to make sense of gender inequalities in the employment of women DJs. She identified five types of accounts used to explain the lack of women DJs, with each centred on a particular claim such as 'women don't apply' or 'the audience prefers male DJs'. She emphasised that 'the DJs and PCs *all* drew on and combined different and contradictory accounts for the lack of women DJs' (p. 76). Gill discussed four of the five accounts in detail: 'women don't apply'; 'audience objections'; 'gender differences'; and 'women's voices'. She noted that when the participants made use of one of these claims they spontaneously offered further accounts to warrant their explanations and make them sound more plausible. Let's consider the example of the most prevalent account, drawn on by four of the five participants, which centred on the claim that 'women don't apply'. Gill identified four types of supporting account for this claim, including that women are not interested in becoming DJs because 'it's a man's world'. She quoted the following extract from her interview with one of the PCs ((.) indicates a short pause):

> And it's where people come from (.) so in hospital radio there aren't many women DJs (.) there aren't many women DJs in pubs (.) there aren't many female DJs (.) especially teenage age which is when we're looking to bring people like (.) who are interested in doing it. (p. 78)

The participant accounted for the lack of women DJs in terms of the lack of women in the traditional recruiting grounds for local radio – pubs and hospitals – but his account did not stop there. He also referred to women's lack of interest in radio broadcasting and so maintained that women lack genuine motivation to become DJs. Gill argued that 'the idea that oppressed groups do not "really" want to change their position, is one frequently drawn on by members of dominant groups in order to justify their actions or inaction' (p. 78). She also argued that this claim serves to ward off criticism of radio stations in general and the participant's radio station in particular. It suggests that radio stations are willing to employ women, but women are not interested in applying. The participant underscored the image of the radio station fighting against women's disinterest by commenting later that they have to look 'extra hard' to find women DJs. This notion allowed the participant to highlight his lack of sexism and place responsibility for the lack of women DJs firmly on women's shoulders.

In the discussion, Gill argued that her approach demonstrates that the participants did not articulate a particular attitude about women DJs; rather they flexibly (and sometimes inconsistently) drew on a range of accounts both to justify a lack of women DJs and to present themselves as non-sexist. She argued that the ideological effect of their accounts is to perpetuate gender inequality at radio stations.

In outlining these approaches, we have aimed to give you a very brief (and limited) sense of the scope of two different approaches to pattern-based DA. These are 'foundational' approaches, developed early on in the life of DA (their advocates have sometimes gone in different directions, such as DP [Box 8.1], CA [Box 8.2] or more narrative and psychoanalytically inspired analysis, e.g. Billig, 2006; Hollway & Jefferson, 2000; Parker, 2005a). The field is constantly evolving: these approaches are still widely used, albeit often with fuzzier boundaries. Approaches sometimes collectively termed *critical discursive psychology* try to synthesise elements of the different traditions, retaining an interest in both resources and practices, and even drawing more widely than DA (Wetherell, 2007). And the term 'thematic discourse analysis' is sometimes used (e.g. Taylor & Ussher, 2001) to refer to an analysis that is akin to a constructionist TA. In TA, the moniker 'critical thematic analysis' is sometimes used to signal a similar approach, primarily thematic, but drawing on discursive insights (e.g. Terry & Braun, 2011b).

Is it feasible to use some version of pattern-based DA in a small-scale or student project? We think it is, but with the proviso that DA is probably one of the more challenging qualitative methods to learn quickly, and get 'right', unless you're already familiar with the theoretical frameworks behind the version of DA you're using, and have a supervisor who is familiar with the approach/theory (see Chapter 3). In relation to coding and analysis (see Chapters 9–11), we draw across both frameworks to provide guidelines for beginning to do DA.

BOX 8.1   WHAT IS DISCURSIVE PSYCHOLOGY?

By Sally Wiggins, School of Psychological Sciences and Health, University of Strathclyde, UK

DP provides a rigorous, empirical methodology through which we can understand how people 'do' things when they talk or write. It is concerned with psychological issues such as accountability, cognition, emotion, identity and embodiment. But rather than treating these as taken-for-granted, pre-existing 'things', DP starts from the premise that these issues are contestable, negotiated and contingent upon interaction. In other words, what is important is not whether people might 'have' an emotion or particular identity, but rather how such categories and concepts are made relevant in the social interactions they engage in. How does someone claim to be an expert in raising children, for example, and how might such claims be acknowledged or challenged by others?

DP treats discourse (i.e. all forms of talk and text), first and foremost as social action, rather than as a window into people's 'interiors'. This is a key point: discourse is *not* treated as a route to other psychological concerns (whether these are cognitions, emotions or physiology). Instead, discourse is in itself *where psychology happens*. It is in interaction, and all the messiness involved in this, that psychology comes to life. That is where identities are constructed, blame attributed and decisions made.

In terms of epistemology, DP takes a critical relativist stance to knowledge. That is, DP seeks to understand the processes through which knowledge is *produced* in everyday practices, as well as the types of knowledge which become ratified as 'truth' in different situations. For instance, how does one person's claim to being 'full' at a mealtime become accepted by others? What if this person is a child? Is simply saying 'I've had enough to eat' acceptable, or must this be evidenced in some other way? DP differs from other forms of discourse analysis in that it usually focuses more closely on the detail of interaction, at the level of turn-taking, pauses and intonation in people's speech (in this it has close links to CA; see Box 8.2).

DP therefore allows us to answer research questions which focus on the 'how' of social practices: how are social actions carried out? What are the social and interactional implications of different ways of talking? The advantages are that it provides a lens through which we can examine social life in all its rich and complex detail: psychological concerns are examined for their impact on social life, and 'truth' is always questioned.

One of the challenges of DP for the new qualitative researcher is that it requires a commitment to a relativist position, which cannot straight-forwardly be combined with other methodologies. We cannot simply move from asking about the 'causes of X on Y', for example, to examining how 'X' is contested in interaction. It's a whole different paradigm! DP also requires a rigorous examination of audio, and more often video, data. Detailed transcripts are required to provide the turn-by-turn analysis and the focus on intonation, pauses and gestures in talk. This is time-consuming work, but the rewards are plentiful.

Further reading

For an overview of the method, see: Wiggins, S. & Potter, J. (2010) Discursive psychology. In C. Willig & W. Stainton Rogers (Eds), *The Sage handbook of qualitative research in psychology* (pp. 73–90). London: Sage.

For an example of DP research, see: Wiggins, S. (2009) Managing blame in NHS weight management treatment: psychologizing weight and 'obesity'. *Journal of Community and Applied Social Psychology. 19*, 374–387.

BOX 8.2   WHAT IS CONVERSATION ANALYSIS?

By Sonja Ellis, Department of Psychology, Sheffield Hallam University, UK

CA arose out of the work of US sociologist Harvey Sacks (Sacks & Jefferson, 1995); following his untimely death in 1975, it was developed by his colleagues Emanuel Schegloff and Gail Jefferson.

(Continued)

BOX 8.2   (*continued*)

Although CA was developed within sociology, it has become increasingly popular in psychology over the past decade or so. Based in an ethnomethodological tradition, CA (like DP; Box 8.1) is the study of talk-in-interaction: talk as the site of social action. In contrast to experiential qualitative approaches which are concerned with understanding people's experiences, views and practices, CA could be regarded as a form of *critical* qualitative research because it is interested in the processes by which truths emerge, and social realities and identities are built. While CA is considered by some to be a form of DA, it departs from other discursive approaches in a number of important respects.

Whereas most discursive (and other qualitative) approaches can be applied to a range of data collection methods, CA is only suited to naturally occurring talk (e.g. telephone conversations; in-person conversations). Unless talk is spontaneously produced (as opposed to researcher-generated) the analyst is simply studying interactions which are a by-product of the research context. Rather than focusing on content, CA studies the structural organisation and orderliness of social interaction, with particular attention to turn-taking (see Sacks, Schegloff, & Jefferson, 1974) and sequence (see Schegloff, 2007). It is suited to language practice research questions (see Table 3.1 in Chapter 3), particularly those which focus on understanding the shared procedures used by speakers to produce and recognise meaningful action.

One of the main ways in which CA differs from other qualitative methods is the extent to which the broader social context is interpreted analytically. In CA, context is only considered relevant if it is *displayed* as relevant by participants in a conversation: for example, if (and then how), the gender of speakers is *invoked* by people in interaction, rather than assuming it *is* impacting on it.

The method itself is highly structured, which also makes it different from many other forms of qualitative analysis. For most qualitative methods, the analyst moves between and within data items in a systematic but fluid way. However, with CA, analysis necessarily happens sequentially, because each turn of talk is responsive to prior turns: any given piece of talk cannot be understood without reference to the construction and delivery of talk which precedes it. Sequential analyses also focus on the way in which the participants have understood and interpreted the prior talk rather than what that talk might mean if taken in isolation. By focusing on language at the micro-level, CA enables qualitative researchers to more specifically identify how speakers use language to bring off particular identities or to achieve particular goals.

Further reading

For an overview of the method, see: Wilkinson, S. & Kitzinger, C. (2007). Conversation analysis. In C. Willig & W. Stainton-Rogers (Eds), *The Sage handbook of qualitative research in psychology* (pp. 54–71). London: Sage.

For an example of CA research, see: Stokoe, E. (2010). 'I'm not gonna hit a lady': conversation analysis, membership categorization and men's denials of violence towards women. *Discourse & Society*, *21*, 1–24.

BOX 8.3   WHAT IS NARRATIVE ANALYSIS?

By Brett Smith, Co-Director, Qualitative Digital Research Lab (LiQuiD), Loughborough University, UK

Narrative analysis (NA) refers to a family of qualitative methods for making sense of 'storied' data. Key in NA is the 'story' (Sarbin, 1986). Narrative analysts believe that people are storytelling creatures (MacIntyre, 1984) and the stories they tell distinctly *do* things (Frank, 2010). For example, stories affect how we behave, they (dis)connect people, and they shape our identities. As NA is grounded in this appreciation of a story, an essential component of NA is that the story told in data is kept *intact* for analysis. Other analytic approaches, like GT and TA, fracture stories as they cut across data for different analytic purposes. Narrative analysts offer insight into both *what* is said in talk and *how* things are said. In contrast, GT, TA, and IPA concentrate primarily on the *whats* of talk whilst (some versions of) DA attend to the *hows*.

NA can be described, like IPA, as case-centred (meaning it focuses closely on small number of individuals or a group) and offering insight into lived experience (Bruner, 1990). The difference between them is that in NA attention is directed more on the socio-cultural constitution of experience: for example, a focus is on experience as constituted – not reflected – through the narratives culture supplies. Somewhat akin to 'discourses' in poststructuralist DA, narratives 'out there' in society are understood as the resources from which people make sense of their 'inner' lives and selectively draw on to frame lived experience (to tell stories about it).

Another distinguishing characteristic of NA is that it has no 'method' in the sense of a canonical sequence of prescribed steps to be followed. Method in NA is a craft wherein the practical wisdom gained through analytic experience is prized (Frank, 2010). Analysts cultivate 'craft skills' and gain experience by critically reading examples of NA. Writing is also integral to the development of 'craft skills'. It is not the last stage in NA; rather, NA takes place in the continuous craft of writing and re-writing about data. Analysis also gets started and occurs through posing questions. Key NA questions include:

- What is told in the story and what happens as a result of telling that story (its effects)?
- How is the story structured?
- What narrative resources shape storytellers' experiences and the story told?
- In what ways do these narratives enable and/or constrain lives?
- How are people's lives defined by the stories they overlook as well as those they get caught up in?
- Who does the story connect the storyteller to?
- Who is placed outside this connection?
- What was the response of the listener (including analyst) to the story?
- What counts in the response from the listener?

(Continued)

BOX 8.3 *(continued)*

In practice, however, NA rarely deals with the interactional business being accomplished in people's everyday storytelling. People tell stories in relation to another person (e.g. an interviewer or friend), but often the role of the researcher in co-constructing stories is overlooked.

NA is not bound to one theoretical position. Some NA is underpinned by phenomenology, some by social constructionism. That said, most narrative analysts commit to an epistemology in which knowledge is seen as constructed, and to a relativist ontology wherein reality is mind-dependent. This does not mean 'anything goes'. Rather, in NA no claims are made to discovering human reality through method, or to produce knowledge independent of us. The strengths of NA include an ability: to reveal the temporal, emotional, and contextual quality of lives; to illuminate experience; and to understand a person as both an individual agent and as someone who is socio-culturally fashioned.

Further reading

For an overview of the method, see: Sparkes, A. & Smith, B. (2008). Narrative constructionist inquiry. In J. Holstein & J. Gubrium (Eds), *Handbook of constructionist research* (pp. 295–314). London: Guilford Publications.

For an example of NA research, see: Smith, B. & Sparkes, A. C. (2008). Changing bodies, changing narratives and the consequences of tellability: a case study of becoming disabled through sport. *Sociology of Health and Illness*, 30, 217–236.

CHAPTER SUMMARY

This chapter:
- set out the scope and range of qualitative analyses;
- introduced and evaluated TA, IPA, GT and pattern-based DA as key qualitative analytic approaches, and ones which are accessible to novice qualitative researchers;
- showcased three other methods (DP, CA, NA).

? QUESTIONS FOR DISCUSSION AND CLASSROOM EXERCISES

1   Working in small groups, design an IPA study. Develop an appropriately experiential research question and answer the following questions: who will you speak to and how will you find them? How will you determine the homogeneity of the sample, and how big will the sample be? How will you collect data? What questions will you ask your participants?

2 IPA (Osborn & Smith, 2006; Smith & Osborn, 2007), GT (Charmaz, 1983, 1995) and TA (Lack et al., 2011; LaChapelle et al., 2008) have all been used in studies of chronic pain and illness. Working in groups of three, select an IPA, GT and TA paper on chronic pain and illness (such as those cited above). Each member of the group should read one of these papers, then as a group identify the similarities and differences in the three studies in relation to the study design (size and constitution of sample, methods of data collection, etc.) and the analysis (not just the main results, but: Are the data situated within a wider social context? Is the emphasis on psychological or sociological interpretation? How are data extracts used – to illustrate analytic claims [illustratively] or to further the analysis [analytically]? See Chapter 11).

3 Using one of the papers from the above exercise, redesign it as a DA study. How will the research question change? How will the study design change? Speculate about how the results might differ (keeping in mind that language is not viewed as a transparent window on participants' concerns within a discursive framework). In general, what are some of the key differences between a discursive approach and an experiential one?

4 Working in small groups, and using the descriptive–interpretative continuum below, decide where to place each of the four Illustrative Research Examples (8.1–8.4) on the continuum (we deliberately chose studies that represent different points on the continuum) – do any of the studies simply describe/summarise the data? Do any interpret the meaning of, or interrogate, the data (with a theoretical framework)? Do any combine elements of both of these types of analysis? (See the *companion website* for the 'answer'.)

Descriptive	*Interpretative*

FURTHER RESOURCES

Further reading:

Short papers provide a quick introduction to methods:

For TA, see: Braun, V. & Clarke, V. (in press) Thematic analysis. In A. C. Michalos (Ed.), *Encyclopaedia of quality of life research*. New York: Springer.

For IPA, see: Reid, K., Flowers, P., & Larkin, M. (2005). Exploring lived experience. *The Psychologist, 18*, 20–23.

For GT, see: Henwood, K. & Pidgeon, N. (1995). Grounded theory and psychological research. *The Psychologist, 8*, 115–118.

For a bit more depth around TA, and a clear outline of the approach, see: Braun, V. & Clarke, V. (2006). Using thematic analysis in psychology. *Qualitative Research in Psychology, 3*, 77–101.

For a bit more depth around IPA, and an outline of the key principles and procedures of IPA, see: Smith, J. A. & Osborn, M. (2003). Interpretative phenomenological analysis. In J. A. Smith (Ed.), *Qualitative psychology: A practical guide to methods*. London: Sage.

The ultimate definitive resource for anyone planning an IPA study (also useful as an introduction to experiential qualitative research more broadly) is: Smith, J. A., Flowers, P., & Larkin, M. (2009). *Interpretative phenomenological analysis: Theory, method and research*. London: Sage.

For a bit more depth around GT from a psychological perspective, see: Pidgeon, N. & Henwood, K. (1997). Using grounded theory in psychological research. In N. Hayes (Ed.), *Doing qualitative analysis in psychology* (pp. 245–273). Hove, UK: Psychology Press.

For detailed and practical guidance for conducting contextualist (constructivist) GT, see: Charmaz, K. (2006). *Constructing grounded theory: A practical guide through qualitative analysis*. London: Sage.

For an accessible introduction including practical guidance to pattern-based DA, see: Coyle, A. (2007). Discourse analysis. In A. Coyle & E. Lyons (Eds), *Analysing qualitative data in psychology* (pp. 98–116). London: Sage.

For an accessible guide to *critical* discursive psychology, which brings theoretical concepts to life through the use of worked examples, see: Edley, N. (2001). Analysing masculinity: interpretative repertoires, ideological dilemmas and subject positions. In M. Wetherell, S. Taylor, & S. J. Yates (Eds), *Discourse as data: A guide for analysis* (pp. 189–228). London: Sage.

For a key foundational introduction to DA, see: Potter, J., & Wetherell, M. (1987). *Discourse and social psychology: Beyond attitudes and behaviour*. London: Sage.

Online resources:

A useful collection of online qualitative analysis learning resources can be found at:
- http://onlineqda.hud.ac.uk/index.php
- Our TA website: www.psych.auckland.ac.nz/thematicanalysis
- Grounded Theory Institute: www.groundedtheory.com/
- Birkbeck College (University of London) IPA website: www.ipa.bbk.ac.uk/
- Loughborough University Discourse and Rhetoric Group (associated with Potter, Edwards, Billig, etc.): http://www.lboro.ac.uk/departments/socialsciences/research/groups/darg/
- The Discourse Unit (associated with Parker, Burman, etc.): www.discourseunit.com/
- University of East London Centre for Narrative Research: www.uel.ac.uk/cnr/

See the **companion website** (**www.sagepub.co.uk/braunandclarke**) for:
- self-test multiple choice questions relating to Section 3;
- the flashcard glossary – test yourself on the definitions of key terms used in this chapter;
- the answer to the descriptive–interpretative continuum exercise;
- further readings (articles from Sage journals).

First analytic steps: familiarisation and data coding

OVERVIEW

Data collection and data analysis: separate stages?
Reading and familiarisation: essential beginnings
What is coding?
Doing complete coding
What role do computer programs have in qualitative coding and analysis?

Once you have data ready for analysis (transcribed or collated), you can begin. In the following three chapters (9–11) we aim to provide practical 'how to' guidance around analysis; as much as we describe *what* you need to do, we provide illustrated worked examples to show *how* you do it, using the weight and obesity focus group (FG) dataset we introduced in Chapter 5 (see the ***companion website***). Showing what analysis *looks like* can take away some of the (anxiety-provoking) uncertainty of qualitative research. Some methods – such as interpretative phenomenological analysis (IPA) and thematic analysis (TA) – provide more detailed guidance than others – such as discourse analysis (DA) (see Table 9.1). We primarily demonstrate a basic TA approach, and discuss how IPA, grounded theory (GT) and pattern-based DA do things differently.

It's tempting to view analytic guidelines as *recipes* that have to be *precisely* followed, as if adhering to these will ensure a successful outcome. This isn't the case. Obviously, being systematic and thorough is crucial (see Chapter 12), but good qualitative analysis is primarily a product of an 'analytic sensibility', not a product of 'following the rules'. An analytic sensibility is often viewed as a rather esoteric skill that some rarefied individuals naturally possess, rather than a skill that can be developed. We think it *can* be developed. An analytic sensibility refers to the skill of reading and interpreting data through the particular theoretical lens of your chosen method. It also refers to being able to produce insights into the meaning of the data that go beyond the obvious or surface-level content

Table 9.1 Stages of coding and analysis described by different qualitative analytic methods

Stage	Thematic Analysis	IPA	Grounded Theory Lite	Pattern-based Discourse Analysis
1	Transcription	Data preparation (transcription)	Transcription	Transcription
2	Reading and familiarisation; taking note of items of potential interest	Reading and familiarisation; taking note of items of potential interest	*Initial* (open) coding (semi-complete) Writing initial memos	Reading and familiarisation; taking note of items of potential interest
3	Coding – complete; across entire dataset	Coding – complete (termed *initial noting*); focusing first on *one* data item	*Intermediate* (focused) coding, including: Memo writing Refining the coding system Linking codes to other codes Identifying categories Defining categories	Coding – selective (developing an inclusive corpus of items of interest); across entire dataset
4	Searching for themes	Developing **emergent themes** (within that data item)	Production of a diagrammatic representation of analysis – shows categories and relationships between them	Analysis

Stage	Thematic Analysis	IPA	Grounded Theory Lite	Pattern-based Discourse Analysis
5	Reviewing themes (producing a map of the provisional themes and subthemes, and relationships between them – aka the 'thematic map')	Searching for connections across emergent themes (within that data item) and generating superordinate themes (with emergent themes nested within them) Producing a figurative or tabular representation of analysis	Writing up – finalising analysis	Writing up – finalising analysis
6	Defining and naming themes	Stages 3–5 repeated with other data items		
7	Writing – finalising analysis	Identifying themes and superordinate themes *across* dataset; producing a figurative or tabular representation of analysis		
8		Writing up – finalising analysis		

of the data, to notice patterns or meanings that link to broader psychological, social or theoretical concerns. Essentially, it relates to taking an inquiring and interpretative position on data (see Chapter 11 for more discussion around interpretative analysis). This is easier if you feel you have a handle on what you're supposed to be doing. Chapters 9–11 are designed to provide that.

The first analytic steps we lay out in this chapter can be done either on hard copy (paper and pen) or electronically, either with one of many different computer programs (discussed later) or in Microsoft Word using the comment feature. We explain the process as if you were using hard copy data. It's good to learn to code using a manual, hard-copy process, even if you eventually do it electronically. Quite apart from anything else, being away from a screen allows for a different mode of interaction with data, and moves you into a different conceptual and physical space for conducting analysis (Bringer, Johnston, & Brackenridge, 2006).

DATA COLLECTION AND DATA ANALYSIS: SEPARATE STAGES?

In quantitative research, analysis generally only begins once all data have been collected. In qualitative research, it isn't essential to have *all* your data collected to start your analysis. In reality, there's not always a clean separation between data collection and analysis – GT even prefers that there *isn't* – which can result from a drawn-out data collection period, where you begin your data coding while still collecting final data items, or from a staged data collection process, where you collect part of your data, review it with an analytic eye for possible patterns, and then refine or reorient subsequent data collection. This is one of the advantages of the flexibility of qualitative research designs.

READING AND FAMILIARISATION: ESSENTIAL BEGINNINGS

The analysis of qualitative data essentially begins with a process of 'immersion' in the data. The aim of this phase is to become intimately familiar with your dataset's content, and to begin to notice things that might be relevant to your research question. For textual data, this process involves reading, and re-reading, each data item; for audio (or visual) data, it involves a similar pattern of repeated listening to (and viewing) the material. During this process, you'll probably start to *notice* things of interest. These might be loose overall impressions of the data (e.g. food seems to be talked about in two ways – as friend and as enemy), a conceptual idea you have about the data (e.g. participants use an implicit model of the person as naturally 'gluttonous' and 'lazy'), or more concrete and specific issues (e.g. that a participant uses euphemistic language around weight and body size). It's good to keep a record of these 'noticings', and record them in a place you can refer back to. This might be a separate file (e.g. your research journal) or notes directly on the data themselves. This process is observational and casual, rather than systematic and precise. Don't agonise over the wording of your noticings; you aren't coding the data yet. Noticings would typically be written down as a stream of consciousness, a messy 'rush of ideas', rather than polished prose. Such notes are written only *for you*, to help you with the process of analysis – think of them as memory aids and triggers for developing your analysis.

These noticings often reflect what we bring to the data, and while they can enrich our analysis, we should be wary of using them as the main or sole basis for developing our analysis, as they are not based in a *systematic* engagement with the data. The things that jump out at you initially are likely either the most obvious aspect of the data, or reflect things that are salient to you as a person. For example, when we were familiarising ourselves with the FG data, one of Virginia's noticings was that physical activity seemed to be framed incredibly negatively by participants, as a *chore* with *no* pleasure attached. This likely reflects the fact that she has always been an enthusiastic participant in a variety of exercise that ranges from school PE to football to hiking, and people's lack of enthusiasm doesn't resonate with her experience in any way. The negativity around exercise was *not* one of Victoria's noticings, which likely reflects that her own experience of exercise is similar to that which participants' expressed. The point is not that one of us is 'right' and one 'wrong', but that our personal experiences shape how we read data; they can be a great resource for analysis, but they can also limit what we see in data. You need to recognise this, and reflect on it during the analytic process (see Box 13.2 in Chapter 13).·

Familiarisation is not a passive process of just understanding the words (or images); it is about starting to *read data as data*. Reading data as data means not simply absorbing the surface meaning of the words (or images), as you typically absorb a crime novel or a Hollywood blockbuster, but reading the words *actively*, *analytically* and *critically*, starting to think about *what the data mean*. This involves asking questions like:

- How does a participant make sense of their experiences?
- Why might they be making sense of their experiences in *this* way (and not in another way)?
- In what *different* ways do they make sense of the topic discussed?
- How 'common-sense' is their story?
- How would I feel if I was in that situation? (Is this different from or similar to how the participant feels, and why might that be?)
- What assumptions do they make in talking about the world?
- What kind of world is 'revealed' through their account?

The more you engage with the data, the more they 'open up' to you, so don't worry if you feel that you don't 'see' anything beyond the obvious in your data at first. An analytic sensibility is essential for moving beyond a surface, summative reading of the data, and questions like the above will help in developing an analytic sensibility. You don't need to be overly concerned at this point about the theoretical coherence of your initial noticings either.

Different analytic approaches to analysis treat these noticings differently. In approaches like TA they may become the initial blocks in the process of coding then building your final analysis. In IPA, in contrast, where the focus is on capturing and interpreting the *participants'* experiences, it is recommended that you note down your ideas and observations and then *put them aside* (basically forget them for a while), so that your analytic eye remains focused on the participants' meanings and experiences. You may revisit *your* noticings later as you move to the more researcher-interpretative stages of IPA, but initially you want to stay with the participants' meanings (Smith et al., 2009).

WHAT IS CODING?

Coding is a process of identifying aspects of the data that relate to your research question. There are two main approaches to coding in pattern-based forms of qualitative analysis (see Table 9.1), which we call **selective coding** and **complete coding**.

SELECTIVE CODING

Selective coding involves identifying a corpus of 'instances' of the phenomenon that you're interested in, and then selecting those out. The purpose here is one of 'data reduction'. Imagine your dataset was a bowl of multi-coloured M&Ms. The process of selective coding is akin to pulling out only the red or yellow ones, and leaving the rest in the bowl. What you gather is a collection of data of a certain *type*. This approach to coding is often seen as a pre-analytic process, the pragmatic selection of your data corpus, rather than as part of your analysis (e.g. Potter & Wetherell, 1987). However, it does inevitably have an analytic element, in that you need to work out what counts as an instance of what you're looking for, and where that instance starts and finishes. It also requires pre-existing theoretical and analytic knowledge that gives you the ability to identify the analytic concepts that you're looking for. The process of reading and familiarisation may be more involved and take longer with this approach than for a complete coding approach, as you have to come to 'see' what it is that you will identify, and then selectively code for, in the data. In complete coding, the process itself develops and refines what it is that you are interested in, analytically. Selective coding is most typically used for narrative, discursive and conversation analytic approaches, as well as pattern-based DA, to build a corpus of instances of the phenomenon you're interested in (Arribas-Ayllon & Walkerdine, 2008; Potter & Wetherell, 1987) – for instance, from Virginia and colleagues' DA work, all interview talk that invoked the concept of reciprocity when discussing heterosex (Braun, Gavey, & McPhillips, 2003).

COMPLETE CODING

Complete coding is a rather different process. Instead of looking for particular instances, you aim to identify *anything* and *everything* of interest or relevance to answering your research question, within your entire dataset. This means that rather than selecting out a particular corpus of instances which you then analyse, you code all the data that's relevant to your research question, and it's only later in the analytic process that you become more selective.

In complete coding, codes identify and provide a label for a feature of the data that is potentially relevant for answering your research question. A code is a *word* or *brief phrase* that captures the essence of why you think a particular bit of data may be useful. In qualitative research, coding is not an exclusive process, where an excerpt of data can only be coded in one way. Any data extract can and should be coded in as *many* ways as fits the purpose. For example, if you look at the extract of coded data in Table 9.2, we coded Judy's line 'Yeah if people are working hard they want something quick which tends to be the unhealthy food rather than the healthy food' in three different ways, each capturing different elements in the data that might be useful in our developing analysis: i) common-sense association: working hard and wanting 'convenient' (i.e. quick) food; ii) categorisation of food: healthy/unhealthy; good/bad; iii) unhealthy food = quick/convenient; healthy food = slow/inconvenient.

Codes provide the building blocks of analysis: if you imagine your analysis is a brick-built, tile-roofed house, your *themes* are the walls and roof; your *codes* the individual bricks and tiles. In broad terms, codes can either reflect the semantic content of the data (we call these **data-derived** or **semantic codes**) or more conceptual or theoretical interpretations of the data (we call these **researcher-derived** or **latent codes**). Different approaches have different labels for these types of codes (see Table 9.1).

DATA-DERIVED AND RESEARCHER-DERIVED CODES

Data-derived codes provide a succinct summary of the explicit content of the data; they are *semantic* codes, because they are based in the semantic meaning in the data. When coding participant-generated data, they mirror participants' language and concepts. In the example of coding in Table 9.2, the codes *modern technology facilitates obesity* and *kids don't know how to cook* directly map onto the content of what the participant has said. As analysts, we haven't put an interpretative frame around their words.

Researcher-derived codes go beyond the explicit content of the data; they are *latent* codes which invoke the researcher's conceptual and theoretical frameworks to identify *implicit* meanings within the data. By implicit meanings, we mean the assumptions and frameworks that underpin what is said in the data. In the example in Table 9.2, the code *humans as naturally lazy* is a clear example of a researcher-derived code. The participants never actually express this sentiment, but many of the things they say around exercise and modern lifestyles rely on this particular understanding of what humans are like. The theoretical and knowledge frameworks you bring will allow you to 'see' particular things in the data, and interpret and code them in certain ways; no two analysts will code in exactly the same way. Going back to the idea of the analyst as a sculptor rather than an archaeologist (Chapter 2), two sculptors with different tools, techniques and experiences would produce (somewhat) different sculptures from the same piece of marble. Likewise, two researchers would code the same dataset somewhat differently (see also Chapter 12).

This separation between semantic and latent codes is not pure; in practice codes can and do have both elements. A good example of this is the code *Gendered safety: (women) feeling unsafe running alone* (which you see in the extended version of Table 9.2 on the **companion website**). It captures the explicit content of what the participant has said – she doesn't feel safe to run by herself – but then applies an interpretative lens – gender – to it, derived from

Table 9.2   Coding in thematic analysis: a worked example of the early stages

Data	Codes
Moderator: What do you think about the modern lifestyle and weight and obesity? Do you think that's had a big effect?	
Sally: I think it's had a huge effect because I remember, say forty years ago, we had a lot more industry in this country, so people were actually what you might call working harder. I know we all work hard, but erm working more…	Important factor influencing obesity Modern lifestyles are sedentary Lack of physical work nowadays Hard physical work is beneficial to avoid obesity Times have changed
?: ((in overlap)) Physically.	
Sally: …physically harder. Erm and, you know, we didn't all have cars. So like my Mum used to walk two or three miles to go to the train station to go another ten miles to work, you know, it was like there was a lot more impact. There was no bus for her so she had to walk. And nowadays we think 'oh I can't do that, can't miles to go and do that' ((laughs)).	Lack of exercise Times have changed Choice and exercise (none in past) Physical activity was an integral part of life in the past Humans as naturally lazy Exercise as negative (chore and burden) Implicit *ideal* person is fit/physically active and thin
Rebecca: Take the car yeah.	Humans as naturally lazy
Sally: Yeah exactly.	
Rebecca: Yeah.	
Sally: Erm and I think over the decades as technology's advanced, we've suddenly… our lifestyle has changed and it's had an impact on society now. So we've got kids growing up who are going um ((pause)) who are growing up thinking 'oh well if I just jump in the car', you know, 'Mum'll take me to so and so' or…and they're not in that sort of exercise is a luxury. You go and you have to motivate yourself to go to the gym. Where at one time you didn't have to go to a gym because you worked physically or whatever, and now we have to motivate and I'm not motivated. ((laughs))	Times have changed Negative impacts of technology Different lifestyles Kids learn bad habits from parents (laziness is learnt behaviour) Exercise as negative (inherently unpleasant) Exercise is not a natural desire or activity for humans (humans are naturally lazy) Exercise is a necessary evil of modern life Exercise isn't part of *everyday* life Choice and exercise (we have it, but won't do it) Exercise as exceptional and expensive Exercise requires something extra (willpower/discipline)

Data	Codes
	Not being motivated is a common story (laughter suggests *ideal* person is motivated to exercise)
Judy: I think modern technology, like allows you to be lazy as well cos you don't have to do things for yourself. You can get machines and stuff to do things for you.	Modern technology facilitates obesity Convenience of modern lifestyles is hard to resist Humans are naturally lazy
?: Mm-hm.	
Anna: My friends that live up in Manchester and London, they find it's actually erm easier to buy food on the way home, kind of like take-out and stuff or go out for a meal, than it is actually to go home and start cooking something if you like finish work at eight or nine o'clock at night or something.	Big cities = modern lifestyles Modern lifestyles = long working hours Time poor (money rich) Convenience (pre-prepared food) Home cooking as onerous (time, effort)
?: Mm-hm.	
Anna: Erm which I guess fuels the fact that people essentially may not be eating food that's, you know, healthy ((laughs)).	Forced into unhealthy eating by modern lifestyles Eating out/not cooking = unhealthy eating Categorisation of food (healthy/unhealthy; good/bad)
Judy: Yeah if people are working hard they want something quick which tends to be the unhealthy food rather than the healthy food.	Common-sense association of working hard and wanting 'convenient' (i.e. quick) food Categorisation of food (healthy/unhealthy; good/bad) Unhealthy food = quick/convenient; healthy food = slow/inconvenient
?: Yeah.	
?: Yeah.	
Carla: And then their children are growing up not know- having the faintest idea to even cook or prepare food. And also, like you said, the modern technology, it's like MSN, kids live on it.	Modern lifestyle: bad for adults; bad for children Kids don't know *how* to cook Children engage in sedentary 'play' Children's socialisation is inadequate Who is responsible (for children's 'not knowing')? Implicit parent blaming Technology is unhealthy

our theoretical and topic-based knowledge. Here, she doesn't suggest her safety has anything to do with her being a woman. However, we suggest 'safety' in relation to exercise is a concern typically experienced *differently* by women and men, reflecting wider gendered safety concerns commonplace in western societies (e.g. Valentine, 1989).

New qualitative researchers tend to initially generate mostly data-derived codes as they are easier to identify, and rely less on having conceptual and theoretical knowledge through which to make sense of the data. The ability to generate researcher-derived codes develops with experience, as they require a deeper level of engagement with the data and with fields of scholarship and theorising. This doesn't mean that researcher-derived codes are inherently *better* than data-derived ones, but they do assist in developing an interpretative analysis which goes beyond the obvious (see Chapter 11). In certain forms of pattern-based analysis, particularly DA and more theoretical forms of TA, there is a much stronger focus on researcher-derived codes.

DOING COMPLETE CODING

With complete coding, you begin with your first data item, and systematically work through the whole item, looking for chunks of data that potentially address your research question. You can code in large chunks (e.g. 20 lines of data), small chunks (e.g. a single line of data), and anything in between, as needed. Data that don't contain anything relevant to the research question don't need to be coded at all. If you are starting with a very broad research question, which you may refine during the analytic process, you want to code widely and comprehensively; if you already have a very specific research question, you may find that large sections of the data are not relevant and don't need to be coded. The outcome of a first (but thorough) coding of an excerpt of our FG data is provided in Table 9.2 (see the ***companion website*** for an extended version). In coding this extract, we were working with a broad research question informed by a constructionist position: 'In the context of an "obesity epidemic", how do people make sense of obesity?'

Basically, every time you identify something potentially relevant, code it. Remember, you can code a chunk of data in as many ways as you need (as Table 9.2 shows; but note this shows very detailed coding and coding doesn't always need to be that detailed, as it depends on your focus). Coding on hard-copy data, clearly writing down the code name, and marking the text associated with it in some way, is common. Other techniques include using specialised computer software (see below), using the comments feature in Microsoft Word, using some kind of a file card system – keep a card for each code, with data summary and location information listed – or cutting and pasting extracts of text into a new word-processing file, created for this purpose (making sure you record where each extract came from). Some methods allow you to collate coded text *as you code*, which is helpful, but there is no right or wrong way to manage the mechanics of coding. Work out what suits you best. What is important is that coding is inclusive, thorough and systematic, working through each data item in full, before proceeding to the next, except in IPA (we discuss this more below).

What makes a *good* code? Codes should be as concise as possible – except in IPA, where coding can be more akin to writing brief commentaries on the data (see Table 9.3). A code captures the essence of what it is about that bit of data that interests you. Codes should 'work' when separated from the data (imagine, horror of horrors, that you lost your data – good codes would be informative enough to capture what was in the data, and your analytic take on it), because you initially develop candidate themes from your codes, and then your coded data, rather than directly from the full data items. This means developing codes may take some thought. When coding the extract in Table 9.2, in Sally's first response, we first had a code 'different lifestyles', but 'different lifestyles' doesn't really tell us anything without the data. After thinking it through, and talking about it, we decided that 'times have changed' was a better code: it works without the data, and better captures her point that the organisation of our *world* has changed, meaning people do things differently now.

The process continues in the same way for the rest of the data item, and indeed the whole dataset. For each new bit of text you code, you have to decide whether you can apply a code you have already used, or whether a new code is needed to order to capture what it is you've identified. Coding is an organic and evolving process. As your coding progresses and you start to understand the shape and texture of your data a bit more, you will likely modify existing codes to incorporate new material. Once you've finished the first coding of the dataset, it's worth revisiting the whole thing, as your codes will probably have developed during coding.

Each code should be distinct in some way, so if you have codes that almost completely overlap, a broader code might usefully be developed to reflect the general issue. For instance, if you had some data coded as 'hates exercise' and other data coded as 'doesn't like exercise' you might want to merge them into a single code called 'dislike of exercise'. However, this isn't always the case, as you may want to preserve such nuanced differences in your coding. In our coded extract (Table 9.2) two similar codes are 'exercise as negative (chore and burden)' and 'exercise as negative (inherently unpleasant)'. These *may* want to be refined down to a broader 'exercise is negative' code, depending on the rest of the dataset, and also on the research question. Subtle distinctions in codes are about staying close to the data during coding. Some overlap is likely and not a problem – such overlaps are partly how patterns are formed (see Chapter 10). Ultimately, you want a comprehensive set of codes that differentiates between different concepts, issues and ideas in the data, which has been applied consistently to the dataset.

Your motto should be inclusivity. If you are unsure about whether something in the data may be relevant to addressing your research question, code it. It's much easier to discard codes than go back to the data and recode it all later – although, as noted above, some recoding is typically part of the analytic process. Depending on your topic, dataset and precision in coding, you will have generated any number of codes – there is no maximum, and no minimum. You want to ensure that you have enough codes to capture both the patterning and the diversity within the data. You also want to ensure that the coding of each data item is not entirely idiosyncratic; most of your codes should be evident in more than one data item, and you want some that are evident in many if not most data items.

The main exception to this general approach to complete coding occurs with GT, where you aren't aiming to identify *all* instances of a code in the dataset, but rather map all the *different* facets of the concept you're coding around (Charmaz, 2006; Pidgeon & Henwood, 1996). This is because GT seeks to understand a phenomenon in its entirety, and selects data on that basis (often through theoretical sampling; see Box 3.3 in Chapter 3). In contrast, other approaches, like TA and IPA, seek to understand a phenomenon as it appears *within*

Table 9.3 Coding (initial noting) in IPA: a worked example

Original data	Exploratory comments
Sally: I mean metabolism does seem to have a lot to do with it because erm as you say you you seem to have a lot of junk food and yet you're sorry for saying this but you're really slim I wish I was that slim ((Group laughter)) but whatever I eat, even if I really limit what I eat, I seem to put pounds on. If I look at a cream cake I put pounds on. It's like ((laughs)) it just seems to have that cos I have a very slow metabolism and I don't know there's nothing I can do to change it	*Descriptive comments*
	Weight gain as caused by internal factors (metabolism)
	Sally expresses 'envy' (?) of and a desire for slimness
	Weight gain as extremely easy
	Weight gain is an ever-present threat in Sally's life
	Linguistic comments
	Commenting on another person's body size as sayable (if slim, and admiring)
	Group laughter in response to Sally's expression of size 'envy' – recognition of a social norm? Awkwardness?
	'...look at a cream cake' – language is interesting. This is both an 'extreme case' (patently not 'true') but also seems idiomatic...humour? Self-deprecation?
	Conceptual comments
	Given her metabolism, avoiding gaining weight becomes hard if not impossible for Sally (even if she only looks at a cream cake). Sally tells a story of weight gain as beyond her control. There's no agency in her story of how she puts on weight, it's something her body does *to* her, rather than something she does to her body. There's helplessness in the story here, she is at the mercy of a force beyond her control or ability to change (her metabolism). Similar to lack of agency in relation to factors 'causing' obesity (physical incapacitation, depression) in other data. Is this about managing a stigmatised identity?
	Is there a sense of her body as a source/site of betrayal? That she doesn't have a body that does what it 'should' – stay slim?

Original data	Exploratory comments
Sally: Well I know when I was at my biggest and this wasn't this was after all the surgeries and everything I was walking back normally again erm I was having back ache leg ache god knows what else, and it was affect- I mean I've lost seven stone so far and (.) it really has had a dramatic impact on the way I walk around but I think it's all had a bigger impact on how I feel about myself cos I'm not I don't think I'd have started the university course had I been the weight I was cos I'd have been too ashamed I would have been too ashamed and felt I can't do that cos I can't go out in public where there's all these nice slim people and they're all going to look at me and think 'oh look at you' you know so I didn't whereas because I'd lost the weight it gave me so much more confidence it was amazing	*Descriptive comments*
	A fat self means a painful/hard life, a life of suffering
	Shame as a powerful emotion associated with being fat
	Revelation of dramatic weight loss
	Dramatic weight loss experienced as transformative and dramatic, physically and psychologically
	Confidence is gained through weight loss; the slim(mer) self is a confident, engaged self
	Linguistic comments
	'…all the surgeries and everything' – suggests a lot to contend with (a lot pushing her toward obesity)
	Use of first person I pronouns throughout, no depersonalising in this story (which is one of triumph over fatness)
	Sally's valuing of slimness evident in language 'nice slim people' – but it's a curious turn of phrase, because not only does it suggest slimness is desirable, it equates being slim with being nice
	By emphasising the negatives of being fat, Sally's narratives reinforce the desirability of being slim
	'Amazing' is powerful and dramatic language which bolsters the enormity of the transformation
	Conceptual comments
	A fat self seems to mean a life of restriction. Talk of physical pain in exercise evokes restricted physical possibility. Restriction here though is far more psychological, a result of Sally self-policing herself due to her shame associated with fatness, and fear of being the target of judgmental gazes, fear of standing out, fear of social stigma – which she manages by staying at home (imprisoned by fatness)
	Sally talks about her experience in a very individualised way, her experience of shame is real and true, but she does not make external attributions around this and blame a 'nasty' fat-phobic society which produces that shame
	A non-fat life is a liberated and free life – this seems also to be about an experience where weight is a dominant and defining feature in this person's life

the dataset collected. Approaches like TA and IPA are also interested in diversity, but identify it through a comprehensive coding approach. We discuss some of the specifics of GT coding briefly outlining the IPA approach to coding.

CODING IN IPA

Coding *in IPA* is referred to as noting or commenting, and unlike other coding, doesn't aim to produce succinct codes – a code is more like a brief commentary on the data. This commenting occurs at three main levels: *descriptive* comments focus on the lived worlds and meanings of participants; **linguistic comments** focus on the language participants' use and how they use it to communicate their experiences; *abstract* or *conceptual* comments stay with the participant's experience but interpret it from the researcher's perspective. Coding in IPA can involve 'sweeps' of (reading through) the data – coding at these different levels: 1) to make descriptive comments; 2) to make linguistic comments; 3) to make conceptual comments. IPA coding also includes 'free associating' where you note whatever comes to mind when reading the data (Smith et al., 2009). In Table 9.3 we provide an example of IPA initial noting ('coding') of two excerpts from our weight and obesity FG where one of the participants, Sally, talked about her experience of fatness and weight gain. The extracts come from different points in the FG (see the ***companion website*** for the full transcript) – different segments are separated by horizontal black lines. We provide quite detailed comments on these rich extracts, and separate them by 'type' of comment. The broad research question is 'What is the subjective experience of "obesity"?'

CODING IN GROUNDED THEORY

Coding *in GT* covers the whole analytic process; the early stages are typically known as *initial coding* (Charmaz, 2006) or *open* coding (Pidgeon & Henwood, 2004). Throughout coding, codes should be refined as necessary until the best possible *fit* with the data has been determined.

Coding in GT has a number of named features. Key is the *constant comparative* analytic technique, which aims to ensure that the complexity of the data are represented in the analysis by requiring the analyst to constantly move back and forth, to flip flop (Henwood & Pidgeon, 1994), between their developing codes, categories, concepts and the data (Charmaz, 2006). (Although identified here as a key feature of GT, we recommend a recursive approach like this as essential for rigorous qualitative analysis in general.) Codes are the smallest unit of analytic information in GT. As in TA, they are a label applied to a segment of data. They condense, summarise, and potentially provide some analytic 'handle' on the data (Charmaz, 2006). Categories are higher-level concepts derived during analysis through clustering codes (Birks, Chapman, & Francis, 2008), akin to themes in TA. Both codes and categories aim to capture concepts (ideas) in the data.

Like other methods, GT distinguishes between data-derived codes (in their language: **in vivo** or *member* codes) and researcher-derived codes, and coding happens from the very focused and specific to the broader, more conceptual levels, as in TA. Two useful GT techniques are indexing and memo-writing. *Indexing* refers to the way GT records concepts derived through coding. The aim of indexing is to include all relevant coded material so as to demonstrate fully the *diversity* of the concept captured by the code. Indexing can take place using a computer or manually, for instance using index cards or Post-it notes (Birks et al., 2008; Pidgeon & Henwood, 1997).

Memo writing is a process of recording analytic insights that provide more depth and complexity than codes. Memo writing starts as soon as you have any analytic ideas that that you may want to pursue, and continues throughout the research process, with *early memos* giving way to *advanced memos* as the coding (i.e. analysis) develops. Charmaz (2006: 80) recommends you 'use early memos to explore and fill out your qualitative codes'. Memo writing offers a process for refining and developing your analytic ideas, as you return to past memos and write additional memos on that topic. Memos are the step between analysis and write-up (Charmaz, 2006): in writing memos, you set up the basis for your analytic write-up through the ideas they capture. There are no rules as to how many memos you need, or how frequently you need to write them; they can also serve many different functions (Birks et al., 2008). You shouldn't struggle over wording – they aren't polished prose; they're analytic notes-to-self that can be more or less developed, and may or may not include relevant data extracts. Box 9.1 provides an example of an early memo from our GT analysis of the focus group data. The research question we were working to was 'What factors are influential in becoming "obese"?'

BOX 9.1   A GT MEMO

The ways participants understand obesity (13 July 2010)

In order to understand how participants make sense of the causes of obesity, we have to understand how they view obesity itself. In the opening sequences of the data, obesity is framed in a most 'extreme' way, and a consensual view is being built up around this – until one participant 'comes out' as formerly obese, and still on the 'boundaries' (Carla, L71) of obesity, and another participant reveals a similar 'obese' past. But even in revealing this 'fact' they question the validity of the medical 'fact' of obesity; obesity to them is very 'overweight', not just 'overweight'. So even though they speculate that the media probably influence their views in this, they still implicitly work with a model of obesity that is quite different from, and more extreme than, the medical one. They talk about things like 'averagely overweight' (Sally, L432) people who are classed as obese, and dispute the validity of this. They present obesity as a rare and non-normative condition (e.g. 'Britain's fattest man' [Sally, L1141-2]; 'people that you know can't fit in their bed or can't fit on a chair' [Rebecca, L600]), whereas 'overweight' is presented as a normative condition, something common (and thus shouldn't be considered obesity).

In addition, GT analysis can also be distinguished by its particular focus on processes, rather than topics (Charmaz, 2006), and so coding often focuses on data related to actions and processes. This stems from the social interactionist orientation (of some forms of GT), and a view of 'human beings as active agents in their lives' (Charmaz,

2006: 7). Charmaz (2006: 55) suggests asking a series of questions, including the following, when coding, to stay focused on action and process in the data:

- What process(es) are at issue here? How can I define it?
- How do the research participant(s) act while involved in this process?
- What are the consequences of the process?

Charmaz also suggests the use of *gerunds* to help keep the focus on actions and processes. In GT, this refers to using verbs which end in 'ing', such as 'describing' or 'leading' (in grammar, gerunds are 'ing'-ending verbs which function as nouns). Using an 'ing' word keeps the focus on practices and actions, rather than states our outcomes. So a code using a gerund could be 'fat shaming'; the code captures the idea that shaming is a *process* fat people experience (a code 'fat shame' would, by contrast, emphasise a state). It also contains enough information to be informative without the data present.

FINISHING UP COMPLETE CODING

The final stage of complete coding is collating the coded data. For each individual code, you need to collate together all instances of text where that code appears in the dataset. If some codes cluster together (e.g. have fine distinctions between them, such as '*exercise as negative [chore and burden]*' and '*exercise as negative [inherently unpleasant]*'), it would probably make sense to collate all data excerpts for the *similar* codes in one place, instead of collating them for each code individually. This should be determined by the level of similarity in your codes, and how important fine-grained distinctions are likely to be for answering your research question. Codes should be clearly titled, and excerpts of data should be identified to indicate what data item they came from, and where they can be found in that item (e.g. FG1, lines 99–101). Table 9.4 provides examples of some collated coded data for three codes from the FG. IPA is an exception to this, as you code and analyse each data item *sequentially*. This means that you don't collate codes and coded data. Instead, after coding a data item, you develop your analysis of that particular data item (see Table 10.2 and Box 10.3 in Chapter 10), before moving to the next one. A detailed comparison of coding in TA, IPA and GT is provided on the **companion website**.

DOING SELECTIVE CODING IN PATTERN-BASED DISCOURSE ANALYSIS

We briefly outline the different process for doing selective coding, particularly in relation to pattern-based DA. To do selective coding, you need to know what you're looking to code before you begin; data familiarisation is thus particularly vital. The basic elements of selective coding include:

- *Identifying what you're coding for*: this involves a) knowing before you start coding what is that you're looking for; b) looking for it; and c) marking those instances in some way (e.g. on a hard copy of the data). A novice qualitative researcher *may* benefit by doing more complete coding of the data first, to help identify the instances that you'll then selectively code for.

Table 9.4 Examples of some extracts of data collated for three codes

Eating badly leads to obesity	Children are being brought up in a way which promotes obesity	Humans are naturally lazy
Carla: I think there is more of an issue of what we eat and the crap that we eat and people not cooking and not using real food.	Sally: We've got kids growing up who are going um ((pause)) who are growing up thinking 'oh well if I just jump in the car', you know, 'Mum'll take me to so and so' or...	Sally: [...] And nowadays we think 'oh I can't do that', can't walk four miles to go and do that ((laughs)).
Rebecca: Then that's the individual's choice if they want to eat because nobody asks them, even if you are a bit depressed, you have got that... that mentality to think 'oh I'm not going to eat my fifth cream cake today' because that's just a bit piggish.	Carla: And then their children are growing up not know- having the faintest idea to even cook or prepare food. And also, like you said, the modern technology, it's like MSN, kids live on it.	Rebecca: Take the car yeah.

Sally: Yeah exactly.

Rebecca: Yeah.

Sally: You go and you have to motivate yourself to go to the gym. Where at one time you didn't have to go to a gym because you worked physically or whatever, and now we have to motivate and I'm not motivated ((laughs)). |
| Sally: Yeah cos I remember seeing a programme about the uh what is it, Britain's Fattest Man or something. And I mean he just really pigged out.

Judy: But then if they don't want to be that fat they shouldn't eat it. | ?: Yeah ((laughs)).

Carla: It's like we've got a trampoline outside. I have to drag them out by their hair to try and get them to get on it, you know. Sort of constantly just talking to seven different people. 'I'm on MSN, I'll be there in a minute.' ((laughs)) You know. It's not good.

Rebecca: I think it starts at home really. Like the Government can stick their labels on and schools can not give kids chips, but you spend... I think you spend most of your time at home and I think a lot of it is down to erm parents and how you have dinner time at home. And when I was a kid we all used to sit round the table, whereas now everyone just makes their own meals and just sits in front of the TV and it's dangerous I think. | Sally: I think there's got to be some sort of push towards physical education in school. Although they... we obviously do PE and stuff, erm without... I don't want to get over into the nanny state type thing cos I hate that, erm but something to actually motivate kids into exercise. Not making it a chore. Making it fun.

Judy: I think modern technology, like allows you to be lazy as well cos you don't have to do things for yourself. You can get machines and stuff to do things for you. |

- *Determining the boundaries of instances*: this involves deciding when an instance begins and ends. In some cases, it may be really obvious; in others, you may have to make a judgement. If so, err on the side of over-inclusivity, and include at least a few lines of data on either side of the instance.
- *Collating instances*: this involves compiling all instances into a single file. If you are simultaneously coding for two or more phenomena, keep a separate file for each phenomenon you're looking at (the same data extracts can appear in more than one place, if relevant).

Ideally, code as inclusively as possible (Potter & Wetherell, 1987) – for all instances of a phenomenon and anything that vaguely resembles it. It might involve collating *all* data in which a particular word or topic appears (e.g. talk about *causes* of obesity). It might be tempting to see selective coding as data selection, rather than analysis, but it is part of the analysis, and is not one step in a linear analytic process. Often additional coding occurs throughout the development of the analysis, as the shape of the analysis takes form. This means some instances will be rejected as no longer relevant, and other data may need to be collated to fully develop and complete the analysis. Continuing our earlier M&M example, after selecting the red and yellow M&Ms as your data, you may decide that the yellow ones don't fit – and you put them back in the bowl. But you realise that blue M&Ms should be coded, so you need to go back to the bowl (your data) and select out all blue ones and add them to your already selected data (the red M&Ms).

Pattern-based DA coding involves a strong focus on researcher-derived codes: rather than developing an analysis that represents the participants' words or perspectives, the discourse researcher is interested unpicking the language used, to understand its effects within (and beyond) the data (see Chapter 8). They bring their theoretical understanding of language – as productive – to the analysis, and look 'beneath the semantic surface' of the data when coding, in order to identify how language produces or reproduces different versions of reality or particular effects (Arribas-Ayllon & Walkerdine, 2008; Potter & Wetherell, 1987). Coding can occur from quite micro – a few lines of talk – to a more macro focus. In poststructuralist DA, for example, it's often oriented at a broader level: if we were interested in discourses around obesity, for instance, much of the extract of data in Table 9.4 might be 'coded' as evidencing a discourse of *modern life*.

Pattern-based discourse analytic approaches can combine complete and selective coding styles: very broad complete coding followed by selective coding to extract data excerpts of interest, which would then be coded in more detail. So while the requirement to be systematic applies, the actual mechanics of coding in pattern-based discourse approaches are less defined than for TA, IPA or GT (hence we provide no recommended further reading on coding in pattern-based DA).

WHAT ROLE DO COMPUTER PROGRAMS HAVE IN QUALITATIVE CODING AND ANALYSIS?

Discussions about the role of computers in qualitative analysis have been happening for over two decades (e.g. Fielding & Lee, 1991). A range of programs, often collectively termed **CAQDAS** (computer-assisted qualitative data analysis software), is available (widely used

Table 9.5   The strengths and limitations of using computer programs in data coding

Strengths	Limitations
Can increase the organisation of data, coding and analysis through functioning as on online 'filing' system	Cost – if you have to buy a program, it may not be affordable; commercialisation has been raised as a concern in this area in general
Allows quick searching for codes, data, and (often) the generation of visual connections	May not be possible to spend time learning to use (well) new software in a time-limited (e.g. seven-month) project
Can increase efficiency, making the process of coding and analysis quicker. However, this only applies if you're competent with the program, or a quick learner (otherwise it can take longer)	For some forms of analysis, such as DA, it can take *longer* (and be unsatisfactory, MacMillan, 2005)
Can give reassurance of comprehensiveness of coding (but this does depend on you doing it well in the first place)	Risk of 'usability frustration, even despair and hopelessness" (Lu & Shulman, 2008: 108) if not tech-savvy
Subsequently, may increase the rigour of qualitative coding and analysis	Risk of technologically mediated 'distancing' from the data – less 'immersion' leading to less insight
May facilitate visualisation and (thus) theoretical/analytic development (Konopásek, 2008)	Can work as a distraction; the technologies can be seductive, and assist (fear-induced) analytic-avoidance – aka procrastination (Bong, 2002)
May increase transparency of qualitative research process, as there are clear 'audit trails' (see Chapter 12)	Carries the temptation to over-code or use features of the program not necessary for your analysis (Mangabeira, 1995)
Can you be very useful for managing a large dataset	Risk of producing a focus on quantity – with *frequency* being mistaken for *meaningfulness*
Can be useful for team projects	Risk that the software can promote certain forms of analysis (e.g. tendency towards GT in many programs, MacMillan & Koenig, 2004), rather than facilitating the use of a chosen method – this risks analysis being determined by techniques and technologies, rather than conceptual or other factors (see Chapter 3), a process referred to as methodolatry (Chamberlain, 2000; Reicher, 2000)
Some have particularly argued for the compatibility of CAQDAS and GT (Bringer et al., 2006)	Programs can contain embedded methodological and theoretical assumptions (often derived from GT), and these need to be critically considered (MacMillan & Koenig, 2004; Mangabeira, 1995)

ones include NVivo and ATLAS.ti). Some qualitative researchers revere CAQDAS; others revile it (Lu & Shulman, 2008). Traditionally, CAQDAS has been separable into programs that just allow you to 'code' data and then 'retrieve' all coded data, and those that allow some 'conceptual mapping' of coded data to explore relationships between codes (Fielding & Lee, 1998). While the sophistication and scope of programs have increased over the years (Mangabeira, Lee, & Fielding, 2004), resulting in user-friendly tools that can assist in the production of very complex and nuanced analyses, and *may* aid interpretation and theorising (Silverman, 2005), none escape the fact that qualitative analysis is an interpretative process driven by what the analyst sees in, and makes of, the data. So before you get excited at the thought that a computer can *do* your analysis, such programs only offer a tool to *assist* with coding and analysis.

That said, they do offer exciting – if still quite modest (Silver & Fielding, 2008) – possibilities, and, if used in a critical, thoughtful, creative and flexible way that serves the needs of the project, driven by the researcher, research questions and research design, have the potential to enhance the process and the outcome of qualitative analysis. Ultimately, whether or not CAQDAS in general is right for you and for a particular project will depend on a number of factors, such as the scope and scale of the project, the research questions, data type and analytic approach (MacMillan, 2005; MacMillan & Koenig, 2004) and your familiarity and comfort with different technologies (Mangabeira et al., 2004).

The CAQDAS site at Surrey University, and the hands-on guide they have published (Lewins & Silver, 2007), offer a useful resource for CAQDAS-related decisions. Table 9.5 summarises some strengths and limitations noted around CAQDAS programs (Bourdon, 2002; Lu & Shulman, 2008; Mangabeira et al., 2004; Roberts & Wilson, 2002; Silver & Fielding, 2008). Whether or not you use CAQDAS, doing analysis requires understanding of the analytic method you are using, and the frameworks in which it is embedded, rather than knowing how to use a CAQDAS program (MacMillan & Koenig, 2004), so any use of CAQDAS does not replace knowledge of an analytic approach.

CHAPTER SUMMARY

This chapter:
- outlined the first stages of analysis: familiarisation with your data;
- defined different types of coding: selective vs. complete; data-driven vs. researcher-driven;
- demonstrated the process of complete coding;
- outlined and illustrated differences in complete coding for IPA and GT;
- discussed the process of selective coding in pattern-based DA;
- considered the use of computer software in qualitative analysis.

? QUESTIONS FOR DISCUSSION AND CLASSROOM EXERCISES

1   For the coded data in Table 9.2, determine whether each of the codes is data-derived, researcher-derived, or a mix of both.

2   The following data come from a female respondent to the *story completion task* discussed in Chapter 6, in which a father tells his children he wants to have a 'sex change' (see Material Example 6.1). The data are recorded as written, including

errors. Working alone, code the data in relation to two broad research questions: i) 'How do people make meaning of trans parenting?'; ii) 'How do people make meaning of the impact of trans parenting on children?' Record your codes in the space to the right of the extract. After you have finished your coding, form a small group, and compare your codes. Did you code the same segments of data? How much overlap is there between each of your codings? What are *your* overall impressions of the story in relation to the two research questions? Are those shared among the group? How would you make sense of any differences in overall impressions?

The children look at their Dad very confused. The youngest child begins to cry and tells his Dad that he doesn't want him to change. The oldest child becomes angry and says some hurtful things to his Dad about 'why can't he just be normal' and that he is a freak. He storms off upstairs. Brian is now worried and thinks that telling his children at this stage was a mistake and wishes he had waited until they were older. He tries to talk to his eldest but he is still angry and quiet with his Dad. The son tells his Dad that children at school will take the mick out of him and gets confused because he won't have a 'Dad' anymore. Brian explains that he will still be exactly the same person; he will just look different. The child starts to understand the situation a bit better. The child can see that his Dad will be much happier if he goes ahead with this as it's something he has kept quiet about for ages and just wants his Dad to be happy. Eventually after the surgery, all the family are back to how they were before. Maybe even better than they were because Brian is now truly happy and himself. All children get on very well with the new 'Brian'.	

3 Write a (grounded theory) memo about your first impressions of the *story completion task* data presented in Exercise 2.

4 Code a longer extract of data. The different transcripts and sample datasets available on the **companion website** offer the chance to code participant-generated data. Coding a long segment (e.g. from an FG) can give insights into the reality of the coding process for qualitative researchers, including the choices you face and the ways codes evolve throughout the process. To maximise your learning, we recommend trying out all the different *types* of coding discussed in this chapter.

FURTHER RESOURCES

Further reading:

For a data-based worked example of the coding and analytic steps in thematic analysis, see: Braun, V., & Clarke, V. (2012). Thematic analysis. In H. Cooper (Ed.), *Handbook of research methods in psychology* (pp. 57–71). Washington, DC: APA Books.

For a really clear and practical account of coding in grounded theory, see: Chapter 3 in Charmaz, K. (2006). *Constructing grounded theory: A practical guide through qualitative analysis*. Thousand Oaks, CA: Sage.

A practical over view of coding and analysis in IPA, using worked examples, see: Chapter 5 (especially pp. 83–91 on 'Initial comments') in Smith, J. A., Flowers, P., & Larkin, M. (2009). *Interpretative phenomenological analysis: Theory, method and research*. London: Sage.

For a good introduction to CAQDAS, with helpful visual illustrations, see: Silver, C., & Fielding, N. (2008). Using computer packages in qualitative research. In C. Willig & W. Stainton Rogers (Eds), *The Sage handbook of qualitative research in psychology* (pp. 334–351). Los Angeles: Sage.

Online resources:

Our TA website: www.psych.auckland.ac.nz/thematicanalysis

The site of the Computer Assisted Qualitative Data Analysis (CAQDAS) Networking Project provides comprehensive resources understanding and making decisions around the use of computers in qualitative analysis: www.surrey.ac.uk/sociology/research/researchcentres/caqdas/

See the *companion website* (**www.sagepub.co.uk/braunandclarke**) for:
- self-test multiple choice questions relating to Section 3;
- the flashcard glossary – test yourself on the definitions of key terms used in this chapter;
- a detailed comparison of coding in TA, GT and IPA;
- transcripts and sample datasets: the weight and obesity and body art FG transcripts; sample data from surveys (the 'views on pubic hair' and 'experiences of orgasm and sexual pleasure' surveys) and our trans parent story completion task;
- extended versions of Tables 9.2, 9.3 and 9.4, illustrating more fully our coding of the weight and obesity FG data;
- further readings (articles from Sage journals).

Identifying patterns across data

OVERVIEW

Searching for patterns: from codes to candidate themes
Reviewing and revising candidate themes
Other ways of identifying patterns across data
Can and should I go beyond looking for patterns?

After coding the data, it's time to shift to looking for larger patterns across the dataset. We focus again on thematic analysis (TA) in this chapter, and describe and illustrate key differences in other pattern-based approaches (i.e. interpretative phenomenological analysis [IPA], grounded theory [GT], and pattern-based discourse analysis [DA]).

At its most basic, a pattern-based analysis allows you systematically to identify and report the salient features of the data. But much pattern-based analysis goes beyond this, and interrogates and interprets the patterns identified (Chapter 11 covers analysis and interpretation of patterns). Pattern-based analysis rests on the presumption that ideas which recur *across* a dataset capture something psychologically or socially meaningful. In working out which patterns are relevant and important in relation to your research question, it's not just a question of which are the most frequent. While frequency is an important factor, it's also about capturing the different elements that are most *meaningful* for answering your research question. So it's about meanings, rather than numbers (Chapter 11 discusses this further). New Zealand health researcher Stephen Buetow (2010) has developed an approach based on, but extending, TA, called *saliency analysis*, which captures the point that something in data can be important without appearing very frequently.

SEARCHING FOR PATTERNS: FROM CODES TO CANDIDATE THEMES

As you work from codes and coded data to identify broader patterns – themes – you get deeper into the analysis. A theme 'captures something important about the data in relation to the research question, and represents some level of *patterned* response or meaning within the data set' (Braun & Clarke, 2006, p. 82). It's typically broader than a code in that it contains many facets. Remember our brick and tile house example: a theme is like the wall or roof panel of a house, made up of many individual bricks or tiles (codes). A good code will capture one idea; a theme has a **central organising concept**, but will contain lots of different ideas or aspects related to the central organising concept (each of those might be a code). For example, one of themes we developed from our coding of the weight and obesity focus group (FG) is called *modern life is rubbish*. The central organising concept of this theme is that contemporary lifestyles encourage obesity. Particular facets of the theme include ideas around the availability of convenience food, not having time to cook, ubiquitous advertising of 'unhealthy' foods and safety concerns curtailing children's activity. Although a rich and complex code may become a theme without much expansion, the distinction between codes and themes is generally a good one to work with: codes combine to form themes.

It's also useful to distinguish whether you're identifying a theme or what we would call a *feature* of the data. Both capture something that's recurring in the data, but a theme has a central organising concept, which tells us something about the content of the data that's *meaningful*, something about how, and in what way, that concept appears in the data: it tells us something meaningful in relation to our research question. For example, when analysing the story completion task data (explained in Chapter 6; for sample data, see the ***companion website***), many of Victoria's students identified *gender* as a key *theme*. However, gender should more accurately be described as a *feature* of the data, rather than a theme. Why? Because it doesn't have a central organising concept and simply clusters together a whole lot of *different* ways gender is evident in the data. This isn't to say that gender was irrelevant to the analysis. It wasn't – it was really important. But a theme around gender had to be built around a central organising concept and tell us something *meaningful* how gender appeared in the data. *Good* gender themes included 'stereotyped gender roles' (the stories typically contained very traditional ideas about appropriate gender roles) and 'the gendering of emotion' (male respondents often wrote angry stories; female participants typically wrote nurturing stories). In determining if you have identified a theme or a feature, it's also worth making sure that it's not just that you have given your theme a terrible title, which fails to demonstrate the central organising concept (see Box 10.1).

IDENTIFYING THEMES AS AN ACTIVE PROCESS

It's quite common to read about 'themes emerging from the data'. We get quite – maybe even very – grumpy when we read this! Why? Because it falsely suggests analysis is a passive process where you identify something that *already exists* (Ely, Vinz, Downing, & Anzul, 1997). Developing themes from coded data is an *active* process: the researcher examines the codes and coded data, and starts to create potential patterns; they do not 'discover' them (Taylor & Ussher, 2001). Searching for patterns is *not* akin to an archaeologist digging to find hidden treasures buried within the data, pre-existing the process of searching for them. It's more akin to the process of sculpture. Analysts, like sculptors, actively make choices about how they shape and craft their 'raw data' (e.g. their piece of marble) into an analysis (like a work of art, such as Michelangelo's *David*). Like the sculptor's block of marble, the dataset provides a material basis for the analysis; it provides some limits or boundaries on what it is possible to produce. However, it does not completely determine the shape of the analysis; it's possible to create many different analyses from qualitative data, just as it's possible to create many different sculptures from one piece of marble. Different researchers, with different tools, can produce different analyses from the same data (e.g. see Coyle & Lyons, 2007; Forrester, 2010) and, like sculpture, the resulting analysis can vary in quality (see Chapter 12).

So how do you identify themes? To identify patterns in the data, you need to review the codes and the collated data relating to each code, with the aim of identifying similarity and overlap between codes. It might help to look for concepts, topics or issues which several codes relate to, and which could be used as a central organising concept for a theme; some codes, if they are large, rich and complex enough, may themselves be 'promoted' to a theme (Charmaz, 2006), a process referred to as subsumption in IPA (Smith et al., 2009). Basically, you want to identify a number of themes (with central organising concepts) that capture the most salient patterns in the data relevant to answering your research question. This makes it sound straightforward, but it's not always easy; sometimes meaningful, interesting or important, or indeed *any*, patterns seem elusive. Box 10.1 provides useful questions to ask yourself as you shift from codes to themes. If you're still having trouble, don't panic! It would be *very unlikely* that there are no patterns in the data. It may be that you haven't given it enough time, and aren't 'immersed' in the data enough and close enough to it (do you feel you know it intimately?). At the same time, you do need *some* distance from the data. This all takes time! You need to leave *lots of time* for coding and analysis – they always take far longer than you ever anticipate (practically every student we have ever supervised has made this comment, even though we warn each and every one about how long it takes). So don't do this in a rush; it won't help in pattern identification.

Sometimes identifying patterns is made harder by the data you have. For instance, we have found that qualitative *survey* data, where the data are typically quite short responses to particular questions, pose unique and particular challenges for identifying patterns across the dataset (see Box 10.2).

**BOX 10.1   GOOD QUESTIONS TO ASK YOURSELF IN
DEVELOPING THEMES**

- Is this a theme (is it just a code or a subtheme)?
- Is there a *central organising concept* that unifies the data extracts?
- What is the quality of this theme? Does the central organising concept tell me something meaningful about a pattern in the data, in relation to my research question?
- Can I identify the boundaries of this theme? What does it include and exclude?
- Are there enough (meaningful) data to support this theme? Is the theme too 'thin'?
- Is there too much going on in the theme, so that it lacks coherence? Are the data too diverse and wide-ranging? Would using subthemes resolve this problem? Or should it be better split into two or more themes, each with their own central organising concept?
- How does this (potential) theme relate to other (potential) themes? Is the relationship between (potential) themes hierarchical or linear?
- What's the overall story of my analysis? How does this theme contribute to that overall story?
- Is the central organising concept reflected in the title I have given to the theme (see Chapter 11)?

CANDIDATE THEMES IN THE WEIGHT AND OBESITY FG DATA

To provide an example of pattern identification, when reviewing our coded FG data, we identified a number of clusterings of codes. For a start, there were some very obvious, semantic-level clusterings:

- lots of codes related to negative descriptions of contemporary life;
- lots of codes provided rosy views of life in the past, compared to the present, in relation to obesity and exercise;
- a large number also clustered around the idea that children's current socialisation and education is inadequate.

Each of these clusterings has a clear and distinct central organising concept, which is captured by these descriptions. Looking a bit more *deeply* at the data, around the underlying *assumptions* or latent ideas informing the things people said, we identified codes clustering around another two central organising concepts:

- the idea that human beings are *naturally* gluttonous;
- the idea that human beings are *naturally* lazy and exercise is an inherently negative activity.

Table 10.1 illustrates the codes we clustered to produce these five candidate themes (the **companion website** has an extended version of Table 10.1). The five themes are organised underneath two **overarching themes** – *human nature* and *modern life*. There are also two subthemes, which we discuss later. In Table 10.1, the number for each overarching theme, theme and subtheme indicate the hierarchical structure of relationships between them (discussed further later).

BOX 10.2   IDENTIFYING PATTERNS IN QUALITATIVE SURVEY DATA

Qualitative survey data can present some particular challenges for a pattern-based analysis. We think this stems from certain features:

- the questions themselves often give a very dominant structure to the data. This impact is potentially exacerbated if you collate data by question for coding and analysis, rather than collating by data item;
- response to any one question is often quite short;
- the data are potentially quite 'bitty'– rather than a longer flowing narrative. You get more discrete responses to particular questions, and these can cover a wide range of issues, but not in much depth.

One of the key challenges in identifying patterns is moving away from the organising structure provided by your questions. Remember, it's important not to confuse *questions* with patterns or themes. Although sometimes we may want to know the sorts of answers given to particular questions (e.g. 'What is a feminist'?), in general a pattern-based analysis will not just look *within* a question, but across the whole dataset to determine themes. Some of the key themes we identified in our critical constructionist thematic analysis of New Zealand responses to the pubic hair survey (discussed in Chapter 6) included: *hair removal as personal choice* (evident semantically and latently), constructions of pubic hair as *private*, as *interfering with sex*, and of removed or reduced pubic hair as *cleaner* and *more attractive* (see Braun, Tricklebank & Clarke, under submission). These constructions were not just found around one question, or in relation to one issue; they cut across responses.

In more essentialist (or semantic or inductive) TA, it can be harder to move beyond the *questions*/topics explored to identify themes across responses to different questions. Keeping data collated *by participant,* rather than *by question,* which we typically do, should help in seeing patterns *across* the dataset rather than around questions. In some ways, doing a more constructionist (or latent or theoretical) form of TA or other analysis may be easier with qualitative survey data, because you don't focus entirely on the explicit content of the data. By trying to get to the meanings and logic underpinning data responses, or in approaching data particular theoretical issue or question in mind (e.g. gendering pubic hair), you remove yourself from the structure imposed by the questions and responses.

IMPORTANT POINTS TO REMEMBER AT THIS STAGE

There are some important points to note at this stage. The first is that themes identified at this point in the process are provisional; they are *candidate* themes, and will be revised or refined through the developing analysis. You have to be prepared to let them go. Sometimes, it will be a case that your supervisor or co-researcher does not think they work; sometimes it may be that you realise the analysis either doesn't fit the data well, or that it doesn't provide the best or most interesting answer to the research question. You

Table 10.1 Candidate themes showing *selected* associated codes (see the ***companion website*** for an extended version)

1. Human Nature			2. Modern Life			
1.1. Sins and sinners	**1.1.1. Deserving/undeserving obesity**	**1.2. Exercise is evil**	**2.1. Those halcyon days of yore**	**2.2. Modern life is rubbish**	**2.2.1. Technology trumps all**	**2.3. They don't get no education**
'Liking food' as negative; associated with overeating	'Deserving' and 'undeserving' obesity: if in control, can judge them; if not, can't	Choice and exercise (none in past; now we have it, but won't do it)	'Dadadada' – common story – a past we all recognise	Cost as a bottom line that determines what you eat	Children engage in sedentary 'play'	Adequate socialisation: cooking needs to be learned (taught in home or school)
Convenience (pre-prepared food); convenience of modern lifestyles is hard to resist	Blaming (eat what he likes) and *not* blaming (he's fed bad food)	Constraints and supports for regular exercise	Different lifestyles	Time poor (money rich)	Modern technology encourages/facilitates obesity/lack of exercise	Children's socialisation is important (but inadequate)
Emotional eating/'overeating' has no validity – not an 'eating disorder'; it's just gluttony!	Doesn't take a lot to cause obesity	Exercise as negative: boring (common story); chore and burden; inherently unpleasant; inherently lacking fun	Past – no such thing as 'exercise'; physical activity an integral part of life	'Bad foods' associated with positive things in ads/marketing	Negative impacts of technology	Irresponsible parenting: adults pander to children; don't regulate children's eating towards healthy foods; feed them unhealthy food
Home cooking as onerous (time, effort); cooking is a hassle	External factors/life events: obesity impinges *upon* you (you have little control)	Exercise as self-indulgent	Times have changed	Advertising/marketing of junk food (to children)	She's not responsible for her children's behaviour: tries to promote good behaviour but powerless in face of technology and 'modern life'	Kids have an inherent desire to be able to cook, but education system denies them this
Humans are naturally gluttonous: unless controlled will eat too much/wrong foods; BUT we *should* have restraint		Exercise can be a luxury/pleasure	Times have changed: junk food not *everyday* food in the past	Children engage in sedentary 'play'		Socialisation (school PE teaching) as inadequate
		Exercise easier if part of a regular routine – becomes something you just do		Commodification of exercise		
				Prepared food as cheap and therefore appealing ...		

	1. Human Nature			2. Modern Life			
1.1. Sins and sinners	1.1.1. Deserving/ undeserving obesity	1.2. Exercise is evil	2.1. Those halcyon days of yore	2.2. Modern life is rubbish	2.2.1. Technology trumps all	2.3. They don't get no education	
Labradoring – pure gluttony Obesity: caused by laziness	Emotional eating is still potentially under control (some restraint should be applied; completely unrestrained eating is bad) Humans have a natural propensity for obesity: a constant threat you have to actively work against (if you become obese, you're to blame)	Need a motivation to exercise (getting away from kids); motivation trumps all obstacles to exercise (motivation also rare) Not exercising is easy; exercise requires effort (bother)	Times have changed (the halcyon past – freedom and an active childhood; the hellish present)	Irresponsible to cook if you can buy a pre-prepared meal cheaply Junk food used to be a treat No 'modern pantry': The home no longer contains the basics for cooking Society is no longer safe: children as perceived to be vulnerable – limits outside play as 'child safety' paramount Exercise isn't part of *everyday* life Forced into unhealthy eating by modern lifestyles	Technological inherently addictive (more appealing than exercise as 'leisure' activity) Technology is unhealthy	Socialisation failure; across generations: parents don't necessarily know how to cook; young parents not equipped to socialise their children; current cooking teaching inadequate; government intervention needed (to re-educate) Socialisation is key: early learning sets up later attitudes and practices	

have to make sure you give yourself enough time to get the analysis 'wrong', revise it, or start again; as noted above, time pressure does not generally produce an excellent qualitative analysis (see Chapter 12). As a rule of thumb, analysis is likely to take at least twice as long as you imagine it will.

The second important point is that, as noted above, themes are not determined in some quantitative fashion (see also Chapter 11), and there is no magical equation or cut-off point to determine what counts as a theme across a dataset, and what doesn't. As this form of analysis is about identifying patterns across data, themes need to be identified across a proportion of the data (we cannot specify exactly what proportion, as qualitative analysis does not work like that), but it does not need to be present in every data item, or even most data items (Braun & Clarke, 2006; Buetow, 2010). Similarly, within each individual data item, some themes will be present, and others not. Some themes may be very prominent in certain data items, but less prominent in others. Determining the importance of a theme is not about counting (e.g. frequency overall, frequency within each data item); it's about determining whether this pattern tells us something meaningful and important for answering our research question. This means the themes you discuss in any research report will not *necessarily* be the most common ones (see Braun & Clarke, 2006).

The third important, related, point is that your themes don't have to cover everything in the data – they should be about addressing the *research question,* and since you are reporting patterned meaning, some less patterned or irrelevant codes will be excluded. In our data, a large number of codes didn't obviously address the research question, or didn't sit within these initial candidate themes. We collated those into a 'miscellaneous' category. A category like that can be important to keep at this stage, as the analysis is still very provisional, meanings themes may be radically altered, and new themes developed (for an example, see Frith & Gleeson, 2004). Codes which don't appear to fit anywhere, or cluster with any others, may start to fit as the analysis progresses. Or they may not. Being able to let go of coded material (and indeed, candidate themes) that does not fit within your overall analysis is an important part of qualitative research. Your task in analysing the data is a *selective* one. It's about telling a *particular* story about the data, a story that answers your research question. It isn't to represent *everything* that was said in the data.

Finally, if you're doing your analysis with anyone else involved (supervisor, co-researcher), it's important to realise that some coding and analytic differences are likely when doing qualitative analysis, as we all read data from different perspectives and experiences (see Chapter 12). The key is to work out whether the differences are problematic (e.g. contradictory themes) and, if so, work out where they're coming from (different theoretical takes, perhaps?), and how to resolve them. In our example, as we previously noted, Virginia, who's quite 'sporty', noted the negative tone of talk around exercise, something that Victoria, who's not so 'sporty', did not. After discussing this point, Victoria understood Virginia's analysis of exercise constructions, and this eventually became a theme in our analysis (*exercise is evil*). Qualitative research is not about finding the *right* answer; what you're always looking for is the best 'fit' of analysis to answer the research question.

WHAT MAKES A GOOD THEME?

When developing themes, and your analysis, it's important to consider themes on their own, *and* the relationship between themes. Good themes are distinctive and need to make sense on their own; at the same time, good themes need to fit together to form the overall analysis. A useful comparison could be with the craft of patchwork, which we discussed in Chapter 2. Consider a patchwork quilt made up of six separately patterned squares. Each of the six patterned squares can be understood as akin to a theme in TA (the pieces of fabric which create those patterns are akin to codes). Each of the six squares needs to be organised, coherent and distinct; and combined together, they need to work to create an *overall* patchwork pattern for the quilt. The patterning requires organisation to give it meaning. The patchwork only works if lots of different pieces of fabric (codes) contribute towards creating organised and coherent patterns (themes), which are distinct from other patterns, and which work together to make an overall pattern (the analysis). It's your role as analyst to work out what pieces of fabric (codes) to use, and the *best* way to combine those pieces to create certain patterns (themes), that together produce the overall patchwork quilt (analysis).

Relationships between themes in TA can be hierarchical or non-hierarchical (lateral). In terms of hierarchical relationships, themes occur at three main levels. *Overarching* themes (similar to superordinate themes in IPA) organise and structure the analysis; they tend not to contain codes or data, but instead simply capture an idea encapsulated in a number of themes. The other two levels are *themes* and *subthemes*; subthemes capture and develop notable *specific* aspects of the central organising concept of one theme. In an analysis, one or two overarching themes might provide and organising structure for most or all of your themes, but they are not necessary for analysis. Themes themselves may have subthemes, or they may not. In our example, with our initial candidate themes, as noted above, we identified two overarching themes: *modern life* and *human nature* (see Table 10.1). *Modern life* captures an idea that underpins three themes (which we have called *those halcyon days of yore*, *modern life is rubbish* and *they don't get no education* [we discuss naming themes in Chapter 11]). The idea is that there's something about the way we live our lives now that is inherently unhealthy and encouraging of obesity. Human nature captures an idea that underpins two themes (which we have called *sins and sinners* and *exercise is evil*). The idea is that there's something about our psychology (and maybe physiology) as humans that *naturally* encourages obesity.

Our candidate themes are structured both laterally (five themes) and hierarchically (three layers). That's about as complex as you would ever want to go. One layer – just themes – is fine, and typical of much TA. You don't *need* to have subthemes; you don't *need* to have overarching themes. In general, it's a good idea to avoid thematic structures with lots of nested layers of themes and subthemes; they are complicated, hard to follow, and often detract from both clarity and depth, analytically. Don't force your analysis into a hierarchical structure; only organise your analysis in this way if it's the best way to present your results. For this reason, and to demonstrate the potential for hierarchical and lateral relationships, our worked example describes all three layers.

VISUAL MAPPING AS A USEFUL AID

A visual thematic map can be a useful aid for exploring the relationships between codes and themes, and themes, subthemes, and overarching themes. A thematic map offers a mode to visually explore and refine the connections between these elements (this is not emphasised in IPA). It can be a vital tool for developing the final form of your analysis: essential if you're a visual person, but useful for anyone in that it shifts the developing analysis into a different – visual – framework, and gives you an alternative view of potential relationships between themes and subthemes. Figure 10.1 shows a visual map from the early stages of our thematic analysis of our data, showing our two overarching themes, five themes and two subthemes (and connections between them). It's done here electronically, but we'd typically do it by hand, as we find it quicker, easier and more flexible. Use whatever works for you; as widely available electronic drawing technology evolves, it may become more user-friendly. Such visual representations can also be generated using some CAQDAS programs (Silver & Fielding, 2008).

HOW MANY THEMES?

So how many themes should you have in a pattern analysis? Unfortunately, there is no magic formula; no 'X data items/Y word-length = Z themes'. You're likely to produce more codes with a larger dataset; in turn you're then like to produce more themes. However, more isn't necessarily better. A clear and coherent analysis is what you're aiming for, and beyond a certain number of themes, you increase the likelihood that you lose coherence, depth and focus (just like with too many layers). Your themes need to be presented in enough depth and detail to convey the richness and complexity of a central concept in your data. If you try to report too many themes, you're unlikely to achieve this; your themes will likely be 'thin' (see Chapters 11 and 12).

The number of themes partly depends on what you're trying to do. If what you want to do is provide a meaningful *overview* of your data, one or two themes will likely be insufficient: you'll need more to demonstrate the *breadth* and *diversity* of patterns in the data. It's good to reiterate at this point that any one reported analysis is never going to tell the 'whole' story about your data. And you can develop different analyses from the same dataset, exploring certain aspects of the data in much more depth, or asking different research questions. For example, one of Virginia's datasets for her research into women's genital meanings was FG data. From this, she produced a general 'overview' of patterns in women's talk (Braun & Wilkinson, 2003), and two more detailed, focused analyses, one around bodies and gendered identity (Braun & Wilkinson, 2005), and one around vaginal size (Braun & Kitzinger, 2001). If you are doing a more detailed, in-depth analysis of one aspect

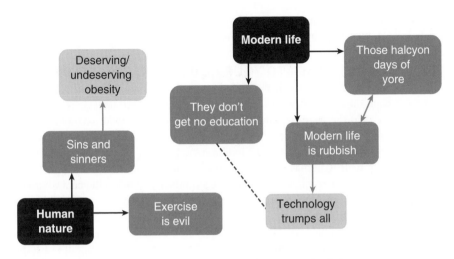

Figure 10.1   Our candidate overarching themes, themes and subthemes

Key: single directional solid arrows demonstrate hierarchical relationships between overarching themes, themes and subthemes; a bi-directional solid arrow signals a close lateral relationship between themes; a dotted line indicates a tentative relationship between a theme and a subtheme of a *different theme*.

of the dataset, one or two themes (with more subthemes) may work well. In an 8,000 word report, which is a common maximum length for qualitative journal articles, we would usually discuss between two and six themes and subthemes (e.g. see Braun, 2008).

After identifying candidate themes, and developing a thematic map or table that outlines these themes, you should collate together all the data extracts relevant to each theme. Once done, you're ready to develop your analysis further, by reviewing the themes.

REVIEWING AND REVISING CANDIDATE THEMES

This phase is essentially one of 'quality control' in relation to your developing analysis – checking to determine whether your candidate themes *fit* well with the coded data, and the dataset you collected. You want your themes to tell a story that 'rings true' with the data – so that if someone read your analysis, then read the dataset, they would go 'yep, I buy it'. Remember, though, this isn't about telling the *one true story* about your data (there's no such thing in qualitative research), but about telling a story that is faithful to the data (even if it moves well beyond the surface meaning, as critical, theoretically informed analyses often do). So what do you need to do to ensure this?

REVISION BY GOING BACK TO YOUR CODED AND COLLATED DATA

You first need to go back to all the coded and collated data and read it to make sure that each candidate theme 'works' in relation to these. How well does it fit with the collated data? Do the candidate themes cover most of the coded data and most of the things you see as important for answering your research question? Does anything else 'jump out' of the data at you? If the candidate themes don't seem to capture the meaning of the data well, you may need to rethink the analysis a bit. First start by seeing if minor tweaks, such as reorienting the themes slightly, by revising the central organising concept slightly, or shifting coded data in and out of different themes, might create a better data-theme fit. If this doesn't help, if may be that a whole theme (or themes) needs to be discarded and a new one developed. Or you may end up collapsing a number of candidate themes together, or splitting a big broad theme into a number of more specific or coherent themes.

REVISION BY GOING BACK TO THE WHOLE DATASET

After you've revised the themes around the coded data extracts, and have a set of candidate themes that are coherent (each has a central organising concept), distinctive (from each other), work together and, importantly, relate to the research question in some way, you then need to further review the candidate themes by going back to your entire (un-coded) dataset (or the subset of the dataset your analysis relates to). By this we mean do a final re-read of all your data items, to ensure that your themes capture the meaning of the dataset *in relation to your research question*. If your candidate themes do capture the meaning and spirit of the dataset, all good! It's time to move on to the most 'analytic' phase of the analysis. If not, you'll need to do further reviewing and refining of the candidate themes in relation to the dataset, to ensure it does capture these elements.

YOU'VE GOT TO BE PREPARED TO LET THINGS GO

Reviewing candidate themes is the key stage where a back and forth between data and developing analysis occurs. This is typically the stage candidate themes are confirmed, revised and/or rejected if they don't work. One fundamental principle to remember is to not force your data into your analysis; you don't want to be like Cinderella's stepsisters, trying to force their feet into the glass slipper. It's therefore vital not to be too attached to your candidate themes! We will keep saying this, because it's really hard not to get too attached to them. And try to remember that qualitative analysis is not a linear process. It is recursive, it goes back and forth on itself, and you have to be prepared to go backwards, and take a different route, to ultimately move forward.

Thorough review is important in any qualitative research, and is part of developing a quality piece of work (see Chapter 12), but it is especially important for new qualitative researchers, or researchers working with a large dataset. Because qualitative analysis is a skill we learn, with more experience we can become more adept at shifting between different levels of 'pattern' in our data (e.g. codes, themes), and identifying 'patterns' for analysis; for newer researchers, these can be harder to identify, and harder to feel confident about. With more experience, your analytic process will become more recursive and less linear; this means that (especially when working with smaller datasets) reviewing themes becomes built into theme development, rather than comprising a separate stage. However, if you're working with a large dataset (and sometimes even with a smaller one), it can be impossible to keep all your data and your analytic ideas 'in your head' and so going back and double-checking is imperative.

REVIEWING CANDIDATE THEMES IN THE WEIGHT AND OBESITY FOCUS GROUP DATA

As a result of our review of our candidate themes, we didn't make substantial changes to our candidate themes – which partly reflects our experience as qualitative researchers, the very small size of the dataset (one FG), and our research question. However, a review of these candidate themes did result in us identifying two potential subthemes: *technology trumps all* as a subtheme of *modern life is rubbish* and *deserving/undeserving obesity* as a subtheme of *sins and sinners* (shown in Table 10.1 and Figure 10.1). Developing a subtheme can highlight a common, distinctive or important aspect of a theme, and can provide a means of organising a larger theme. The subtheme still has to relate to the central organising concept of the theme it sits within, but to be a meaningful subtheme it also has its *own* central organising concept.

In our analysis, the central organising concept of the quite semantic-level candidate theme *modern life is rubbish* is that contemporary lifestyles encourage obesity through a combination of the values we now have, and the demands, constraints and opportunities available to us. One frequently discussed aspect of this related to the place and use of technologies in our lives, and so we created a subtheme, *technology trumps all*. Technologies were invariably framed as both negative (in that they encourage behaviours that encourage obesity – hence it's part of *modern life is rubbish*) but somehow also impossible to resist (captured in the subtheme name). This dual characterisation creates a distinct, but related, central organising concept for the subtheme: technology seduces us to live in ways that encourage obesity.

The central organising concept of the more latent-level candidate theme *sins and sinners* is a construction of human beings as *naturally* lazy and gluttonous, and hence possessing a natural tendency towards obesity. But it also contains an almost religious moralistic element (hence the name), in that these natural propensities, while understandable, *ought* to be resisted. One particular feature of the data was the effective construction of two different groups in relation to obesity, with moral value applied differently to each: a) people whose obesity resulted from factors *beyond their control*, such as being wheelchair bound, were framed as undeserving of their obesity, and deserving of understanding; b) those who were obese through a failure appropriately to control their 'natural' gluttony and sloth were framed as deserving of their obesity, and deserving of (moral) scrutiny and judgement. While clearly related to the overall theme's central organising concept, this was a distinctive aspect; creating a subtheme (*deserving/undeserving obesity*) allowed us to capture and highlight an important patterned element of the data. Subthemes are useful where there are one or two overarching patterns within the data in relation to your question, but each is played out in a number of *different* ways.

Reviewing our candidate themes also affirmed that our candidate theme *those halcyon days of yore* contained enough depth/richness to stand as its own as a theme. Although relatively 'small' as a theme, it contains its own clear central organising concept – a romanticised view of the past as a place where we lived active healthy lives that precluded obesity – which is distinct from the central organising concept of the theme it acts as a contrast to, *modern life is rubbish*. Noting that this theme is relatively 'small' brings us to a final important point about themes: theme size. Your themes don't have to be the same 'size' as each other. Some may be smaller and less complex, with a single core idea that's relatively straightforward and contains only a few different elements; others might be complex and contain a number of distinct ideas in relation to the central organising concept, and thus potentially contain one or more subthemes. It's always good to think about the relationships between themes, both hierarchically and laterally, and to check whether small themes are really subthemes of larger themes. The litmus test for whether or not a theme is its own theme, or the subtheme of something else, is whether it shares a central organising concept with another theme.

WHEN SHOULD I STOP WITH REVIEWING AND MOVE ON WITH THE ANALYSIS?

When is enough reviewing enough? Theoretically, you could keep reviewing your candidate themes indefinitely, because data do not contain a definitive set of pre-existing themes that you will eventually 'discover'. Remember this, and don't be tempted by the idea of finding the *perfect* 'fit'. Your themes continue to take shape in the next phase of analysis – which also takes lots of time – so once you don't want to make any substantial changes to your thematic map, it's a good time to stop and move on. You should end this phase with a set of distinctive, coherent themes, and a sense of how they fit together and the overall story they tell about the data.

OTHER WAYS OF IDENTIFYING PATTERNS ACROSS DATA

The process we have described is based on the methods outlined for TA. It describes a process for a systematic and thorough engagement with the data, based on the assumptions and core principles of that method (Braun & Clarke, 2006, 2012). Different methods of qualitative analysis (e.g. IPA, GT) follow somewhat different processes, which emanate from and align with the theoretical commitments of each approach. Both IPA and GT specify processes for pattern identification beyond coding, which we now outline and illustrate.

WHAT'S DIFFERENT IN PATTERN IDENTIFICATION IN IPA?

For IPA, procedures for pattern generation are very clear and there isn't a lot of disagreement among practitioners. The procedure in IPA is somewhat different from TA. There are two levels at which themes are generated: **emergent themes** and superordinate themes. A key difference from TA is that both levels of theme development are completed *for each data item*, before the next data item is considered. This reflects IPA's idiographic focus, and means that the individual case detail and variation retains a much stronger presence in IPA analysis. Once all data items have been examined, superordinate themes are compared across the whole dataset, to determine the final (master) themes that will be presented in the overall analysis. This comparison involves a further layer of refinement, and a possible shift to more conceptual or theoretically informed themes (Smith et al., 2009).

Emergent themes are developed from the original data item (e.g. interview transcript) *and* the exploratory comments, and are about producing 'concise and pithy statement[s] about what was important' (Smith et al., 2009: 92) in the exploratory comments. Emergent themes aim to capture elements that appear to be crucial for the developing analysis; they reflect a mix of staying *close* to the participant's experience, and the analyst's developing interpretation. They sit somewhere between codes and themes in a TA approach. IPA practitioners recommend writing the emergent themes on left-hand side of the transcript (with exploratory comments on the right). Table 10.2 shows an example on an extract from the FG data we 'coded' with exploratory comments in relation to the research question 'What is the subjective experience of obesity?'.

Superordinate themes broadly map onto themes in TA, and are developed through searching for *patterns* of connection across emergent themes, in any number of ways. These include: *abstraction*, whereby many similar emergent themes are clustered together to form a similarly oriented but slightly more abstracted superordinate theme, closely related to a core issue; *subsumption,* where an emergent theme becomes a superordinate theme, with other emergent themes clustering 'under' this new superordinate theme, somewhat akin to the promotion of codes in GT (Charmaz, 2006); and *polarisation*, where differences rather than similarities are considered (see Smith et al., 2009, for more detail and other techniques). Although IPA doesn't promote the use of visual mapping, this could also be useful.

To illustrate superordinate and master themes, we continue with our analysis of data from our FG (see Box 10.3). Data relating to the instances where two participants, Sally and Carla, talked about their personal experiences of obesity and gastric band surgery for weight-reduction, were selected out from the whole focus group. The superordinate

Table 10.2 Emergent themes in our FG data

Emergent themes	Original data	Exploratory comments
		Descriptive comments
Fatness is painful (physically and psychologically)	Sally: Well I know when I was at my biggest and this wasn't this	A fat self means a painful/hard life, a life of suffering
Being fat equals physical restriction	was after all the surgeries and everything I was walking back	Shame as a powerful emotion associated with being fat
	normally again erm I I was having	Revelation of dramatic weight loss
Weight loss is transformative for the self	back ache leg ache god knows what else, and it was affect- I	Dramatic weight loss experienced as transformative and dramatic, physically and psychologically
		Confidence is gained through weight loss; the slim(mer) self is a confident, engaged self
		Linguistic comments
Fatness is shameful	mean I've lost seven stone so far and (.) it really has had a dramatic	'…all the surgeries and everything' – suggests a lot to contend with (a lot pushing her toward obesity)
Being fat equals psychological restriction	impact on the way I	Use of first person I pronouns throughout, no depersonalising in this story (which is one of triumph over fatness)
	walk around but I think it's all	Sally's valuing of slimness evident in language 'nice slim people' - but it's a curious turn of phrase,
	had a bigger impact on how I feel	because not only does it suggest slimness is desirable; it equates being slim with being nice
Triumph over adversity	about myself cos I'm not I don't think I'd have started	By emphasising the negatives of being fat, Sally's narratives reinforce the desirability of being slim
Slim is good	the university course had I been	'Amazing' is powerful and dramatic language which bolsters the enormity of the transformation
		Conceptual comments
Slim is desirable	the weight I was cos I'd have been	A fat self seems to mean a life of restriction. Talk of physical pain in exercise evokes restricted physical
Fatness is stigmatised	too ashamed sounds awful but	possibility. Restriction here though is far more psychological, a result of Sally self-policing herself due to
	I would have been too ashamed	her shame associated with fatness, and fear of being the target of judgmental gazes, fear of standing out,
	and felt I can't do that cos I can't	fear of social stigma – which she manages by staying at home (imprisoned by fatness)
Surveillance of fatness	go out in public where there's	Sally talks about her experience in a very individualised way, her experience of shame is real and true,
Slimness is liberatory	all these nice slim people and they're all going to look at me and	but she does not make external attributions around this and blame a 'nasty' fat-phobic society which produces that shame
Slimness is confidence	think 'oh look at you' you know so I didn't whereas because I'd lost	A non-fat life is a liberated and free life – this seems also to be about an experience where weight is a dominant and defining feature in this person's life
	the weight it gave me so much more confidence it was amazing	

themes we developed from Sally's experience also applied to Carla's, and so in Box 10.3 we just present one summary of the superordinate (master) themes, with a selection of emergent themes related to the superordinate themes, and selected brief illustrative data extracts. We also provide brief summaries, as we are not including the actual analysis. (NB: Both our emergent and superordinate themes sit at the more 'socially oriented' end of the IPA spectrum; see Chapter 8.) A compiled table of superordinate (and emergent) themes in IPA, like that shown in Box 10.3, should both capture what you want to say about the data, and the order you want to say it in. It's effectively a shorthand road-map for your analysis and we recommend presenting it at the start of your results (for an example, see Eatough et al., 2008; see also Chapter 13). After this stage, the IPA analysis moves into a deeper interpretative level (see Chapter 11).

WHAT'S DIFFERENT IN PATTERN IDENTIFICATION IN GT?

The procedures for GT are in some ways similar to TA, but can *seem* very different, because GT uses quite different language. Furthermore, unlike IPA, there seem to be as many different processes and terms for coding and analysis in GT as there are authors on the subject (see Birks & Mills, 2011). We will briefly outline some of the unique and key elements specific to GT (drawing on Birks & Mills, 2011; Charmaz, 2006; Pidgeon & Henwood, 1996, 2004).

In GT, the shift from the initial to the intermediate stage (Birks & Mills, 2011) of coding signals a different level of engagement with the data, but there's no pre-determined point at which it's time to shift from 'coding' to 'theme development' (unlike TA and IPA); the shift from initial to more 'focused' (Charmaz, 2006), 'core' (Pidgeon & Henwood, 2004) or 'intermediate' (Birks & Mills, 2011) coding in GT does not occur when all data items have been coded. Instead, it's a judgement on the part of the researcher that they have reached a point where they are starting to see *categories*, rather than codes, in the data and think that close (line-by-line) coding is no longer productive (Birks & Mills, 2011). This is partly about reaching code satura-tion, when the initial coding phase stops generating anything new in relation to the concepts explored (this might mean not all data are fully coded or that you have made a number of sweeps through the data). However, the shift between coding 'levels' is not a direct linear, progressive process; it can be recursive (Charmaz, 2006; Pidgeon & Henwood, 2004).

A number of different coding practices can apply in this stage, such as focused and axial coding. Focused coding (to use Charmaz's, 2006, term) involves refining an index-ing system of initial codes to determine ones that are analytically useful, and using these as a basis for re-engaging with the data at a less fine-grained (i.e. not line-by-line) level. The analytic process is essentially about shifting from narrower codes to broader cat-egories, and building a more theoretical or conceptual analytic take on the data. This may involve simply 'raising' codes to categories, or developing categories by divid-ing codes, or by clustering codes (Pidgeon & Henwood, 2004), similar to the process of theme development in TA. This phase also requires writing clear definitions of each category (again, similar to writing theme definitions in TA; see Chapter 11). Exploring

BOX 10.3   SUPERORDINATE THEMES IN OUR FG DATA

The fat self is a restricted self – captures the ways the experience of being fat was described as one of physical restriction, but also importantly one of psychological restriction.

Being fat equals physical restriction

Sally: I was having back ache leg ache god knows what else

Carla: That weight you know really feeling like it was slowing me down and struggling to sort of run after [my children]

Being fat equals psychological restriction

Sally: I would have been too ashamed and felt I can't do [a degree] cos I can't go out in public

The slim self is a free self – captures the way slimness was seen as desirable, and associated with being able to live a freer life, and thus be a different person; and the way losing weight was experienced as liberating

Slimness is liberatory

Sally: Because I'd lost the weight it gave me so much more confidence it was amazing

Weight loss is transformative for the self

Sally: It's all had a bigger impact on how I feel about myself

A spoiled identity: the stigma and shame of fatness – captures the experience of shame relating to social stigma around fatness, highlighting the emotional and relational experience of fatness, such as the emotional aspects of a *diagnosis* of obesity.

Fatness is shameful

Sally: I don't think I'd have started the university course had I been the weight I was cos I'd have been too ashamed

Carla: You look at yourself and think 'oh I'm disgusting'

Diagnosis as obese as a negative experience

Sally: Clinically I was classed as obese I used to find it really degrading and insulting

Carla: 'Oh my god I might as well just go and shoot myself now' you know

My fatness is not my fault – captures the way obesity was characterised as happening to them, rather than something they did themselves.

Response to depression

Sally: Suddenly you feel a little bit depressed as well so (well) you tend to have the knock-on effect of eating

Carla: Depression kicks in and it becomes this vicious cycle

Obesity results from metabolic factors beyond the person's control

Sally: I have a very slow metabolism [...] there's nothing I can do to change it

Carla: I have to have huge doses of steroids which why I'm overweight at the moment

There's no easy way out of obesity – captures the way obesity was experienced as an ever-present threat in their lives.

Weight is hard to lose

Carla: It becomes such a huge mountain to climb

Carla: I fought to get it off

Weight is easy to gain

Sally: If I look at a cream cake I put pounds on

Carla: Half of its gone back on again

---

relationships between categories, and mapping or modelling these relationships (Pidgeon & Henwood, 2004), rather than *just* identifying and defining categories, is important (just as it is in TA).

Axial coding (Corbin & Strauss, 1990) is a formalised technique for conceptually mapping the relationships between categories (and sub-categories) through an 'exhaustive coding' (Pidgeon & Henwood, 2004: 640) process; it is an extra layer of analysis that although potentially useful is not critical (Charmaz, 2006). Charmaz (2006: 61) suggests that axial coding can 'extend or limit your vision' depending on the focus of your research and your 'ability to tolerate ambiguity'. Researchers who prefer more structure will benefit from axial coding whereas those who value a more flexible approach may feel limited by it (see also Pidgeon & Henwood, 2004).

'Advanced' memos, which are more conceptual and relate to the developing conceptual analysis (see Box 10.4), can also be useful for developing the relationships between categories. Through different coding phases and practices, the GT researcher produces

---

BOX 10.4   AN ADVANCED MEMO

Different levels of explanation (18 August 2010)

We're noticing there are three seemingly quite distinct levels of explanation within the data about the factors that seem to cause individuals to become obese, and also to explain the so-called obesity epidemic. The first level we might call structural – this is factors that relate to the very nature and organisation of society (e.g. Sally: 'our lifestyle has changed' [L154]). An example of this would be the idea that we now lead very sedentary lives, compared to what we did in the past, and that this results from the ways our jobs and working lives are organised. NB this explanation seems quite classed; to reflect a middle-class sensibility or conception of what a job entails (not physical labour) and this is applied universally as 'the way things are'. The second level seems to relate to the way we are brought up to be as people – we might term these socialisation – so education and what we are taught or not in schools would relate here (e.g. Carla: 'teaching them to cook at school you know' [L871]). Mostly this is negative. Then there are explanations which are about what individuals do or don't do. Some of these are things that happen to the person, or that the person has no control over (like their biology; e.g. Sally: 'I mean metabolism does seem to have a lot to do with it" [L288]); others are things they themselves 'choose' (e.g. whether they 'overeat'; Rebecca: 'I have a twelve year old brother and he just eats what the hell he likes' [L497]). The levels seem to interrelate (e.g. structural factors enable personal tendencies; Judy: 'modern technology, like allows you to be lazy as well' [L162]). This may form the basis for a model of explanation about why a person becomes obese.

---

lots of information to help them develop their analysis – either a GT-lite version (see Chapter 11 for the model we developed from the FG data), or to continue to move to a full GT. This information includes: definitions of categories; the indexing system; memos; models and maps of the categories and relationships between them; and the coded dataset itself. There are two important points to remember: 1) although the analysis becomes more theorised, and shifts to the more conceptual domain, it needs to remain grounded in the data; 2) the research question can be refined to more clearly fit the developing analysis (Pidgeon & Henwood, 2004).

WHAT ABOUT PATTERN-BASED DA?

Methods of pattern-based DA, in contrast, tend not to offer structured guidance about the steps and processes for identifying 'different' *patterns* in the data, but instead, following selective coding (see Chapter 9), involve reading and re-reading the data to identify and interpret patterns and features of the selected data (Coyle, 2007; Parker, 1992;

Willig, 2008). This means the somewhat mysterious 'analytic sensibility' is particularly important for pattern-based DA. Because the process is at the more interpretative end of analysis, we discuss it in Chapter 11.

CAN AND SHOULD I GO BEYOND LOOKING FOR PATTERNS?

Our focus is on identifying and analysing *patterns* across qualitative datasets, and pattern-based approaches can be applied to almost any qualitative dataset. However, there are other elements that can be explored in qualitative data (e.g. stories, interaction; discussed in Boxes 8.1–8.3), and certain *forms* of data suit particular types of analysis better than others (see Table 3.2 in Chapter 3). *Story-completion tasks* (see Chapter 6) are unique among the participant-based methods of qualitative data collection we've discussed in this book. They require participants to *write stories* (about a hypothetical situation) rather than responding to questions about their experiences or providing their views, which is what other methods ask participants to do. This means that story completion data are rather different from all other forms of qualitative data. And while it's still useful to identify and analyse patterns in story completion data, there are some other questions we can ask when analysing story completion data. These are described in Box 10.5. One strategy we discuss is 'mapping' the stories and Figure 10.2 provides an example of a visual mapping of stories from one of Victoria's student's projects.

BOX 10.5   DIFFERENT THINGS TO DO WITH STORY COMPLETION DATA

In addition to identifying and analysing patterns in story completion data, there are some other questions we can ask when analysing story completion data to make the best use of the unique data generated by story completion tasks:

Is there a 'model' story (or stories) within the dataset? Ask yourself whether you can identify a structure that it common to all or most of the stories, or a subset of stories. Identifying a model story is a clear way to provide an overview of your data, while preserving the integrity of the 'storied' data. Beth Cooper (an undergraduate student of Victoria's) used story completion tasks to explore stories around a daughter ('Sarah') disclosing a non-heterosexual identity to her parents. Her visual overview of her data (see Figure 10.2) provides an excellent example of a map of how stories tended to unfold. Beth's analysis identified that while the stories contained different elements, most started in a

(Continued)

BOX 10.5 (*continued*)

similar way, with the parents portrayed as initially expressing shock in response to their daughter's disclosure. Most stories then took one of two paths – a negative or positive reaction from the parents – and these paths led to three different resolutions (negative, positive or ambiguous). Stories with positive middles all had positive endings: stories with negative middles could end in any one of the three ways.

Is knowing how the story ends important? In looking at story completion data, consider whether categorising the resolutions/endings of stories is particularly pertinent to your research question. It may or may not be. In our story completion research on people's perceptions of trans parenting (see Chapter 6 and the **companion website**), the ways in which the stories are resolved is highly relevant to our research question. So whether stories end 'happily ever after' with acceptance of the parent undergoing a gender transition and the family remaining together (e.g. 'Eventually after the surgery, all the family are back to how they were before. Maybe even better than they were because Brian is now truly happy and himself. All children get on very well with the new "Brian"'; PF008B) or rejection of the parent and disruption of the family unit (e.g. 'He felt empty without his family and out of place in his new body [...] He lived out the rest of his life on the dole abusing lighter fluid and ruing the choices he made'; PM067B) potentially tells us something interesting about the meanings people make of a parent undergoing a gender transition. Furthermore, as we used a comparative design (comparing the responses of male and female participants, and comparing participants' responses to a male and female parent), we could explore, for example, gender differences in portrayals of the acceptance or rejection of the trans parent.

Is reporting numbers useful? In contrast to most qualitative research (see Box 11.6), it may be useful to count and report frequencies when analysing story completion data, depending on your research question. Frequency might be useful when looking at certain concrete features of the data, and in comparisons between different versions of the story and/or different participant groups. In Kitzinger and Powell's (1995) study of perceptions of infidelity in heterosexual relationships (see Illustrative Research Example 6.2 in Chapter 6), for example, they were interested in exploring the assumptions that participants made about the phrase 'seeing someone else'. Given this interest, it made sense to concretely report how many participants interpreted this as (sexual) infidelity or something else, and how many assumed that the unfaithful partner was 'seeing someone' of the opposite or same sex.

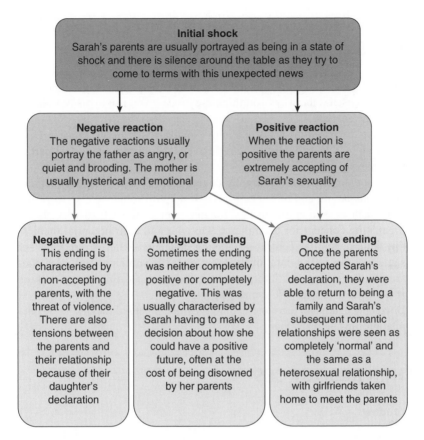

Figure 10.2   Story-map showing key elements in a story-completion task (people's perceptions of Sarah 'coming out' as non-heterosexual to her parents)

CHAPTER SUMMARY

This chapter:

- described the process of searching for patterns (themes) across coded data and a dataset;
- demonstrated the process of reviewing candidate themes identified in the data;
- outlined particular considerations in dealing with qualitative survey and story completion task data;
- described the different processes of pattern recognition when using IPA and GT.

? QUESTIONS FOR DISCUSSION AND CLASSROOM EXERCISES

1   In small groups, identify key differences in process of analysis between TA, IPA and GT. Discuss the ways you think the *process* you use to analyse the data might shape the analysis.

2   We have discussed the ways qualitative analysis is an *active* process. Discuss what we mean by this, and why being reflexive is therefore an important part of qualitative analysis.

3   Using a dataset you have already coded, identify two potential themes – if possible, one latent, and one semantic. Pair up with someone else working with the same dataset, and compare the 'themes' you've identified. Identify the central organising concept for each theme. Do your and their potential themes relate to the same or similar central organising concepts – that is, are you 'seeing' the same patterns in the data, or different ones? If you have both identified similar themes, have you each interpreted the theme in a similar way – why the theme is interesting and how it is meaningful?

4   Develop a candidate thematic map to illustrate potential themes in the data, and the relationships between them.

FURTHER RESOURCES

Further reading:

One of the most useful ways to see the process of analysis is through *worked* examples.

For a worked example of thematic analysis, see: Braun, V., & Clarke, V. (2012). Thematic analysis. In H. Cooper (Ed.), *Handbook of research methods in psychology*. (vol. 2: Research Designs; pp. 57–71) Washington, DC: APA Books.

For a worked example of IPA, see: Storey, L. (2007). Doing interpretative phenomenological analysis. In A. Coyle & E. Lyons (Eds), *Analysing qualitative data in psychology* (pp. 51–64). London: Sage.

For a worked example of GT, see: Appendix in Birks, M., & Mills, J. (2011). *Grounded theory: A practical guide*. London: Sage.

For a worked example of pattern-based DA, see: Edley, N. (2001a). Analysing masculinity: interpretative repertoires, ideological dilemmas and subject positions. In M. Wetherell, S. Taylor, & S. J. Yates (Eds), *Discourse as data: A guide for analysis* (pp. 189–228). London: Sage.

For a worked example of how to do Foucauldian DA, see the chapter on Foucauldian Discourse Analysis in: Willig, C. (2008). *Introducing qualitative research in psychology: Adventures in theory and method* (2nd ed., pp. 112–131). Maidenhead, UK: Open University Press. (Note that there are different 'takes' on 'how to do' Foucauldian DA; Willig outlines one approach in an accessible manner; not all Foucauldian DA analyses follow these guidelines.)

Online resources:

See the *companion website* (**www.sagepub.co.uk/braunandclarke**) for:
- self-test multiple choice questions relating to Section 3;
- the flashcard glossary – test yourself on the definitions of key terms used in this chapter;
- an extended version of Table 10.1;
- the weight and obesity FG transcript, the orgasm survey sample dataset, and the trans parenting story sample dataset;
- further readings (articles from Sage journals).

11 Analysing and interpreting patterns across data

OVERVIEW

The relationship between analysis and writing in qualitative research
Defining themes
Developing the analysis
Analysing patterns across data using other approaches
Doing pattern-based analysis well

Once you've got a good idea of your themes and subthemes, it's time to really work with the data to develop your analysis fully. You've spent a lot of time already engaging, coding and developing your candidate themes; this phase goes a lot deeper. In some ways, although all the other work you have done so far has been *analytic*, it is preparatory for the work you now have to do: deep analytic interpretative work to make sense of, and interpret, the patterns you've identified in the data. This involves the crucial moulding of the analysis into its fine-grained detail. This is also the point at which you start writing in a serious way, as writing goes hand in hand with *doing* qualitative analysis

THE RELATIONSHIP BETWEEN ANALYSIS AND WRITING IN QUALITATIVE RESEARCH

You cannot really *do* qualitative analysis without *writing* it. You can have insights and thoughts, but you can't complete your analysis of the data and *then* write it up, because qualitative analysis *is* writing. It uses words to tell the story about textual (and visual)

data. This means writing *is* the process through which the analysis develops into its final form (see Chapter 13 for more on *writing* skills and tips). Although we have elsewhere separated the stages of thematic analysis (TA) into 'defining themes' and 'writing the report' (Braun & Clarke, 2006, 2012), here we discuss these as a more interwoven process, which is what happens in practice.

The pile of information with which you begin the journey deep into analysis might include: lots of annotated, highlighted transcripts; lists of initial codes and categories; lots of analytic notes; files of excerpted, collated, and coded data for each candidate theme, some kind of visual mapping of your potential analysis; and analytic notes about some data extracts. Through the interlinked processes of analysis and writing, you transform this mass of (messy) information into a complex, nuanced yet streamlined analysis that tells a clear, coherent and compelling story about the data and what they mean.

DEFINING THEMES

In working towards your final analysis, you need to be able to clearly *define* your themes, to state what is unique and specific about each. Writing *theme definitions* is a useful discipline to engage in at this point. It forces you to define the focus and boundaries of your themes, to really distil to an essence (a few short sentences) what each theme is about. You can quickly see if the scope of any theme isn't clear. Box 11.1 presents definitions of the overaching themes and subthemes from our analysis of the weight and obesity focus group (FG) data. Each theme has a clear focus, scope and purpose, is relatively discrete (although the themes are related, and the subthemes in particular build on the previous analysis), and together the themes provide a rich, coherent and meaningful picture of dominant patterns in the data that addresses our research question. (Your explanation should be the most plausible; if there are other plausible interpretations, these should be considered, evaluated and/or discounted.)

DEVELOPING THE ANALYSIS

At this point, you should have a pretty good sense of the scope of each theme. So what does analysis now actually involve? From all your coded and collated data for each candidate theme, you now select the extracts that you will use to illustrate the different facets of each theme, and write a narrative around those extracts, which tells the reader the 'story' of each theme. The analysis you present has been described as 'a deliberate and self-consciously artful creation by the researcher [which] must be constructed to persuade the reader of the plausibility of an argument' (Foster & Parker, 1995: 204). The data you select to quote and analyse are vital in convincing the reader of your analysis, so it's important to select these carefully (see Box 11.2). Ideally, you want extracts that are vivid, and compellingly illustrate the analytic point you are making about your data. For instance, in Virginia's study of sexual health, where she identified 'national identity' explanations around 'risk' for sexually transmitted infections as a key theme, one of the

---

BOX 11.1   THEME DEFINITIONS FROM OUR FG DATA

Human nature

An overarching theme that explains obesity and weight-gain as things that occur as a result of our 'human nature'. Participants constructed human nature in a few particular ways, all of which were largely negative: humans as lazy, gluttonous and ignorant. The theme 'exercise is evil' explores an implicit model of humans as inherently lazy, and thus naturally inclined not to engage in activities that require *effort* (such as exercise), situating weight-gain and obesity as natural propensities. A corresponding construction was of exercise as an inherently unpleasant activity. The theme *sins and sinners* captures another implicit model of humans – as inherently gluttonous, so that given the opportunity, we will 'over' eat, and eat unhealthy things, meaning we have a natural tendency to gain weight and become obese. Across both themes is a tension: the expectation that a good person *should* overcome their human nature, and be neither lazy not gluttonous. This moral tension is explored in the subtheme of *deserving/undeserving obesity*, which illustrates the categorisation of obese people into those who should be condemned (it's their own fault) and those who should be saved or sympathised with (they cannot help their obesity).

Modern life

An overarching theme which explains weight-gain and obesity as a result of the features of our contemporary society (rather than human nature, although these two intersect). Frequent references to an idealised past are discussed in the theme *those halcyon days of yore*. This mythical past was one in which people led healthier lives, and was clearly contrasted with the way the present was talked about. The theme *modern life is rubbish* captures two facets of talk about the present. First, the structural organisation and functioning of society was described as enabling (even demanding) all sorts of *unhealthy* behaviours; second, this was seen to produce 'rubbish' people who (understandably) make unhealthy choices. Within this, modern technology was situated as dominating our lives, and being an enemy of healthiness, described in the subtheme *technology trumps all*. The final theme, *they don't get no education*, highlights contemporary failures of education, both formal and informal, so that people are ignorant of ways to be healthy, and subject to the impacts of subsequent 'unhealthy' choices.

---

subthemes was around a binge-drinking culture. The following quote from one participant, Francesca, captures both 'drinking' and 'cultural' elements of this succinctly: 'like New Zealand in- maybe a cultural thing like, we have quite a binge drinking culture, specially in the teenage population. That may have something to do with it, like every weekend getting smashed' (Braun, 2008: 1819–1820). You also want to draw extracts

---

BOX 11.2   SELECTING AND PRESENTING DATA EXTRACTS

Two purposes of including qualitative data extracts are evidence your analytic claims, and to allow the reader to judge the 'fit' between your data and your understandings and interpretations of them. In addition to selecting vivid and compelling extracts, and avoiding selecting all of your extracts from the same participant (or data item), it is important to:

- Save words by editing out any unnecessary detail or irrelevant material from data extracts. It is good practice to tell the reader that you have edited data extracts, and to use something like '[…]' to signal where you have removed anything more than repetitions or hesitations. It's acceptable to delete hesitation and repetition without acknowledgement (removal of such features can be characterised as 'cleaning up' the data, which should be signalled in your methods section; see Chapter 7) (see Sandelowski, 1994b).

- Add punctuation to transcribed audio data, to accentuate readability, but make sure that it does not change the meaning of the data (see Chapter 7).

- Avoid using the same data extract more than once, unless absolutely necessary.

- Contextualise data extracts if necessary – for example, when quoting a short extract from an interview or FG, it may help the reader to understand the meaning of the extract by telling them something about the discussion it is part of (e.g. 'when discussing her frustration with the mind-set of health professionals, Alia noted that …').

- Always include a way for the reader to identify the speaker (or source) of each extract – this could be the participant's pseudonym, or a data ID code – so that the reader can identify the different sources you have drawn on, and track data from individual participants or sources.

- Humanise participants by using pseudonyms rather than participant codes/numbers, especially when reporting interview and focus group studies, and studies with smaller samples (e.g. interpretative phenomenological analysis [IPA] studies).

- If relevant, identify salient features of the participant (or data item) you are quoting, a process that has been called 'staging' quotes (Sandelowski, 1994b). For example, in a project on the clothing practices of non-heterosexuals, where age and gender are relevant features of the data, at a minimum you would want to identify each participant with a pseudonym and information about their sexuality, gender and age (e.g. 'Ollie, a 21-year-old gay man, noted that …'); in other cases, more or less information may be necessary to contextualise the data extract.

- Present data extracts appropriately. As a general guideline, shorter extracts (roughly less than three lines of text/40 words) should be embedded in the main text, typically within a sentence using quotation marks to show where the quote begins and ends (see Kitzinger & Willmott, 2002, for a good example of how to present short quotations). If presenting a few shorter extracts together, or for longer extracts, show these in their own separate paragraph, which should be indented from the main text. For indented data, the use of quotation marks is not necessary (see Braun, 2008, for an example).

from *across* your data, which shows the breadth or spread of a theme. It's always the case with audio and some written data that some participants are more articulate than others, making it tempting to always use their extracts. But providing extracts from only a few participants could make your analysis seem more *selective* than it actually is (see Chapter 12). Although patterns don't need to be identified in every data item (see Braun & Clarke, 2006), you do want to have – and show – evidence of spread across the dataset, as this *is* the aim of a pattern-based analysis.

TREATING DATA ILLUSTRATIVELY OR ANALYTICALLY

The analysis is the narrative you write around the data, which tells the reader *your* story about the content and meaning of the data – and the extracts themselves are a crucial part of it. There are two main ways data extracts can be treated in qualitative analysis (of all types). One is to treat the extracts as illustrative examples; the other is to actually provide an analysis of the content of the extract itself. This distinction is important. In the illustrative approach, your analytic narrative provides a rich and detailed description and interpretation of the theme, and data quotations inserted throughout are used as examples of the analytic points you are claiming. If you were to remove your extracts of data from the narrative, it would still make sense to a reader. They would want to see 'evidence' from the data, but it would still be a thorough and coherent description. In the treating extracts analytically approach, your analysis would not make sense if the extracts were removed, as your analytic narrative is closely tied to the *content* of the extracts presented. Indeed, in your analytic narrative, you would make specific interpretative claims about the *particular* extracts you present – as well as making more general descriptive or interpretative comments about the patterns in the data overall.

These two different approaches to treating data can map onto two broad styles of TA: a more *descriptive* and often *essentialist* form of analysis, which aims to closely tell the 'story of the data', and so tends to use extracts more illustratively, and a more *conceptual* and *interpretative*, and often *constructionist*, form of analysis, typically focusing on more **latent meanings**, that frequently provides a more detailed analysis of particular extracts. Box 11.3 provides a brief example of these two styles applied to the same extract of data.

Interpretative forms of analysis can be more difficult to 'get' at first; it can take experience in qualitative analysis to be able to look 'beyond' the explicit or semantic meanings in the data, to identify more implicit or latent meanings (questions to assist this are discussed later in this chapter). This of course also depends on the topic, and on your familiarity with the empirical and theoretical literature; if you know an area really well, the latent meanings may be fairly quickly apparent to you (as Virginia's research journal example shows; see Box 3.8 in Chapter 3). Each approach to TA has a different purpose, and it's important that the form you choose maps onto your research question. In some cases, semantic and latent approaches might be combined, with the analysis moving from initially descriptive beginnings to more interpretative endings.

BOX 11.3   TREATING DATA ILLUSTRATIVELY VS. ANALYTICALLY: EXAMPLES FROM THE OVERARCHING THEME 'MODERN LIFE' USING THE SAME DATA EXTRACT

An example of using data illustratively

Participants frequently described contemporary society as unsafe and unhealthy, and contrasted this with an idealised account of the past, which was set up as implicitly healthier than the present. These distinctions related to many aspects of life, from the food we eat and the exercise we get to the ways children play; many are captured in the following comment from Anna:

> I think, you know, kids sit inside and they play their computer games all the time. Erm and maybe it's not even safe in society to go out on your bikes now. Do you know what I mean? Like when my Dad was...he was saying 'I know when I was a boy I'd go out for hours in the country and da-da-da-da'. And now you can't go outside without an adult cos you're worried about being mugged. So it's like it's what do you do really?

An example of using data analytically

Participants frequently described contemporary society as unsafe and unhealthy, and contrasted this with an idealised account of the past, which was set up as implicitly healthier than the present. For example:

> I think, you know, kids sit inside and they play their computer games all the time. Erm and maybe it's not even safe in society to go out on your bikes now. Do you know what I mean? Like when my Dad was...he was saying 'I know when I was a boy I'd go out for hours in the country and da-da-da-da'. And now you can't go outside without an adult cos you're worried about being mugged. So it's like it's what do you do really? (Anna)

Here, Anna contrasts a grim view of the present (see *modern life is rubbish*) with a nostalgic and almost idealised view of the past (see *those halcyon days of yore*). Her father's claimed 'hours out in the country' evoke an image of freedom, adventure and health (fresh air, exercise). This image of the past serves as a direct contrast to the image of the present, a frightening reality where it is not safe for children to occupy space external to the home without supervision. In making a direct contrast in this way, the internal, sedentary, computer-gaming behaviour of contemporary children – often claimed as unhealthy and problematic – is rendered blameless. It is not just that children are lazy; modern life (contemporary society) is responsible for creating a context in which children *need* to remain indoors, for their own good, and people are helpless to do anything different in the face of this unpleasant reality. With this extract, then, Anna manages to render the present undesirable, but our behaviour in the present understandable, even required. Paradoxically, the 'unhealthy' behaviour of contemporary children is rendered almost 'healthy', a result of *good* parenting rather than bad.

ACTUALLY ANALYSING DATA

Making sure you're actually *analysing* the data is absolutely crucial at this stage. Analysis, even when it is descriptive, does not involve paraphrasing what an extract says (Antaki, Billig, Edwards, & Potter, 2002); instead, it has to tell the reader *what is* interesting about the data – and particular data extracts – and *why* that is. Even if you use extracts illustratively, they have to be embedded in your narrative; your narrative guides the reader as to what sense they should make of the extract, and why it's relevant and interesting.

One important thing is getting the balance right between data extracts and analytic narrative. Typically you want to have as much narrative as data extracts (or more, especially if you are doing a more interpretative analysis; Sandelowski, 1994b); otherwise, you risk just bombarding the reader with data, without providing enough interpretation. Remember, data do not speak for themselves; *you* speak for the data. That is what analysis is. Even in the more inductive forms of qualitative pattern analysis (some forms of TA, grounded theory [GT] and interpretative phenomenological analysis [IPA]), when the analysis is descriptive and seemingly stays quite close the content of the data, analysis should move *beyond* the data. The job of pattern-based qualitative analysis is to organise data into patterns, interpret the data patterns and tell a story about them. Analysis *uses data to make a point*. Analysis needs to be driven by the question 'so what?' What is relevant or useful here to answering my question?

BEING PREPARED TO LET THINGS GO (STILL)

Another crucial thing to note is that the candidate themes you enter this phase with are not set in stone. Far from it; the process of analysis and defining themes means that some revision is likely (indeed probable), so that you may develop a new subtheme or theme at this stage. This is partly because, as you get more involved in interpreting the data, and the patterns you've identified in it, you're likely to see things in more depth, and with more nuance. This means you may well refine or reorganise the analysis to tell a story slightly different from what you were envisaging. There is an important caveat: at this stage you should have enough in-depth knowledge about your data and potential themes that these revisions would usually be *tweaks* to the existing structure rather than wholesale redevelopments (like changing your kitchen colour-scheme, rather than getting a whole new kitchen). That said, sometimes an analysis really doesn't 'work' when you get to this stage, and you do need to reject it and do something different. If that's the case, you have to go back a few steps and engage with the whole dataset again.

Box 11.4 provides an example of a final draft analysis from our FG data; we provide an excerpt from our constructionist TA of one of the two themes related to human nature: *exercise is evil* (the **companion website** provides the full write-up of this theme). The analysis, presented as we would write it in a report (e.g. a journal article), demonstrates the interweaving between more summative and descriptive analysis, which illustrates the scope of the theme in relation to the dataset, and detailed and specific interpretative analysis of what happens in a particular data extract.

BOX 11.4   EXTRACT FROM FINAL-DRAFT WRITE-UP OF THE THEME 'EXERCISE IS EVIL'

Exercise is evil

'Exercise is evil' captures a construction of the human as naturally slothful and lazy, and thus disinclined (unless pushed, or taught) to engage in *effortful* activities that are 'healthy' (such as exercise and cooking for yourself). For example, Judy commented that 'if people are working hard they want something quick which tends to be the unhealthy food rather than the healthy food'. The logic that informs a comment like this is that creating your own meal (the healthy option) is *effortful* and that effort is unpleasant. Talking about fast food, Rebecca made the comment 'and it's so cheap as well, just so...Like you can't justify making a...making a meal for like two pounds when you can go and buy something for the same amount of money, you know, you don't have to bother with the washing up.' This extract demonstrates a very narrow cost–benefit analysis, by suggesting that the time and effort involved with food preparation be analysed primarily on monetary terms. Here, again, the logic is that preparation of your own meal is an inherently demanding and unpleasant activity; against a quick and low cost meal, it simply cannot win. This relies on a construction of human beings as inherently motivated to avoid anything that requires time and/or effort, and situates such activities as unpleasant chores (in contrast, for instance, to other construction of cooking as a creative, even de-stressing, and therefore rewarding, activity [e.g. Hollows, 2003], or food as having personal meanings beyond cost, such as nutritional value or taste, or cultural or ritualistic meanings).

Such constructions often also linked into our other overarching theme of 'modern lifestyles' in many ways, for instance through reference to being 'too busy' to cook:

Anna: My friends that live up in Manchester and London, they find it's actually erm easier to buy food on the way home, kind of like take-out and stuff or go out for a meal, than it is actually to go home and start cooking something if you like finish work at eight or nine o'clock at night or something.

Such comments provide examples where the model of the person is one for whom a quick and easily solution is more (inherently) appealing than something constructed as requiring work, effort or physical energy expenditure.

For the most part, 'effort' was discussed in relation to exercise, with accounts of people as inherently disinclined to engage in exercise. Exercise itself was constructed as effortful, and thus unappealing, and possibly even 'evil' (the theme name is both playful, and captures the moral dimension to the theme). This appeared quite obviously in discussion of *motivation* around exercise. For example, in relation to the gym, Sally commented, 'you have to motivate yourself to go to the

(Continued)

BOX 11.4   (*continued*)

gym. Where at one time you didn't have to go to a gym because you worked physically or whatever, and now we have to motivate and I'm not motivated ((laughs)).' This extract evokes a person who only engages in exercise by necessity ('back in the day' we had to work hard), or if something else motivates them. In a context (the FG) where exercise was recognised as the 'right' thing to do (in relation to health; fitting with British public health messages), exercise was positioned implicitly as something that now '*has* to' be done, requiring effort and motivation (something 'extra'), rather than being something that just *is* done as part of daily life. This conceptually separated exercise from the things humans *naturally* do. Given *options*, humans do not 'choose' exercise:

> Sally: [...] my Mum used to walk two or three miles to go to the train station to go another ten miles to work, you know [...] There was no bus for her so she had to walk. And nowadays we think 'oh I can't do that, can't walk four miles to go and do that' ((laughs)).
>
> Rebecca: Take the car yeah.
>
> Sally: Yeah exactly.

'Motivation' becomes a key ingredient for overcoming inherent laziness, the obstacle to getting the exercise we need to be 'healthy' and not obese. In contrast to how she described her mother – getting exercise *because* she has no other options – Sally's account of her own gym-going behaviour suggested that it relied on another person: 'I've actually joined a gym and do I go? No. Because if I had somebody to go with, I'd be motivated to do it. [...] it's nice to have somebody to actually join that sort of thing and actually help you.' The idea that another person can ensure exercise occurs again relies on, and reproduces, the idea that there is nothing inherently attractive in about it, in and of itself. For Carla, a motivator in gym going had been time to *herself*, away from her small children: 'that was a real impetus to get me going. But I don't bother now ((laughs)).' The language she used is revealing – 'bother' evokes effort. The laughter at the end suggests a rueful acknowledgement of the disjuncture between what she *does* and what she *should do* – a 'giving in' to her human nature.

Alongside an inherent human laziness, exercise itself (as noted above) was constructed very negatively, as something that holds no intrinsic appeal. Rebecca, for instance, described being 'bored' with the gym. Although this was a prevalent theme in the data, it is important to consider that the participants in the focus group were all women, and although they did not articulate a *gendered* human being, but rather a non-gendered lazy *person* who dislikes exercise, the prevalence of this construction in our female-only group may reflect the gendered nature of sports and exercise participation, particularly throughout childhood and in educational settings (Flintoff & Scraton, 2005; Kirk, 2002). Indeed, physical exercise (PE) at school was described as unpleasant: 'It was a real chore and I used to think "oh god", you know, "not PE, oh I don't want to do that'" (Sally), and something actively avoided: 'I bunked every PE lesson I could possibly get away with' (Rebecca). Such commentary around sport and exercise at school echoes research which demonstrates girls' disengagement in physical activities and exercise (Whitehead & Biddle, 2008). However, as noted above, in our data this account of exercise and laziness was not overtly gendered.

As discussion of school PE hints at, this inherent laziness was ascribed to both children and adults, suggesting it as a *universal* human trait. Children's leisure activities were typically described as inside, sedentary, and technologically mediated (although the reasons for this were sometimes ascribed to society; see *modern life is rubbish*). Although not always framed as the children's 'fault', children's engagement in outdoor activity was typically framed as rare or unusual, and sometimes forced. For example, Carla described her home situation: 'It's like we've got a trampoline outside. I have to drag them out by their hair to try and get them to get on it, you know (Carla).'

However, this lazy human characteristic was not framed as insurmountable. For example, Judy described gym-going as 'easy' when she had a 'habit':

Judy: I think it's easy once you get in the habit as well cos I joined a gym and then I used to go every day or two or three times every day after work. And then stopped working and then came to uni and then you just get (yeah) you come out of the habit and it's harder to get into the habit again.

Here, a 'habit' could produce a different way of engaging with the world. [Analysis continues; see full version of the final draft analysis on the *companion website*.]

INTEGRATING LITERATURE INTO THE ANALYSIS

There are two things we hope you noticed in looking at our analysis in Box 11.4: i) we develop our analytic points *beyond* just summarising the content of the data; ii) there are some references to relevant literature. This analysis *interprets* the data, connects it to our research question and, importantly, ties our data and analysis in to existing scholarly literature. Linking your analysis to the literature is a vital part of any analysis (qualitative or not); it's about locating your analysis in relation to what already exists, and showing how your analysis contributes to, develops further, or challenges what we already know about a topic (see Box 11.5). How this gets done depends a bit on the style of report being produced. In line with 'mainstream' psychology models, some qualitative research contains a separate 'discussion' session; in others, the 'analysis' *combines* what has traditionally been seen as the content for 'results' and 'discussion' sections (see Chapter 13). That means literature is threaded throughout the analysis, and the analysis is expanded on this basis.

While either approach can work for a pattern-based analysis like TA, there are some advantages to an integrative approach: it avoids repetition between a results and discussion section, and it allows you to develop your analysis more fully, *as* it happens. An integrative approach works well when there are clear and strong connections with existing research, when existing theory or research help extend and develop your analysis, and when the analysis is more theoretical, interpretative, or latent. Times it works less well is when your analysis is primarily semantic and descriptive, where existing literature won't help you deepen or develop your analysis, or when your interpretation is less tied to particular points in the data, but instead related to the overall analysis. For example, in our largely descriptive TA of our experiences of orgasm and sexual pleasure survey data (see the **companion website** for the survey), our results section reported key themes in a straightforward way, and integrated a very small amount of literature; our discussion section explored more conceptual and theoretical issues related to the data analysis overall (Opperman, Braun, Clarke, & Rogers, in press).

Another thing we hope you noticed is that in the analysis of the theme 'exercise is evil' we don't use numbers in reporting on the theme (e.g. 'three of the participants reported …'). The use of numbers in reporting patterns is not common and although some would suggest their use (Maxwell, 2010; Sandelowski, 2001), and some use it (e.g. Dalla, 2002; Kim, 2009), we argue it is typically not good practice (see Box 11.6).

NAMING THEMES

It might seem strange to have a whole section on *naming* themes, but the names you give your themes require thought and creativity. What you call each theme is important – as it can signal both the content of, and your analytic 'take' on, the data. It's also a place where you can be creative! We enjoy theme names that are evocative, catchy, concise and informative. Sometimes a direct quote from the data can capture this perfectly, because it provides an immediate and vivid sense of what a theme is about, while staying close to participants' language and concepts. Other times, a subtitle might be necessary following a brief quotation, to signal the analytic scope. Sometimes you just want to give them your own names. That is what we did with the themes in our analysis of the FG data.

All of our themes have names which are catchy and which capture the essence of the theme's focus and tell you something about our analytic take. *Sins and sinners*, for instance, tells you that this theme is about people's own (bad) behaviours and practices. Moreover, it evokes a moralistic/biblical frame of reference for making sense of the world, which reflects the interpretative frameworks that participants evoked when discussing the causes of obesity. The title of *those halcyon days of yore* tells you that this is about 'the past' but it also is intended to capture the romanticised, idealised image of the past evoked in the data; we kept thinking about bucolic Constable paintings (see www.nationalgallery.org.uk/artists/john-constable) in relation to this theme. Finally, two theme names reference popular culture: *modern life is rubbish* was the title of a Blur album (back in our youth!), which perfectly captures the central organising concept of this theme; *they don't get no education* is a thinly veiled reference to Pink Floyd's song

---

BOX 11.5   USING EXISTING LITERATURE AND THEORETICAL CONCEPTS TO DEEPEN YOUR ANALYSIS

One of the ways you can *deepen* your analysis of your data and move beyond simply summarising and describing them is by using existing research and theoretical concepts to inform your analysis. For example, Eleni Demetriou (one of Victoria's students) used email interviews and an online qualitative survey to explore the experiences of adults who had grown up with a lesbian, gay or transgender (LGT) parent (or parents). When analysing her data, Eleni noticed some similarities between the patterns in her data and the themes identified in previous research on lesbian and gay parenting, specifically qualitative research exploring arguments used by lesbian and gay parents, and their allies, to defend their families in public discourse (e.g. Clarke & Kitzinger, 2004) and more conventional psychological research comparing the outcomes of children in lesbian and gay and heterosexual-headed families (e.g. Golombok & Tasker, 1996). So Eleni used this literature to help her develop and extend her analysis of her data.

For example, one of her themes 'It's not all about my parent's sexuality/gender identity' focused on the ways in which the participants often downplayed the significance of their LGT parent(s)' sexuality/gender identity when describing their upbringing. To illustrate this theme, Eleni quoted from Eva's interview in which she talked about being bullied at school: 'When I was younger it was part of a wider set of things I got teased for. I also got teased about e.g. wearing glasses or being studious, so I was teased because I was teased, not because my mother was lesbian but because I was the kind of kid to get picked on.' In her report, Eleni noted that this statement echoed the findings of comparative mainstream psychological research on lesbian mother families – children of LGBT parents are 'no more likely to get teased or bullied than children of non-LGBT parents' (Tasker & Golombok, 1997: 89–90). She then drew on critical psychological research on homophobic bullying (Clarke et al., 2004) to argue that Eva was *normalising* her experiences of homophobic bullying in order to *minimise* the impact of this bullying, and the implication that her mother was a bad parent because she *chose* to come out as a lesbian when Eva was growing up (just as mainstream psychologists arguably normalise homophobic bullying). Eva, like the other participants, was very protective of her LGT parent and keen to refute the notion that having an LGT parent is damaging to children. Eva individualised (rather than politicised) her experience of bullying (it was about her, and the type of person she was). In drawing on the literature in these ways, Eleni was able to move beyond simply describing that the participants resisted the notion that their parents' sexuality/gender identity was the defining feature of their upbringing, to explore *why* they did this and to theorise about what effects this pattern of meaning may have.

(Continued)

BOX 11.5 *(continued)*

Another of Victoria's students, Beth Cooper, used story completion tasks to explore people's perceptions of how parents react when their daughter (Sarah) comes out to them as non-heterosexual (see Box 10.5 and Figure 10.2 in Chapter 10). As part of her degree, Beth had attended a critical 'gender and sexuality' course, in which she learnt about critical concepts such as heterosexism (Adam, 1998) and heteronormativity (Warner, 1993). Beth applied this theoretical knowledge to her data analysis. She noticed, for example, that even though the story stem did not specify the gender of Sarah's parents, every participant assumed they were a heterosexual couple. She also noted that the parents were portrayed as assuming Sarah to be heterosexual, prior to her disclosure of her non-heterosexuality, and as having expectations of a 'heteronormative life-script' for Sarah – she would find the 'right' man, settle down, get married and have children. Beth's newly gained theoretical knowledge literally allowed her to see her data differently, and to dig deep into the data to identify the assumptions underpinning the stories.

'Another Brick in the Wall' (covered more recently by Marilyn Manson). This name tells you that this theme is about the education system, but also signals that this is a critique of that system (the music reference also signals this). In Ken Loach's (2009) superb film *Looking for Eric*, former football great Eric Cantona describes his desire to give the fans a 'gift' in each game through some special and unexpected play; less dramatically, theme names which reference something else can offer a 'treat' for those readers who recognise the reference. What we really want to signal is that you can have lots of *fun* naming themes. We do. But don't worry if you can't think of creative names. As long as the name captures the theme well, it will work as an effective theme name. What *is* crucial is that you have developed a *good* analysis of the theme (discussed more below), and the theme name captures the essence of your analysis (the same goes for the title of your report; see Chapter 13).

PRESENTING A RICH, INTERCONNECTED, LOGICAL ANALYSIS

Each theme needs to be developed not only in its own right, but in relation to your research question, and in relation to the other themes; the analysis should be interconnected. The order you present your themes in should be logical, with each new theme building on the previously discussed theme(s) to tell a richer, more detailed story about your data. If you have a *key* theme in the data, or one that underpins all other themes, discuss that first. Essentially, think about the logic of the story you are telling; the order you present your themes is determined by that. The way you order your analysis is also a crucial tool in conveying your story and analysis to your audience in a compelling way. When you get to the end of the analysis, the conclusions you reach should be drawn from across *the whole* analysis, and they should relate to the research questions you have set up (see Chapter 13, for more on 'writing up' analysis).

BOX 11.6   SHOULD I USE NUMBERS IN PATTERN ANALYSIS?

Most qualitative pattern analysis uses expressions like 'a common theme …', 'in a majority of the texts analysed …', or 'many participants commented that …' when reporting on the patterns in the data, and typically what such terms mean isn't specified (although see below). But wouldn't it be better to report *actual numbers* (e.g. 27 of the women …)? We argue not, and generally discourage the use of frequency counts in reporting analysis (though the times they can be useful to report in relation to particular practices – e.g. the proportion of about-to-be-married heterosexual women who intended to change their name to that of their future husband's). Phrases like the above are sometimes criticised for being vague – the assumption being that indicating precise numbers of participants provides more meaningful or accurate information (the assumption that numbers are *better* than words also says a lot about the dominance of a quantitative paradigm in psychology). Australian health researcher Prisicilla Pyett (2003: 1174) argued that 'counting responses misses the point of qualitative research', as frequency does not determine value. Whether something is insightful or important for elucidating our research questions is not necessarily determined by whether large numbers of people said it (Braun & Clarke, 2006; Buetow, 2010; Wainwright, 1997).

Furthermore, the use of numbers in qualitative research reporting is not straightforward. A main reason for this relates to the open way (interactive) qualitative data are collected, compared to quantitative data. For instance, consider a quantitative survey, where you ask people to select from a number of options. Reporting, and comparing, the proportions who select each of a series of response options is meaningful, because they have all been asked the same thing, and given the same response options. But when you collect qualitative research interactively, the data generated from each participant can be quite different. For example, because interviews are fluid and flexible data collection tools, and interview questions are responsive to the participants' developing account, it's not the case that every participant in an interview study discusses exactly the same issues. So if someone reports in an interview study with 15 participants that 'six of the women thought …', we *can't* assume that the remaining nine participants *didn't* think this, or thought the *opposite* (see Huxley, Clarke, & Halliwell, 2011). They simply might not have discussed it in their interview. We have no way of interpreting what is not reported in qualitative data. Likewise, imagine an FG where someone raises one particular 'reason' for why people are fat (they're lazy), but other participants do not elaborate on this point. In such situations, we have no way of knowing what the other people's views are: do they agree but haven't said anything? Do they disagree but haven't said anything? These examples demonstrate the complexities of using frequencies or numbers when reporting qualitative pattern analysis (although see Box 10.5 in Chapter 10 on story-completion task data). The use of more critical theories of language, which treat it as productive rather than as reflective of reality

(Continued)

BOX 11.6   *(continued)*

(see Chapters 2 and 8), further complicate the assumption that frequency is key in reporting qualitative analysis, because language is not seen as the vehicle by which truth is accessed.

In some cases, you may want or be required (by an editor, or a supervisor) to indicate some level of 'frequency' in relation to patterns in qualitative data. Ginny's former PhD student Gareth Terry studied New Zealand men's experiences of vasectomy using a mix of methods, including individual interviews, analysed using thematic analysis. In his doctoral thesis, he included the following description: 'when a theme is discussed within this chapter, some quantifying language will be used to discuss its prevalence across the data corpus. It is important to note that these terms are not in any way attempting to "count" the instances of a theme's occurrence (as per content analysis), but rather to provide some indication of the strength or consistency of a theme. Where the term "many" is used, it refers to occurrences of the theme within at least ten of the 17 "typical" participant's accounts. When I use "most" or "almost all", this will mean at least 12 to 14 occurrences are being referred to, and "some" as six to eight. Terms such as "commonly" and "typically" or "often" will more broadly refer to occurrences of the theme in anywhere between ten and 17 interviews and "occasionally" or "uncommon" will refer to less than half of the participants' (Terry, 2010: 108). This approach takes a 'middle ground' one, and works to alleviate concerns around vagueness and imprecision (although, as noted, these are problematic). However, it also avoids the implication that numbers reveal the truth in the data better than other ways of reporting pattern 'frequency' or 'saliency'.

ANALYSING PATTERNS ACROSS DATA USING OTHER APPROACHES

Just as in the earlier stages of analysis discussed in Chapters 9 and 10, different pattern-based approaches to qualitative analysis follow somewhat different processes for interpretative analysis. They also differ in the theoretical lens that they provide, and hence the analytic 'slant' given to data. So part of the difference between different versions of pattern-based analysis is the theoretical orientations they bring, and hence the questions that they work with. IPA, being grounded in phenomenology, is oriented to questions of experience, and interpretation of experience (a TA could produce a similar analysis and interpretation, if using similar theoretical frameworks). GT tends to be more interested in social factors and social processes, rather than experience (again, TA using a similar theoretical framework *could* produce similar analysis). Table 11.1 provides a useful comparison of the sorts of *different* questions and analytic interpretations that stem from an IPA and a GT study of a similar topic. While IPA is typically about seeking a description (and interpretation), GT is typically about seeking an *explanation*, and to this end, models can be a useful tool (see Box 11.7 and Figure 11.1)

Table 11.1 Comparing IPA and GT analyses: the study of chronic pain/illness

Comparison points	Smith & Osborn (2007) 'Pain as an assault on the self: An interpretative phenomenological analysis …'	Charmaz (1983) 'Loss of self: A fundamental form of suffering in the chronically ill'
What is the research question/focus?	Experience of the self in chronic pain	How suffering undermines the self and the social psychological factors that underpin that suffering
What is the theoretical framework?	Idiographic and phenomenological; emphasis on the subjective experience of participants	Symbolic interactionism
View of the self?	The self has a social dimension (but is also separate from the social context)	The self is fundamentally social (the self-concept can change across the lifespan)
What is the sample?	Homogenous purposive sample of six people with chronic benign lower back pain	53 chronically ill people (with a variety of diagnoses) who vary in age and income/social class
What is the dataset?	Transcripts of six semi-structured interviews	Transcripts of 73 in-depth interviews (dataset limited to participants with the most debilitating illnesses and/or who were housebound)
Is there an argument?	Yes, stated in the conclusion: the self is an important aspect of the experience of chronic pain; chronic pain 'assaults' the self (this assault can be more unpleasant than the physical pain)	Yes, stated in the introduction: chronic illness leads to a loss of self (not just physical discomfort)
Analysis	Negative impact of pain on the self; continuum and trajectory (negative impact of pain is a developmental process: positive original self – negative pain self; public arena makes it worse (participants worried about the impact of pain on their relationships/families and how they were viewed by others); directing negativity at others (the pain self contaminates significant others); sting in the tail (pain –> negative thoughts –> self-loathing –> negative behaviour towards others –> punishment)	Sources of suffering (that produce a loss of self): living a restricted life (which provides fewer possibilities for constructing a valued self); social isolation (a major consequence of a restricted life); discrediting definitions of self (discrediting occurs in interaction with others and commonly results from the 'failure of the ill person to fulfil their expectations' (p. 182); the significance of discrediting depends on the perceived magnitude and the importance of who discredits; as discrediting reoccurs, the chronically ill accept the discredited self; becoming a burden

(Continued)

Table 11.1 (Continued)

Comparison points	Smith & Osborn (2007) 'Pain as an assault on the self: An interpretative phenomenological analysis ...'	Charmaz (1983) 'Loss of self: A fundamental form of suffering in the chronically ill'
Presentation of results and discussion	Separate (with short conclusion)	Interwoven (with a longer conclusion [labelled 'discussion'])
Use of data-extracts?	Illustratively *and* analytically, but primarily analytically, commenting on the particular ways in which participants' describe their experiences ('bit of man', p. 525) and the psychological processes underpinning particular accounts ('Simon seems to move in and out of self-identification with the pain', p. 523) (roughly 40% extracts and 60% analytic commentary)	Illustratively to evidence analytic observations (e.g. under the heading of 'living a restricted life', the author notes that 'the greater the loss of control and the amount of potential embarrassment ... the more likely that individual's self concepts suffers and he or she will restrict his or her life ... For example, an elderly lady ... whispered to me, "I just can't go our anymore dear; it's the bladder...", p. 175) (roughly 30% extracts and 70% analytic narrative)
Is the analysis descriptive?	Yes: the authors describe the participants' subjective experiences of chronic pain (especially the impact of pain on the self). For example, under the heading 'the public arena makes it worse', the authors describe how 'the threats to the participants' self-regard were at their most acute when in a social or relational context' (p. 524) and provide illustrations of this from the data	Yes: the author describes the social and psychological processes that underpin the loss of self (however, this description is underpinned by a theoretical argument that chronic illness leads to a loss of self). For example, the author notes that the unpredictable nature of chronic illness promotes uncertainty and fear and as a consequence 'some patients voluntarily restrict their lives more than need be' (p. 174)
Is the analysis interpretative?	Yes: the authors offer a number of interpretations of the psychological processes underpinning the accounts (e.g. one participant [Helen] refers to her two selves: 'a nice person' and the 'mean me', and the authors comment that 'it may be that Helen is convinced that she is still a nice person but is worried that publicly other people perceive her to be something else ... Alternatively ... she may see herself engaged in a battle for her identity itself', p. 522); the authors also provide tentative theories ('there is the suggestion of a possibility of a developmental process', p. 523) in relation to the emergence of the pain self) and models (how fear of social judgement and punishment results from the experience of chronic pain; see above) to make sense of how chronic pain assaults the self	Yes: as well as arguing that chronic illness leads to a loss of self, the author explains how this happens, and how wider social/cultural values of independence and individual responsibility (see below) underpin this (social and psychological) process. For example, under the heading 'living a restricted life' the author argues that 'the world is set up for the healthy and able' (p. 174), and this is not something that is questioned by the chronically ill; as such "the lives of the chronically ill are sometimes more restricted that they need to be" (p. 174)

Comparison points	Smith & Osborn (2007) 'Pain as an assault on the self: An interpretative phenomenological analysis …'	Charmaz (1983) 'Loss of self: A fundamental form of suffering in the chronically ill'
		Chronically ill people judge themselves by the standards and expectations pertaining to the healthy and able-bodied and in so doing inadvertently contribute to the restrictedness of their lives. The author gives the example of a man with back pain who avoids going to the movies because he cannot sit for several hours – the man does not consider that if he got up and walked around for a while this would enable him to go to the movies, because getting up and walking around for a bit is not what 'normal' people do
Is the analysis contextualised in relation to the wider social context?	No (but in the discussion the 'socialness' [p. 528] of chronic pain is noted)	Yes, in the introduction: US values of 'independence, privacy and family autonomy' (p. 169) influence the management of chronic illness; Protestant **ideology** (independence, hard work and individual responsibility) leads chronically ill people to blame themselves for their dependency on others/the state
Is the analysis contextualised in relation to the wider literature?	Yes, in the discussion: the results are related to research on the psychological aspects of chronic pain, sociological research on chronic illness, theories of the social (and moral) nature of chronic illness, literature on shame (the ways in which the current study is similar to or extends existing literature are noted; literature is also used to interpret the results)	Yes but not in any detail; sociological literature on chronic illness and stigma is simply cited throughout the analysis

Overall: The studies draw very similar conclusions (although some of the similarities are concealed by the use of different language and concepts and very different presentations – partly the result of disciplinary differences), but the emphasis is different – Smith and Osborn emphasise the psychological experience of chronic pain; Charmaz emphasises the social processes underlying individual experiences of chronic illness.

BOX 11.7   DEVELOPING A MODEL IN GT

GT can be useful if you're wanting to develop models of explanation for a *process* (e.g. Clifford & Orford, 2007) or an issue. With a GT-lite analysis, you would not be aiming to develop an all-encompassing theory, but could offer a theoretical/conceptual explanation of the data that related to your research question. For us, this meant developing a conceptual mapping of how participants in the FG explained the increases in obesity at the societal level and how individuals themselves become obese. Any model developed through GT needs to be clearly grounded in, and derived from, the data. However, it doesn't directly stem from the data, but involves *interpretation* on the part of analyst. This interpretation is about working out how the different codes, concepts and categories in the analysis 'fit together' to create a theoretically informed explanation of the social and psychological processes underlying the phenomenon of interest. In the model we have developed (see Figure 11.1), the participants didn't necessarily say these things, or make these connections, directly; instead, our process of analysis interrogated the things they said in relation to 'becoming obese', and made sense of how the different elements they identified (directly and indirectly) interrelated. So the process of interpretation in GT is not just about telling a story about the data; it's about developing an *explanation from* the data. In this way, it differs from both TA and IPA.

Our model focuses on factors that are seen to influence *becoming* obese; it's not about the *experience* of being obese (which was the focus of our IPA analysis example; see Chapter 8 and 9) or the understandings around obesity and the obesity epidemic (which was the focus of our TA analysis example, developed in Chapter 8, 9 and here). Although we only present the model in graphic form, any analysis would develop a full analytic narrative with embedded data extracts. Just as TA would sequentially discuss themes, an analysis around this would sequentially describe the different levels and elements in the model. In doing so, we would also note certain caveats or specificities, such as that within the data, some kinds of fatness were quite normalised and not seen as wholly negative, and that participants shifted between individual and social levels of explanation around a person becoming obese.

Although this is sufficient for a GT-lite analysis, a *full* GT would go further. Unlike the two stages of initial (open) and intermediate (focused) coding we've explicated (in Chapters 9 and 10), a full GT requires an additional one (Birks & Mills, 2011) or two (Charmaz, 2006) further coding stages towards full theory development, and also theoretical sampling (see Box 3.3 in Chapter 3) to ensure saturation of the concepts being explored in the theory development.

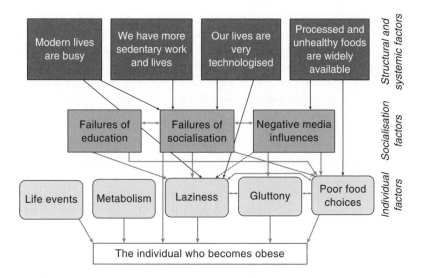

Figure 11.1   Explanatory factors for becoming obese: a grounded theory model

Key: arrows signal a relationship between factors; arrow direction signals the direction of influence in the model; a broken arrow signals a tentative relationships.

DA in all varieties can be viewed as a theoretically-informed critical analytic engagement with data, which seeks to identify patterned features of language, and to interpret those within an understanding of language as productive and constitutive, as *doing something*, rather than as providing information. Most 'methodological guidelines' (Arribas-Ayllon & Walkerdine, 2008: 98) for DA (e.g. Parker, 1992; Potter & Wetherell, 1987; Willig, 2008) tend to point to features of language or theoretical concepts that the analyst explores or examines, through 'a sensitivity to language' (Parker, 2004: 310), and then interrogates and interprets their functions and implications of language-use. DA effectively requires the researcher to look for 'answers' to a series of questions posed of the data; analysis also requires a reflexive researcher, who asks, constantly, of themselves: 'Why am I reading this passage in this way?' (Potter & Wetherell, 1987: 168).

Different versions of pattern-based DA bring their different theoretical orientations and different conceptual tools to bear on analysis (discussed in Chapter 8). A poststructuralist (Foucauldian) version is likely to employ and explore concepts like discourses or subject positioning (Arribas-Ayllon & Walkerdine, 2008; Parker, 1992; Willig, 2008). For example, as part of a study of being 'large', British psychologists Irmgard Tischner and Helen Malson (2008) examined the multiple subject positions and discourses through which women talked about the (in)visibility of their large bodies, identifying surveillance as a key part of their experience. They identified the ways women positioned themselves both as subject to surveillance from society, and as surveillers (of self, and others). Their analysis explored the complex power dynamics of visibility and invisibility, through the multiple, and contradictory, positions taken up by their participants, some of which complied with, and some of which resisted, dominant discourses and constructions of large bodies (see Further Reading). Critical discursive psychology or repertoire-based DA approaches are more likely to employ and explore concepts like interpretative repertoires or ideological dilemmas (Edley, 2001a; Potter & Wetherell, 1987). For example, as part of their classic study of the language of racism in Aotearoa/New Zealand, Margaret Wetherell and Jonathan Potter (1992) identified two repertoires around (Māori) culture – culture as *heritage* (something fixed in the past) and culture as *therapy* (a form of 'salvation'). Identification of such repertoires was just the beginning; their analysis moved to consider the quite different ideological implications of these two patterned ways of constructing 'culture', for Māori generally, and for race-relations and the socio-political organisation of New Zealand society. This highlights an important point: in pattern-based DA, description is never sufficient for an analysis. Interpretation is *essential*, as is examination and consideration of the functions and implications of language and language-use.

DOING PATTERN-BASED ANALYSIS WELL

Issues related to doing *quality* qualitative research are covered more fully in Chapter 12; here we briefly outline some key aspects of good (and poor; see Box 11.8) pattern-based analysis (see Table 11.2). A good analysis will go beyond *just* summarising data and be thorough, plausible, sophisticated and most of all interpretative. Interpretation, which we've already mentioned quite a few times, is vital. It's how we make sense of data, and provides the basis for why we should care about it. In analysing the data, you need to take the reader *beyond* just the words of participants or the words in secondary texts. Imagine you have a pile of data of talk about being fat. If your interest is in how *fatness* is constructed, you would collate data related to that, organise them into themes (e.g. fatness as genetic infliction, fatness as moral failing, fatness as liberation from cultural pressures), tell a rich story about them and then tell the reader *why* they should care about these constructions. Why they should care is a pretty open book – it might be at theoretical, scientific, social, medical, psychological, political, policy and/or other levels. What is crucial is that you provide reasons for why the story you have told about the data is important.

The sorts of questions that can be useful to helping to develop an *interpretative* analytic orientation include:

- What meanings, ideas or assumptions underpin this pattern of meaning-making?
- What are the implications of this pattern for the participants?
- What are the implications of this pattern for the issue at hand?
- What are the implications of this pattern for society?
- What are the implications of this pattern for the academic knowledge of the field?

Such questions can usefully be applied both to each pattern you identify, and to the whole analysis (see Braun & Clarke, 2006, 2012). For instance, continuing the example above, for a theme of 'fatness as genetic infliction' we might note that this meaning exists because of a biomedical framework which situates weight (both being fat and being thin) as a result of genetics and metabolism. The implications of this for fat individuals might be positive (lack of blame) but also negative (sense of futility if they wish to lose weight). If this is a commonly understood, common-sense meaning, any societal attempts to address the issue ('the obesity epidemic') would need to take into account these 'lay explanations' (Blaxter, 1997), so your analysis might impact both policy and the practices of health professionals. Academic knowledge would be enhanced by greater understanding of the everyday explanations, and how these map onto existing scientific framings (do they echo them or are they at odds?).

UK-based health psychologists Carla Willig and Wendy Stainton Rogers (2008: 9), however, sound an important word of caution in relation to interpretation in qualitative analysis:

The challenge to qualitative researchers is … to go beyond what presents itself, to reveal dimensions of a phenomenon which are concealed or hidden, whilst at the same time taking care not to impose meaning upon the phenomenon, not to squeeze it into pre-conceived categories or theoretical formulations, not to reduce it to an underlying cause.

This invites us to remember the emergence of qualitative methods as a way of capturing the messy complexities of everyday realities, of centring participants' experiences and meanings, and of avoiding the imposition of the all-powerful researcher's interpretative frameworks (see Chapter 1). This does not mean interpretation should be avoided; it suggests we should not engage in it with a disregard for our data. Likewise, it's not a call to provide only analysis which 'honours' the data.

Is interpretation relevant to a more descriptive study? Absolutely. IPA (Smith et al., 2009) is a good example of a method which aims to both capture and interpret experience. So even if your aim is to capture the *experience of being fat*, for example, and your analysis of shared experiences sticks closely to what the participants report, with an analysis that is typically inductive and semantic, you still need to *make sense of* the patterns that you report, and you need to address the '*so what?*' question. Combined, these produce an interpretative analysis, and they are always oriented to your (potentially evolved) research question. To just summarise and/or paraphrase the data is not (good) qualitative analysis; it is a step on the way to analysis.

Inadequate interpretation also applies to other forms of analysis, such as DA (see Antaki et al., 2002). These British discursive psychologists identified one practice of 'under analysis' as 'taking sides'. Something similar we see our students struggle with is how to treat text *as data* and not as something to *argue* with. This can be a tricky distinction to get, but when you treat text as data, your purpose is not to ascertain the truth or falsity of what is contained within, or whether you agree or disagree with it; your purpose is to organise, interpret and report on the patterns you identify. Keeping with the example above, if most of your participants identified that the cause of their fatness was because the government had been putting high calorie but tasteless artificial sweeteners into tap water for the last decade, this would be a dominant theme,

Table 11.2   Good and bad practices in pattern-based analysis

Examples of good practices	Examples of bad practices
A good balance between analytic commentary and data extracts (at least half analytic commentary)	Too many data extracts and little or no analytic commentary OR analytic claims not supported by adequate examples from the data
Strong evidence of a systematic and thorough analytic process; the analytic commentary provides original and novel insights into the meaning of the data	Little or no analytic work has been done – analysis is based on a surface skim of the data, and simply paraphrases the data OR presents more obvious features of the data as themes with data extracts are selected that support these 'themes'
There is a good fit between the data and analytic claims; interpretation of the data is convincing and compelling	Poor fit between the data and the analytic claims: analytic claims are not supported by the data or are unconvincing; alternative explanations seem more compelling
Each theme has a clear central organising concept. An appropriate number of coherent themes are presented; together they provide a 'thick description' of the data. Each theme is discussed in sufficient depth and detail	Themes are incoherent and don't have a clear single central organising concept. Too many themes (themes are thin and scrappy) OR too few themes (themes are unwieldy and overly complex) are presented
Themes have primarily been identified *across* the entire dataset, regardless of what questions participants were asked (best practice)	Themes have been derived from the questions asked – for example, the responses to each interview/survey question have simply been summarised and presented as themes
Each theme is distinctive	Themes overlap; the analysis is repetitive
The themes work *together* to *tell a story* about the data. During the analysis equal attention has been paid to individual themes and the relationship between them; the analyst has had the confidence to discard codes/themes that do not fit the overall developing analysis	The relationship between themes is unclear (or, even worse, non-existent) and the themes do not form a coherent whole. Little or no thought has been given to the overall analysis when generating themes
The analysis is descriptive *and* interpretative, providing a conceptual and theoretical analysis of the data. Existing research and theoretical concepts are drawn on to deepen the analysis of the data	The analysis is limited to describing/summarising the data (simply 'giving voice' to the participants); there is no interpretation; nothing to tell the reader why it is interesting or important
The analysis provides a critical analysis of the assumptions underpinning the data and the implications of the data	Analysis *of* the data is substituted with arguing with the data
The data are located in the wider social context	The analysis ignores the links between the data and the wider social context; the data are interpreted in a social vacuum
The analysis captures the different 'stories' in the data and considers other plausible interpretations of the data	The analysis does not consider other, obvious, interpretations of the data, or the complexity and contradiction in the data

Examples of good practices	Examples of bad practices
The analysis explains why the data are interesting and significant or important in relation to the research question; it potentially highlights this at both semantic or 'overt' levels, and more latent or 'hidden' levels	The meaning of the data is assumed to be self-evident; the data are left to 'speak for themselves'
The analysis makes an argument, often developed in relation to theoretical, conceptual, or other empirical work	The analysis simply represents key features of the data
The analytic claims fit with the overall theoretical position of the analysis AND are consistent. For example, a constructionist analysis around fatness does *not* describe people's attitudes to fat people, or fat people's experiences of being fat	The analysis and theoretical frameworks are contradictory OR the analysis is inconsistent. For example, an experiential analysis of fatness focuses on how the participant *constructs* 'fatness' in their talk rather than reporting the participants' *experiences* of being fat
The analysis answers the research question	The analysis does not answer the research question OR does not provide a clear research question to start with

a dominant 'lay theory' of fatness. While there *may* be evidence of traces of artificial sweeteners in tap water (Scheurer, Brauch, & Lange, 2009), if we can find no credible evidence of claims that this was a deliberate government action, we assume that such 'lay explanations' are *false*. However, your task as an analyst is not to directly argue this point, not to prove that your participants are wrong in what they believe, by identifying the falsity of their claims, and backing it up with 'evidence'. Instead, your role is interpretative, coming back to those 'so what?' and 'what does this mean?' questions. Your interpretative analysis *may* offer an evaluation of this lay theory in the context of other evidence (e.g. that there is no evidence sweeteners in water are the cause of the 'obesity epidemic'), but this would not be done by disagreeing *with* the data. So you wouldn't bluntly say something like: 'the participants were deluded in their belief that artificial sweeteners added to tap water, as there is no evidence this is the case (REFS)'; you might say something like 'in the spectrum of scientific research on causes of fatness (e.g. REFS), artificial sweeteners do not feature, but were frequently raised by participants. Potential implications of this common lay explanation for fatness are …'.

Many other features of good and bad pattern-based qualitative analysis are presented in Table 11.2. Because it can be hard to imagine what 'bad' analysis looks like, which correspondingly can be anxiety-provoking (how do you know what to avoid?) we have provided an example of a bad analysis in Box 11.8. We have used the same theme ('exercise is evil') we illustrated in Box 11.4, to provide an easy and useful comparison point.

BOX 11.8   A 'BAD' ANALYSIS OF THE THEME 'EXERCISE IS EVIL'

The theme 'exercise is evil' identifies the idea that humans are naturally lazy, which seemed to inform participants' talk and be the implicit model of what humans are naturally like. The idea was that the typical human being did not like to engage in exercise and activity, or do things that require energy expenditure. For instance, Rebecca talked about meals you can get at McDonald's, and observed that:

> And it's so cheap as well, just so...Like you can't justify making a...making a meal for like two pounds when you can go and buy something for the same amount of money, you know, you don't have to bother with the washing up. (Rebecca)

In this extract, Rebecca identifies that if food costs the same amount to buy as to make, then it 'cannot be justified' – especially as you don't have to 'to bother with the washing up', an activity that nobody enjoys! So here humans are 'naturally lazy', because if there is a cheaper/easier way to prepare food, they will take it. Indeed, people were only described as engaging in any activity *if* they had no other option. For instance, Sally talked about her mother having to walk miles to catch the train to work each day:

> My Mum used to walk two or three miles to go to the train station to go another ten miles to work, you know [...] There was no bus for her so she had to walk. (Sally)

When describing their own lives, where they typically did not engage in physical activity, this was typically put down to 'motivation':

> I've actually joined a gym and do I go? No. Because if I had somebody to go with, I'd be motivated to do it. (Sally)

Our participants were not exercisers. They described a long-standing laziness on their parts, going as far back as school, where physical education (PE) was a hated part of the curriculum:

> I bunked every PE lesson I could possibly get away with. (Rebecca)
>
> It was a real chore and I used to think 'oh god', you know, 'not PE, oh I don't want to do that'. (Sally)

This dislike for physical activity was still described in children today:

> It's like we've got a trampoline outside. I have to drag them out by their hair to try and get them to get on it, you know. (Carla)

Here Carla describes her household situation, where her children don't want to take part in a fun childhood toy – a trampoline. Of course, Carla doesn't literally drag her children out by the hair (if she did, we would need to be calling social services to take them away!), but they clearly are naturally lazy, and reluctant to go outside and play when they could stay indoors playing on the computer. Hence Carla has to force them outdoors. This demonstrates the ways that laziness is present in children, right from a young age, and isn't just something that should be associated with adults, like the women in our sample.

These extracts and our analysis demonstrate the theme 'exercise is evil', and show that human beings were assumed to be naturally lazy by the participants in the focus group. But it may just be that this reflects their own biases, as they were an unusually lazy group – none of them currently engaged in regular physical activity.

CHAPTER SUMMARY

This chapter:
- discussed the relationship between writing and analysis in qualitative research;
- clarified the outcome of pattern-based analysis;
- described and illustrated the processes of developing and defining a thematic analysis;
- discussed different processes for different versions of pattern-based analysis;
- highlighted key practices to ensure a good pattern-based analysis.

? QUESTIONS FOR DISCUSSION AND CLASSROOM EXERCISES

1   Write theme definitions for the two themes you developed across your coding (Chapter 9) and theme development (Chapter 10) exercises.
2   Select a couple of extracts from the data you have previously coded (Chapter 9) and developed potential themes for (Chapter 10). For each, write a paragraph or two of analysis, once using the data illustratively, and once using it analytically.
3   In small groups, identify the key differences in process of analysis between TA and pattern-based DA. What ways do you think the *process* you use to analyse the data might shape the analysis produced?
4   Looking at the *bad* analysis in Box 11.8, identify the things that are 'wrong' with it. Work out how it might have been done better (see the ***companion website*** for 'answers' to this exercise).

FURTHER RESOURCES

Further reading:

For a really good discussion of the use of data extracts in qualitative research, see: Sandelowski, M. (1994). The use of quotes in qualitative research. *Research in Nursing & Health, 17,* 479–482.

For an example of the potential of interpretative (critical) TA, see: Braun, V. (2008). 'She'll be right'? National identity explanations for poor sexual health statistics in Aotearoa/New Zealand. *Social Science & Medicine, 67,* 1817–1825.

For an example of an interpretative IPA study, see: Smith, J. A., & Osborn, M. (2007). Pain as an assault on the self: an interpretative phenomenological analysis of the psychological impact of chronic benign low back pain. *Psychology & Health, 22,* 517–534.

For an example of an interpretative GT study, see: Rose, L., Mallinson, R. K., & Walton-Moss, B. (2002). A grounded theory of families responding to mental illness. *Western Journal of Nursing Research, 24,* 516–536.

For an example of a short poststructuralist DA study, see: Tischner, I., & Malson, H. (2008). Exploring the politics of women's in/visible 'large' bodies. *Feminism & Psychology, 18*, 260–267.

For a longer example of a poststructuralist DA study, see: Gavey, N., & McPhillips, K. (1999). Subject to romance: heterosexual passivity as an obstacle to women initiating condom use. *Psychology of Women Quarterly, 23*, 349–367.

For a detailed example of a large 'interpretative repertoire' style DA study, see: Wetherell, M., & Potter, J. (1992). *Mapping the Language of Racism*. Hemel Hempstead, UK: Harvester.

 Online resources:

See the ***companion website*** (**www.sagepub.co.uk/braunandclarke**) for:

- self-test multiple choice questions relating to Section 3;
- the flashcard glossary – test yourself on the definitions of key terms used in this chapter;
- the answer to the bad analysis exercise;
- an extended version (full write-up) on the 'exercise is evil' theme (Box 11.4);
- the weight and obesity FG transcript;
- further readings (articles from Sage journals).

SECTION
4

Successfully
completing
qualitative research

12 Quality criteria and techniques for qualitative research

OVERVIEW

What makes a good piece of qualitative research?
Can we apply quantitative quality criteria to qualitative research?
Quality criteria and techniques suitable for qualitative research
Checklist criteria for qualitative research

What grade should we give this project?

Should this person be awarded a PhD?

Should this research proposal be funded?

Should this paper be published?

Should I change my (clinical) practice on the basis of these results?

Such questions illustrate the very practical need to evaluate the quality of qualitative research, and reflect on good and bad practice. Various criteria have been developed to both ensure and judge the quality of the research conducted. Understanding these criteria is vitally important for conducting (good) qualitative research, for reflecting on whether your research is any good, for writing up and disseminating your research, *and* for evaluating qualitative research in general. We have explored and emphasised *quality* in lots of different ways throughout the book: for example, in relation to what makes a good interview, or how best to present your analysis. Belgian health researcher Karin Hannes and colleagues (Hannes, Lockwood, & Pearson, 2010: 1737) make a useful distinction between quality criteria and techniques: 'we define *criteria* as the standards to be upheld as ideals in qualitative research, and *techniques* as the methods employed to diminish validity threats' (emphasis in original). In this chapter we consider the issue of the more *general* criteria we should use to ensure – and judge – the quality of qualitative research.

WHAT MAKES A GOOD PIECE OF QUALITATIVE RESEARCH?

Unfortunately there are no *absolute* criteria for judging whether a piece of qualitative research is any good. As British sociologist Clive Seale (1999: 471) noted, '"quality" is a somewhat elusive phenomenon' in qualitative research. But this doesn't mean we cannot differentiate between a good and a poor quality study. Qualitative research is a bit like films in this respect. There are no universal criteria agreed on by film critics (or the film-going public) for judging the quality of a film but, as a community, film critics have implicit knowledge of what makes a film good or bad. Most critics would agree that *The Godfather: Part II*, the winner of six Oscars including 'Best Picture' in 1974, is a *good* film, whereas *Sex and the City 2*, a nominee for the Razzie Awards' worst picture of 2010, is a *bad* one. Experienced qualitative researchers similarly often use implicit criteria for judging qualitative research; these criteria can be hard to know and understand if you are a new member of the qualitative research community, so guidelines can be useful.

The example of *Sex and the City 2* also highlights different dimensions on which we might judge a film: whether we enjoy it and whether it is 'quality': the enormous popularity of *Sex and the City 2* led to it being dubbed 'critic proof' (Pulver, 2010) because almost universally bad reviews did not stop people viewing it in droves. Translating this to the domain of qualitative research, it's important to differentiate between approaches or topics we find interesting, and research we can judge to be of good quality. For instance, you don't have to agree with the principles of grounded theory (GT) to assess whether a particular study is a good example of that approach. What is important is that you know the criteria on which you *should* judge it. First we consider whether the criteria used to evaluate quantitative research can also be applied to qualitative research, then outline quality criteria and techniques specific to qualitative research.

CAN WE APPLY QUANTITATIVE QUALITY CRITERIA TO QUALITATIVE RESEARCH?

The (formal) criteria for evaluating *quantitative* research are widely agreed upon and are often presented as *the* criteria for evaluating all research (see Gilbert & Mulkay, 1984, for a discussion of the more *informal* criteria): good research is reliable and valid, and the purpose is to generalise beyond the sample to the wider population. Do these criteria apply for qualitative research?

RELIABILITY

Broadly speaking, **reliability** refers to the possibility of generating the same results when the same measures are administered by different researchers to a different participant group (Yardley, 2008). It is important because quantitative researchers are often interested in developing *generalisable* laws, and so seek to minimise the influence of the researcher – which is seen as a source of error or 'bias'. The paradigm requires that their tools must not be influenced by the person collecting the data, the participants or the context of data collection. Hopefully, you can immediately see the problems for qualitative research. Qualitative researchers acknowledge that the researcher *inevitably* influences the research process and the knowledge produced, and they seek to 'maximise the benefits of engaging actively with the participants in the study' (Yardley, 2008: 237). As Yardley (2008: 237) notes, seeking to minimise the influence of the researcher 'would make it very difficult to retain the benefits of qualitative research', such as the generation of data and analysis through the researcher's active personal engagement with the participants and/or the phenomenon of interest (McLeod, 2001). The kinds of things said in an interview or a focus group, for instance, depend on the (embodied) presence and the skill of the researcher. Similarly, the types of themes or categories generated in the analysis depend on the standpoint and experience of the researcher. For example, Kitzinger and Willmott (2002) conducted their interview study of women's experiences of polycystic ovarian syndrome (PCOS, see Illustrative Research Example 4.1 in Chapter 4) within a feminist framework; a different group of researchers who didn't subscribe to feminist values may have interpreted the women's accounts differently. Qualitative researchers are also often interested in *individual* meanings and experiences, and consider context important in creating or impacting on those meanings (Yardley, 2008); therefore, they do not treat knowledge as *ideally* removed from the context it was generated in. Reliability (and alongside it, replicability) is also 'rooted in a realist view of a single external reality knowable through language' (Seale, 1999: 41), whereas qualitative approaches acknowledge multiple realities or the context-bound nature of reality (and critical qualitative approaches view language as producing, rather than reflecting, reality or reali*ties*; see Chapter 2).

This means that reliability is *not* an appropriate criterion for judging qualitative work and procedures such as calculating the 'inter-rater reliability' of qualitative coding are problematic (because of the assumption that coding can and *should* be objective). Calculating inter-rater reliability involves two or more researchers coding data independently, then comparing their codes; the level of agreement between their codes is calculated using Cohen's Kappa (a Kappa of > .80 indicates a very good level of agreement and supposedly 'reliable' coding) (Yardley, 2008). However, if we think of reliability more broadly as being about the 'trustworthiness' or 'dependability' of our methods of data collection and analysis (McLeod, 2001), then some version of reliability *is* applicable. As we discuss further below, qualitative researchers have identified ways we can meaningfully judge the trustworthiness of qualitative research.

VALIDITY

Validity can be defined very broadly as a piece of research showing what it claims to show (Goodman, 2008a). A narrower definition is whether a measure accurately captures 'reality', which is obviously problematic in qualitative research, given the emphasis on multiple realities (see Chapter 2). There are many different forms of validity for quantitative researchers to consider. Four common ones include (Goodman, 2008a):

- *construct validity*, which is concerned with whether a data collection measure measures what it aims to measure. This also includes consideration of whether the results from a measure (e.g. a racism scale) can be generalised to the wider construct (e.g. racist attitudes);
- *internal validity*, which is concerned with whether the effects identified are in fact being caused by the variable(s) under study, rather than some other, confounding, factor;
- *external validity*, which is concerned with whether the results from the study can be generalised from the sample to the wider population;
- *ecological validity*, which is concerned with the relationship between the 'real world' and the research. This sometimes manifests as whether the context of data collection resembles the real world context (and is so meaningful to 'real life') and sometimes as whether the results can be applied to real world settings.

The first three of these are considered essential for 'valid' (good) quantitative research; the last is desirable but not essential. Of these four criteria, *ecological validity* is considered most relevant to qualitative research. Qualitative research is often seen as more ecologically valid because it *tends* to gather data in ways that are less removed from the real world than quantitative measures, although this is not always the case; an interview is not a person in their 'real life' (Fine & Gordon, 1989). Ecological 'validity' as a construct for evaluating qualitative research also assumes a certain view of language (representational; see Chapter 2) and so does not fit all qualitative research.

GENERALISABILITY (AND TRANSFERABILITY)

Generalisability refers to whether or not the results generated in one study can be applied to wider or different populations – for instance, can we assume that body hair removal practices of British women are accurately captured by what a sample of over 600 British women report doing (Toerien, Wilkinson, & Choi, 2005)? If a US and German collaborative study identifies strategies to reduce men's neo- and modern-sexist beliefs (Becker & Swim, 2011), should we apply those in Aotearoa/New Zealand, Iceland, or Brazil? Here, generalisation is about the 'horizontal' extension of your results (Stephens, 1982). Essentially, its importance reflects the generation of (universal) laws as an aim of research. Some researchers argue that generalisability is not a meaningful goal for qualitative research, because of assumptions about the context-bound nature of knowledge in qualitative research and an interest in the *detail* of the phenomenon being investigated (Johnson, 1997; Schofield, 1993; see also Chapter 2).

Others (Sandelowski, 2004; Stephens, 1982) argue that qualitative research results are (potentially) generalisable, just not in the same way as quantitative results are. Indeed, as Yardley (2008: 238) noted, 'there would be little point in doing research if every situation was totally unique, and the results in one study had no relevance to any other situation!' For example, British discourse analyst Simon Goodman (2008a: 265) argued that the results of discursive analyses 'can be considered generalizable to the extent that they can show how a particular discursive strategy will often bring about the same interactional result'. He illustrates this with reference to a common discursive strategy of 'using existing prejudice to justify further prejudice', which has been demonstrated in different settings from discussions of lesbian and gay parenting (Clarke, 2001; Clarke et al., 2004) to the rights of asylum seekers in the UK (Goodman, 2008b) and immigrant communities in the Netherlands (Verkuyten, 2005) and Greece (Figgou & Condor, 2006). In Victoria and colleague's (Clarke et al., 2004) study, claims that children will be subject to homophobic bullying (existing prejudice) were *routinely* used to justify opposition to lesbian and gay parenting (further prejudice).

Goodman's (2008a) argument about the generalisability of discursive work related not to *statistical* generalisability (e.g. if 70 per cent of my sample diet, 70 per cent of the population can be assumed to diet) but to a concept of *flexible* generalisability. Goodman argued that in order to make a claim of flexible generalisability, the analyst should be able to show that:

- a discursive strategy achieves a certain function (e.g. existing prejudice is used to justify further prejudice);
- the strategy achieves this function in a range of settings and when used by a range of speakers (this may not be possible to demonstrate in one study; a researcher can draw on existing research to demonstrate it).

Because language is a flexible tool, any generalised discursive strategy is likely to be subject to change, and unlikely to persist for ever. This means considering generalisability in discursive research requires sensitivity to context and to the flexible nature of language. The same could be said of generalisability in qualitative research more widely.

Different versions of generalisability have been proposed that may be useful to capture the wider relevance of qualitative results, including *vertical generalisability* (Stephens, 1982) and *analytic* or *idiographic generalisability* (Sandelowski, 2004), where it is about building and creating deep interpretative analysis from the specifics of the study, which can contribute to wider knowledge. We'll consider generalisability in relation to Kitzinger and Willmott's (2002) study of women with PCOS (see Illustrative Research Example 4.1 in Chapter 4). They didn't make any explicit comments on generalisability; they only noted that further research was warranted given the small-size of their sample. However, given that their central theme of 'freakishness' was so pervasive, we can reasonably assume that it captures a common aspect of women's experiences of PCOS (certainly for women who share the characteristics of the sample). Moreover, the fact this theme was strongly tied to wider gender norms (the women felt like failures in relation to the norms of 'proper' femininity or womanhood) increases the likelihood of its broader relevance. That is, the results were strongly situated in an interpretation of the wider social context. The authors made claims about normative femininity in western cultures and tied the participants' claims about 'proper womanhood' to a critical feminist analysis of the supposedly 'natural' feminine woman. The study appears, then, to fit criteria for some form of flexible generalisability.

A concept more frequently used in relation to the 'flexible generalisability' of *qualitative* (but not quantitative) research is **transferability**. Transferability stems from one of the earliest sets of quality criteria for qualitative research, compiled by US education researchers Yvonna Lincoln and Egon Guba (1985), and refers to the extent to which (aspects of) qualitative results can be 'transferred' to other groups of people and contexts. The key to enhancing the transferability of a study is to describe the *specific* contexts, participants, settings and circumstances of the study in detail, so the reader can evaluate the potential for applying the results to other contexts or participants. In Lincoln and Guba's formulation of transferability, the burden of transferring results is placed on the *reader*: the reader has to decide whether *their* circumstances and settings are enough like those of the original study to warrant a 'safe' transfer.

QUALITY CRITERIA AND TECHNIQUES SUITABLE FOR QUALITATIVE RESEARCH

Instead of starting from, or relying on versions of, quantitative criteria, qualitative researchers have developed quality criteria and techniques specific to, or suitable for, qualitative research. Two of the best known, yet controversial, are member checking and **triangulation**.

MEMBER CHECKING

Member checking (or 'member validation'; Seale, 1999: 61) refers to the practice of checking your analysis with your participants. It typically involves presenting a draft written or oral report of the research, or just of the analysis, to some or all participants, and asking them to comment on the trustworthiness or authenticity of what has been produced (sometimes it can be more extensive; see Box 12.1). Researchers choose to do this for a number of reasons including a concern to avoid 'misrepresenting' the views of their participants (particularly if members of vulnerable or socially marginalised groups; see Chapter 3) or, if they are aiming to 'give voice' to participants' experiences, to ensure that there is a good fit between their interpretations and representation of their participants' experiences and the participants' *own* understandings of their experiences. Lincoln and Guba (1985) presented member checking as a type of 'credibility check'. It could be regarded as a qualitative version of 'reliability' – it aims to determine that the results are credible and dependable, from the point of view of the participants. If using this 'verification step', it needs to be built into the research design; when participants are recruited they need to be informed of this process and invited to participate in it.

BOX 12.1   EXPLORING THE POSSIBILITIES FOR MEMBER CHECKING IN DEVELOPING YOUR ANALYSIS

British clinical psychologists Clair Clifford and Jim Orford's (2007) GT-informed study of the experience of becoming trans aimed to develop a model to capture this process. Participants were invited to assist with developing, refining or validating the model. First, on the basis of interviews with eight trans people, an initial three-phase 'biographical, developmental' (p. 199) model of the process of becoming trans was developed. This provisional model was then presented to a *different* group of 12 participants, who were invited to reflect on 'the relevance of the model to their own experience, and to identify aspects of the model that were either unclear or did not fit with their experiences' (p. 200). On the basis of their feedback, some of the categories in the model were collapsed or combined; others were divided. The refined three-phase model was then presented to another group of eight different participants, for a 'final check of the explanatory power of the model and an opportunity to identify any further material for negative case analysis' (p. 201). Negative case analysis is a quality technique that can mean different things (e.g. see Henwood & Pidgeon, 1992, on negative case analysis in GT; Potter, 1996, on deviant case analysis in DA). In this instance, negative case analysis involved identifying cases that did not fit with the developing model and reporting separately the data that did not fit. The authors *could* have chosen at this stage to further refine the model to improve its explanatory power and ability to account for such 'negative' cases (see Henwood & Pidgeon, 1992).

It's important to distinguish member checking, where the analysis can be revised on the basis of feedback, from 'returning research' to participants on ethical or political grounds (Taylor, 2001) which, for some researchers, is an important practice, but is not part of 'quality control'. For example, Kitzinger and Willmott (2002: 352) described presenting a version of their completed study at a meeting of the support group from which they recruited their participants, and noted that the presentation was 'very enthusiastically received'. They presented this as evidence of their commitment to feminist research ethics ('giving back' the results of the study to the participants), rather than a formal credibility check.

For qualitative researchers engaged in research that emphasises the importance of understanding participants' (subjective and situated) meanings and experiences, member checking can be an important way of establishing the credibility and quality of the analysis. In research designs that include member checking, participants (arguably) play a more active role in the research process, and are given the opportunity to correct (perceived) 'errors' or inappropriate interpretations of their experiences. Member checking has its roots in phenomenological approaches to research (Smith, 1996), which aim to record as closely as possible how an individual perceives something, and in the development of more democratic and participant-centred approaches to research (where it can still present challenges; Fine et al., 2003). At first sight, member checking seems eminently sensible. If your aim is to represent the experiences of a particular group (such as women with PCOS, trans people), doesn't it make good sense to ask them whether you have 'got it right'? Yes, but ... There are critiques and questions around using member checking as a key quality criterion that need to be considered.

First, there are potential *practical* problems with member checking (McLeod, 2001):

- Some participants may be reluctant to engage in the process: they may not have time to participate in this 'extra' process, or perceive no value in doing so, for a whole host of reasons. Obviously, participants cannot be compelled to take part, but explaining on the participant information sheet that participation involves both data collection and verification of the analysis and explaining *why* this is important may help to increase engagement. Alternatively, you can recruit an additional (smaller) group of participants to validate the analysis (see Box 12.1).

- Another factor is researcher power and authority: some participants may feel reluctant to express doubts or criticisms about the credibility of the analysis. Such potential problems can partly be addressed in the instructions provided to participants offering feedback (e.g. by emphasising that the participant is the 'expert' on their experience, and the researcher needs to understand it from their point of view).

- Some participants may be more forthcoming with comments and criticism, but may be motivated by something other than aiding the researcher to produce the most credible report (e.g. disputes and tensions within the participant group), so their comments may not be particularly helpful in validating the analysis (e.g. because their feedback strongly reflects their own agenda).

- What happens if member checking produces contradictory feedback – some love the analysis and believe it's a true reflection; others hate it and see nothing of their experience there? How would you resolve this kind of tension? In a situation like this, you have the ultimate responsibility for how you interpret data, so you need to make a judgement call on the content of your analysis. If this happens, one solution might be to note that some participants endorsed the analysis, while others didn't (and if possible, explain why they didn't).

- What happens if the member checking process does not 'verify' the analysis? You need to be prepared to 'let go' of some or all of your analysis. If member checking is to be more than a 'quality ritual' (Bloor, 1997), enough time must be allocated for reworking the analysis in light of participants' feedback, and possibly engaging in a second round of member checking (which is beyond the scope of most small projects).

- Do you have enough time to complete the process? For a small project, member checking can easily take *at least* a month to complete (e.g. two weeks for participants to read and comment on your draft analysis; two weeks to revise your analysis in light of their comments). This needs to be included in your research timetable right from the start (see Box 3.7 in Chapter 3). You also need to think about the practicalities of *how* the participants feed their comments back (will they post or email you written comments or will you arrange individual or group meetings to discuss your analysis?).

- A final important practical question is when you stop. The process of credibility checking is potentially limitless, so you need to decide when you are going to stop the process.

The theoretical and methodological assumptions that underpin the concept of member checking also need to be considered. Member checking typically assumes that participants are the ultimate authority on, and have complete insight into, their experiences. As such, it works well with experience-type questions (see Chapter 3). However, even when the aim of qualitative research is to 'give voice' to participants (e.g. Smith et al., 2009), we cannot simply 'represent' participants' experiences. Understanding and representing participants' experiences requires interpretative activity; this is always informed by our own assumptions, values and commitments. Moreover, as researchers we view participants' experiences from a different angle to what they do; we identify and interpret aspects of their experiences that they may not be fully aware of; we ask different questions than they do (often moving beyond common-sense understandings). Ontologically, member checking is situated within a realist framework, and so is underpinned by an assumption that seeking to depict '*the* truth' of participants' experiences is worthwhile. For qualitative researchers whose goal is not to represent participants' experiences, member checking is even more problematic. If we understand our results from a more critical position, where they are an *interpretation*, underpinned by theory (and subjectivity), 'there is no reason why non-academic participants should be especially qualified to validate it' (Taylor, 2001: 322). The participants' approval cannot 'prove' or 'disprove' the analysis, because it is not intended as a reflection of their experience as they understand it (see Chapter 2). US communication researcher Sarah Tracy (2010: 844) has proposed a broader strategy of 'member reflections', which does not assume a 'single true reality', as an alternative to member checking. Member reflections entail 'sharing and dialoguing with participants about the study's findings, and providing opportunities for questions, critique, feedback, affirmation, and even collaboration'. Member reflections can involve participant validation, but they can also be an opportunity for 'reflexive elaboration' of the results rather than *testing* whether the researcher has 'got it right'.

This discussion of member checking reveals the main 'take home' message of this chapter: most quality criteria are not theoretically 'neutral.' They are also underpinned by assumptions about the goals of research. It's important to understand the theoretical and methodological assumptions that underpin quality criteria, and to select those that 'fit' with the aims and frameworks of the research you are evaluating.

TRIANGULATION

Triangulation is a millennia-old mathematical process for determining the distance or location of an object, combining independent measures from separate locations to provide an accurate reading. In research, triangulation traditionally refers to a process whereby two or more methods of data collection or sources of data are used to examine the same phenomenon, with the aim of getting as close to the 'truth' of the object of study as possible. The use of triangulation in qualitative research was first promoted by the US sociologist Norman Denzin (1970). Some qualitative researchers also use triangulation in relation to using the different standpoints and perspectives of a team of researchers to develop the analysis of data (see Lincoln & Guba, 1985). If you are conducting a realist qualitative study assuming a single, knowable truth, then either view of triangulation makes sense. But both are rather problematic for (most) qualitative researchers, who view meaning as fundamentally tied to the context in which it is produced. If you don't assume a single (objective) knowable 'truth', then using different data sources, methods, approaches or analysts cannot take you closer to *the* truth, because such a thing doesn't exist for you.

Smith (1996) argued that some qualitative researchers view triangulation as a way of strengthening analytic claims, and of getting a richer or fuller story, rather than a more accurate one. This argument is similar to Australian-based health psychologist Jane Ussher's (1999: 43) use of a jigsaw metaphor to advocate 'multi-methods': 'it is only when we put the different pieces of the jigsaw together that we see a broader picture and gain some insight into the complexity' of our research. Triangulation becomes a way of capturing the multiple 'voices' or 'truths' that relate to the topic, rather than being understood as way to access the one right 'result' (Silverman, 1993). As an example of this form of triangulation, Smith (1996) described a (hypothetical) study of bullying in schools, in which a team of researchers collected interview data from teachers, children and parents, used participant observation within the schools, and also used textual methods (diaries, vignettes, story completion tasks; see Chapter 6 and *companion website*) to examine the issue. This involved three forms of triangulation: via data (collecting from different sources); via methods (using different methods of data collection and, possibly, data analysis); via researchers (using a team of researchers to collect and analyse the data) (Gliner, 1994; see also King et al., 2008 for an example of 'polyvocal' analysis of a qualitative interview by a group of phenomenological researchers). This approach to triangulation could also involve the use of multiple theoretical lenses (Tracy, 2010). Tracy (2010) advocates the replacement of the imagery of triangulation with that of *crystallisation* (from poststructuralist theory), which transcends the 'rigid, fixed, two-dimensional' (Richardson, 2000: 934) triangle with the multi-faceted crystal. The goal of crystallisation is to use multiple sources of data, methods, researchers and theoretical frameworks 'to open up a more complex, in-depth, but still thoroughly partial, understanding of the issue' (Richardson, 2000: 844) under investigation.

CHECKLIST CRITERIA FOR QUALITATIVE RESEARCH

In our approach to thematic analysis (TA; Braun & Clarke, 2006), we identified a checklist of 15 criteria for a good TA (see Table 12.1) – many of which can be applied to qualitative research more generally. Others have developed general criteria for assessing the quality of qualitative research (see 'Further Resources' below for details of some online appraisal tools, and Hannes et al., 2010, for a comparison and evaluation of these tools), which aim to transcend the theoretical assumptions associated with particular qualitative approaches. For example, North American psychologists Robert Elliott, Constance Fischer and David Rennie (1999) synthesised a wide range of validity criteria into what they called 'evolving guidelines for the publication of qualitative research studies in psychology and related fields'. Box 12.2 provides an abbreviated version of their guidelines. Although the criteria are oriented towards getting a study published, they should not be seen as limited to that, and do offer useful criteria to ensure you do good qualitative research. Their guidelines have, however, been controversial. Although Elliott et al.'s

Table 12.1   A 15-point checklist of criteria for good thematic analysis (Braun & Clarke, 2006)

Process	No.	Criteria
Transcription	1	The data have been transcribed to an appropriate level of detail, and the transcripts have been checked against the tapes for 'accuracy'
Coding	2	Each data item has been given equal attention in the coding process
	3	Themes have not been generated from a few vivid examples (an anecdotal approach), but instead the coding process has been thorough, inclusive and comprehensive
	4	All relevant extracts for all each theme have been collated
	5	Themes have been checked against each other and back to the original data set
	6	Themes are internally coherent, consistent, and distinctive
Analysis	7	Data have been analysed – interpreted, made sense of – rather than just paraphrased or described
	8	Analysis and data match each other – the extracts illustrate the analytic claims
	9	Analysis tells a convincing and well-organised story about the data and topic
	10	A good balance between analytic narrative and illustrative extracts is provided
Overall	11	Enough time has been allocated to complete all phases of the analysis adequately, without rushing a phase or giving it a once-over-lightly
Written report	12	The assumptions about, and specific approach to, thematic analysis are clearly explicated
	13	There is a good fit between what you claim you do, and what you show you have done – i.e. described method and reported analysis are consistent
	14	The language and concepts used in the report are consistent with the epistemological position of the analysis
	15	The researcher is positioned as *active* in the research process; themes do not just 'emerge'

aim was to create guidelines that could be applied to *all* forms of qualitative research, and they mention the importance of evaluating qualitative research on its own terms (rather than on those derived from quantitative research), some qualitative researchers have highlighted ways their guidelines failed to meet these aspirations. British social psychologist Steve Reicher (2000), for example, argued that their guidelines didn't take account of the theoretical assumptions of discursive research, which can be quite different (see Chapter 8, and Elliott et al.'s, 2000, response to Reicher). Reicher emphasised the importance of qualitative research being judged as excellent on its own terms, and suggested that, given the diversity of theoretical approaches employed across the broad field (see Chapters 2 and 8), it might not be possible to develop a *single* set of guidelines that apply to *all* forms of qualitative research (for discussion of criteria related to specific methods, see Antaki et al., 2002; Charmaz, 2005; Potter, 1996; Smith et al., 2009).

BOX 12.2　ROBERT ELLIOTT, CONSTANCE FISCHER AND DAVID RENNIE'S (1999) EVOLVING GUIDELINES FOR PUBLICATION OF QUALITATIVE RESEARCH STUDIES IN PSYCHOLOGY AND OTHER FIELDS

(A) Publishability guidelines shared by both qualitative and quantitative approaches

1　*Explicit scientific context and purpose*. The manuscript specifies where the study fits within relevant literature and states the intended purposes or questions of the study.

2　*Appropriate methods*. The methods and procedures used are appropriate or responsive to the intended purposes or questions of the study.

3　*Respect for participants*. Informed consent, confidentiality, welfare of the participants, social responsibility and other ethical principles are fulfilled. Researchers creatively adapt their procedures and reports to respect both their participants' lives, and the complexity and ambiguity of the subject matter.

4　*Specification of methods*. Authors report all procedures for gathering data, including specific questions posed to participants. Ways of organising the data and method of analysis are also specified. This allows readers to see how to conduct a similar study themselves, and to judge for themselves how well the reported study was carried out.

5　*Appropriate discussion*. The research data and the understandings derived from them are discussed in terms of their contribution to theory, content, method and/or practical domains, and are presented in appropriately tentative and contextualised terms, with limitations acknowledged.

6　*Clarity of presentation*. The manuscript is well organised and clearly written, with technical terms defined.

7　*Contribution to knowledge*. The manuscript contributes to an elaboration of a discipline's body of description and understanding.

(B) Publishability guidelines especially pertinent to qualitative research

1　*Owning one's perspective*. Authors specify their theoretical orientations and personal anticipations, both as known in advance and as they become apparent during the research. In developing and communicating their understanding of the phenomenon under study, authors attempt to recognise their values, interests and assumptions and the role these play in the understanding. This disclosure of values and assumptions helps readers to interpret the researchers' data and understanding of them, and to consider possible alternatives.

2　*Situating the sample*. Authors describe the research participants and their life circumstances to aid the reader in judging the range of people and situations to which the findings might be relevant.

3　*Grounding in examples*. Authors provide examples of the data to illustrate both the analytic procedures used in the study and the understanding developed in the light of them. The examples allow appraisal of the fit between the data and authors' understandings of them; they also allow readers to conceptualise possible alternative meanings and understandings.

4 *Providing credibility checks*. Researchers may use any one of several methods for checking the credibility of their categories, themes or accounts. Where relevant, these may include: (a) checking these understandings with the original informants or others similar to them; (b) using multiple qualitative analysts, an additional analytic 'auditor', or the original analyst for a 'verification step' of reviewing the data for discrepancies, overstatements or errors; (c) comparing two or more varied qualitative perspectives, or (d) where appropriate, 'triangulation' with external factors (e.g. outcome or recovery) or quantitative data.

5 *Coherence*. The understanding is represented in a way that achieves coherence and integration while preserving nuances in the data. The understanding fits together to form a data-based story/narrative, 'map', framework, or underlying structure for the phenomenon or domain.

6 *Accomplishing general vs. specific research tasks*. Where a *general* understanding of a phenomenon is intended, it is based on an appropriate range of instances (informants or situations). Limitations of extending the findings to other contexts and informants are specified. Where understanding a *specific* instance or case is the goal, it has been studied and described systematically and comprehensively enough to provide the reader a basis for attaining that understanding. Such case studies also address limitations of extending the findings to other instances.

7 *Resonating with readers*. The manuscript stimulates resonance in readers/reviewers, meaning that the material is presented in such a way that readers/reviewers, taking all other guidelines into account, judge it to have accurately represented accurately the subject matter or to have clarified or expanded their appreciation and understanding of it.

It *is* important to assess qualitative research in relation to the 'logic of justification' and theoretical assumptions employed by the authors (Madill et al., 2000) – in other words, constructionist research should be evaluated according to constructionist criteria; experiential research by experiential criteria. But might it be possible to develop more generic criteria that can be applied flexibly across different orientations? British health psychologist Lucy Yardley (2000, 2008) developed a set of four theoretically 'neutral' validity principles (see Box 12.3) that could be applied to qualitative research of experiential (e.g. interpretative phenomenological analysis [IPA]) or constructionist (e.g. discourse analysis [DA]) forms. Each of her four criteria can be interpreted and demonstrated in different ways, appropriate to the methods used, and she notes that 'it is not necessary or even possible for any single study to exhibit all these qualities' (Yardley, 2008: 248). Yardley's criteria are open and flexible, and represent one of the most successful attempts to develop theoretically 'neutral' quality criteria (see also Tracy's, 2010, eight flexible, trans-theoretical criteria).

BOX 12.3   LUCY YARDLEY'S (2000, 2008) 'OPEN-ENDED, FLEXIBLE' QUALITY PRINCIPLES

1 *Sensitivity to context* – a qualitative researcher can be sensitive to context by:
   - contextualising the research in relation to relevant theoretical and empirical literature;
   - being sensitive to participants' perspectives and the socio-cultural context (during both data collection – by, for example, asking open-ended questions that encourage participants to talk about what is important to them – and during data analysis by exploring how the participants' socio-cultural context shapes their accounts);
   - being sensitive to ethical issues such as the extra responsibility of care when representing the stories of marginalised or vulnerable participants (see Chapter 3);
   - being sensitive to the data by not simply imposing the researcher's meanings on the data and being open to alternative interpretations of, and the complexities and inconsistencies in, the data.

2 *Commitment and rigour* – can be demonstrated by:
   - thorough data collection;
   - breadth and/or depth of analysis;
   - methodological competence and skill;
   - in-depth engagement with topic (both professionally and personally).

3 *Transparency and coherence* – can be demonstrated through presentation of the analysis that exhibits:
   - clarity and power of description or argument through a persuasive and convincing interpretation of data;
   - fit between the research question, the theoretical framework and the methods used to collect and analyse data;
   - a transparent account of how data were collected and analysed; presentation of data extracts to allow the reader to judge for themselves the adequacy of interpretations;
   - reflexivity through considering how the researcher, or the use of particular methods, shaped the research.

4 *Impact and importance* – 'can only be assessed in relation to the objectives of the analysis, the application it was intended for, and the community for whom the results were deemed relevant' (Yardley, 2000: 223). So a piece of research might have:
   - practical or applied impact for a particular user-group or community, or for practitioners or policy makers;
   - theoretical impact through increasing our understanding of a particular issue or creating new understandings;
   - socio-cultural impact through contributing to positive social change for a particular group.

Madill et al. (2000) concluded that qualitative researchers have a responsibility to make their theoretical position and epistemological assumptions clear, to conduct their research in a manner consistent with that position and those assumptions and to present their results in a way that they can be evaluated appropriately. This is because 'ultimately, evaluation operates through persuading the academic community' (Taylor, 2001: 324); researchers can and do persuade their peers of the value of their work (their research gets published and gets cited in other journal articles and academic books). Table 12.2 provides an evaluation of Kitzinger and Willmott's (2002) study using ten suitable criteria discussed in this chapter, taking into account the constraints of academic publishing (see Chapter 13).

Table 12.2   An evaluation of Kitzinger & Willmott (2002) using appropriate quality criteria

Criteria	Comments	Evaluation (Poor– Excellent)
Sensitivity to context of existing research and theory (Yardley)	The authors discuss what is already known about PCOS and develop a new research question about women's experiences of PCOS.	Excellent
Sensitivity to participants' perspectives and the socio-cultural context (Yardley)	The interview guide 'was designed to allow women to tell their own stories' (p. 350); the women's accounts are located within the wider socio-cultural context of 'norms of "proper" womanhood or femininity' (p. 352).	Excellent
Owning one's perspective (Elliott et al.)	The authors acknowledge that the research is conducted 'within a feminist framework' (p. 349) and adheres to basic feminist principles of 'drawing attention to women's experiences' (p. 352) and 'empowering the "socially marginalised"' (p. 352). They also acknowledge that the second author, who conducted all of the interviews, had PCOS herself and was open about this with the participants. The authors could have provided a more detailed reflection on how Jo Willmott's 'insider' status shaped the data collection and analysis.	Good
Situating the sample (Elliott et al.)	The authors present a relatively thorough description of the participants, providing both generic socio-demographic information (age, race/ethnicity/culture, sexuality, relationship status, employment/occupation) and information specific to the study (whether or not they have children and, if so, whether they were conceived as a result of fertility treatment). They note also that the participants reflect the typical PCOS support group member (largely white, able-bodied, heterosexual, aged 25–34). They could have situated the sample further by providing information on social class, ability and geographic location, and by considering the specifics of the British context of the sample.	Good

(Continued)

Table 12.2   (Continued)

Criteria	Comments	Evaluation (Poor– Excellent)
Grounding in examples (Elliott et al.)	The key finding that women with PCOS experience themselves as 'freaks' is very well grounded in the data. The analytic claims are supported by vivid and compelling data extracts.	Excellent
A good balance between analytic narrative and data extracts (Braun & Clarke)	With an approximate 60/40 split between data extracts and analytic commentary, there is scope for further development of the analytic commentary.	Good
The researcher is positioned as active in the process (Braun & Clarke)	The authors describe how they collected and analysed the data; however more detail could be provided on the process of 'organising sections of the data into recurrent themes' (p. 351) and, as noted above, they could have reflected on how Jo Wilmott's personal experience of PCOS informed the analysis and development of the key theme of 'freakishness'.	Good
Transferability (Lincoln & Guba)	The authors provide a reasonably 'thick description' of the participant group (see above) to enable readers to make judgements about the 'safe' transfer of the results.	Good
Sensitivity to the data – (being open to) capturing different 'stories' in the data (Yardley)	The authors acknowledge that the women did sometimes problematise the notion of 'proper womanhood'. They discuss and provide evidence of 'some muted and inconsistent resistance to the socially constructed notion of "normal" women as the effortless feminine hair-free, 28-day cycle creatures of advertising copy and male fantasy' (p. 259).	Excellent
Impact and importance (Yardley)	The paper is the first to 'give voice' to the experiences of women with PCOS; the authors hope 'that the publication of these research findings will contribute to de-stigmatising PCOS, will influence the understanding PCOS women have of themselves, and will contribute to medical practitioners' understandings of how PCOS affects women' (p. 359). How can we measure if these aspirations have been achieved? A quick Google search reveals that the paper is cited on various health information web sites and in popular books aimed at women with PCOS; it has also achieved over 100 academic citations – a very impressive citation count for a social science journal article, and strong evidence that the authors have persuaded the academic community of the value of their work (Taylor, 2001).	Excellent

Overall assessment: a very good example of qualitative research. That this paper is based on Jo Willmott's *undergraduate* psychology project shows that small student research projects can reach the highest standards!

The development of such guidelines has not closed the debate on how to judge the quality of qualitative research, and a problem remains with how to interpret guidelines; most are not absolute. For example, in relation to Elliott et al.'s (1999) criteria of 'owning one's perspective' (see Box 12.2), the process has been described as potentially limitless, and given the dominant requirement of anonymous peer review within journal publishing (where reviewers of a manuscript do not know the identity of the authors), there are likely to be practical limitations on how far it is possible to 'own one's perspective' (McLeod, 2001). Another important question is how we could judge whether a perspective has been appropriately 'owned' and authentically conveyed? And who gets to determine it? The key point is that quality criteria are not *absolute* yardsticks by which to judge the quality of a piece of research; like all aspects of qualitative research, they require active interpretation and application appropriate to the study in hand (Meyrick, 2006). This takes us back to the notion of *implicit* criteria and communities of knowledge discussed at the start of the chapter: as you become a more experienced researcher, you will *know* quality when you see it.

When evaluating research, it is also important to keep in mind that 'no research is perfect in that all can be criticised' (Taylor, 2001: 317): there is always room for improvement (a mantra our students are very familiar with) and reports of research always bear the imprint of the researcher who created them. As Taylor (2001: 321) noted, many quality criteria draw our attention to 'the importance of the way in which the research is written up', and it is this final step in the research journey that we turn to in the next chapter.

CHAPTER SUMMARY

This chapter:
- discussed whether the quantitative criteria of reliability, and validity, and the aim of generalisability, can apply to qualitative research;
- discussed quality criteria specific to qualitative research, including checklist criteria;
- emphasised the need to evaluate any particular qualitative study *on its own terms*.

? QUESTIONS FOR DISCUSSION AND CLASSROOM EXERCISES

1   Working in small groups, choose a qualitative study that the group broadly agrees is a good example of qualitative research (such as one of the examples from this book) and identify the key theoretical and methodological assumptions underpinning the study. Guided by these assumptions, select ten quality criteria discussed in this chapter that would be appropriate for evaluating the study and critically assess the study using these criteria. Do the results of this evaluation cohere with your instinct that this is a good example of qualitative research?

2   What assumptions underpin the use of an 'analytic auditor' (Elliott et al., 1999)? Which qualitative analytic methods is this quality technique most and least applicable to?

3   Identify ten quality criteria appropriate to the evaluation of an *experiential* TA of interactive data such as interviews or focus groups. If you were going to evaluate a constructionist TA of secondary sources, which of these criteria could you retain, which would you have to change, and what would you replace them with?

4   Three researchers are each planning to conduct and complete a small IPA study over eight months. Their participant groups and methods of data collection are:

a   gay men with intellectual disabilities, who will participate in face-to-face interviews (see Bennett & Coyle, 2007);

b   geographically dispersed university students who are heavy internet users/internet 'addicts', who will participate in email interviews (see Chou, 2001);

c   injecting drug users, who will complete diaries and then participate in face-to-face interviews (see Singer et al., 2000).

Each researcher wants to use member checking to help establish the credibility of their results, but are aware there may be some practical (and theoretical) problems with implementing member-checking with their participant group. Working in small groups, what advice would you give to each researcher on their use of member checking? What practical problems might they encounter and how can they manage these? On balance, would you recommend the use of member checking or other quality techniques?

FURTHER RESOURCES

Further reading:

For a worked example of an evaluation of qualitative study, see: Chapter 2, Narrative analysis. In E. R. Girden (2001), *Evaluating research articles: From start to finish*, (2nd ed). Thousand Oaks, CA: Sage.

For a more detailed discussion of Lucy Yardley's flexible and open-ended quality criteria and a worked example of the appropriate application of these criteria, see: Yardley, L. (2008). Demonstrating validity in qualitative psychology. In J. A. Smith (Ed.), *Qualitative psychology: A practical guide to research methods* (pp. 235–251). London: Sage.

For an alternative set of universal quality criteria for qualitative research, see: Tracy, S. J. (2010). Qualitative quality: eight 'big-tent' criteria for excellent qualitative research. *Qualitative Inquiry, 16*, 837–851.

For a discussion and comparison of the evaluative criteria associated with three different epistemological frameworks (realist, contextualist and radical constructionist qualitative research), see: Madill, A., Jordan, A., & Shirley, C. (2000). Objectivity and reliability in qualitative analysis: realist, contextualist and radical constructionist epistemologies. *British Journal of Psychology, 91*, 1–20.

Online resources:

HCPRDU Evaluation Tool for Qualitative Studies: http://usir.salford.ac.uk/12970/

Critical Appraisal Skills Programme (CASP) Qualitative Appraisal Tool (ten questions to help you make sense of qualitative research): http://www.caspinternational.org/mod_product/uploads/CASP_Qualitative_Studies%20_Checklist_14.10.10.pdf

See the *companion website* (**www.sagepub.co.uk/braunandclarke**) for:
- self-test multiple choice questions relating to Section 4;
- the flashcard glossary – test yourself on the definitions of key terms used in this chapter;
- further readings (articles from Sage journals).

13

Writing and communicating qualitative research

Congratulations! You have reached the final stage of your qualitative research journey: communicating your results. Just as qualitative analysis involves developing a compelling and coherent story about your data, writing a report, presenting a talk or designing a poster involve telling a story *about your research*, turning the messy process of *doing* qualitative research into a coherent and informative research narrative. And this requires writing. Writing is a fundamental skill for qualitative research; *writing* and *thinking* go hand-in-hand. But writing can be a daunting and even terrifying process – particularly if faced with writing a 10,000- or 20,000-word research report for the first time. But it needn't be. This chapter is designed to teach good writing (and editing) practice, to help you feel more confident (you may even soon be wondering how you'll fit everything in – the very problem we tend to have with writing, including writing this book!).

IT'S ALL ABOUT THE EDIT!

For those new to research, the model of writing that's probably most familiar is the 'static writing model' (Richardson, 2000): first you do something (read, think, plan), then you write it up, communicating *what you already know*. Writing is the end point of a linear journey (Cameron, Nairn, & Higgins, 2009). For experienced scholars, writing about (qualitative) research is more of 'a messy and iterative process of bringing ideas into being' (Cameron et al., 2009: 270), a way of thinking (Howitt, 2010; Miles & Huberman, 1994). Writing is used to *generate* ideas, rather than simply to report them, and we encourage this more creative style of writing. As we noted in Chapter 11, it is through writing that analytic ideas are crystallised and refined; we often 'find our argument' (Charmaz, 2006) through drafting and re-drafting our research. This means that experienced researchers typically write *multiple* drafts of a manuscript before they submit it for publication. Our writing process is fairly typical. We write a first draft, edit the draft, by reading a hard copy and annotating it with comments, and then make changes. When we have repeated this process a number of times to produce a second or third draft (or even a fourth or fifth) we might circulate it to a few trusted colleagues for feedback. We revise the manuscript again in light of our colleagues' feedback; only then would we consider submitting it for publication. The ***companion website*** includes a comparison of the first draft, and final version of a paragraph from one of our papers on thematic analysis, to give an indication of *how much* we tend to change our work from our first attempt.

This process demonstrates that writing is a *craft*, and a recursive process. It is rare for any researcher to be able to produce a perfect report like a rabbit out of a magician's hat. New Zealand-based literary scholar Helen Sword (2010) advises that academic writers should 'write first, edit later'. Rather than editing *as you go* – writing and (immediately) rewriting each sentence to get it 'perfect' – try to write whole chunks of text in one go, and then edit it once a whole section or the whole report has been produced. The vast majority of writing time should be allocated to editing rather than writing the *first* draft (Woods, 1999, recommended 90 per cent of your time, which gives an indication of how important editing is seen to be). Editing as a process involves 're-writing, rephrasing, re-ordering, re-structuring, moving parts of the text around, adding to and deleting text, clarifying ... removing ambiguities, sharpening, tightening, tidying up grammar, and so on' (Woods, 1999: 81). Woods (1999) recommended careful editing to remove (among other things):

- *faulty grammar* such as sentences that aren't grammatical, sentences that are far too long, spelling errors, unclear meaning, punctuation errors, or mixing past and present tense (for guidance on grammar and punctuation, see Seely, 2009; Taggart, 2008; Truss, 2003).
- *stylistic problems* such as repetition, using excessive numbers of words or providing unnecessary detail (a cluttered text), too many or too lengthy quotations from academic sources, inappropriate use of slang and colloquial language, or inconsistent presentation;
- *structural problems* such as sections that are not closely linked, a structure that is basically a list of points rather than a developing argument, loose ends, repetition across sections.

When we edit, we ask ourselves questions like: 'Is the point of this sentence clear?'; 'Do we need to provide more detail here?'; 'Does this section have a logical and coherent structure?'; 'What point(s) am I making in this section?'; and 'Is my overall argument clear?' You should plan to draft and then re-draft your report a number of times, using the writing and the editing process to develop and polish your ideas.

At a certain point, it can become very difficult to 'see the wood for the trees' in your own writing. For this reason, it's also good to give yourself time to put your writing down, and let it sit for at least a few days. Also consider circulating a (good) draft to trusted peers for feedback (this might also be provided by your supervisor). Although formal assessment of students at university tends to encourage working in isolation, this does not replicate how many academics produce their articles and books. To make the most of any feedback (from your supervisor or from others), only ask for feedback when you think your report (or a section of your report) represents your best effort, and you can't see any obvious ways to improve it – or if you're completely stuck. There's little point asking for feedback when you know which bits need clarification and tightening, or are missing crucial information; you will simply be told things you already know. The advantage of feedback is that it provides a fresh (outsider) perspective on your work – someone who can tell you if a sentence isn't clear, if you have provided enough (or too much) detail, if the analysis isn't convincing, etc. It's really useful for people to know what kind of feedback you need (Belcher, 2009); you can use the *comments* function in Microsoft Word to ask questions about specific aspects of your report. The feedback you receive, especially from supervisors, should ideally be treated as a springboard for significantly developing your writing and scholarship. Try to see the general principles behind the given feedback, rather than just applying that feedback *literally* to a specific place in the report.

SKILLS FOR ACADEMIC WRITING

Australian human geographer Jenny Cameron and colleagues (Cameron et al., 2009) identified the following knowledge and skills as necessary components of academic writing:

- *creative skills* such as getting ideas onto the page and finding your own voice, which includes recognising that you have a contribution to make;
- *critical skills* that enable you to *revise* the words on the page;
- *technical writing skills* such knowing how to construct sentences and paragraphs, structure an argument, write clearly, when to use the passive and active voice (e.g. 'the data were collected' vs. 'I collected the data');
- *procedural writing skills* including understanding that writing is recursive, knowing how to deal with writer's block, knowing how to move between reading, writing and thinking, understanding the importance of a disciplined writing schedule and the importance of breaks – and exercise – and understanding that digressions and failures are not mistakes but an inevitable part of recursive process of writing.

It's also important to understand that writing is an *emotional* process that can rouse difficult emotions – self-doubt is a particularly devilish one – for new qualitative researchers *and* the most experienced academics (Cameron et al., 2009). Even among successful academics, there are few who 'find the writing process easy' (Sword, 2010: 1) – we know of very few academics who experience writing as an entirely positive process without struggles and negative feelings. Grounded theorist Kathy Charmaz's (2006) tips for writing for grounded theory (GT) are useful ones to follow in learning to write qualitative research reports. One particular element we like is the 'free writing' exercise, which can help overcome the writing paralysis that fear or anxiety can produce. A 'free-writing' exercise can help you to find your 'voice', produce fresh material and work through your fears (see Box 13.1).

BOX 13.1   A FREE-WRITING EXERCISE (CHARMAZ, 2006)

If you're suffering from writer's block or are struggling to articulate your ideas, spend ten minutes writing whatever comes to mind (in relation to your analysis/report), following these guidelines:

- write for yourself (don't write for an audience);
- don't worry about grammar, sentence structure and organisation;
- give yourself permission to write badly;
- write as quickly as you can;
- write as though you are talking (to yourself).

AVOIDING DISCRIMINATORY LANGUAGE IN WRITING

To conform to good, ethical research practice (see Chapter 3), our writing (and presentations) should avoid sexist, racist, homophobic, heterosexist and other pejorative language and assumptions (Schwartz, Landrum, & Gurung, 2012). While the terms racism, sexism and homophobia are widely understood, heterosexism is less familiar. It refers to the assumption that everyone is, or should be, heterosexual (Braun, 2000): heterosexist assumptions include the assumption that all participants are heterosexual, that all partner relationships are between men and women, and that the values and practices of heterosexuality are 'normal'.

The avoidance of all forms pejorative language and assumptions 'cannot be fully reduced to a list of dos and don'ts' (Howitt & Cramer, 2008: 74). Language is a fluid and flexible tool, and it is possible to offend without intending to, and without using overtly offensive language. However, some useful rules are:

- *Avoid 'he-man' language*: this refers not to the name of the main character in the *He-Man and the Masters of the Universe* US cartoon series, but to terms such as 'he', 'man' and 'mankind', 'chairman', 'man-made' being used as supposedly generic, gender-neutral terms. Research shows that these terms do not make people think of men *and* women, but of men only, and such terms present men as the 'norm' and render women invisible (Crawford & Unger, 2004). Gender-neutral pronouns and words like 'people' and 'humankind' do the job perfectly. Also avoid stereotyped terms such as 'male nurse' and 'lady doctor', unless the gender of the person is relevant. And think about the assumptions embedded when dominant groups are placed first in lists or pairings, such as 'men and women' (see Hegarty, Watson, Fletcher, & McQueen, 2011), 'straight and gay,' etc.

- *Use the terms that socially marginalised groups use to describe themselves*: for example, terms such as 'gay man', 'lesbian' or 'bisexual woman' are ones most non-heterosexual people would use to describe themselves, rather than 'homosexual' – this term should not be used because it is vague (see Schwartz et al., 2012) and it has associations with deviance, mental illness and criminal behaviour (Committee on Lesbian and Gay Concerns, 1991). 'Non-heterosexuals' and 'LGB people' are good substitutes for 'homosexuals'.

- *Be precise (and culturally specific) about race and ethnicity*: the American Psychological Association (APA) recommends being as precise as possible about participants' race/ethnic identity (Schwartz et al., 2012) – but do avoid compromising anonymity. It's important to be aware that racial/ethnic/cultural identity categories are incredibly culturally variable, with localised uses and meanings (British Sociological Association, 2005). For example, in Aotearoa/New Zealand, 'European' or 'New Zealand European' is shorthand for a racial (white) identity; in the UK, European would mean something quite different. Many white New Zealanders prefer to use an indigenous Māori term (Pākehā) to refer to their racial/ethnic/cultural identity because it is socio-politically and geographically specific (Bell, 1996) and meaningful; others don't, or reject the label. Similarly, in the UK, the broad category 'Asian' generally refers to people from South Asian countries like India and Pakistan; in Aotearoa/New Zealand, 'Asian' tends to be applied to people from South-East Asia. It is generally better to be more specific and refer to particular national identities such as Indian or Vietnamese.

- *Put the person first*: this means not defining people by an experience or condition. For example, instead of labelling people as 'schizophrenics' or 'autistics', put the person *before* the condition, and refer to 'people with a diagnosis of schizophrenia' or 'people with autism' (Schwartz et al., 2012). In using terms such as 'the schizophrenic sample' or 'the black sample' you present people's medical condition or race as their most relevant and important characteristic; something like 'the sample of people with schizophrenia' would be preferable. However, note that this approach isn't universally supported. Some, such as British writer Clare Sainsbury (Sainsbury, 2009), who has Asperger's, argue that such 'putting the person first' language reinforces 'shame' around conditions, and also treats it as something separate from the person, like an appendage.

- *Avoid implicit (normative) moral judgements*: avoid using language which situates certain social arrangements (e.g. heterosexuality) as 'normal', because they are either common or taken for granted. The use of 'normal' implies that different social arrangements (e.g. anything other than heterosexuality) are *abnormal*. The word 'normative', in contrast, refers to what is *deemed* normal, or exists as 'the norm' within dominant social or psychological values. Many expressions we commonly use have inbuilt assumptions – for instance, the phrases 'fatherless families' (as opposed to single-parent [or lesbian] families) or 'childless women' (as opposed to 'child-free') (Denmark et al., 1988) situate *not* having (involved) fathers in a family or *not* having children as abnormal and undesirable. Given that there is almost always another way to describe someone or something, think about what assumptions and implications are embedded in the terms you are using. Sometimes these reflect the origins of language, and we may choose not to use words that carry negative social values. For instance, one of our PhD supervisors taught us that the commonly used term 'denigrate' stems from the Latin dénigrâre, meaning 'to blacken' (http://en.wiktionary.org/wiki/denigrate), and hence can be understood as reiterating racist values.

If you are unsure about the correct terminology, ask your supervisor or consult published guidance on non-sexist (Stark-Adamec & Kimball, 1984), non-racist (British Sociological Association, 2005), non-ableist (British Sociological Association, 2004; Committee on Disability Issues in Psychology, 1992; *Guidelines for reporting and writing about people with disabilities*, 2008), non-ageist (Schaie, 1993) and non-heterosexist (Clarke et al., 2010; Committee on Lesbian and Gay Concerns, 1991) language; general advice is also available (American Psychological Association, 2010; Kessler & McDonald, 2012; Schwartz et al., 2012).

PLANNING FOR WRITING

Helen Sword (2010) suggests a number of useful time-planning strategies for starting, progressing, and completing writing projects:

- Set short-term writing goals: what will I write *today*?
- Also set longer-term writing goals: what will I write this *week/month*?

Combined, these help keep writing on track. Viewing your project in terms of daily or weekly targets, or chunks of writing, rather than one *huge* report, can also help to manage fears and anxieties. Sword also advises avoiding 'binge writing' – such as trying to write the entire report in a week. As writing is an integral part of your research, writing a little, often, rather than a lot, infrequently, helps with remaining engaged with your report. She also suggests that you try to allow time to reflect, ponder, draw and redraw mind maps, or simply stare out of the window. We fully agree. It's often when we walk away from our computers that ideas suddenly take shape. The benefit of unpressured 'thinking time' cannot be overestimated.

WRITING A RESEARCH REPORT

In this section, we orient to the British context, and particularly the requirements for undergraduate psychology project reports. Some of this will be easily translatable to other contexts. The most important thing when writing a report is having a clear understanding of the specific requirements of your report (whether it's an undergraduate project, a PhD, or a manuscript for a journal).

WHAT MAKES A GOOD RESEARCH REPORT?

British psychologist Brendan Gough and colleagues (Gough et al., 2003) drew on the views of 50 psychologists who supervise qualitative projects to identify the features of a good qualitative research project. The top five features were:

- displaying an awareness of the differences between quantitative and qualitative paradigms and grounding the chosen approach epistemologically;
- developing research questions that display originality and are relevant to the wider social context;
- qualitative analyses that move beyond description and summary to conceptual analysis;
- making 'a serious effort to be reflexive' (see Box 13.2);
- Developing a 'coherent narrative' about the whole project.

We agree that a 'coherent narrative' is crucial. All the different elements of the report should be organised around a central storyline (White, Woodfield, & Ritchie, 2003); 'what you did' and 'what you found' should be presented in a logical and clear way. If you compare your research process to that described in published reports of qualitative research, you might think 'my research process was a lot messier than their research process'. In truth, their process was probably as 'messy' as, if not 'messier' than, yours; coherence develops in the process of writing about the research. This is not to say that professional researchers are dishonest, just that in writing about their research, researchers often edit out the messiness and focus on the main elements of the story (primarily because this is what academic conventions demand). As Cameron et al. (2009: 271) noted, students:

> see academic work in its most finished form – the published refereed journal article or the published book – when all evidence of the recursiveness of writing, of the numerous iterations that a piece of writing usually goes through, has been obliterated. So working alone, and with other's published work as the standard, it is not surprising that many novices become filled with self-doubts. They experience their own writing in all its messiness, while the work they are reading seems to spring fully formed onto the page.

To achieve this coherence, do you need to write your report in a linear fashion? The short answer is no! If you consult the research project timetable in Box 3.7 in Chapter 3, you'll see that we encourage you to get writing straight away, starting to draft your literature review (and introduction) in the first month of your project. We have also discussed the ways in which writing more generally is integral to the process of qualitative research in terms of practices such as keeping a research journal or memo-writing in GT (see Chapter 9). This means that when it comes to actually 'writing up' your research, you will already have done a lot of writing, and while writing your report involves

BOX 13.2   TO BE OR NOT TO BE REFLEXIVE?

Throughout this book we have emphasised the active role of the researcher in the research process and in constructing knowledge, and the fact that all of us have values, interests and standpoints that shape our research. Reflexive research is, broadly speaking, research in which the researcher acknowledges and reflects on this role. The 'idea of reflexivity implies a certain capacity for "bending back" or "turning back" one's awareness on oneself' (McLeod, 2001: 195); in practice, this 'turning back' tends often to be rather minimal (e.g. a researcher might note that she is white and middle class – because she perceives these aspects of her identity to be relevant to the research). This is often for practical reasons: the constraints of journal and other academic publishing are such that there is typically little if any scope for extended discussions of reflexivity. There can also be a risk that the researcher's reflection becomes the focus of the research, and while this can be useful for exploring reflexivity (e.g. Rice, 2009), it can lead to paralysis when it comes to actually reporting the results of research.

Should *you* be reflexive in your research project? Although some researchers are critical of statements such as 'I am a white, middle class, heterosexual woman ...', we think even such limited reflexive statements, which 'own your perspective' (Elliot et al., 1999), are important – it seems rather odd to provide such information about participants, to 'situate your sample', but not about yourself. Locating your standpoint is especially important if an aspect of your identity is particularly pertinent to the research topic (see our evaluation of Kitzinger & Willmott's, 2002, study of women's experiences of PCOS in Table 12.2 in Chapter 12). *However*, and this is a fairly big however, reflexive writing is difficult to do well. The 'reflexive bits' in student projects can seem flippant or frivolous if not carefully thought through (Howitt, 2010) – reflexive writing is often either overly casual and colloquial or stiff and excessively formal. In *general*, we would advise against having a separate 'reflexive section' in your report (although some courses may require one), as it nearly always works better to weave your (personal) reflection throughout your report in relevant sections (e.g. introduction, methods, discussion).

To provide an example of good practice in reflexive writing, one of Victoria's students, Eleni Demetriou, who conducted her undergraduate research project on the experiences of adults who had grown up with a lesbian, gay or trans (LGT) parent (or parents), acknowledged in her methods section her personal investment in the topic as the daughter of a gay father and discussed how she disclosed her 'insider' status to the participants and often drew on her personal experiences in her interviews. When evaluating the study in the discussion section of her report, Eleni further explored how her insider status shaped the research process,

(Continued)

(Continued)

noting that 'it was difficult for me not to see the participants' stories through the lens of my own personal experience' (Demetriou, 2011: 27). She also discussed how her firsthand experience of anti-gay prejudice against gay families informed her desire to explore the impact of heteronormativity on the participants' experiences. Eleni's reflexive observations were interwoven throughout her report, highly relevant to the description and evaluation of her research and written in an appropriately personal but scholarly style. For some further examples of reflexive writing, see Virginia's reflexive analysis of her and her participants' heterosexism in her focus group research on the vagina (Braun, 2000), Victoria's exploration of how her 'insider' status shaped her research on lesbian and gay parenting (Clarke et al., 2004), and New Zealand feminist psychologist Maree Burns's discussion of the embodied nature of interviewing (Burns, 2003, 2006).

more (new) writing, it is also a process of assembling and editing, rather than writing a (say) 10,000-word report completely from scratch – including re-drafting your literature review and introduction to 'fit' the analysis, emphasising existing research and theories important for your analysis.

Returning to the issue of a coherent narrative or line of argument, a good test of whether you have achieved this is whether you can summarise your project to someone who knows nothing about it in a few sentences (can you easily identify the main strengths or contributions of your project?)? If yes, then you have, to paraphrase grounded theorist Kathy Charmaz (2006), 'found your argument'. If no, then you need to do some more writing and thinking. Another thing to keep in mind when writing your report is rationale, rationale, rationale! Although it is important to adhere to good (ethical) research practices, you can be original and make unusual choices as long as you have a clear justification for the choices you have made in conducting your research. Indeed, every aspect of your research (from your choice of sampling strategy to your analytic method) should be justified in your report. In some psychology departments, your use of a qualitative methodology itself may require justification (discuss this with your supervisor).

Look at examples of published qualitative research, ideally from journals that routinely publish qualitative research, such as *Qualitative Research in Psychology* and *Feminism & Psychology*, as models on which to base your report; articles that use a similar approach to yours are particularly helpful (Howitt, 2010). One particular feature you will note is that qualitative research often uses a language quite different from quantitative research; we note some salient differences in Box 13.3.

BOX 13.3   LANGUAGE IN QUALITATIVE RESEARCH REPORTS (AND PRESENTATIONS)

Because of the nature of qualitative analysis, when writing about your analysis we suggest using language like: 'identify' 'categorise' and 'report' – terms which acknowledge that the researcher has an active role in analysis. For example, use sentences like: 'We identified two discourses in the data ...'; 'We categorised the data into five main themes'; The patterns we report in our analysis ..." If you're astute, you'll have picked up that all of these are written in the first person. Writing in qualitative research often involves putting yourself in the text and writing in the first person. Some examples of the different types of language and writing approaches used in quantitative and qualitative paradigms are provided below. But it's also important to remember that you are also always writing for a specific purpose, so check the specific requirements for your report.

Quantitative paradigm	Qualitative paradigm
Hypotheses	Research questions
Experiment	Study/project
Subjects	Participants
Found	Identified (e.g. themes)
Findings/results	Analyses/results
Significant	Noteworthy/key/important
Third person	First person
Passive tense	Active tense
Researcher absent in the written article	Researcher present in the written article; first person language

---

ELEMENTS IN THE RESEARCH REPORT

In general, a student report of qualitative research should contain the elements listed below. We have based our advice on section lengths on a 10,000-word report, which includes all data extracts, but excludes the reference list and any appendices; adjust to whatever your own requirements are (e.g. if it's 12,500 words, increase the length of the main sections by 25 per cent).

Title page

This should include the title of your report and your name. A good title tells the reader something about your topic (and/or your key results) and your approach, uses language and concepts appropriate to qualitative research, and is as short as possible (avoid redundant words such as 'A study into ...'; Howitt, 2010). (Box 13.4 has advice on titles – and other information – specific to interpretative phenomenological analysis [IPA] projects.) A good clear example is: 'Students' perceptions of international adoption: A story completion study.' It concisely specifies the topic, sample and method used. A bad example is: 'Students' attitudes toward foreign adoption.' The use of the social-cognitive construct 'attitude' and the failure to specify a qualitative method suggest a quantitative project. Moreover, the use of term 'foreign' has a rather pejorative tone; as noted above, ensuring we use *respectful* language in research reporting is important. Qualitative report titles typically have two parts: a title and a subtitle (connected with a colon). A short data quote that captures a key aspect of your results can make the title vivid and engaging – for example, '"Real men don't diet": An analysis of contemporary newspaper representations of men, food and health' (Gough, 2007).

Acknowledgements

This can be as informal or formal as you like (it's not marked), but remember to thank anyone who helped you with your project (however small their contribution) including your supervisor and participants. Many people also choose to thank people who offered less directly research-related support, such as their partner, family and friends.

Abstract (around 100–200 words)

Your abstract should introduce the general topic and the research question/aims, explain the methods of data collection and analysis used, including describing the sample, outline your results (e.g. your themes), what you think they mean, and their significance for psychological theory, research and/or practice. In academic journal articles, a *key* function of an abstract is to enable a reader to decide whether or not to read the full journal article – you're summarising your research for someone who knows nothing about your project, and you want to 'entice them in'. For this reason, a catchy topic-related first sentence can be a good idea – such as 'Should we view nuns as oppressed or agentic?' (Brock, 2010: 473).

Contents page

The contents can either just list the major sections of the report (those discussed now), with relevant page numbers, or also include any subheadings within sections. If you have tables or figures or other illustrations, these need their own separate contents listing.

Introduction (2,000–3,000 words)

The purpose of the introduction is to contextualise, and provide a rationale for, your research. It should provide a discussion of relevant literature (see 'reviewing the literature for qualitative research reports' below), but is far more than just a literature *review*. If relevant it should also contextualise your topic in relation the wider social context, and explain why it is an important (social, health etc.) issue. It should also specify and justify your aims/research question, and often your broad methodological and theoretical approach (depending on the nature of your report, it might be more appropriate to include this information later, at the start of the methods section under the subheading 'methodology'). The introduction can also achieve the task of 'owning your perspective' (Elliott et al., 1999; see Chapter 12), by disclosing your values, interests and assumptions and the roles these played in researching your chosen topic. After reading the introduction, you want the reader to have a strong sense of why your project is important and interesting, how it relates to what we already know about the topic, and how it will offer something new. A few (topic-based) subheadings can be useful to organise the introduction. In general, 'funnel' from the broader context to the 'particular considerations most relevant to your research' (Crowley, 2010: 233), and write in the *past tense* (Banister, 1994). This section can combine both passive and active writing styles (Crowley, 2010) – passive when discussing relevant literature, active when describing research questions (and methodology).

Methods section (1,000–1,500 words)
The purpose of the method section is to tell the reader what you did, and how and why you did it. This section needs to do a range of things (not necessarily in this order):

- outline and justify the methods used to collect and analyse data (and methodology and research question/aims if not discussed in the introduction). It should explain *how* you developed any data collection tools such as interview guides or story completion tasks and how the data were prepared for analysis – e.g. transcribing audio data or typing up and compiling survey data;
- 'situate the sample' (Elliott et al., 1999) by providing a detailed description of what it is, and how it was obtained, specifying selection and/or recruitment processes. If you used participants, a summary of any demographic information should be provided (when reporting numbers such as the age of participants provide ranges and means, but avoid standard deviations and percentages);
- explain how the data were collected, including, if relevant, what information was given to participants;
- note institutional ethical approval (with some types of secondary data, this may not be required; see Chapters 3 and 6) and discuss the ethical guidelines and procedures followed. A more extended discussion of ethical issues will be necessary if your research generated particularly interesting or problematic ethical concerns (Howitt, 2010);
- 'own your perspective' (Elliott et al., 1999) by reflecting on the role your values and interests have played in the process of collecting and analysing your data (if you have not included this in your introduction);
- finally, if appropriate, discuss any quality techniques used (such as member checking or auditing; see Chapter 12).

Subheadings can be useful for organising this section; avoid the traditional sub-headings used in quantitative reports (e.g. 'materials,' 'procedure') unless they are appropriate. Useful subheadings for qualitative reports include 'Participants and recruit-ment', 'Data collection' (or something oriented to your chosen method – e.g. 'Collecting focus group data') and 'Data analysis'. Overall, the methods section should provide appropriate levels of detail while being pithy and focused. Like the introduction, this section should generally be written in the past tense (Banister, 1994); it can be written passively or actively depending on preference, and should be fully referenced (e.g. refer-ences for methods of data collection and analysis, ethics).

The results and discussion can be presented in one of two ways as we discuss further below (see also Chapter 11):

1 a combined *results and discussion* section (where the results are presented *and* contextualised in relation to the wider literature), followed by a longer *conclusion* (where which the overall results are summarised, the study is evaluated and sug-gestions are made for future research);

2 a *results* section (where the results are presented), a *discussion* section (where the results are summarised and contextualised in relation to the wider literature, the study is evaluated and suggestions are made for future research), and a short *con-clusion* (which provides an overall summary of the research).

Results section (4,000–5,000 words) or a combined results and discussion section (5,000–6,000 words)

This section, the longest in your report, should ideally begin with an overview of your results. This can be a simple list of your themes, or a summary table, model or figure (see Chapter 11). Then you should have a sub-section for each key theme (or analytic pattern) being discussed: use theme names as subheadings. For some projects, combining the results and the discussion sections will work best. In this model, which suits a lot of qualitative research (especially critical approaches; see Chapter 11), you contextu-alise your results in relation to the relevant literature, expanding your interpretation beyond the data (explained further in the next paragraph). For other projects, a more traditional model, with separate results and discussion sections will work best (see Box 13.4 for advice specific to IPA projects). As we noted in Chapter 11, if you keep spotting links between your analysis, and the wider literature, and/or want to use existing research and theoretical concepts to deepen your analysis of your data, then combine your results and discussion. This section can either be written in the present or the past tense, depending on preference. (This section may also be titled *analysis* or *analysis and discussion*.)

Discussion (up to 1,500 words)

The discussion section should provide a clear summary of your *overall* results, looking *across* your themes to highlight the general points (see Box 13.5 for an example), and, if not addressed in a results and discussion section, should contextualise your research

---

BOX 13.4   WRITING UP IPA: HINTS AND TIPS FROM SMITH ET AL. (2009)

- A common way to title IPA projects is: essence of results (title) and approach (subtitle). So for a project on shyness, for example, this would be something like: *What it is to be shy: an interpretative phenomenological analysis*. It's appropriate to use a short data quote as a title but only if the quote 'really does encapsulate ... the most important thing you want to say' (p. 111).
- Begin the results section with a summary of your results – either an abbreviated table of the group themes (present the full table in an appendix) or a figurative representation of the themes (like the thematic map in Chapter 10).
- Start your discussion of each theme with a brief description of the theme and then show how it applies to each participant in your sample (this is the case within a theme approach; with IPA it may sometimes be appropriate to prioritise the participant and use a theme-within-case approach, where the themes for each participant are discussed together).
- An IPA write-up is a weaving together of the 'P' (extracts from the participants) and the 'I' (your analytic commentary). It can be good to draft your analysis relatively quickly and then edit and revise at leisure. First drafts written by novice qualitative researchers tend to be rather descriptive, with lots of P (data quotes) and little I (analytic commentary). The revised draft should be more interpretative, but analytic claims should still be supported with evidence from the data.
- It is usual to separate out the results and discussion in an IPA report – the results section should provide a close reading of the participants' experiences without reference to the wider literature. In the discussion section you should consider both how your results relate to existing literature and how existing research and theory can elucidate your results (it is acceptable to introduce new literature in the discussion to achieve this). You need to be selective here – you won't be able to contextualise your research in relation to every relevant body of literature.

---

in relation to existing literature, discussing how it adds to, fits with, extends or challenges what we already knew about the topic. Ask yourself: are there any similarities between my results and those discussed in the introduction? Do my results challenge existing research in any way? Why might this be? Reflect on the wider implications of your results – read a few discussion sections of published qualitative reports and you'll notice that experienced qualitative researchers avoid making grand claims for their results (such as 'this research has revolutionised our understanding of ...'); good academic writing is rather tentative and cautious, only claims that are well evidenced and justified are made. Refer back to our discussion of the generalisability (or transferability) of qualitative research results in Chapter 12, and think carefully about what claims you can reasonably make for your results. You should also evaluate the strengths and weaknesses of your research (on qualitative grounds, see Chapter 12) and explore how your study could be improved and expanded (Marvasti, 2011). This is another opportunity to 'own your perspective' by reflecting on how your values and interests shaped the research. Any suggestions for future research should *arise* from your study and your results. We have read many reports in which the suggestions for future research are often completely unrelated to the project being reported or apply quantitative standards to qualitative research (e.g. assume that bigger samples are better). An obvious suggestion for future research might arise from your *sample* – imagine your project was on women's feelings about their bodies in relation to the media. If you have only spoken to young women in their twenties, might it be appropriate to speak to older groups of women? Is there any evidence (research and/or anecdotal) to suggest these groups might have different views and experiences? Or did some of your participants mention something interesting, but you didn't have enough data to form a coherent theme? This issue could be a focus for future research. You might have made a tentative interpretation or drawn a cautious conclusion about something that requires further exploration (see Box 13.5).

Conclusion (up to 300 words if results and discussion are separate; 500–1000 words if results and discussion are combined)

This should contain a short (one or two paragraph) summary of your main results. It should also discuss the implications, to leave the reader with a clear 'take home' message, a punchy synthesis of the 'so what' of the research. This is not the moment to be introducing new material and new ideas but, if appropriate, you should still reference in this section. If you combined your results and discussion, your evaluation, suggestions for future research and overall conclusions should be incorporated into the conclusion.

References list (at least 40 sources)

This needs to include all (and only) the references you have cited in your report. It should be consistently formatted in an appropriate style, contain all necessary information and be free from errors.

Appendices

The appendices of a report include a range of supplementary materials that have been referred to in the body of the main report (e.g. 'participants were then asked to sign a consent form [see Appendix B] ...'), and which provide additional information for the reader. If there are quite a few, it's best to include a contents page for the appendices. Ideally, they should be organised according to the order they are referred to in the report: the first time you refer the reader to the appendix, call it Appendix A; the second time,

---

BOX 13.5   EXAMPLE OF AN OVERALL SUMMARY AND INTERPRETATION OF RESULTS

British social psychologists Hannah Frith and Kate Gleeson's (2004) thematic analysis of men's clothing practices provides a good example of summarising results appropriately which makes meaningful suggestions for future research (see Illustrative Research Example 6.1 in Chapter 6 for a summary of their four main themes). In the discussion section of their paper, they sum up their results as follows:

- the participants intentionally and strategically used clothing to 'manipulate their appearance to meet the cultural ideals of masculinity' (Frith & Gleeson, 2004: 45);
- many men expressed dissatisfaction with some aspect of their body which they try to disguise, cover or detract from using clothing;
- men felt that they should express disinterest in clothing and appearance.

These conclusions do not map on exactly to the four themes presented in the paper; rather the discussion of the themes gives rise to these overall conclusions about men's relationship with clothing. Their main argument was that men use clothing to manipulate their appearance in a way that is more traditionally associated with women. The possibility of making this argument was established in the introduction when Frith and Gleeson argued that men are assumed to be less interested in clothing than women (see Box 13.6). Their analysis makes an important contribution in that it challenges perceived wisdom about clothing, appearance and masculinity, but further questions remain and arise from it; they made the following suggestions for future research:

- exploring the ways pressures to conform with an ideal masculine body, and to appear unconcerned about their appearance, intersect with other aspects of men's identities such as age, race, class and sexuality and 'pathological' (vs. 'average') relationships with the body;
- examining men's subjective experiences of their bodies and the ways in which 'body image', rather than being fixed and internal, 'is fluid, contradictory, and constantly renegotiated' (Frith & Gleeson, 2004: 45);
- mapping men's embodied clothing practices and appearance regimes (shopping for clothes, the role of style magazines and partners and friends), and the ways in which these intersect with other aspects of identity.

Note that these suggestions relate either to the constraints of the study design (such as the limitations of the sample – mostly white, young, middle-class, heterosexual, 'average' men) or issues that were apparent in the data that could not be explored more fully.

Appendix B, and so on. Then collate – and clearly label – each appendix *in that order*: Appendix A, Appendix B ... Most of the materials in the appendices will relate to what you discuss in the 'Method' section, and include research materials, like copies of your recruitment materials, Participant Information Sheet (PIS), consent form, data collection 'tool' (e.g. interview guide, survey), and materials to show your analytic paper trail, such as evidence of coding, collated codes, thematic maps and theme definitions (but note that appendices are rare in journal articles). Sometimes, you may be required to append copies of your data; if so, you must have the permission of your participants to do so (this should be included in the ethics application and the PIS; see Chapter 3).

In addition to writing academic reports, many qualitative researchers 'return' their results to the participants, or to people and organisations who helped with their research, in the form of a brief (one–two A4-pages) written summary of their research, or a short presentation. Consider whether this is appropriate, or necessary; if you promise this, you must deliver!

REVIEWING THE LITERATURE FOR QUALITATIVE RESEARCH REPORTS

A key aspect of your report is first 'reviewing', and later situating your results in relation to, relevant literature. The purpose of a literature review in *quantitative* research reports is to tell the 'up the mountain' story of scientific research (Rorty, 1979), where current research builds, and improves, on previous research, until we reach the peak of scientific understanding. Literature reviews in quantitative reports are oriented to questions such as: What do we know? What are the limits of existing knowledge (are there contradictory results)? What are the methodological flaws of existing research (poorly constructed samples, weak construct validity)? How will my research 'fill a gap' in the literature and overcome the flaws of existing research? This is *not* an appropriate model for literature reviews in *qualitative* research reports, because it is based on a (post)positivist scientific model of research.

There are two main 'types' of literature 'review' in qualitative research reports:

- A relatively conventional literature review, which aims to provide a comprehensive overview of existing research (within the constraints provided by the length limits of the report, obviously). This type of literature review needs to identify key results and discuss the limitations of existing understandings; it 'makes a case' for the reported research on the basis of gaps and inadequacies in what we currently know. It is more common in reports of qualitative research in applied areas of psychology (see Box 13.6 for an example).
- A specifically qualitative – and *critical* – literature 'review'. This type discusses relevant literature in the context of developing a theoretically informed *argument* that frames the analysis. It 'makes a case' for the reported research on the basis of an important, interesting, and contextualised question. For example, in taking a discursive approach to a topic which had primarily been studied other ways, the

literature review would be used to build a theoretical case for a discursive approach, and to outline how and why a discursive approach would view the topic differently from quantitative and experiential qualitative approaches (see Speer & Potter, 2000, for a good example), thus providing a clear 'rationale' for your research (see Box 13.7 for an example).

Regardless of which type of literature review you are writing, you should discuss the most relevant research, either qualitative or quantitative – though we'd usually anticipate more emphasis on the qualitative. This is about *contextualising* your research; you should not ignore research solely on the basis of its methodology if it

---

BOX 13.6   GOOD EXAMPLE OF A MORE CONVENTIONAL LITERATURE REVIEW: HOW DO MEN'S FEELINGS ABOUT THEIR BODIES INFORM THEIR CLOTHING PRACTICES?

This paper was published in a journal that is not totally sympathetic to qualitative research; hence Frith and Gleeson (2004) provided a more conventional literature review. The introduction framed and provided a rationale for the study and enabled the authors to make certain arguments in their conclusions (see Box 13.5). First they established why a seemingly trivial topic, one that doesn't generally interest psychologists – men's embodied clothing practices – *is* interesting and important. They provided evidence that clothing practices are an important part of appearance regimes and that men are developing new relationships to their clothed selves. The rest of the introduction was divided into two main – thematic – sections: 'Clothing practices' and 'Appearance and body image' (the two areas deemed most relevant to their chosen topic and research question). Under 'Clothing practices', they noted (again) the marginalisation of appearance and clothing research within psychology and the fact that most clothing research focuses on how clothing is perceived by others. This section mainly focused on the handful of studies to have examined the relationship between body image and clothing (in women). They identified two key themes in this literature: i) that women use clothing to manage their appearance; ii) most research focuses in individual differences in body satisfaction and clothing practices. They highlighted contradictory findings in the literature, and the assumption that men are uninterested in clothing, and ended this section by arguing for a need for research on men and clothing. Under 'Appearance and body image' they noted that most research on this topic focuses on women and has found that women alter their bodies and appearance to conform to cultural ideals. They discussed evidence of increasing pressures on men to conform to cultural ideals (growing numbers of men are dissatisfied with their bodies) and problems with measuring men's dissatisfaction (existing scales for women emphasise thinness). They provided an overview of the types of appearance management men engage in. Finally, they provided a direct rationale for their study, noting that there is no research on men's clothing practices, which is a mundane form of appearance management, but may be more ubiquitous than other (extreme) forms.

BOX 13.7   GOOD EXAMPLE OF A LESS CONVENTIONAL LITERATURE REVIEW: HETEROSEXUALS ACCOUNTING FOR INTERCOURSE

New Zealand feminist psychologist Nicola Gavey and colleagues (Gavey, McPhillips, & Braun, 1999) began their qualitative, interview study of heterosexual people's explanations of why they engage in coitus with a short introduction (just over two pages of their 30-page article), which provided a theoretical and political framework for their study. Drawing on feminist research, they began by highlighting the taken-for-granted status of penis-in-vagina-intercourse. Then they asked a question that framed their research: 'While both women and men have described "liking" intercourse in various complex ways ... we pose the question: Is it always worth it?' (Gavey et al., 1999: 35). They outlined the risks associated with intercourse, identified by feminist researchers, for men and particularly for women (HIV/AIDS and other sexually transmitted infections, negative health effects of contraception and unwanted pregnancies). They gave the example of a qualitative interview study that illuminated the situation of women living under the Ceausescu regime in Romania: contraception was illegal; abortion was illegal to women under 40; many women died of complications associated with illegal abortions. They presented this as an extreme example of the strength of the 'coital imperative' (a feminist concept, which captures, and critiques, the normative notion that coitus is integral to sex). Next, they problematised the notion that women 'always have a real choice about whether they engage in intercourse' (p. 37), highlighting the pervasive social representation of women as passive recipients of men's sexual desire and the use of rape and sexual violence as punishments for sexual refusal. Then they clearly stated their research question, and the focus of the article (what reasons do heterosexuals give for having intercourse?) and the theoretical assumptions underpinning their approach (that sex is discursively constituted). Finally, they briefly discussed, and problematised, the discourses that shape heterosexual sex, such as British feminist psychologist Wendy Hollway's (1984, 1989) 'male sexual drive' and 'permissive' discourses. Although their introduction is very brief, the study is clearly framed as a feminist, critical, constructionist/discursive (qualitative) exploration of accounting for coitus, that will develop and extend a small body of critical feminist research on heterosexuality and heterosex, and has wider relevance to the lives of ordinary women (and men) and practical implications for sexual health promotion.

---

has something relevant to say. It is also acceptable to include research from outside your main academic discipline, as qualitative research is generally more interdisciplinary than quantitative research.

Very occasionally, you will be researching something completely novel, a topic no-one has researched (qualitatively) before (e.g. our story completion research on perceptions of trans parents – see Chapter 6 – is, to the best of our knowledge, the first study of its kind), which begs the question of what literature you should discuss. The same principle – 'making a case' – applies and you typically want to discuss research most closely related to your research question, (broader) topic and approach. For our study of trans parents, this included: psychological research on trans parenting, and its effects on children; quantitative attitude research on transphobia; and critical qualitative research on perceptions of lesbian and gay parents. Table 13.1 provides additional tips on things to aim for – and to avoid – in writing a qualitative literature 'review'.

Table 13.1   Overview of good and bad practices in literature reviews

Examples of good practices	Examples of bad practices
Identifying key themes and debates in the relevant literature, and using these to organise the literature review; using the literature to make an argument and provide a theoretical framework for your study	Describing the findings of study after study in a long list. For example, Clarke and Kitzinger (2004) found that ... Riggs (2006) found that ... Hicks (2005) found that ...
Assessing qualitative studies on their own terms (see Chapter 12)	Using quantitative criteria to evaluate qualitative research. For example, criticising qualitative studies for bias, unrepresentative samples, limited generalisability ...
Organising discussion of the literature logically (using key topic areas as subheadings), starting with the mostly *broadly* relevant areas and finishing with the most *directly* relevant	Constructing a literature review that lacks a coherent organisation and overall structure
The literature review conveys a thorough understanding of relevant literature; the emphasis is on the most directly relevant studies	Selection of literature that seems rather ad hoc and is not suggestive of a thorough knowledge of the literature; important studies are missed out

PRESENTING YOUR RESEARCH

In addition to writing for assessment (and publication; see later), research is often *presented* at academic conferences, in seminars and for student assessment. There are two main formats for presenting research (we base our discussion on psychology conferences): 1) *the oral presentation* – a spoken account of the research, typically accompanied by Microsoft PowerPoint slides, which usually lasts 15–20 minutes, with an additional five–ten minutes allocated to audience questions; 2) *the poster presentation* – a printed depiction of the research, usually displayed with other posters in a large room at a certain allocated time, during which authors will stand next to their posters and answer questions about their research from other conference delegates. It can be a challenge to squeeze a rich and complex qualitative research narrative into either of these formats!

ORAL PRESENTATIONS

Typically, the structure of oral presentations broadly echoes that of a written report. To illustrate this, we provide and discuss an example presentation from Virginia's research on sexual health in Aotearoa/New Zealand (see Braun, 2008, for the written report), which was presented at the British Psychological Society's Social Psychology Section Annual conference (a more general rather than specialist audience) (see Material Example 13.1; see the *companion website* for this in full colour, and further oral presentation examples).

MATERIAL EXAMPLE 13.1

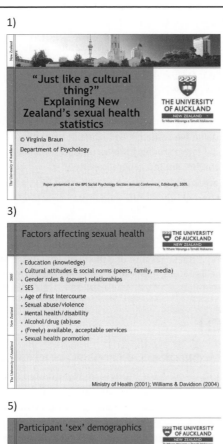

1)

"Just like a cultural thing?"
Explaining New Zealand's sexual health statistics

THE UNIVERSITY OF AUCKLAND
NEW ZEALAND
Te Whare Wānanga o Tāmaki Makaurau

© Virginia Braun
Department of Psychology

Paper presented at the BPS Social Psychology Section Annual Conference, Edinburgh, 2005.

2)

Sexual 'health' in NZ: a gloomy picture

THE UNIVERSITY OF AUCKLAND

- Sexual health and sexually transmitted infections (STIs)
- Recent increases in STI incidence:
  - Gonorrhoea 44% since 2000
  - Chlamydia 28% since 2000 (most common STI)
  - Gen. warts 20% since 2000 (most common viral STI)
  - Syphilis 53% since 2003
- Limitations in our knowledge
- International STI comparisons:
  - STI increases in many western countries
  - NZ prevalence appears comparatively high
  - But caution is necessary in making international comparisons

3)

Factors affecting sexual health

THE UNIVERSITY OF AUCKLAND

- Education (knowledge)
- Cultural attitudes & social norms (peers, family, media)
- Gender roles & (power) relationships
- SES
- Age of first intercourse
- Sexual abuse/violence
- Mental health/disability
- Alcohol/drug (ab)use
- (Freely) available, acceptable services
- Sexual health promotion

Ministry of Health (2001); Williams & Davidson (2004)

4)

Research details

THE UNIVERSITY OF AUCKLAND

- Qualitative project
- 15 focus groups: 6 female only, 4 male only, 5 mixed
- 58 participants in total: 38 female, 20 male
- Average age: 25 (range 16-36)
- Majority were:
  - heterosexual
  - Pākehā
  - Employed/middle class
- Lived in NZ most of their lives
- Thematic analysis of data

5)

Participant 'sex' demographics

THE UNIVERSITY OF AUCKLAND

average # sexual partners	12
average # sexual relationships	6
currently in a relationship	64%
average relationship length	3+ years
casual sex	75%
'unsafe' sex at some point	virtually all
1> sexual health check	73%
known STI	25%
>1 STI	7% (27%)
no check & 'no' STI	57%

6)

Explaining New Zealand's STI statistics

THE UNIVERSITY OF AUCKLAND

- 2 broad categories of explanation
  - National 'socio-structural' explanations
    - Lack of knowledge/(sex) education
    - Easy cures & safety nets
    - Social woes
    - NZ as 'safe by nature'
  - 'National identity' explanations
    - 'Binge-drinking: "we're such a huge drinking culture"
    - NZers as poor communicators
    - Self-sufficiency & stoicism
    - Conservatism & "old fashioned values"
    - Highly/complacently sexual: "we're just so damn horny"
    - The "Kiwi persona": "we're very laid back people"

7)

National 'socio-structural' explanations

THE UNIVERSITY OF AUCKLAND
NEW ZEALAND
Te Whare Wānanga o Tāmaki Makaurau

* Lack of knowledge and (sex) education

Ana: *I think the fact that we couldn't even name you know STIs and STDs we didn't even know the symptoms um would indicate to me that there's a complete lack of knowledge and that when we did talk about things like sexual health we talked about in relation to you know, kind of classes at school but we vaguely remember as not being that good*

Stella: *I certainly don't really remember at school learning about sexually transmitted diseases* (FG1)

* Easy cures & safety nets

Hermione: *I think that maybe um there's so much pregnancy and stuff now it's cos there's like such easy cures and it's so easy to access like you can just get an abortion* (Bob/Gertrude: *mm*) *and and like yeah maybe it's why we don't care as much* (FG12)

8)

National 'socio-structural' explanations

THE UNIVERSITY OF AUCKLAND
NEW ZEALAND
Te Whare Wānanga o Tāmaki Makaurau

* Social 'woes'

Sally: *now um that our like youth suicide rate is so high is probably somehow related i- the fact that um teens don't s'of have enough-young people don't have enough to do* (FG15)

Mrs Smith: *there seems to be a lot of hopelessness out there* (FG11)

* NZ as 'safe by nature'

Joey: *I think a lot of people see New Zealand as a very sheltered place as well cos it's not America* (Ginny: *uhuh*) *it's not g- it's not America it's not Britain you know nothing like that happens here* (FG10)

9)

National 'identity' explanations

THE UNIVERSITY OF AUCKLAND
NEW ZEALAND
Te Whare Wānanga o Tāmaki Makaurau

* We have a conservatism about us

Brandon: *well the only perception I have with New Zealand sexually um and just comparing it to you know what you said of overseas it's it going back to what I said before we just seem very conservative about it so you know when when something like that does happen um you know it's not really something you like talking about you know that may be why the abortion rate's so high or something like that you know it's not it's almost the shame factor behind it or I'm not too sure but it just I I know we are a very conserva- we seem like a very conservative country like that (std is not something that people would)-*

Jason: *my impression is that although there's a sort of conservative ah attitude when it comes to broadcasts like tv and print and the media that an act- like in actual fact people generally are extremely sexually active and*

James: *and laid back about it* (continues)

10)

National 'identity' explanations

THE UNIVERSITY OF AUCKLAND
NEW ZEALAND
Te Whare Wānanga o Tāmaki Makaurau

Jason: *and really laid back about it like it's just no big deal it's just you know meet someone you go home with them you have sex it's just normal like everyday the majority of people are doing it and it's*

Brandon: *shaking hands*

Jason: *yeah it's it's like it's really not much beyond shaking hands or you know*

Brandon: *mmm as trivial as that*

Jason: *yeah it's just like just casual sex it's that's it that's it it's just casual it's just no big deal and um (pause) so kind of the opposite of conservative like just really really I don't know if you'd call it liberal but really laid back about it and she'll be right you know it's like a like a New Zealand kind of thing it's like oh whatever you know it's no big deal it's just*

Dylan: *my opinion on New Zealand is from just from what I've seen and travelling a little and stuff in general I think we seem we come across quite conservative but I actually think we're quite extreme in a lot of ways ah in sex in a lot of things it's just not really talked about...* (FG7)

11)

National 'identity' explanations

THE UNIVERSITY OF AUCKLAND
NEW ZEALAND
Te Whare Wānanga o Tāmaki Makaurau

* 'We're very laid-back people'

BK: *maybe it's like maybe it's like um how New Zealanders pret-really do have the no worries attitude that we*

KS: *market ourselves* ((laughter))

Kimberly: *believe our own hype yeah*

BK: *market ourselves and to you know I think um all through history well all through our history um New Zealanders have been known as people who don't worry too much about things that go wrong go badly you know like*

Arnold: *she'll be right*

BK: *the storm comes in and blows your farm down and you know that was a bit of a bit of a bugger but you know*

Kimberly: *she'll be right*

BK: *yeah she'll be right and no worries is pretty much a New Zealand motto um*

Kimberly: *it is yeah* (FG2)

12)

Implications for sexual health promotion

THE UNIVERSITY OF AUCKLAND
NEW ZEALAND
Te Whare Wānanga o Tāmaki Makaurau

* National 'socio-structural' explanations offer:
  * lack of individual culpability/responsibility
  * potential for sexual health improvement
  * sexual health change as requiring structural change

* 'National identity' explanations offer:
  * lack of individual culpability/responsibility
  * construct sexual safety as 'un-Kiwi'
  * sexual health statistics as less likely to improve
  * sexual health change as requiring national identity change

13)

Key question for sexual health promotion

THE UNIVERSITY OF AUCKLAND
NEW ZEALAND
Te Whare Wānanga o Tāmaki Makaurau

* How might we reconstruct our 'national identity' as a 'sexually safe' one?
  * Or use 'identity' as a useful basis for sexual health promotion?
  * An example from anti-littering campaigns - 'be a tidy kiwi'

Virginia's presentation has the following components:

- a title slide;
- a *short* introduction (which contextualises the study in relation to existing research and the wider social context);
- an equally short overview of the study design and methods (focusing on the characteristics of the sample);
- the analysis (the longest section of the presentation);
- a short discussion (focusing on the implications of the study for sexual health promotion and questions for future research and practice).

The goal of an oral presentation is not to provide a detailed discussion of every aspect of the project; it's about paring back your research to tell a concise story, organised around a central argument. The content of the presentation should be determined in relation to the *specific audience* – what information is crucial for *this* audience and what can be left out? In Virginia's presentation, the theoretical and methodological approach is barely mentioned; she was speaking to an audience familiar with these approaches so a detailed explanation was not necessary. For a specialist sexual health audience, it would have been appropriate to include more methodology, and less topical background information.

Depending on your audience, you may present a general overview of your results, or you may look at one aspect of the analysis in depth. How you present and discuss the analysis depends on your style of analysis: if you used data illustratively (see Chapter 11), you can weave data extracts and analytic commentary together in the discussion of your themes/ categories/discourses, revealing and reading each extract when appropriate, or for each theme/category/discourse, you can provide a brief introduction, present and read some illustrative extracts, then discuss the theme in more detail. If you treated data analytically (see Chapter 11), select a *few* extracts to focus on in detail in the presentation, reading each extract first, and then presenting your analysis of it. Having worked on your analysis for months and months, what appears immediately obvious to you will likely not be to people who are encountering your data for the first time, so you need to consider how much explanation is necessary.

Microsoft PowerPoint is virtually de rigueur these days; it provides an excellent visual tool to structure and enhance your talk. In Virginia's presentation, PowerPoint is used to structure the presentation, highlight key information, and present data extracts (she did a lot more talking in relation to each slide than just reiterating the material covered in the slides). The general principles of effective Microsoft PowerPoint use are adhered to:

- the text is an appropriate size (easily readable from the back of a large room), headings are larger than the main text, the typeface is one that is easy to read, a darker-coloured font is placed on a lighter-coloured background (much easier to read than dark font on a dark background or light font on a light background);
- there's an appropriate amount of information on each slide – the slides aren't crammed, but neither do they have lots of blank space;

- colour is used sparingly, consistently and for effect – a lighter blue background, a brighter and darker blue for headings, and purple to highlight data quotes (see the colour version on the ***companion website***);
- images are used for emphasis on the final slide (see Boynton, 2005);
- there are a total of 15 slides for a 20-minute presentation.

One third of the slides in this material example are data extracts. Data extracts are good to show – they vividly convey the content of the data, and provide a 'grounding' for the audience in interpreting your analysis. However, one mistake qualitative researchers often make is expecting people to read and absorb an extract of data at the same time as they present their analysis of it (usually to save time). This is expecting too much of an audience. Plan to read out the data yourself, or pause from speaking to give the audience time to read extracts (and yourself time to take a sip of water).

ORAL PRESENTATION PERFORMANCE

An oral presentation is not just about the content, and the visual presentation of that content; it's also crucially about *how* you present: 'you impart significance through the rhythm and pacing of your speech, emotional nuances and enthusiasm, body language, and eye contact with the audience' (Charmaz, 2006: 155). So think about elements of your own presentation style, and how they may be a help or hindrance to effective presentation. Reflect on your natural speaking speed – if you're a fast speaker (like Victoria), you may need to slow down a bit; if you're slower speaker (like Virginia), you may need to speed up a bit. Practise *varying* speed, volume and intonation to highlight particular points, and to signpost the shift from one section of the presentation to another. Gestures are another way to emphasise particular points and to signpost changes, but should be used sparingly (for general advice on effective oral presentations, see Bradbury, 2006; Chivers & Shoolbred, 2007; Van Emden & Becker, 2010).

Practice is *critical* for an effective presentation. Practice in front of an audience (trusted peers, family members, your dog ...), and *time your presentation carefully*. We cannot emphasise timing your presentation enough! There is a tendency for qualitative researchers to cram in too much detail, and then run out of time. We know this from experience; we always have to edit our talks down after a first practice 'run through' – sometimes substantially. But, when preparing and timing, also be mindful of the fact that when nervous we *can* speak *faster* (a presentation precisely timed to last 15 minutes when spoken slowly at home may be done and dusted in 12). If you think you will speak too fast, write a reminder to yourself in your presentation notes to check your pace, and breathe deeply and slow down if you're going too fast. *However*, that said, in all the hundreds of qualitative research presentations we have seen, we have *virtually never* seen a presentation that is too short – even perfectly timed talks are rare. A *substantial* proportion are too long – something we ourselves are occasionally guilty of, despite our best timing efforts. A tendency to 'ad lib' and add material 'on the spot' is the chief culprit here. Try to avoid this, as it's an easy trap for not finishing your presentation (or allow time for it). Timing notes (of how long a slide or section *should* take to talk through) are quite handy for keeping you on track. Finally, it's useful to practice answering questions on your talk (obviously, you will need a human audience for this).

Should you write a full text for your talk, or just notes? That's up to you – we have different preferences (Virginia writes hers in full; Victoria writes notes) – but regardless of what you do, you have to remember that this is a *talk*, to an audience, and not the reading-out, in a room of people, of a written text (or talking to your notes, the projector, or the computer screen). You should direct your presentation *to* the audience; if you're feeling really nervous, borrow a trick from theatre actors and direct your presentation to a point on the back wall, just above the heads of the audience. If you have your talk written down (which can alleviate nerves somewhat), be wary of reading without *any* audience eye contact, and speaking in a rapid 'monotone of terror' – this doesn't make for an engaging presentation!

Finally, if the idea of an oral presentation scares you, keep in mind that even the most experienced academics can feel nervous when giving a presentation – it is a rare person who doesn't experience nerves, or at least a rush of adrenaline, before and during a presentation. For most people, these nerves soon dissipate once they start speaking and become absorbed in the flow of the presentation.

POSTER PRESENTATIONS

The poster presentation is an even more challenging format for qualitative researchers, and there is 'no one right way' (Russell, Gregory, & Gates, 1996: 551) to construct a qualitative poster. As (Wilson & Hutchinson, 1997: 65) noted:

> if the constraints of a page-limited article pose barriers to reporting qualitative work through the scientific journal medium, the research poster looms as an ever greater challenge for the qualitative researcher because posters are by definition concise and visual rather than richly detailed and dependent on language.

The trick of a poster is to catch the eye of the viewer – usually it's competing with lots of other posters for attention (Russell et al., 1996). A poster should stand alone without any additional information needed from the presenter (Russell et al., 1996). Effective qualitative posters: have a clear message; make it easy for the viewer to follow the flow of information, and to read and understand the information presented; keep the amount of words to a minimum; and use visuals to assist the viewer in understanding the textual information presented (see Box 13.8 for further guidance; Ellerbee, 2006; MacIntosh-Murray, 2007; Russell et al., 1996; Wilson & Hutchinson, 1997). One of the main challenges of poster design is reducing the content down (MacIntosh-Murray, 2007). Decide on your key message, narrow the focus as much as possible, and display information 'simply, clearly, and concisely' (Russell et al., 1996: 544). As with oral presentations, you should allocate about half the poster to presenting your results. You will need to think carefully about how to present your results – providing a brief overview of your themes, in the form of table or simple thematic map, and selecting a few themes to discuss in more detail, can work well; use brief and vivid quotes to illustrate themes (Wilson & Hutchinson, 1997).

BOX 13.8   SOME *RELATIVELY* INFLEXIBLE GUIDANCE FOR POSTER DESIGN

Content
- Keep titles short – while still informative of research question and approach – and catchy (e.g. 'Should lecturers wear gay slogan t-shirts in the classroom?');
- Keep information to a minimum while leaving the overall message clear – it should take only 30 seconds to get the key message (and no more than five minutes to read most or all of the poster);
- The poster should work as a stand-alone information package – avoid too little, or too much, information;
- Pay attention to detail – check for typographical, grammatical and spelling errors before printing; don't handwrite changes on the poster.

Text
- Dark typeface on a light background is generally easier to read than the reverse;
- Titles and headings should be visible from 1–2 metres away, the main text from 0.5–1 metre away;
- Use a slightly larger typeface for headings and a much larger typeface for titles;
- Use italics, underlining, capitalisation and bold for emphasis; otherwise regular typeface is best (the selective use of colour is also useful for emphasis);
- Use only one or two different fonts (sparingly use one font for emphasis);
- Avoid fancy fonts such as **Franklin Gothic Medium** and *Segoe Script*. Serif fonts such as Times New Roman are easier to read for the main text; sans-serif fonts such as Arial and Verdana are good for headings and titles; the humanist sans-serif font Calibri is now the default font on Microsoft Word and PowerPoint and is a good all-rounder.

Colour and visual elements
- Avoid busy backgrounds;
- Have one or two background colours, and use one or two colours in the main text and headings to accent the background colour. Some people have problems seeing red and green, so use sparingly. Warm colours (red or yellow) convey power and happiness; cool colours (blue, beige and pastels) are soothing and relaxing. A colour wheel can help with selecting complementary or contrasting colours. Avoid fluorescent colours, and harsh colours and combinations; avoid *boring* colour schemes (not black and white!);
- Use visual elements to create interest and emphasise important areas – tables (to present demographic information), figures (simple thematic maps), clipart, images, photographs (check

(Continued)

BOX 13.8   *(continued)*

the copyright status of any images you intend to use; taking your own photographs – as we have done for the posters shown in this chapter and on the ***companion website*** – can be a [fun] way to avoid problems with copyright);

- Any visual materials should be meaningful (and clearly related to the topic) and enticing. Images of people are particularly good for creating warmth and interest. Avoid stereotypical images;
- Less can be more: 'too many fonts and too many colours and designs will detract from the message that you are trying to convey' (Ellerbee, 2006: 167); the visual elements shouldn't overpower the poster – avoid too many visuals, or poorly placed visuals, or visuals that are too small;
- Make sure any tables and figures have clear captions.

Text
- Avoid long blocks and lines of text – keep line length to 50–70 characters, including spaces and punctuation; keep any paragraphs short;
- Use short sentences or phrases (and short words); bullet points, lists and short chunks of text (remove unnecessary text and condense information wherever possible);
- Avoid a feeling of clutter and busyness by having some blank space in the poster around headings, blocks of text and visuals.

Layout
- The material should be placed in a easy to understand order, content should flow from top to bottom (and left to right) in each section of the poster; use sequential numbers or arrows to direct the reader from one section to the next (colour is also useful here);
- Sections should be aligned;
- Text should be left-justified only. The uneven gaps between words with left *and* right-justified text make it is much harder to read;
- Place the most important material at eye-level.

The main components or sections of a poster are broadly similar to those in a written report (or oral presentation), with each section of information clear and succinct:

- *title* and author(s)'s name(s) and affiliation(s);
- *introduction* and purpose of the study, including a sentence on the theoretical/ methodological framework;
- *methods* for collecting and analysing data, study design, details of sample/participants;
- *results*;

- *conclusion and implications* – Russell et al. (1996) found that this section is the one most often missing from qualitative posters, but is frequently the one people read first, to decide if they want to read the rest of the poster; it's a bit like the abstract in a published report;
- some acknowledgement may also be included (e.g. to a supervisor, participants).

When preparing your poster, give equal attention to the content *and* the overall design and layout. As Bushy (1991: 11) noted, 'a good poster display cannot rescue a bad idea, but a poor one can easily sink the best idea – as well as viewers' impression of the author'. Posters contain the following *visual* elements (as outlined by Russell et al., 1996; Wilson & Hutchinson, 1997):

- text (which font you use, what size it is and whether you italicise, bold or underline any of it);
- layout (flow of information);
- visuals (relevant to the topic);
- colour scheme.

The poster in Material Example 13.2 provides an example of good poster design. The poster uses a large font size for the title, which is short, lucid and catchy. Images that are clearly relevant to the topic create warmth and visual interest. The overall layout and organisation is comprehensible and logical; the design is visually pleasing and balanced. A slightly different background colour is used for the results section, which draws the readers' attention to the most important information (see the *companion website* for the full-colour version). Even though full sentences and blocks of text are used, the poster is still very visually readable (paragraphs are used effectively to organise the content). The aims of the study are very clearly stated, the method section is concise and pithy, three themes are presented in the results section (one per paragraph), with all the themes briefly introduced at the start of the section. By contrast, some of the other posters on the *companion website* use bullet points and listing rather than full sentences and paragraphs. It's important to note that the 'rules' for poster design are not completely rigid (hence the title of Box 13.8); it is possible to break *some* of the rules and still produce an effective poster.

WHAT ABOUT PUBLISHING?

Do small qualitative student projects get published? Yes, definitely. Small student projects – sometimes – get published, and they can be of the highest academic standards (see Table 12.2 in Chapter 12). But it's unlikely that all student work will get published, and there's usually a big leap between a student report and a manuscript ready for submission (not least because manuscripts often need to be much shorter, and because they are written for a different purpose). Because supervisors often play a significant role in shaping and developing student projects, and have expertise in writing for publication, any publications based on student projects are usually co-authored with the supervisor.

MATERIAL EXAMPLE 13.2

Eating Disorder Counsellors with an Eating Disorder History
An Interpretative Phenomenological Analysis

University of the
West of England

Nicola Rance
(UWE)
Naomi Moller
(UWE)
Barbara Douglas
(BPS DCoP Registrar)

Introduction

Some have argued that counsellors with an eating disorder (ED) history may not be fit to practise with clients with EDs; others, meanwhile, have argued that an ED history makes a practitioner working in the field *more effective* (Johnston, Smethurst & Gowers, 2005). Despite general acknowledgement that working with EDs can be incredibly demanding for practitioners (Zerbe, 2008) – in part because of the way it can affect their physical perceptions of themselves (DeLucia-Waack, 1999) and their behaviours surrounding food, eating and appearnace (Warren, Crowley, Olivardia & Schoen, 2009) – there is almost no research exploring the actual experiences of recovered ED counsellors. Given that the number of practitioners believed to have such a history is thought to be between one in three (Barbarich, 2002; Johnston et al., 2005; Warren et al., 2009) and one in four (Bloomgarden, Gerstein & Moss, 2003; Shisslak et al., 1989), understanding their experiences is clearly important.

The study thus aimed to explore recovered practitioners' countertransference experiences in relation to their body image, weight and relationship with food, their perceptions about the impact, if any, of such experiences and their beliefs about the effects (both positive and negative) of their own eating disorder history.

Method

Using semi-structured interviews, the experiences of seven female counsellors (aged 32 to 52, with a variety of theoretical orientations and 2 to 17 years practice experience) were investigated using Interpretative Phenomenological Analysis (IPA; Smith , Flowers and Larkin, 2009). Particular emphasis was given to their beliefs about the impact of their work on their own body image, weight and relationship with food.

Results

Three themes were derived from the IPA: 'Double-edged history', 'Emphasis on normality' and 'Selective attention'. The theme *double-edged history* represented the participants' apparent awareness of both benefits and dangers of their ED history. They saw themselves as having *"insider knowledge"* that enabled them to truly understand their clients' experiences *"you can, understand …. umm why they did, what they did or said what they did umm and that, and that, can work very well"* (Laura) and know that recovery is possible, but also as at risk of overidentification/enmeshment with their clients and criticism/negative judgement from others in relation to their history *"[being interviewed] was sort of, a BIT uncomfortable…. because of maybe, YOU judging me"* (Sandy).

The participants appeared to navigate this double-bind with an *emphasis on normality* that stressed their lack of ED symptoms, the absence of any impact of their work on their self-experiences and behaviours *"I don't think it's [body image], altered … no it [relationship with food] hasn't changed … my appetite hasn't changed … my experience of my body image or my view of body image HASN'T altered."* (Sam), and firmly located their ED in the past *"I know I'm never going to go back to eating disorder behaviour"* (Laura).

Finally, the participants seemed to employ a number of cognitive and attentional strategies to back up and justify their overt assertions of normality. For example, they appeared to hold a binary view of recovery which meant that, as 'recovered', they were thus safe to practise. Additionally, they appeared to have selective attention such that certain areas of their practise were unquestioned *"I don't know what it would be like ….to consider how does an anorexic person …. look at you …. in a WAY that just has not occurred to me"* (Julie).

Discussion

Given that society in the main is not free from disordered eating and what constitutes a good relationship with food and a healthy weight is not only culturally determined but also prone to change with the fashions of the time (Nasser, 1997), the counsellors' apparent felt need to minimise/place far in the past their ED history and normalise their current cognitions, emotions and behaviours related to their relationships with food, their bodies and weight appeared to put them into the impossible position of claiming normality in a world where the norm is not "normal".

It is of course possible that the study participants' recovery processes may have involved them in deep engagement with their body image, weight and relationship with food thus enabling them to develop particularly healthy relationships with each. Yet, even the healthiest of such relationships can be challenged from time to time and being able to voice this (e.g. in supervision, to colleagues) seems important. It would thus be problematic if it were indeed the case that the interviewees (and possibly other practitioners with an ED history) were in a position where they felt unable to do so.

Key reference

Johnston, C., Smethurst, N. & Gowers, S. (2005). Should people with a history of an eating disorder work as eating disorder therapists? European Eating Disorders Review, 13, 301-310.

Publication of small (undergraduate and honours) student projects is usually initiated by supervisors. But if you want to consider this, don't be shy to ask your supervisor: worst case scenario, they say 'no'.

Authorship is a very important conversation to have early on. Order of authorship on academic papers can be a complex thing, but is often largely determined by who takes the lead in writing the paper; activities such as data collection are generally viewed as less important in determining order of authorship. Supervisors will often take the lead on writing a publication from a small (undergraduate and honours) project, and often substantially revise, or even redo, the analysis of the data. In such cases, the supervisor is usually the first author (Clarke & Spence, in press; Clarke & Turner, 2007; Gavey & Braun, 1997; Kitzinger & Frith, 1999; Kitzinger & Willmott, 2002). In other cases, where students take the lead in writing up their research, and the supervisor does not substantially rework the analysis, the student would typically be first author. This is almost always the case for students completing postgraduate study (e.g. Adams et al., 2007; Hayfield & Clarke, 2012; Huxley et al., 2011; Terry & Braun, 2011c); very occasionally, undergraduate projects may result in a first author publication for the student (e.g. Willmott, 2000).

CHAPTER SUMMARY

This chapter:
- provided general guidance on writing and emphasised the critical importance of editing to produce high-quality research reports;
- offered guidance on writing reports of qualitative research, including hints and tips on how to structure and organise your report and what information to include in each major section;
- discussed two different models for a 'literature review' in qualitative research reporting;
- provided advice on presenting qualitative research in the form of posters and oral presentations;
- briefly outlined issues related to publication of (student) research.

? QUESTIONS FOR DISCUSSION AND CLASSROOM EXERCISES

1 Select a piece of academic qualitative writing that you really like and reflect on why you like it. In small groups, discuss your chosen pieces and why you like them. What features of good academic writing can you identify as common to all or most of the papers? (This exercise is based on one in Cameron et al., 2009.)

2 Bring a short piece (two–four pages) of your own academic writing (ideally, a draft of a section of your project report) to share with a small group. Working on the assumption that no piece of writing is perfect (there is *always* room for improvement), read each other's work, and, taking one piece of writing at a time, offer the writer 'constructive criticism' *on their writing*. For example, rather than saying 'this paragraph isn't clear' you could say something like 'the clarity of this paragraph could be improved by …' and offer concrete suggestions on how to improve the paragraph. When reading other people's work, ask yourself the following types of question: Is this whole piece of writing clear? Is this sentence/paragraph clear? Could the structure and organisation be improved? Are there crucial pieces of information missing? Is further explanation of key concepts and terminology needed? Please note that this can be a challenging exercise, but it is also rewarding. (This exercise is based on one in Cameron et al., 2009.)

3 View the 'really bad qualitative poster' on the **companion website**. In small groups, identify everything that's wrong with this poster. Then, discuss how you would improve it so it would be an example of a 'really good qualitative poster', and you would easily be able to answer Wilson and Hutchinson's (1997) four questions about posters: 1) Where can I find out what the poster is about? 2) Where do I find the take-home message? 3) Where do I begin reading? 4) How far through am I?

4 Identify the main argument in Chapter 12. (Hint: at one point, we state this very explicitly.) Looking at the chapter as a whole, work out how the various sections and components of Chapter 12 contribute to and develop this argument.

5   Cameron et al. (2009) have written about the emotional challenges in writing. In small groups, brainstorm the challenges of writing (What are the worst bits of writing for you? Your worst fears about writing?) Now identify some of the positive aspects of writing. Which did you find easier to identify (more of)? Why do you think that is? Finally, brainstorm strategies for managing the challenges of writing you have identified. What have you learnt from this exercise?

6   Read the following really badly written paragraph from an imaginary methods section of a qualitative report of a project using email interviews and an online qualitative survey. Identify the problems with the paragraph and rewrite it with the aim of resolving the problems and reducing the word count, so the paragraph is pithy and economical while still providing all the crucial details.

The data was collected using email interviews. Email interviews involve a dialogue between the researcher and participants over email – questions are posed to participants in an email and the participant replies to these questions via email. The email text was cut and pasted into a word file. Five people participated in email interviews. Participants were asked ten initial questions; we also asked them follow-up questions to clarify understanding and for gaining further detail about their experiences and understanding of the issues. The remaining ten participants participated in an online survey constructed using Qualtrics. The same questions were used in the survey and in the email interview, but in the email interviews, questions were tailored to the individual circumstances of each participant. This means that a total of 20 people participated in the research – ten in email interviews and ten in an online survey. The guide for the email interviews and the online survey questions were designed on the basis of a review of the relevant literature and our own interests in conducting the research, participants were given a choice of whether to participate in an email interview or an online survey in order to address concerns about anonymity of participation, participation in the online survey was completely anonymous (there was no way of tracking the identity of participants taking part), whereas participation in the email interviews was only partially anonymous – we knew participants' names and their email addresses.

FURTHER RESOURCES

Further reading:

For an excellent discussion of editing qualitative reports (and an example of hand-written edits on a page of a report), see: Chapter 5, Editing. In P. Woods (1999). *Successful writing for qualitative researchers*. London: Routledge.

For a detailed discussion of writing a qualitative research report, including the characteristics of a good report, see: Chapter 13, Writing a qualitative report. In D. Howitt (2010). *Introduction to qualitative methods in psychology*. Harlow, UK: Pearson Education.

For general advice on presentation skills, see: Chivers, B. & Shoolbred, M. (2007). *A student's guide to presentations: Making your presentation count*. London: Sage.

For a (30-item) tool for assessing posters, see: Bushy, A. (1991). A rating scale to evaluate research posters. *Nurse Educator*, *16*, 11–15.

For a shortened ten-item version, see: Garrison, A., & Bushy, A. (2004). The research poster appraisal tool (R-PAT-II): designing and evaluating poster displays. *JHQ Online, July/August*. www.nahq.org/uploads/researchposter.pdf

Online resources:

For advice around writing and referencing in psychology, look at the online advice given by the American Psychological Association: www.apastyle.org/index.aspx

See the *companion website* (**www.sagepub.co.uk/braunandclarke**) for:
- self-test multiple choice questions relating to Section 4;
- the flashcard glossary – test yourself on the definitions of key terms used in this chapter;
- the first and final versions of a paragraph from one of our papers – demonstrating the importance of editing;
- further examples of posters and Microsoft PowerPoint presentations;
- tools for evaluating posters and oral presentations;
- qualitative research project checklist;
- the 'really bad qualitative poster' for Exercise 3;
- further readings (articles from Sage journals).

Glossary

Bias: associated with positivist research, bias refers to the idea that our research or data might be contaminated by our lack of objectivity. Bias as a concept does not apply as a valid critique of qualitative research. (see *Subjective*; *Subjectivity*)

Big Q qualitative research: the application of the qualitative methods of data collection and analysis within a qualitative paradigm, rather than a positivist one. (see *Small q qualitative research*)

CAQDAS: computer assisted qualitative data analysis software.

Central organising concept: the essence of a *Theme* in *Thematic analysis*; an idea or concept that captures a coherent and meaningful pattern in the data, and provides a succinct answer to the research question.

Coding: the process of examining data, identifying and noting aspects that relate to your research question. Coding can be *Complete*, where the whole dataset is coded, or *Selective*, where only material of interest is selected and coded.

Construct: refers to a particular social artefact or object, which is the focus of analysis or interest. Fitting with a *Social constructionist* position, meaning is seen not as inherent in the object, but as socially produced. For example, consider the construct 'the child': what westerners now understand as the essence and meaning of childhood is very different to the meanings ascribed 200 years ago; policies and practices around children similarly differ. (see *Construction*; *Social constructionism*)

Construction: can be used to refer to both a process and a product. As a process, it is about the production of meaning and reality through language, representation and other social processes, such as the production of meaning around 'obesity'. As a product, it refers to a particular or specific object or meaning that has been produced through this process – 'obesity' is a good example of a construction (or *Construct*). (see *Social constructionism*)

Contextualism: a theoretical approach informing some qualitative research, which assumes that meaning is related to the context in which it is produced.

Constructivism: a theoretical approach, sometimes used instead of, or interchangeably with, constructionism, concerned with the production of meaning (by people). Although related, the approaches are somewhat different, applied in different ways in different fields; can be applied more individualistically and psychologically oriented than constructionism. (see *Social constructionism*)

Convenience sampling: a very common a way of sampling, where participants or data are selected based on *accessibility* rather than some other criterion. (see *Purposive sampling; Snowball sampling; Theoretical sampling*)

Conversation analysis (CA): a form of qualitative analysis that attempts to describe the orderliness, structure and sequential patterns of interaction in everyday conversation or institutional (formal) talk.

Critical psychology: an umbrella term for a range of different approaches that challenge core assumptions of mainstream psychology. The key components of critical research are the questioning of taken-for-granted truths about subjectivity, experience, and the way the world is, combined with recognition of the cultural, political and historical factors which shape experience.

Critical realism: a theoretical approach that assumes an ultimate reality, but claims that the way reality is experienced and interpreted is shaped by culture, language and political interests.

Critical qualitative research: does not take data at face value. It takes an interrogative stance to the meanings expressed in data, and unpacks the ideas and concepts associated with them; often ties in to broader social meanings.

Data: materials collected or generated that are analysed.

Data-derived code: closely tied to the explicit or semantic content of the data; provides a succinct summary of an aspect of the data. Also known as a *Descriptive code* or *Semantic code*. (see *Researcher-derived code*)

Data item: an individual unit of *Data* (e.g. an interview; a newspaper story).

Dataset: all the *Data items* collected for a particular study or analysis.

Deconstruction: a critical form of analysis (and a philosophy) which is concerned with exposing unquestioned assumptions and internal contradictions.

Descriptive code: see *Data-derived code*.

Descriptive analysis: a semantic approach to analysis which aims to investigate, document and describe the nature of some issue.

Discourse: a word with various meanings. Most broadly, it refers to patterned meaning within spoken or written language; to systems of meaning and talk which form readily identifiable ways of interpreting or understanding a particular object, or set of objects, in the world, which are theorised to create reality. (see *Power*; *Subject position*)

Discourse analysis (DA): a cluster of forms of qualitative analysis that centre on the detailed examination of patterns of meaning within texts, and the effects and implications of particular patterns of meaning. Theoretically underpinned by the idea that language creates meaning and reality, rather than reflecting it.

Discursive psychology (DP): the application of discourse analysis to psychological phenomena, associated with a 'fine-grained' approach to discourse analysis and detailed analyses of textual data.

Email interview: an interactive data collection method, with a researcher and a participant, that takes place over email. (see *Interview*; *Telephone interview*; *Virtual interview*)

Emergent theme: used in *Interpretative phenomenological analysis* to describe initial low-level themes. 'Emergent' signals that these themes are preliminary, rather than that they 'emerged' from the transcript.

Empiricism: theoretical position that sees truth as revealed through observation and experimentation or empirical research.

Epistemology: a theory of knowledge, which determines what counts as valid or accepted knowledge, and also therefore how do we go about obtaining or producing that knowledge.

Essentialism: the idea that events result from fixed qualities 'inside' people (essences) that are impervious to the social context. Not the same as biology, but frequently closely linked to biology in explanations of human behaviour.

Ethics: theory, codes and practices concerned with ensuring we do research in a moral and non-harmful manner.

Experiential qualitative research: seeks to understand people's own perspectives, meanings and experiences.

Feminism: broad range of theoretical and political approaches which at their core assume the rights of women.

Field notes: notes written very soon after (or during) data collection which record commentary about, and reflection on, the data collection session as well as ideas for analysis.

Focus group: a method of collecting data, where a group of participants discuss a topic of interest, guided by a moderator, either face-to-face or virtually. A key and unique aspect of this method is the interaction and conversation between members of the group. (see *Virtual focus group*)

Focus group moderator: the person who guides the discussion in a *Focus group* and moderates the group dynamics. Sometimes a member of a pre-existing group, rather than the researcher, can take on this role.

Framework: see *Methodology*.

Generalisability: the ability to apply the results of a study to the wider population; most strongly associated with quantitative research. (see *Transferability*)

Grounded theory: a qualitative methodology which offers a way of developing theory grounded in data. As the theory evolves throughout the process of the research, data analysis and collection are linked. Often used in a 'lite' manner, without full theory-development.

Hard to engage populations: groups who might not feel a strong connection to, investment in, or understanding of, research, or might have had very negative experiences of research in the past, or for whom participation might be risky. (see *Hidden populations*; *Vulnerable groups*)

Hermeneutics: the theory and practice of interpretation.

Heteronormativity: a concept developed in queer theory that describes the social privileging of heterosexuality and the assumption that heterosexuality is the only natural and normal sexuality.

Heterosexism: the assumption that individuals are heterosexual; the privileging and promotion of heterosexuality over other sexualities. Infuses both individual and institutional practices.

Hidden populations: those whose group memberships are not necessarily very visible, or may be stigmatised in some way, so they are not likely to be necessarily easy to identify as a member of that group. (see *Hard to engage populations*; *Vulnerable groups*)

Idiographic: an approach to knowledge production which is based on the specific and the individual (e.g. case study methods), rather than the shared and generalisable (e.g. quantitative survey methods).

Ideology: an organised collection of ideas; a way of looking at things.

Interview: a one-on-one method of collecting qualitative data, where a participant responds to a researcher's questions. Traditionally conducted in person, but can also be conducted virtually. (see *Email interview*; *Telephone interview*; *Virtual interview*)

Insider researcher: a researcher who belongs to the groups/communities they are researching.

Interpretation: a process of making sense of, and theorising the meanings in, data; goes beyond summarising the obvious semantic content of data and puts an interpretative framework around it.

Interpretative phenomenological analysis (IPA): an approach to qualitative research concerned with understanding experiences of the 'person in context;' prioritises participants' experiences and their interpretations of them. Theoretically developed from *Phenomenology* and *Hermeneutics*.

Interpretative repertoire: concept in *Discourse analysis* that refers to a patterned and relatively coherent meaning in talk about an object or concept. (see *Discourse*)

In vivo code: concept in *Grounded theory*, essentially a *Data-derived code*.

Language practice: the ways language is used to create particular versions of reality.

Latent meaning: meaning not explicitly evident in the data; the ideas, assumptions or concepts that underpin what is explicitly stated in the data. Both *Codes* and analysis can focus at the latent or semantic level. (see *Semantic meaning*)

Linguistic comment: type of code in *Interpretative phenomenological analysis*, which focuses on the language being used by the participant to convey the meaning of their experiences.

Member checking: practice of checking your analysis with your participants, to ensure it does not misrepresent their experiences; often treated as a form of validation in qualitative analysis.

Memo: analytic tool in *Grounded theory*; note written by the researcher to record and develop ideas related to coding and analysis.

Method: a technique or tool for data collection or analysis; often confused with *Methodology*.

Methodology: theory of how research proceeds, including consideration of such things as *Methods*, *Participants* and the role of the researcher, *Ethics* and so forth.

Mixed method research: the combination of different methods of data collection and/ or data analysis within a single study, frequently combing qualitative and quantitative approaches. Often conducted within a *Realist* framework; qualitative research within mixed methods approach is rarely *Big Q qualitative research*.

Narrative: an account of events or more than one event, characterised by having some sort of structure, often temporal in western cultures, and other story-elements.

Narrative analysis: uses the person as the unit of analysis, and looks within the person's account to find meanings; the analysis may draw together elements from multiple stories to construct an overarching narrative.

Naturalistic data: data that exist in the world (such as newspaper reports or doctor-patient interactions) rather than being collected specifically for the purposes of research.

Ontology: refers to the study of being, and is concerned with the state/nature of the world; with questions of what exists, and what relationship exists between the world and our human understandings and interpretations of the world.

Orthographic transcript: records the spoken words and other linguistic utterances in audio or audiovisual data. (see *Transcript*)

Outsider researcher: a researcher who is not a member of the groups/communities they are researching.

Overarching theme: may be used to organise and structure a *Thematic analysis*; tends not to contain its own codes or data, but instead simply captures an idea encapsulated in a number of *Themes*. (see *Subtheme*; *Superordinate theme*)

Paradigm: a conceptual framework within which scientific (and other) theories are constructed, and within which scientific practices take place. Major changes in thought and practice have been referred to as paradigm shifts.

Paralinguistic: non-linguistic features of speech, such as coughs, laughter, pauses; inclusion of such features in a *Transcript* provides far richer detail about how the information was conveyed and this type of transcription is typically used in *Conversation analysis* and *Discursive psychology*.

Participant: a person who takes part in research.

Participant information sheet (PIS): Written information given to potential participants that specifies the parameters of a study and the scope of any involvement they might have, including the potential risks and benefits.

Participatory methods: involve the participants and/or the community the research is about as active members of the research, even as co-researchers.

Pattern-based discourse analysis: versions of *Discourse analysis* primarily focused on identification of patterned features of language; often retain some interest in the content of language, not just its function.

Phenomenology: an influential philosophy in qualitative research. There are many varieties of phenomenology, but broadly speaking it is concerned with understanding people's subjective experiences.

Positioning: process by which *Subject positions* within *Discourse* are mobilised through language; refers to the locating of individuals (including the researcher) in systems of *Representation* about particular objects.

Positivism: a theoretical framework for making sense of the world which assumes a world that exists independent of our ways of getting to know it, and that if we observe it properly, we can discover the reality of the world.

Postmodernism: notoriously resistant to definition (and anti-definition in itself), postmodernism is a worldview that challenges the linear and 'progressive' model of the world promoted by modernism. Instead, it offers an approach to society and/or knowledge that stresses the uncertainty of knowledge and the existence of multiple truths. It theorises individual experiences as fragmented and multiple rather than coherent and linear. It is often seen as ironic and self-aware.

Postpositivism: beyond *Positivism*, a theoretical position that acknowledges that researchers are influenced by their contexts, but still seeks (uncontaminated) knowledge about the true nature of the world.

Poststructuralism: refers to a loose collection of theoretical positions (and analytic approaches) developed in France in the 1960s from structuralist theories of language. The different approaches labelled poststructuralist share assumptions about language, meaning, and subjectivity. Language (*Discourse*) is seen as constitutive of the world, the organisation of society, and individual subjectivity. Meaning is thus produced and created within language and discourse.

Power: a *Poststructuralist* view sees power as a productive force, rather than just as oppressive one, meaning it creates rather than suppresses; linked to theories of *Discourse* and language as productive.

Practice(s): a term that captures the very diverse 'things people do'; often used in place of the term 'behaviour' within critical psychology research, but is conceptually much broader than a traditional understanding of behaviour because it includes things like language use.

Pseudonym: a fake named used in place of a real name, to protect a participant's anonymity.

Purposive sampling: a mode of sampling typical of qualitative research; involves selecting participants or data on the basis that they will have certain characteristics or experience. (see *Convenience sampling*; *Snowball sampling*; *Theoretical sampling*)

Qualitative survey: a method of qualitative data collection consisting of a series of open-ended questions that participants write responses to.

Rapport: sense of positive emotional connection between people; often relates to inter-active data collection; putting participants at ease and creating an environment where they feel relaxed, open, and willing to answer questions.

Raw data: data in their original form, such as audio data before transcription.

Realism: an *Ontological* and *Epistemological* position which assumes that the world has a true nature which is knowable and real, discovered through experience and research; that we 'know' an object because there are inherent facts about it that we can perceive and understand.

Reflexivity: reflexivity has many meanings, but here it is concerned with a critical reflection on the research, both as process and as practice, on one's own role as researcher, and on one's relation to knowledge. Reflexive research is that which acknowledges the role of the researcher in the production of knowledge, and in which the researcher reflects on their various positionings and the ways these might have shaped the collection and analysis of their data.

Relativism: a theoretical position that holds that there are multiple, constructed realities, rather than a single, knowable reality; holds that all we have is representations or accounts of what reality is, and that, at least *Epistemologically*, all accounts are of equal theoretical value (even if they might not be, based on other criteria); there is no foundation on which to claim some version of reality as more true and right than another version. (see *Ontology*)

Reliability: the extent to which the results generated could be generated again (e.g. by another researcher, in another context, at another time ...); a key component of *Positivist* research.

Representation: in writing up research, refers to the process of saying something about what participants think, feel, say, believe, etc; representation is what we do with research. As a form of qualitative research, refers to an interest in factors which shape or create meaning and the effects and implications of particular patterns of meaning in particular contexts.

Research design: effectively the plan for what a study will involve, and how it will be conducted. Ideally it should incorporate the goals of the study, the theoretical framework(s), the research questions, ethics, and methods of generating and analysing data.

Research object: the thing that we are studying; the thing we want to understand more about. Can be theoretical or conceptual (love, creativity) or more concrete (cancer, eating).

Researcher-derived code: goes beyond the explicit content of the data, to identify a latent or implicit meaning in the data; driven by the researcher's theoretical and conceptual knowledge; sometimes called latent codes or conceptual codes. (see *Latent meaning*)

Rich data: data which provide detailed, complex and contradictory accounts about the *Research object*. (see *Thick description*)

Safety buddy: a third party who knows from whom you are collecting data, when, and where, and with whom you check in before and after completing data collection.

Saturation: the point at which new data stop generating any substantially new ideas; developed out of/associated with *Grounded theory*.

Secondary sources (of data): information that has been generated for purposes other than research, but that can be used as data in empirical research, such as parliamentary debates or blogs.

Small q qualitative research: the use of qualitative methods of data collection within a positivist or essentialist paradigm; the occasional use of qualitative questions within a primarily quantitative method of data collection. (see *Big Q qualitative research*)

Snowball sampling: an approach to sampling where new participants are invited from the networks of people who have already taken part. (see *Convenience sampling*; *Purposive sampling*; *Theoretical sampling*)

Social constructionism: a broad theoretical framework, popular in qualitative research, which rejects a single ultimate truth. Instead, it sees the world, and what we know of it, as produced (constructed) through language, representation and other social processes, rather than discovered. The terms in which the world is understood are seen related to specific socio-political, cultural, historical contexts, and meanings are seen as social artefacts, resulting from social interaction, rather than some inherent truth about the nature of reality.

Story completion task: a method of data collection, where participants are given the start of a story and asked to complete (or continue) it.

Story cue: a very 'bare bones' scenario for a *Story completion task*. (see *Story stem*).

Story stem: the start of a story involving a hypothetical scenario and characters as part of the *Story completion task* method. (see *Story cue*)

Subject positions effectively a 'way of being' or identity created by *Discourse*, which individuals can take up; subject positions offer ways of thinking about oneself in relation to the world, and delimit the options available for action. (see *Subjectivity*)

Subjective: the idea that the researcher brings their personal and cultural history, values, assumptions, perspectives and mannerisms into their research, and these inevitably influence research, making it subjective, rather than objective; seen as a strength by most qualitative researchers. (see *Bias*; *Subjectivity*)

Subjectivity: people's sense of themselves; their ways of being in, and relating to, the world. Within *Poststructuralist* (and *Postmodern*) thought, the individual is a contradictory, fragmented subject, whose identity is constituted in and through *Discourse*.

Subtheme: in *Thematic analysis*, a subtheme captures and develops one notable *specific* aspect of one *Theme,* but shares the *Central organising concept* of that theme. (see *Overarching theme*)

Superordinate theme: a concept from *Interpretative phenomenological analysis*; broad or higher-order themes under which other themes cluster. (see *Overarching theme*)

Telephone interview: an interactive data collection method between a researcher and a participant that takes place over the telephone. (see *Email interview*; *Interview*; *Virtual interview*)

Thematic analysis: a form of analysis which has the *Theme* as its unit of analysis, and which looks across data from many different sources to identify themes.

Theme: patterned meaning across a dataset that captures something important about the data in relation to the research question, organised around a *Central organising concept*. (see *Overarching theme*; *Subtheme*)

Theoretical sampling: an approach to sampling most associated with *Grounded theory*, where the developing analysis shapes the selection of subsequent data; sampling driven by theoretical considerations. (see *Convenience sampling*; *Purposive sampling*; *Snowball sampling*)

Thick description: originally referred to data in which the contexts of behaviour were described; now often used to refer to detailed, complex, contradictory data. (see *Rich data*)

Transcript: a textual version of audio or audiovisual data, produced through the process of *Transcription*. (see *Orthographic transcript*)

Transcription: the process of turning audio or audiovisual data into written text (a *Transcript)* by writing down what was said (and if audiovisual material, what was done), and in some instances how it was said, so that data can be systematically coded and analysed.

Transferability: the extent to which qualitative research results can be 'transferred' to other groups of people or contexts. (see *Generalisability*)

Triangulation: using two or more data sources, methods, or researchers to try to gain a fuller or multi-faceted understanding of a topic.

The 'usual suspects': the people who most regularly feature as the sample for western psychology: white, middle class, heterosexual, able-bodied (and in the past, male) individuals; often psychology students.

Validity: refers most basically to whether research actually shows what it claims to show. There are different forms of validity, with ecological validity the most commonly used in qualitative research. Ecological validity is about whether or not research captures meaning in a way closely related to real life situations.

Vignette: a short hypothetical scenario; as a method for qualitative data collection, a vignette is presented to participants, often in a series of 'stages', after which they answer a series of open-ended questions relating to it. (see the ***companion website***)

Virtual focus group: a *Focus group* conducted using some form of mediated communication, such as the internet or telephone, rather than face-to-face.

Virtual interview: an *Interview* conducted using the internet, email, or telephone, rather than face-to-face.

Vulnerable groups: groups marginalised within society, or potentially at risk of harm. (see *Hard to engage* and *Hidden populations*)

References

Abrahamson, M. (2004). Alcohol in courtship contexts: focus-group interviews with young swedish women and men. *Contemporary Drug Problems, 31*, 3–29.

Adam, B. D. (1998). Theorising homophobia. *Sexualities, 1*, 387–404.

Adams, J., McCreanor, T., & Braun, V. (2007). Alcohol and gay men: consumption, promotion and policy responses. In V. Clarke & E. Peel (Eds), *Out in psychology: Lesbian, gay, bisexual and trans and queer perspectives* (pp. 369–390). Chichester, U.K: John Wiley.

Adler, C. L., & Zarchin, Y. R. (2002). The 'virtual focus group': using the internet to reach pregnant women on home bed rest. *Journal of Obstetric, Gynecologic, & Neonatal Nursing, 31*, 418–427.

Ahmed, B., Reavey, P., & Majumdar, A. (2009). Constructions of 'culture' in accounts of South Asian women survivors of sexual violence. *Feminism & Psychology, 19*, 7–28.

Alm, C., & Frodi, A. (2008). Tales from the shy: interviews with self- and peer-rated shy and non-shy individuals concerning their thoughts, emotions, and behaviors in social situations. *Qualitative Research in Psychology, 5*, 127–153.

Altheide, D. L. (1996). *Qualitative media analysis*. Thousand Oaks, CA: Sage.

American Psychological Association. (2010). *Publication manual of the American Psychological Association* (6th ed.). Washington, DC: American Psychological Association.

Anderson, J. A. (2008). Thinking qualitatively: hermeneutics in science. In D. W. Stacks & M. B. Salwen (Eds), *An integrated approach to communication theory and research* (2nd ed., pp. 40–58). Mahwah, NJ: Lawrence Erlbaum Associates.

Antaki, C., Billig, M., Edwards, D., & Potter, J. (2002). Discourse analysis means doing analysis: a critique of six analytic shortcomings. *DAOL Discourse Analysis Online 1.* [Online: extra.shu.ac.uk/daol/articles/v1/n1/a1/antaki2002002-paper.html].

Arcury, T. A., & Quandt, S. A. (1999). Participant recruitment for qualitative research: a site-based approach to community research in complex societies. *Human Organization 58*, 128–133.

Arksey, H., & Knight, P. (1999). *Interviewing for social scientists*. London: Sage.

Aronson, J. (1994). A pragmatic view of thematic analysis. *The Qualitative Report, 2* [Online: www.nova.edu/ssss/QR/BackIssues/QR2-1/aronson.html].

Arribas-Ayllon, M., & Walkerdine, V. (2008). Foucauldian discourse analysis. In C. Willig & W. Stainton Rogers (Eds), *The SAGE handbook of qualitative research in psychology* (pp. 91–108). London: Sage.

Asher, N. S., & Asher, K. C. (1999). Qualitative methods for an outsider looking in: lesbian women and body image. In M. E. Kopala & L. A. Suzuki (Eds), *Using qualitative methods in psychology* (pp. 135–144). Thousand Oaks, CA: Sage.

Ashworth, P. (2003). The origins of qualitative psychology. In J. A. Smith (Ed.), *Qualitative psychology: A practical guide to research methods* (pp. 4–24). London: Sage.

Atkinson, J. M., & Heritage, J. (1984). *Structures of social action: Studies in conversation analysis*. Cambridge: Cambridge University Press.

Augoustinos, M., & Every, D. (2007). The language of 'race' and prejudice: a discourse of denial, reason and liberal-practical politics. *Journal of Language and Social Psychology, 26*, 123–141.

Augoustinos, M., Tuffin, K., & Every, D. (2005). New racism, meritocracy and individualism: constraining affirmative action in education. *Discourse & Society, 16*, 315–340.

Baarts, C. (2009). Stuck in the middle: research ethics caught between science and politics. *Qualitative Research, 9*, 423–439.

Bailey, A. (2008). Let's tell you a story: use of vignettes in focus group discussions on HIV/AIDS among migrant and mobile men in Goa, India. In P. Liamputtonh (Ed.), *Doing cross-cultural research: Ethical and methodological perspectives* (pp. 253–264). New York: Springer.

Banister, P. (1994). Report writing. In P. Banister, E. Burman, I. Parker, M. Taylor & C. Tindall (Eds), *Qualitative methods in psychology: A research guide* (pp. 160–179). Buckingham, UK: Open University Press.

Barbour, R. S. (2005). Making sense of focus groups. *Medical Education, 39*, 742–750.

Barker, M. (2007). Heteronormativity and the exclusion of bisexuality in psychology. In V. Clarke & E. Peel (Eds), *Out in psychology: Lesbian, gay, bisexual, trans and queer perspectives* (pp. 95–117). Chichester: Wiley.

Baxter, J. (2002). Competing discourses in the classroom: a post-structuralist discourse analysis of girls' and boys' speech in public contexts. *Discourse & Society, 13*, 827–842.

Becken, S. (2007). Tourists' perception of international air travel's impact on the global climate and potential climate change policies. *Journal of Sustainable Tourism, 15*, 351–368.

Becker, J. C., & Swim, J. K. (2011). Seeing the unseen: attention to daily encounters with sexism as a way to reduce sexist beliefs. *Psychology of Women Quarterly, 35*, 227–242.

Belcher, W. L. (2009). *Writing your journal article in twelve weeks: A guide to academic publishing success*. Thousand Oaks, CA: Sage.

Bell, A. (1996). 'We're just New Zealanders': Pakeha identity politics. In P. Spoonley, C. Macpherson & D. Pearson (Eds), *Nga Patai: Racism and ethnic relations in Aotearoa/ New Zealand* (pp. 144–158). Palmerston North, New Zealand: The Dunmore Press.

Bennett, C., & Coyle, A. (2007). A minority within a minority: experiences of gay men with intellectual disabilities. In V. Clarke & E. Peel (Eds), *Out in psychology: Lesbian, gay, bisexual, trans and queer perspectives* (pp. 125–145). Chichester, UK: Wiley.

Berger, P. L., & Luckmann, T. (1967). *The social construction of reality: A treatise in the sociology of knowledge*. London: Allen Lane.

Bernard, H. R., & Ryan, G. W. (2010). *Analyzing qualitative data: Systematic approaches*. Los Angeles: Sage.

Billig, M. (1978a). *Fascists: A social psychological view of the National Front.* London: Academic Press.

Billig, M. (1978b). Patterns of racism: interviews with National Front members. *Race & Class, 20,* 161–179.

Billig, M. (1987). *Arguing and thinking: A rhetorical approach to social psychology.* Cambridge: Cambridge University Press.

Billig, M. (2006). A psychoanalytic discursive psychology: from consciousness to unconsciousness. *Discourse Studies, 8,* 17–24.

Birks, M., Chapman, Y., & Francis, K. (2008). Memoing in qualitative research: probing data and processes. *Journal of Research in Nursing, 13,* 68–75.

Birks, M., & Mills, J. (2011). *Grounded theory: A practical guide.* London: Sage.

Blaxter, M. (1997). Whose fault is it? People's own conceptions of the reasons for health inequalities. *Social Science & Medicine, 44,* 747–756.

Blee, K. M. (1998). White-knuckle research: emotional dynamics in fieldwork with racist activists. *Qualitative Sociology, 21,* 381–399.

Bloor, M. (1997). Techniques of validation in qualitative research: a critical commentary. In G. M. R. Dingwall (Ed.), *Context and method in qualitative research* (pp. 37–50). London: Sage.

Bloor, M., Frankland, J., Thomas, M., & Robson, K. (2001). *Focus groups in social research.* London: Sage.

Blumer, H. (1969). *Symbolic interactionism: Perspective and method.* Berkeley, CA: University of California Press.

Bondas, T. (2002). Finnish women's experiences of antenatal care. *Midwifery, 18,* 61–71.

Bong, S. A. (2002). Debunking myths in qualitative data analysis. *Forum Qualitative Sozialforschung/Forum: Qualitative Social Research, 3.* [Online: http://www.qualitative-research.net/index.php/fqs/article/view/849/1845].

Bourdon, S. (2002). The integration of qualitative data analysis software in research strategies: resistances and possibilities. *Forum Qualitative Sozialforschung/Forum: Qualitative Social Research, 3.* [Online: http://www.qualitative-research.net/index.php/fqs/article/view/850/1847].

Bowen, G. A. (2008). Naturalistic inquiry and the saturation concept: a research note. *Qualitative Research, 8.*

Bowker, N., & Tuffin, K. (2004). Using the online medium for discursive research about people with disabilities. *Social Science Computer Review, 22,* 228–241.

Boyatzis, R. E. (1998). *Transforming qualitative information: Thematic analysis and code development.* Thousand Oaks, CA: Sage.

Boynton, P. (2005). *The research companion: A practical guide for the social and health sciences.* Hove, UK: The Psychology Press.

Brackertz, N. (2007). *Who is hard to reach and why?* [ISR Working Paper]. Melbourne: Swinburne Institute of Technology. [Online: http://www.sisr.net/publications/0701brackertz.pdf].

Bradburn, N., Sudman, S., & Wansink, B. (2004). *Asking questions: The definitive guide to questionnaire design – for market research, political polls, and social and health questionnaires* (revised edition). San Fransisco: Jossey-Bass.

Bradbury, A. (2006). *Successful presentation skills* (3rd ed.). London: Kogan Page.

Braun, V. (2000). Heterosexism in focus group research: collusion and challenge. *Feminism & Psychology, 10*, 133–140.

Braun, V. (2008). 'She'll be right'? National identity explanations for poor sexual health statistics in Aotearoa/New Zealand. *Social Science & Medicine, 67*, 1817–1825.

Braun, V. (2009). Selling the 'perfect' vulva. In C. Heyes & M. Jones (Eds), *Cosmetic surgery: A feminist primer* (pp. 133–149). Farnham, UK: Ashgate.

Braun, V. (2010). Female genital cosmetic surgery: A critical review of current knowledge and contemporary debates. *Journal of Women's Health, 19*, 1393–1407.

Braun, V., & Clarke, V. (2006). Using thematic analysis in psychology. *Qualitative Research in Psychology, 3*, 77–101.

Braun, V., & Clarke, V. (2012). Thematic analysis. In H. Cooper (Ed.), *APA Handbook of research methods in psychology* (vol 2: Research designs, pp. 57–71). Washington, DC: APA books.

Braun, V., & Gavey, N. (1999). 'With the best of reasons': cervical cancer prevention policy and the suppression of sexual risk factor information. *Social Science & Medicine, 48*, 1463–1474.

Braun, V., Gavey, N., & McPhillips, K. (2003). The 'fair deal'? Unpacking accounts of reciprocity in heterosex. *Sexualities, 6*, 237–261.

Braun, V., & Kitzinger, C. (2001). The perfectible vagina: size matters. *Culture, Health & Sexuality, 3*, 263–277.

Braun, V., Schmidt, J., Gavey, N., & Fenaughty, J. (2009). Sexual coercion among gay and bisexual men in Aotearoa/New Zealand. *Journal of Homosexuality, 56*, 336–360.

Braun, V., Terry, G., Gavey, N., & Fenaughty, J. (2009). 'Risk' and sexual coercion among gay and bisexual men in Aotearoa/New Zealand – key informant accounts. *Culture, Health & Sexuality, 11*, 111–124.

Braun, V., Tricklebank, G., & Clarke, V. (under submission). 'It shouldn't stick out from you bikini at the beach': gender, public hair, and pubic hair removal. *Psychology of Women Quarterly*.

Braun, V., & Wilkinson, S. (2003). Liability or asset? Women talk about the vagina. *Psychology of Women Section Review, 5*, 28–42.

Braun, V., & Wilkinson, S. (2005). Vagina equals woman? On genitals and gendered identity. *Women's Studies International Forum, 28*, 509–522.

Breakwell, G. M., & Wood, P. (1995). Diary techniques. In G. M. Breakwell, S. Hammond & C. Fife-Schaw (Eds), *Research methods in psychology* (pp. 293–301). London: Sage.

Briggs, C. L. (1986). *Learning how to ask: A sociolinguistic appraisal of the role of the interview in social science research*. Cambridge: Cambridge University Press.

Bringer, J. D., Johnston, L. H., & Brackenridge, C. H. (2006). Using computer-assisted qualitative data analysis software to develop a grounded theory project. *Field Methods, 18*, 245–266.

Brinkman, S., & Kvale, S. (2005). Confronting the ethics of qualitative research. *Journal of Constructivist Psychology, 18*, 157–181.

Brinkmann, S., & Kvale, S. (2008). Ethics in qualitative psychological research. In C. Willig & W. Stainton Rogers (Eds), *The Sage handbook of qualitative research in psychology* (pp. 263–279). London: Sage.

British Sociological Association. (2004). *Language and the BSA: Disability*. [Online: http://www.britsoc.co.uk/equality/].

British Sociological Association. (2005). *Language and the BSA: Ethnicity & race*. [Online: http://www.britsoc.co.uk/equality/].

Brock, M. P. (2010). Resisting the Catholic Church's notion of the nun as self-sacrificing woman. *Feminism & Psychology, 20*, 473–490.

Brocki, J. M., & Wearden, A. J. (2006). A critical evaluation of the use of interpretative phenomenological analysis (IPA) in health psychology. *Psychology & Health, 21*, 87–108.

Brown, L. S. (1997). Ethics in psychology: Cui bono? In D. Fox & I. Prilleltensky (Eds), *Critical psychology: An introduction* (pp. 51–67). London: Sage.

Bruner, J. (1990). *Acts of meaning*. Cambridge, MA: Harvard University Press.

Bryman, A. (1988). *Quantity and quality in social research*. New York: Routledge.

Buetow, S. (2010). Thematic analysis and its reconceptualization as 'saliency analysis'. *Journal of Health Services Research Policy, 15*, 123–125.

Burgoyne, C., Clarke, V., Reibstein, J., & Edmunds, A. (2006). 'All my worldly goods I share with you'? Managing money at the transition to heterosexual marriage. *The Sociological Review, 54*, 619–637.

Burke, L. A., & Miller, M. K. (2001). Phone interviewing as a means of data collection: Lessons learned and practical recommendations. *Forum: Qualitative Social Research, 2*. [Online: www.qualitative-research.net/index.php/fqs/article/viewArticle/959].

Burman, E., & Parker, I. (Eds). (1993). *Discourse analytic research: Repertoires and readings of texts in action*. London: Routledge.

Burns, M. (2003). Interviewing: embodied communication. *Feminism & Psychology, 13*, 229–236.

Burns, M. (2006). Bodies that speak: examining the dialogues in research interactions. *Qualitative Research in Psychology 3*, 3–18.

Burns, M., Burgoyne, C., & Clarke, V. (2008). Financial affairs? Money management in same-sex relationships. *Journal of Socio-Economics, 37*, 481–501.

Burns, M., & Gavey, N. (2004). 'Healthy weight' at what cost? 'Bulimia' and a discourse of weight control. *Journal of Health Psychology, 9*, 549–565.

Burr, V. (1995). *An introduction to social constructionism*. London: Routledge.

Burr, V. (2002). *The person in social psychology*. London: The Psychology Press.

Burr, V. (2003). *Social constructionism* (2nd ed.). London: Psychology Press.

Burton, L. J., & Bruening, J. E. (2003). Technology and method intersect in the online focus group. *Quest, 55*, 315–327.

Bushy, A. (1991). A rating scale to evaluate research posters. *Nurse Educator, 16*, 11–15.

Buttny, R. (1997). Reported speech in talking race on campus. *Human Communication Research, 23*, 477–506.

Cameron, J., Nairn, K., & Higgins, J. (2009). Demystifying academic writing: reflections on emotions, know-how and academic identity. *Journal of Geography in Higher Education, 33*, 269–284.

Capdevila, R., & Callaghan, J. E. M. (2008). 'It's not racist. It's common sense'. A critical analysis of political discourse around asylum and immigration in the UK. *Journal of Community & Applied Social Psychology, 18*, 1–16.

Carrington, C. (1999). *No place like home: Relationships and family life among lesbians and gay men.* Chicago, IL: University of Chicago Press.

Chamberlain, K. (2000). Methodolatry and qualitative health research. *Journal of Health Psychology, 5*, 285–296.

Charmaz, K. (1983). Loss of self: a fundamental form of suffering in the chronically ill. *Sociology of Health & Illness, 5*, 168–195.

Charmaz, K. (2002). Qualitative interviewing and grounded theory analysis. In J. F. Gubrium & J. A. Holstein (Eds), *Handbook of interview research: Context & method* (pp. 675–694). Thousand Oaks, CA: Sage.

Charmaz, K. (2005). Grounded theory for the 21st Century: applications for advancing social justice studies. In N. K. Denzin & Y. S. Lincoln (Eds), *The Sage handbook of qualitative research* (3rd ed., pp. 507–535). Thousand Oaks, CA: Sage.

Charmaz, K. (2006). *Constructing grounded theory: A practical guide through qualitative analysis.* Thousand Oaks, CA: Sage.

Charmaz, K., & Henwood, K. (2008). Grounded theory. In C. Willig & W. Stainton Rogers (Eds), *The Sage handbook of qualitative research in psychology* (pp. 240–259). London: Sage.

Chase, L., & Alvarez, J. (2000). Internet research: the role of the focus group. *Library & Information Science Research, 22*, 357–369.

Chen, P., & Hinton, S. M. (1999). Realtime interviewing using the world wide web. *Sociological Research Online, 4*. [Online: www.socresonline/4/3/chen].

Chiu, L. F. (2003). Transformational potential of focus group practice in participatory action research. *Action Research, 1*, 165–183.

Chivers, B., & Shoolbred, M. (2007). *A student's guide to presentations: Making your presentation count.* London: Sage.

Chou, C. (2001). Internet heavy use and addiction among Taiwanese college students: an online interview study. *CyberPsychology & Behavior, 4*, 573–585.

Christianson, M., Lalos, A., Westman, G., & Johansson, E. E. (2007). 'Eyes Wide Shut' sexuality and risk in HIV-positive youth in Sweden: A qualitative study. *Scandanavian Journal of Public Health, 35*, 55–61.

Clark, A. M. (1998). The qualitative – quantitative debate: moving from positivism and confrontation to post-positivism and reconciliation. *Journal of Advanced Nursing, 27*, 1242–1249.

Clarke, V. (2001). What about the children? Arguments against lesbian and gay parenting. *Women's Studies International Forum, 24*, 555–570.

Clarke, V. (2005). 'We're all very liberal in our views': students' talk about lesbian and gay parenting. *Lesbian & Gay Psychology Review, 6*, 2–15.

Clarke, V. (2006). 'Gay men, gay men and more gay men': traditional, liberal and critical perspectives on male role models in lesbian families. *Lesbian & Gay Psychology Review, 7*, 19–35.

Clarke, V. (2007). Men not included? A critical psychology analysis of lesbian families and male influences in child rearing. *Journal of GLBT Family Studies, 3*, 309–349.

Clarke, V., Burgoyne, C., & Burns, M. (2006). Just a piece of paper? A qualitative exploration of same-sex couples' multiple conceptions of civil partnership and marriage. *Lesbian and Gay Psychology Review, 7*, 141–161.

Clarke, V., Ellis, S. J., Peel, E., & Riggs, D. W. (2010). *Lesbian, gay, bisexual, trans queer psychology: An introduction*. Cambridge: Cambridge University Press.

Clarke, V., & Kitzinger, C. (2004). Lesbian and gay parents on talk shows: resistance or collusion in heterosexism. *Qualitative Research in Psychology, 1*, 195–217.

Clarke, V., Kitzinger, C., & Potter, J. (2004). Kids are just cruel anyway: lesbian and gay parents' talk about homophobic bullying. *British Journal of Social Psychology, 43*, 531–550.

Clarke, V., & Spence, K. (2013). 'I am who I am': Navigating norms and the importance of authenticity in lesbian and bisexual women's accounts of their appearance practices. *Psychology of Sexualities, 4*(1), 25–33.

Clarke, V., & Turner, K. (2007). Clothes maketh the queer? Dress, appearance and the construction of lesbian, gay and bisexual identities. *Feminism & Psychology, 17*, 267–276.

Clifford, C., & Orford, J. (2007). The experience of social power in the lives of trans people. In V. Clarke & E. Peel (Eds), *Out in psychology: Lesbian, gay, bisexual, trans and queer perspectives* (pp. 195–216). Chichester: Wiley.

Colls, R. (2006). Outsize/outside: bodily bignesses and the emotional experiences of British women shopping for clothes. *Gender, Place & Culture: A Journal of Feminist Geography, 13*, 529–545.

Colucci, E. (2007). 'Focus groups can be fun': the use of activity-oriented questions in focus group discussions. *Qualitative Health Research, 17*, 1422–1433.

Committee on Disability Issues in Psychology (1992). *Guidelines for nonhandicapping language in APA journals*. [Online: http://www.apastyle.org/manual/related/ nonhandicapping-language.aspx].

Committee on Lesbian and Gay Concerns (1991). Avoiding heterosexual bias in language. *American Psychologist, 46*, 973–974.

Corbin, J., & Strauss, A. (1990). *Basics of qualitative research: Grounded theory techniques and procedures*. Newbury Park, CA: Sage.

Cotterill, P. (1992). Interviewing women: issues of friendship, vulnerability, and power. *Women's Studies International Forum, 15*, 593–606.

Coxon, A. P. M. (1994). Diaries and sexual behaviour: the use of sexual diaries as method and substance in researching gay men's response to HIV/AIDS. In M. Boulton (Ed.), *Challenge and innovation: Methodological advances in social research on HIV/AIDS* (pp. 125–148). London: Taylor & Francis.

Coyle, A. (2006). Discourse analysis. In G. M. Breakwell, S. Hammond & C. Fife-Schaw (Eds), *Research methods in psychology* (3rd ed., pp. 366–387). London: Sage.

Coyle, A. (2007). Discourse analysis. In A. Coyle & E. Lyons (Eds), *Analysing qualitative data in psychology* (pp. 98–116). London: Sage.

Coyle, A., & Lyons, E. (Eds) (2007). *Analysing qualitative data in psychology*. London: Sage.

Coyne, I. T. (1997). Sampling in qualitative research. Purposeful and theoretical sampling; merging or clear boundaries? *Journal of Advanced Nursing, 26*, 623–630.

Coyne, J. C., & Calarco, M. M. (1995). Effects of the experience of depression – application of focus group and survey methodologies. *Psychiatry: Interpersonal and Biological Processes, 58*, 149–163.

Crawford, M., & Unger, R. (2004). *Women and gender: A feminist psychology* (4th ed.). New York: McGraw-Hill.

Cromby, J., & Nightingale, D. J. (1999). What's wrong with social constructionism? In D. J. Nightingale & J. Cromby (Eds), *Social constructionist psychology: A critical analysis of theory and practice* (pp. 1–19). Buckingham: Open University Press.

Crossley, M. L. (2007). Childbirth, complications and the illusion of 'choice': a case study. *Feminism & Psychology, 17*, 543–563.

Crossley, M. L. (2009). Breastfeeding as a moral imperative: an autoethnographic study. *Feminism & Psychology, 19*, 71–87.

Crowley, C. (2010). Writing up the qualitative methods research report. In M. A. Forrester (Ed.), *Doing qualitative research in psychology: A practical guide* (pp. 229–246). London: Sage.

Dalla, R. L. (2002). Night moves: a qualitative investigation of street-level sex work. *Psychology of Women Quarterly, 26*, 63–73.

Davies, B., & Harré, R. (1990). Positioning: the discursive production of selves. *Journal for the Theory of Social Behaviour, 20*, 43–63.

Day, K., Gough, B., & McFadden, M. (2004). Warning! Alcohol can seriously damage your feminine health: a discourse analysis of recent British newspaper coverage of women and drinking. *Feminist Media Studies, 4*, 165–183.

Day, M., & Thatcher, J. (2009). 'I'm really embarrassed that you're going to read this...': reflections on using diaries in qualitative research. *Qualitative Research in Psychology, 6*, 249–259.

Demetriou, E. (2011). *'Instead of dad coming out of the closet, I suppose we all jumped in with him': A qualitative analysis of the experiences of adult children of lesbian, gay and trans parents*. Dissertation. University of the West of England.

Denmark, F., Russo, N. F., Frieze, I. H., & Sechzer, J. A. (1988). Guidelines for avoiding sexism in psychological research: a report of the Ad Hoc Committee on Nonsexist Research. *American Psychologist, 43*, 582–585.

Denzin, N. K. (1970). *The research act in sociology: Theoretical introduction to sociological methods*. London: Butterworth.

Denzin, N. K., & Lincoln, Y. S. (2005a). Introduction: The discipline and practice of qualitative research. In N. K. Denzin & Y. S. Lincoln (Eds), *The Sage handbook of qualitative research* (2nd ed., pp. 1–32). Thousand Oaks, CA: Sage.

Denzin, N. K., & Lincoln, Y. S. (Eds). (2005b). *The Sage handbook of qualitative research* (2nd ed.). Thousand Oaks, CA: Sage.

DeVault, M. J. (1990). Talking and listening from women's standpoint: feminist strategies for interviewing and analysis. *Social Problems, 37*, 96–116.

Dey, I. (1999). *Grounding grounded theory: Guidelines for qualitative inquiry*. San Diego, CA: Academic Press.

Digman, J. M. (1990). Personality structure: emergence of the five-factor model. *Annual Review of Psychology, 41*, 417–440.

Docherty, S., & Sandelowski, M. (1999). Focus on qualitative method interviewing children. *Research in Nursing & Health, 22*, 177–185.

Dunbar, J. C., Rodriguez, D., & Parker, L. (2002). Race, subjectivity and the interview process. In J. F. Gubrium & J. A. Holstein (Eds), *Handbook of interview research: Context and method* (pp. 279–298). Thousand Oaks, CA: Sage.

Eatough, V., & Smith, J. A. (2006). I feel like scrambled egg in my head: an idiographic case study of meaning making and anger using interpretative phenomenological analysis. *Psychology and Psychotherapy: Theory, Research and Practice, 79*, 115–135.

Eatough, V., Smith, J. A., & Shaw, R. (2008). Women, anger and aggression: an interpretative phenomenological analysis. *Journal of Interpersonal Violence, 23*, 1767–1799.

Eder, D., & Fingerson, L. (2002). Interviewing children and adolescents. In J. F. Gubrium & J. A. Holstein (Eds), *Handbook of interview research: Context and method* (pp. 181–202). Thousand Oaks, CA: Sage.

Edley, N. (2001a). Analysing masculinity: interpretative repertoires, ideological dilemmas and subject positions. In M. Wetherell, S. Taylor & S. J. Yates (Eds), *Discourse as data: A guide for analysis* (pp. 189–228). London: Sage.

Edley, N. (2001b). Unravelling social constructionism. *Theory & Psychology, 11*, 433–441.

Edley, N., & Wetherell, M. (1997). Jockeying for position: the construction of masculine identities. *Discourse & Society, 8*, 203–217.

Edwards, D., & Potter, J. (1992). *Discursive psychology*. London: Sage.

Edwards, R. (1990). Connecting method and epistemology: a white woman interviewing black women. *Women's Studies International Forum, 13*, 477–490.

Ellerbee, S. M. (2006). Posters with artistic flair. *Nurse Educator, 31*, 166–169.

Elliott, H. (1997). The use of diaries in sociological research on health experience. *Sociological Research Online, 2*. [Online: http://www.socresonline.org.uk/socresonline/2/2/7.html].

Elliott, R., Fischer, C. T., & Rennie, D. L. (1999). Evolving guidelines for publication of qualitative research studies in psychology and related fields. *British Journal of Clinical Psychology, 38*, 215–229.

Elliott, R., Fischer, C. T., & Rennie, D. L. (2000). Also against methodolatry: a reply to Reicher. *British Journal of Clinical Psychology, 39*, 7–10.

Ellis, S. (2001). Doing being liberal: implicit prejudice in focus group talk about lesbian and gay human rights issues. *Lesbian & Gay Psychology Review, 2*, 43–49.

Ellis, S. J., & Kitzinger, C. (2002). Denying equality: an analysis of arguments against lowering the age of consent for sex between men. *Journal of Community & Applied Social Psychology, 12*, 167–180.

Ely, M., Vinz, R., Downing, M., & Anzul, M. (1997). *On writing qualitative research: Living by words*. London: Routledge/Falmer.

Etherington, K. (2004). *Becoming a reflexive researcher: Using our selves in research*. London: Jessica Kingsley Publishers.

Evans, A., Elford, J., & Wiggins, D. (2008). Using the internet for qualitative research. In C. Willig & W. Stainton Rogers (Eds), *The Sage handbook of qualitative research in psychology* (pp. 315–333). London: Sage.

Eysenbach, G., & Till, J. E. (2001). Ethical issues in research on internet communities. *BMJ, 323*, 1103–1105.

Fairclough, N. (2010). *Critical discourse analysis: The critical study of language* (2nd ed.). London: Longman.

Farnsworth, J., & Boon, B. (2010). Analysing group dynamics within the focus group. *Qualitative Research, 10*, 605–624.

Farrell, A. E. (2011). *Fat shame: Stigma and the fat body in American culture*. New York: NYU Press.

Farvid, P., & Braun, V. (2006). 'Most of us guys are raring to go anytime, anyplace, anywhere': male and female sexuality in *Cosmopolitan* and *Cleo*. *Sex Roles, 55*, 295–310.

Fassinger, R. E. (2005). Paradigms, praxis, problems, and promise: grounded theory in counseling psychology research. *Journal of Counseling Psychology, 52*, 156–166.

Feldman, M. B., & Meyer, I. H. (2007). Eating disorders in diverse lesbian, gay, and bisexual populations. *International Journal of Eating Disorders, 40*, 218–226.

Fenaughty, J., Braun, V., Gavey, N., Aspin, C., Reynolds, P., & Schmidt, J. (2006). *Sexual coercion among gay men, bisexual men and Tākatāpui Tāne in Aotearoa/New Zealand*. Auckland: The University of Auckland.

Ferguson, C., Kornblet, S., & Muldoon, A. (2009). Not all are created equal: differences in obesity attitudes between men and women. *Women's Health Issues, 19*, 289–291.

Fielding, N., & Thomas, H. (2008). Qualitative interviewing. In N. Gilbert (Ed.), *Researching social life* (3rd ed., pp. 245–265). London: Sage.

Fielding, N. G., & Lee, R. M. (1991). *Using computers in qualitative research*. London: Sage.

Fielding, N. G., & Lee, R. M. (1998). *Computer analysis and qualitative research*. London: Sage.

Figgou, L., & Condor, S. (2006). Irrational categorization, natural intolerance and reasonable discrimination: lay representations of prejudice and racism. *British Journal of Social Psychology, 45*, 219–243.

Finch, J. (1984). 'It's great to have someone to talk to': the ethics and politics of interviewing women. In C. Bell & H. Roberts (Eds), *Social researching: Politics, problems and practice* (pp. 70–87). London: Routledge & Kegan Paul.

Fine, M. (1992). *Disruptive voices: The possibilities for feminist research*. Ann Arbour: University of Michigan Press.

Fine, M., & Gordon, S. M. (1989). Feminist transformations of/despite psychology. In M. Crawford & M. Gentry (Eds), *Gender and thought: Psychological perspectives* (pp. 146–174). New York: Springer-Verlag.

Fine, M., & Macpherson, P. (1992). Over dinner: feminism and adolescent female bodies. In M. Fine, *Disruptive voices: The possibilities of feminist research* (pp. 175–203). Ann Arbour, MI: University of Michigan Press.

Fine, M., & Torre, M. E. (2004). Re-membering exclusions: participatory action research in public institutions. *Qualitative Research in Psychology, 1*, 15–37.

Fine, M., Torre, M. E., Boudin, K., Bowen, I., Clark, J., Hylton, D., Martinez, M. 'Missy', Rivera, M., Roberts, R., Smart, P. & Upegui, D. (2003). Participatory action research: from within and beyond prison bars. In P. M. Camic, J. E. Rhodes & L. Yardley (Eds), *Qualitative research in psychology: Expanding perspectives in methodology and design* (pp. 173–198). Washington, DC: American Psychological Association.

Finlay, L. (2002a). Negotiating the swamp: the opportunity and challenge of reflexivity in research practice. *Qualitative Research, 2*, 209–230.

Finlay, L. (2002b). 'Outing' the researcher: the provenance, process, and practice of reflexivity. *Qualitative Health Research, 12*, 531–545.

Finlay, L., & Gough, B. (Eds) (2003). *Reflexivity: A practical guide for researchers in health and social sciences*. Oxford: Blackwell Science.

Finlay, S.-J. (2001). *Pleasure and resistance? Feminism, heterosexuality, and the media.* Doctoral dissertation, Loughborough University, Loughborough, UK. [Online: http://hdl.handle.net/2134/7537].

Fish, J. (1999). Sampling lesbians: how to get 1000 lesbians to complete a questionnaire. *Feminism & Psychology, 9*, 229–238.

Fish, J. (2006). Exploring lesbians' health behaviours and risk perceptions. *Diversity in Health and Social Care, 3*, 163–169.

Fish, J., & Wilkinson, S. (2003a). Explaining lesbians' practice of breast self-examination: results from a UK survey of lesbian health. *Health Education Journal, 62*, 304–315.

Fish, J., & Wilkinson, S. (2003b). Understanding lesbians' healthcare behaviour: the case of breast self-examination. *Social Science & Medicine, 56*, 235–245.

Fisher, C. B. (2009). *Decoding the ethics code: A practical guide for psychologists* (2nd ed.). Thousand Oaks, CA: Sage.

Flintoff, A., & Scraton, S. (2005). Gender and physical education. In K. Green & K. Hardman (Eds), *Physical education: Essential issues* (pp. 161–179). London: Sage.

Flood, M. (2008). Men, sex, and homosociality: how bonds between men shape their sexual relations with women. *Men and Masculinities, 10*, 339–359.

Forrester, M. A. (Ed.) (2010). *Doing qualitative research in psychology: A practical guide*. London: Sage.

Foster, J. J., & Parker, I. (1995). *Carrying out investigations in psychology: Methods and statistics*. Leicester: BPS Books.

Foucault, M. (1977). *Discipline and punish: The birth of the prison*. London: Allen Lane.

Foucault, M. (1978). *The history of sexuality (Volume 1: An introduction)* (R. Hurley, Trans.). London: Penguin.

Fox, D., Prilleltensky, I., & Austin, S. (Eds) (2009). *Critical psychology: An introduction* (2nd ed.). Los Angeles: Sage.

Fox, F. E., Morris, M., & Rumsey, N. (2007). Doing synchronous online focus groups with young people. *Qualitative Health Research, 17*, 539–547.

Frank, A. (2010). *Letting stories breathe: A socio-narratology*. Chicago: University of Chicago Press.

Frith, H. (2000). Focusing on sex: using focus groups in sex research. *Sexualities, 3*, 275–297.

Frith, H., & Gleeson, K. (2004). Clothing and embodiment: men managing body image and appearance. *Psychology of Men & Masculinity, 5*, 40–48.

Frith, H., & Gleeson, K. (2008). Dressing the body: the role of clothing in sustaining body pride and managing body distress. *Qualitative Research in Psychology, 5*, 249–264.

Frith, H., Riley, S., Archer, L., & Gleeson, K. (2005). Editorial: imag(in)ing visual methodologies. *Qualitative Research in Psychology, 2*, 187–198.

Gaiser, T. J. (1997). Conducting on-line focus groups: a methodological discussion. *Social Science Computer Review, 15*, 135–144.

Gaiser, T. J. (2008). Online focus groups. In N. Fielding, R. M. Lee & G. Blank (Eds), *The Sage handbook of online research methods* (pp. 290–306). Los Angeles: Sage.

Gallais, T. L. (2008). Wherever I go there I am: reflections on reflexivity and the research stance. *Reflective Practice: International and Multidisciplinary Perspectives, 9*, 145–155.

Garfinkel, H. (1967). *Studies in ethnomethodology*. Cambridge: Polity Press.

Garton, S., & Copland, F. (2010). 'I like this interview; I get cakes and cats!': the effect of prior relationships on interview talk. *Qualitative Research, 10*, 533–551.

Gavey, N. (1989). Feminist poststructuralism and discourse analysis: contributions to feminist psychology. *Psychology of Women Quarterly, 13*, 459–475.

Gavey, N., & Braun, V. (1997). Ethics and the publication of clinical case material. *Professional Psychology: Research and Practice, 28*, 399–404.

Gavey, N., & McPhillips, K. (1999). Subject to romance: heterosexual passivity as an obstacle to women initiating condom use. *Psychology of Women Quarterly, 23*, 349–367.

Gavey, N., McPhillips, K., & Braun, V. (1999). Interruptus coitus: heterosexuals accounting for intercourse. *Sexualities, 2*, 35–68.

Gavey, N., Schmidt, J., Braun, V., Fenaughty, J., & Eremin, M. (2009). Unsafe, unwanted: sexual coercion as a barrier to safer sex among men who have sex with men. *Journal of Health Psychology, 14*, 1021–1026.

Geertz, C. (1973). *The interpretation of cultures: Selected essays*. New York: Basic Books.

Gergen, K. J. (1985). The social constructionist movement in modern psychology. *American Psychologist, 40*, 266–275.

Gergen, K. J. (1990). Toward a postmodern psychology. *The Humanistic Psychologist, 18*, 23–34.

Gergen, K. J. (1999). *An invitation to social construction*. London: Sage.

Gilbert, G. N., & Mulkay, M. (1984). *Opening Pandora's box: A sociological analysis of scientists' discourse*. Cambridge: Cambridge University Press.

Gilbert, K. R. (Ed.) (2001). *The emotional nature of qualitative research*. Boca Raton, FL: CRC Press.

Gill, R. (1993). Justifying injustice: broadcasters' accounts of inequality in radio. In E. Burman & I. Parker (Eds), *Discourse analytic research: Repertoires and readings of texts in action* (pp. 75–93). London: Routledge.

Gill, R. (2008). Empowerment/sexism: figuring female sexual agency in contemporary advertising. *Feminism & Psychology, 18*, 35–60.

Gill, R., Hadaway, C. K., & Marler, P. L. (1998). Is religious belief declining in Britain? *Journal for the Scientific Study of Religion, 37*, 507–516.

Girden, E. R. (2001). *Evaluating research articles: From start to finish* (2nd ed.). Thousand Oaks, CA: Sage.

Glaser, B. G. (1992). *Basics of grounded theory analysis: Emergence vs. forcing*. Mill Valley, CA: Sociology Press.

Glaser, B. G. (1978). *Theoretical sensitivity: Advances in the methodology of grounded theory*. Mill Valley, CA: Sociology Press.

Glaser, B. G., & Strauss, A. L. (1965). *Awareness of dying*. New Brunswick, NJ: Aldine.

Glaser, B. G., & Strauss, A. L. (1967). *The discovery of grounded theory: Strategies for qualitative research*. Mill valley, CA: Sociology Press.

Gleeson, K., & Frith, H. (2006). (De)constructing body image. *Journal of Health Psychology, 11*, 79–90.

Gliner, J. A. (1994). Reviewing qualitative research: proposed criteria for fairness and rigor. *Occupational Therapy Journal of Research, 4*, 78–90.

Golombok, S., & Tasker, F. (1996). Do parents influence the sexual orientation of their children? Findings from a longitudinal study of lesbian families. *Developmental Psychology, 32*, 3–11.

Goodman, S. (2008a). The generalizability of discursive research. *Qualitative Research in Psychology, 5*, 265–275.

Goodman, S. (2008b). Justifying the harsh treatment of asylum seekers through the supports of social cohesion. *Annual Review of Critical Psychology, 6*, 110–124.

Gough, B. (2007). 'Real men don't diet': an analysis of contemporary newspaper representations of men, food and health. *Social Science & Medicine, 64*, 326–337.

Gough, B., & Conner, M. T. (2006). Barriers to healthy eating amongst men: a qualitative analysis. *Social Science & Medicine, 62*, 387–395.

Gough, B., Lawton, R., Maddill, A., & Stratton, P. (2003). *Guidelines for the supervision of undergraduate qualitative research in psychology*. Leeds, UK: School of Psychology, University of Leeds.

Graffigna, G., & Bosio, A. C. (2008). The influence of setting on findings produced in qualitative health research: a comparison between face-to-face and online discussion groups about HIV/AIDS. *International Journal of Qualitative Methods, 5*, 55–76.

Griffin, C., & Bengry-Howell, A. (2008). Ethnography. In C. Willig & W. Stainton Rogers (Eds), *The Sage handbook of qualitative research in psychology* (pp. 15–31). London: Sage.

Grogan, S., & Richards, H. (2002). Body image: focus groups with boys and men. *Men and Masculinities, 4*, 219–232.

Guba, E. G., & Lincoln, Y. S. (2005). Paradigmatic controversies, contradictions, and emerging influences. In N. K. Denzin & Y. S. Lincoln (Eds), *Handbook of qualitative research* (3rd ed., pp. 191–215). Thousand Oaks, CA: Sage.

Gubrium, J. F., & Holstein, J. A. (2002). From the individual interview to the interview society. In J. F. Gubrium & J. A. Holstein (Eds), *Handbook of interview research: Context and method* (pp. 3–32). Thousand Oaks, CA: Sage.

Guenther, K. M. (2009). The politics of names: rethinking the methodological and ethical significance of naming people, organizations, and places. *Qualitative Research, 9*, 411–421.

Guest, G., MacQueen, K. M., & Namey, E. E. (2012). *Applied thematic analysis*. Los Angeles: Sage.

Guidelines for reporting and writing about people with disabilities. (2008). (7th ed.). Lawrence, KS: RTCIL Publications.

Hall, M., & Gough, B. (2011). Magazine and reader constructions of 'metrosexuality' and masculinity: a membership categorisation analysis. *Journal of Gender Studies, 20*, 67–86.

Hall, S. (Ed.) (1997). *Representation: Cultural representations and signifying practices*. London: Sage.

Hallowell, N., Lawton, J., & Gregory, S. (Eds) (2005). *Reflections on research: The realities of doing research in the social sciences*. Maidenhead, UK: Open University Press.

Hamilton, R. J., & Bowers, B. J. (2006). Internet recruitment and e-mail interviews in qualitative studies. *Qualitative Health Research, 16*, 821–835.

Hammersley, M., & Atkinson, P. (1989). *Ethnography: Principles in practice*. London: Routledge.

Hannes, K., Lockwood, C., & Pearson, A. (2010). A comparative analysis of three online appraisal instruments' ability to assess validity in qualitative research. *Qualitative Health Research, 20*, 1736–1743.

Harding, S. G. (Ed.) (2004). *The feminist standpoint theory reader: Intellectual and political controversies*. New York: Routledge.

Hay-Gibson, N. V. (2009). Interviews via VoIP: benefits and disadvantages within a PhD study of SMEs. *Library and Information Research, 33*, 39–50.

Hayfield, N., & Clarke, V. (2012). 'I'd be just as happy with a cup of tea': women's accounts of sex and affection in long-term heterosexual relationships. *Women's Studies International Forum, 35*, 67–74.

Heath, C., & Hindmarsh, J. (2002). Analysing interaction: video, ethnography and situated conduct. In T. May (Ed.), *Qualitative research in practice* (pp. 99–121). London: Sage.

Hegarty, P., Watson, N., Fletcher, L., & McQueen, G. (2011). When gentlemen are first and ladies are last: effects of gender stereotypes on the order of romantic partners' names. *British Journal of Social Psychology, 50*, 21–35.

Henrich, J., Heine, S. J., & Norenzayan, A. (2010). The weirdest people in the world? *Behavioral and Brain Sciences, 33*, 61–83.

Henriques, J., Hollway, W., Urwin, C., Venn, C., & Walkerdine, V. (1984). *Changing the subject: Psychology, social regulation and subjectivity*. London: Methuen.

Henwood, K., & Pidgeon, N. (1992). Qualitative research and psychological theorizing. *British Journal of Psychology, 83,* 97–111.

Henwood, K., & Pidgeon, N. F. (1994). Beyond the qualitative paradigm: a framework for introducing diversity within qualitative psychology. *Journal of Community & Applied Social Psychology, 4*, 225–238.

Henwood, K., & Pidgeon, N. (2003). Grounded theory in psychological research. In P. M. Camic, J. E. Rhodes & L. Yardley (Eds), *Qualitative research in psychology: Expanding perspectives in methodology and design* (pp. 131–155). Washington, DC: American Psychological Association.

Henwood, K., & Pidgeon, N. (2006). Grounded theory. In G. M. Breakwell, S. Hammond, C. Fife-Schaw & J. A. Smith (Eds), *Research methods in psychology* (3rd ed., pp. 342–364). London: Sage.

Herdt, G., & Kertzner, R. (2006). I do, but I can't: the impact of marriage denial on the mental health and sexual citizenship of lesbians and gay men in the United States. *Sexuality Research and Social Policy, 3*, 33–49.

Herek, G. M. (1984). Beyond 'homophobia': a social psychological perspective on attitudes towards lesbians and gay men. *Journal of Homosexuality, 10*, 1–21.

Herlitz, C., & Ramstedt, K. (2005). Assessment of sexual behavior, sexual attitudes, and sexual risk in Sweden (1989–2003). *Archives of Sexual Behavior, 34*, 219–229.

Hesketh, K., Waters, E., Green, J., Salmon, L., & Williams, J. (2005). Healthy eating, activity and obesity prevention: a qualitative study of parent and child perceptions in Australia. *Health Promotion International, 20*, 19–26.

Hicks, S. (2005). Is gay parenting bad for kids? Responding to the 'very idea of difference' in research on lesbian and gay parents. *Sexualities, 8*, 153–168.

Hislop, J., & Arber, S. (2003). Sleepers wake! The gendered nature of sleep disruption among mid-life women. *Sociology, 37*, 695–711.

Hislop, J., Arber, S., Meadows, R., & Venn, S. (2005). Narratives of the night: the use of audio-diaries in researching sleep. *Sociological Research Online, 10*. [Online: http://www.socresonline.org.uk/10/4/hislop.html].

Hodgetts, D., & Chamberlain, K. (1999). Medicalization and the depiction of lay people in television health documentary. *Health, 3*, 317–333.

Hodgson, S. (2004). Cutting through the silence: a sociological construction of self-injury. *Sociological Inquiry, 74*, 162–179.

Holland, J., Ramazanoglu, C., Sharpe, S., & Thomson, R. (1998). *The male in the head: Young people, heterosexuality and power*. London: The Tufnell Press.

Hollander, J. A. (2004). The social context of focus groups. *Journal of Contemporary Ethnography, 33*, 602–637.

Holliday, R. (1999). The comfort of identity. *Sexualities, 2*, 475–491.

Holliday, R. (2004). Filming 'the closet': the role of video diaries in researching sexualities. *American Behavioral Scientist, 47*, 1597–1616.

Hollows, J. (2003). Oliver's Twist: leisure, labour and domestic masculinity in 'The Naked Chef'. *International Journal of Cultural Studies, 6*, 229–248.

Hollway, W. (1984). Gender difference and the production of subjectivity. In J. Henriques, W. Hollway, C. Urwin, C. Venn & V. Walkerdine (Eds), *Changing the subject: Psychology, social regulation and subjectivity* (pp. 227–263). London: Methuen.

Hollway, W. (1989). *Subjectivity and method in psychology: Gender, meaning and science*. London: Sage.

Hollway, W., & Jefferson, T. (2000). *Doing qualitative research differently: Free association, narrative and the interview method*. London: Sage.

Holstein, J. A., & Gubrium, J. F. (1995). *The active interview*. London: Sage.

Holstein, J. A., & Gubrium, J. F. (1997). Active interviewing. In D. Silverman (Ed.), *Qualitative research: Theory, method and practice* (pp. 113–129). London: Sage.

Hookway, N. (2008). 'Entering the blogosphere': some strategies for using blogs in social research. *Qualitative Research, 8*, 91–113.

Hoppe, M. J., Wells, E. A., Morrison, D. M., Gillmore, M. R., & Wilsdon, A. (1995). Using focus groups to discuss sensitive topics with children. *Evaluation Review, 19*, 102–114.

Howitt, D. (2010). *Introduction to qualitative methods in psychology*. Harlow: Pearson Education Ltd.

Howitt, D., & Cramer, D. (2008). *Introduction to research methods in psychology* (2nd ed.). Harlow: Prentice Hall.

Howitt, D., & Owusu-Bempah, K. (1994). *The racism of psychology: Time for a change*. Hemel Hempstead: Harvester Wheatsheaf.

Hsieh, H.-F., & Shannon, S. E. (2005). Three approaches to qualitative content analysis. *Qualitative Health Research, 15*, 1277–1288.

Humphreys, L. (1970). *Tearoom trade: Impersonal sex in public places*. London: Duckworth.

Hussain, Z., & Griffiths, M. D. (2009). The attitudes, feelings, and experiences of online gamers: a qualitative analysis. *CyberPsychology & Behavior, 12*, 747–753.

Hutchby, I. (2002). Resisting the incitement to talk in child counselling: aspects of the utterance 'I don't know'. *Discourse Studies, 4*, 147–168.

Hutchby, I., & Wooffitt, R. (2008). *Conversation analysis* (2nd ed.). Cambridge: Polity Press.

Huxley, C., Clarke, V., & Halliwell, E. (2011). 'It's a comparison thing isn't it?' Lesbian and bisexual women's accounts of how partner relationships shape their feelings about their body and appearance. *Psychology of Women Quarterly, 35*, 415–427.

Inglis, V., Ball, K., & Crawford, D. (2005). Why do women of low socioeconomic status have poorer dietary behaviours than women of higher socioeconomic status? A qualitative exploration. *Appetite, 45*, 334–343.

James, N., & Busher, H. (2006). Credibility, authenticity and voice: dilemmas in online interviewing. *Qualitative Research, 6*, 403–420.

James, N., & Busher, H. (2009). *Online interviewing*. London: Sage.

Jankowicz, J. (2004). *The easy guide to repertory grids*. Hoboken, NJ: Wiley.

Jefferson, G. (2004). Glossary of transcript symbols with an introduction. In G. H. Lerner (Ed.), *Conversation analysis: Studies from the first generations* (pp. 13–31). Philadelphia: John Benjamins.

Jensen, A. R. (1969). How much can we boost IQ and school achievement? *Harvard Educational Review, 39*, 1–123.

Joffe, H. (2012). Thematic analysis. In D. Harper & A. R. Thompson (Eds), *Qualitative research methods in mental health and psychotherapy: A guide for students and practitioners* (pp. 209–223). Chichester, UK: Wiley.

Joffe, H., & Yardley, L. (2004). Content and thematic analysis. In D. Marks & L. Yardley (Eds), *Research methods for clinical and health psychology* (pp. 56–68). London: Sage.

Johnson, J. L. (1997). Generalizability in qualitative research: excavating the discourse. In J. M. Morse (Ed.), *Completing a qualitative project: Details and dialogue* (pp. 191–208). London: Sage.

Kamberelis, G., & Dimitriadis, G. (2005). Focus groups: strategic articulations of pedagogy, politics, and inquiry. In N. K. Denzin & Y. S. Lincoln (Eds), *The Sage handbook of qualitative research* (3rd ed., pp. 887–907). Thousand Oaks, CA: Sage.

Kemmis, S., & McTaggart, R. (2005). Participatory action research: communicative action and the public sphere. In N. K. Denzin & Y. S. Lincoln (Eds), *The Sage handbook of qualitative research* (3rd ed., pp. 559–603). Thousand Oaks, CA: Sage.

Kessler, L., & McDonald, D. (2012). *When words collide: A media writer's guide to grammar and style* (8th ed.). Boston, MA: Wadsworth.

Kidder, L. H., & Fine, M. (1987). Qualitative and quantitative methods: when stories converge. *New Directions for Program Evaluation, 35*, 57–75.

Kim, J. L. (2009). Asian American women's retrospective reports of their sexual socialization. *Psychology of Women Quarterly, 33*, 334–350.

Kime, N. (2008). Children's eating behaviours: the importance of the family setting. *Area, 40*, 315–322.

King, N. (1998). Template analysis. In G. Symon & C. Cassell (Eds), *Qualitative methods and analysis in organizational research: A practical guide* (pp. 118–134). Thousand Oaks, CA: Sage.

King, N. (2004). Using templates in the thematic analysis of texts. In C. Cassell & G. Symon (Eds), *Essential guide to qualitative methods in organizational research* (pp. 256–270). London: Sage.

King, N., Finlay, L., Ashworth, P., Smith, J., Langdridge, D., & Butt, T. (2008). 'Can't really trust that, so what can I trust?' A polyvocal, qualitative analysis of the psychology of mistrust. *Qualitative Research in Psychology, 5*, 80–102.

Kirk, D. (2002). Physical education: a gendered history. In D. Penney (Ed.), *Gender and physical education: Contemporary issues and future directions* (pp. 24–37). London: Routledge.

Kitzinger, C. (1987). *The social construction of lesbianism*. London: Sage.

Kitzinger, C., & Frith, H. (1999). Just say no? The use of conversation analysis in developing a feminist perspective on sexual refusal. *Discourse & Society, 10*, 293–316.

Kitzinger, C., & Powell, D. (1995). Engendering infidelity: essentialist and social constructionist readings of a story completion task. *Feminism & Psychology, 5,* 345–572.

Kitzinger, C., & Willmott, J. (2002). 'The thief of womanhood': women's experience of Polycystic Ovarian Syndrome. *Social Science & Medicine, 54,* 349–361.

Kitzinger, J. (1994a). Focus groups: method or madness? In M. Boulton (Ed.), *Challenge and innovation: Methodological advances in social research on HIV/AIDS* (pp. 159–175). London: Taylor & Francis.

Kitzinger, J. (1994b). The methodology of focus groups: the importance of interaction between research participants. *Sociology of Health and Illness, 16,* 103–121.

Kjelsås, E., Bjørnstrøm, C., & Götestam, K. G. (2004). Prevalence of eating disorders in female and male adolescents (14–15 years). *Eating Behaviors, 5,* 13–25.

Konopásek, Z. (2008). Making thinking visible with Atlas.ti: computer assisted qualitative analysis as textual practices. *Forum Qualitative Sozialforschung/Forum: Qualitative Social Research, 9.* [Online: http://www.qualitative-research.net/index.php/fqs/article/view/420/911].

Krueger, R. A., & Casey, M. A. (2009). *Focus groups: A practical guide for applied research* (4th ed.). Thousand Oaks, CA: Sage.

Kuebler, D., & Hausser, D. (1997). The Swiss hidden population study: practical and methodological aspects of data collection by privileged access interviewers. *Addiction, 92,* 325–334.

Kuhn, T. S. (1962). *The structure of scientific revolutions.* Chicago: The University of Chicago Press.

Kurz, T. (2002). The psychology of environmentally sustainable behavior: fitting together pieces of the puzzle. *Analyses of Social Issues and Public Policy, 2,* 257–278.

Kvale, S. (1996). *InterViews: An introduction to qualitative research interviewing.* Thousand Oaks, CA: Sage.

Kvale, S. (2007). *Doing interviews.* London: Sage.

Kvale, S., & Brinkmann, S. (2009). *Interviews: Learning the craft of qualitative research interviewing* (2nd ed.). Thousand Oaks, CA: Sage.

Lang, K. R., & Hughes, J. (2004). Issues in online focus groups: lessons learned from an empirical study of peer-to-peer filesharing system users. *Electronic Journal of Business Research Methods, 2,* 95–110.

Langdridge, D. (2007). *Phenomenological psychology: Theory, research and method.* Harlow, UK: Pearson Education Ltd.

Larkin, M., Eatough, V., & Osborn, M. (2011). Interpretative phenomenological analysis and embodied, active, situated cognition. *Theory & Psychology, 21,* 318–337.

Larkin, M., Watts, S., & Clifton, E. (2006). Giving voice and making sense in interpretative phenomenological analysis. *Qualitative Research in Psychology, 3,* 102–120.

Lavie, M., & Willig, C. (2005). 'I don't feel like melting butter': an interpretative phenomenological analysis of the experience of 'inorgasmia'. *Psychology & Health, 20,* 115–128.

Leask, J., Hawe, P., & Chapman, S. (2001). Focus group composition: a comparison between natural and constructed groups. *Australian and New Zealand Journal of Public Health, 25*, 152–154.

Lee, D. (1997). Interviewing men: vulnerabilities and dilemmas. *Women's Studies International Forum, 20*, 553–564.

Lewins, A., & Silver, C. (2007). *Using software in qualitative research: A step-by-step guide*. London: Sage.

Liamputtong, P. (2007). *Researching the vulnerable: A guide to sensitive research methods*. London: Sage.

Liamputtong, P. (2011). *Focus group methodology: Principles and practice*. London: Sage.

Lincoln, Y. S. (2009). Ethical practices in qualitative research. In D. M. Mertens & P. E. Ginsberg (Eds), *The handbook of social research ethics* (pp. 150–169). Los Angeles: Sage.

Lincoln, Y. S., & Guba, E. G. (1985). *Naturalistic inquiry*. Newbury Park, CA: Sage.

Litovich, M. L., & Langhout, R. D. (2004). Framing heterosexism in lesbian families: a preliminary examination of resilient coping. *Journal of Community & Applied Social Psychology, 14*, 411–435.

Livingston, J. A., & Testa, M. (2000). Qualitative analysis of women's perceived vulnerability to sexual aggression in a hypothetical dating context. *Journal of Social and Personal Relationships, 17*, 729–741.

Loach, K. (Writer, Director) (2009). *Looking for Eric*. London: Icon Film Distribution.

Lovering, K. M. (1995). The bleeding body: adolescents talk about menstruation. In S. Wilkinson & C. Kitzinger (Eds), *Feminism and discourse: Psychological perspectives* (pp. 10–31). London: Sage.

Lu, C.-J., & Shulman, S. W. (2008). Rigor and flexibility in computer-based qualitative research: introducing the coding analysis toolkit. *International Journal of Multiple Research Approaches, 2*, 105–117.

Lupton, D. (1994). The condom in the age of AIDS: newly respectable or still a dirty word? A discourse analysis. *Qualitative Health Research, 4*, 304–320.

Lyons, A. C. (2000). Examining media representations: benefits for health psychology. *Journal of Health Psychology, 5*, 349–358.

MacIntosh-Murray, A. (2007). Poster presentations as a genre in knowledge communication: a case study of forms, norms and values. *Science Communication, 28*, 347–376.

MacIntyre, A. C. (1984). *After virtue: A study in moral theory*. Notre Dame, IN: university of Notre Dame Press.

MacMillan, K. (2005). More than just coding? Evaluating CAQDAS in a discourse analysis of news texts. *Forum Qualitative Sozialforschung/Forum: Qualitative Social Research, 6*. [Online: http://www.qualitative-research.net/index.php/fqs/article/view/28].

MacMillan, K., & Koenig, T. (2004). The wow factor: preconceptions and expectations for data analysis software in qualitative research. *Social Science Computer Review, 22*, 179–186.

Madge, C., & O'Connor, H. (2002). On-line with e-mums: exploring the internet as a medium for research. *Area, 34*, 92–102.

Madge, C., & O'Connor, H. (2004). Online methods in geography educational research. *Journal of Geography in Higher Education, 28*, 143–152.

Madill, A., & Gough, B. (2008). Qualitative research and its place in psychological science. *Psychological Methods, 13*, 254–271.

Madill, A., Jordan, A., & Shirley, C. (2000). Objectivity and reliability in qualitative analysis: realist, contextualist and radical constructionist epistemologies. *British Journal of Psychology, 91*, 1–20.

Malcomson, K. S., Lowe-Strong, A. S., & Dunwoody, L. (2008). What can we learn from the personal insights of individuals living and coping with multiple sclerosis? *Disability & Rehabilitation, 30*, 662–674.

Malik, S. H., & Coulson, N. (2008). The male experience of infertility: a thematic analysis of an online in fertility support group bulletin board. *Journal of Reproductive and Infant Psychology, 26*, 18–30.

Malseed, J. (1987). Straw men: a note on Ann Oakley's treatment of textbook prescriptions for interviewing. *Sociology, 21*, 629–631.

Malson, H. (1998). *The thin woman: Feminism, post-structuralism and the social psychology of anorexia nervosa*. London: Routledge.

Mangabeira, W. C. (1995). Computer assistance, qualitative analysis and model building. In R. M. Lee (Ed.), *Information technology for the social scientist* (pp. 129–146). London: University College Press.

Mangabeira, W. C., Lee, R. M., & Fielding, N. G. (2004). Computers and qualitative research: Adoption, use, and representation. *Social Science Computer Review, 22*, 167–178.

Mann, C., & Stewart, F. (2000). *Internet communication and qualitative research: A handbook for researching online*. London: Sage.

Mann, C., & Stewart, F. (2002). Internet interviewing. In J. F. Gubrium & J. A. Holstein (Eds), *Handbook of interview research: Context and methods* (pp. 603–627). Thousand Oaks, CA: Sage.

Marecek, J. (2003). Dancing through the minefields: toward a qualitative stance in psychology. In P. M. Camic, J. E. Rhodes & L. Yardley (Eds), *Qualitative research in psychology: Expanding perspectives in methodology and design* (pp. 49–69). Washington, DC: American Psychological Association.

Marshall, M. N. (1996). Sampling for qualitative research. *Family Practice, 13*, 522–526.

Marvasti, A. (2011). Three aspects of writing qualitative research: practice, genre, and audience. In D. Silverman (Ed.), *Qualitative research* (3rd ed., pp. 383–396). London: Sage.

Maubach, N., Hoek, J., & McCreanor, T. (2009). An exploration of parents' food purchasing behaviours. *Appetite, 53*, 297–302.

Maxwell, J. A. (2010). Using numbers in qualitative research. *Qualitative Inquiry, 16*, 475–482.

Mayring, P. (2004). Qualitative content analysis. In U. Flick, E. von Kardorff & I. Steinke (Eds), *A companion to qualitative research* (pp. 266–269). London: Sage.

McCoyd, J. L. M., & Kerson, T. S. (2006). Conducting intensive interviews using email: a serendipitous comparative opportunity. *Qualitative Social Work, 5*, 389–406.

McLeod, J. (2001). *Qualitative research in counselling and psychotherapy*. London: Sage.

Meezan, W., & Martin, J. I. (2003). Exploring current themes in research on gay, lesbian, bisexual and transgender populations. *Journal of Gay & Lesbian Social Services, 15*, 1–14.

Meho, L., I. (2006). E-mail interviewing in qualitative research: a methodological discussion. *Journal of the American Society for Information Science and Technology, 57*, 1284–1295.

Mertens, D. M. (2005). *Research and evaluation in education and psychology: Integrating diversity with quantitative, qualitative, and mixed methods* (2nd ed.). Thousand Oaks, CA: Sage.

Merton, R. K. (1975). Thematic analysis in science: notes on Holton's concept. *Science, 188*, 335–338.

Merton, R. K. (1987). The focused interview and focus groups: continuities and discontinuities. *Public Opinion Quarterly, 51*, 550-566.

Merton, R. K., & Kendall, P. L. (1946). The focused interview. *American Journal of Sociology, 51*, 541–557.

Meth, P. (2003). Entries and omissions: Using solicited diaries in geographic research. *Area, 35*, 195–205.

Meyrick, J. (2006). What is good qualitative research? A first step towards a comprehensive approach to judging rigour/quality. *Journal of Health Psychology, 11*, 799–808.

Michell, J. (2004). The place of qualitative research in psychology. *Qualitative Research in Psychology, 1*, 307–319.

Michie, H. (1987). *The flesh made word: Female figures and women's bodies*. Oxford: Oxford University Press.

Michie, S., McDonald, V., & Marteau, T. (1996). Understanding responses to predictive genetic testing: a grounded theory approach. *Psychology and Health, 11*, 455–470.

Miles, M. B., & Huberman, A. M. (1994). *Qualitative data analysis: An expanded sourcebook* (2nd ed.). Thousand Oaks, CA: Sage.

Milgram, S. (1974). *Obedience to authority: An experimental view*. London: Tavistock.

Miller, C. (1995). In-depth interviewing by telephone: some practical considerations. *Evaluation & Research in Education, 9*, 29–38.

Milligan, C., Bingley, A., & Gatrell, A. (2005). Digging deep: using diary techniques to explore the place of health and well-being amongst older people. *Social Science & Medicine, 61*, 1882–1892.

Mishler, E. G. (1986). *Research interviewing: Context and narrative*. Cambridge, MA: Harvard University Press.

Moore, M. R. (2006). Lipstick or Timberlands? Meanings of gender presentation in black lesbian communities. *Signs: Journal of Women in Culture and Society, 32,* 113–139.

Morgan, D. L. (1997). *Focus groups in qualitative research* (2nd ed.). Thousand Oaks, CA: Sage.

Morgan, D. L. (2002). Focus group interviewing. In J. F. Gubrium & J. A. Holstein (Eds), *Handbook of interview research: Context and method* (pp. 141–159). Thousand Oaks, CA: Sage.

Morse, J. M. (1995). The significance of saturation. *Qualitative Health Research, 5,* 147–149.

Morse, J. M. (2000). Determining sample size. *Qualitative Health Research, 10,* 3–5.

Morse, J. M., & Field, P. A. (2002). *Nursing research: The application of qualitative approaches* (2nd ed.). Cheltenham: Nelson Thornes.

Morse, J. M., & Richards, L. (2002). *Read me first for a user's guide to qualitative methods.* Thousand Oaks, CA: Sage.

Murray, C. D., & Sixsmith, J. (1998). Email: a qualitative research medium for interviewing? *International Journal for Social Research Methodology: Theory and Practice, 1,* 102–121.

Myerson, M., Crawley, S. L., Anstey, E. H., Kessler, J., & Okopny, C. (2007). Who's zoomin' who? A feminist, queer content analysis of 'interdisciplinary' human sexuality textbooks. *Hypatia, 22,* 92–113.

Nelson, F. (1996). *Lesbian motherhood: An exploration of Canadian lesbian families.* Toronto: University of Toronto Press.

Nicolson, P., & Burr, J. (2003). What is 'normal' about women's (hetero)sexual desire and orgasm?: a report of an in-depth interview study. *Social Science & Medicine, 57,* 1735–1745.

Nightingale, D. J., & Cromby, J. (Eds). (1999). *Social constructionist psychology: A critical analysis of theory and practice.* Buckingham: Open University Press.

Norris, C. (2002). *Deconstruction* (3rd ed.). London: Routledge.

Norris, S. (2002). The implication of visual research for discourse analysis: transcription beyond language. *Visual Communication, 1,* 97–121.

Novick, G. (2008). Is there a bias against telephone interviews in qualitative research? *Research in Nursing & Health, 31,* 391–398.

O'Hara, L., & Meyer, M. (2004). Keeping it real: the self-directed focus group as an alternative method for studying the discursive construction of prejudice. *The Journal of Intergroup Relations, 31,* 25–54.

Oakley, A. (1981). Interviewing women: a contradiction in terms. In H. Roberts (Ed.), *Doing feminist research* (pp. 30–61). London: Routledge & Kegan Paul.

Ochs, E. (1979). Transcription as theory. In E. Ochs & B. Schieffelin (Eds), *Developmental pragmatics* (pp. 43–72). New York: Academic Press.

Odendahl, T., & Shaw, A. M. (2002). Interviewing elites. In J. F. Gubrium & J. A. Holstein (Eds), *Handbook of interview research: Context and method* (pp. 299–316). Thousand Oaks, CA: Sage.

Oliffe, J. L., & Bottorff, J. L. (2007). Further than the eye can see? Photo elicitation and research with men. *Qualitative Health Research, 17*, 850–858.

Onwuegbuzie, A. J., & Leech, N. L. (2005). The role of sampling in qualitative research. *Academic Exchange Quarterly 9,* 280–284.

Opdenakker, R. (2006). Advantages and disadvantages of four interview techniques in qualitative research. *Forum: Qualitative Sozialforschung/ Forum: Qualitative Social Research, 7.* [Online: www.qualitative-research.net/indexphp/fqs/article/viewArticle/175].

Opperman, E., Braun, V., Clarke, V., & Rogers, C. (in press, 2013). 'It feels so good it almost hurts': young adults, experiences of orgasm and sexual pleasure. *Journal of Sex Research.*

Oringderff, J. (2008). 'My way': Piloting an online focus group. *International Journal of Qualitative Methods, 3*, 69–75.

Palmer, M., Larkin, M., de Visser, R., & Fadden, G. (2010). Developing an interpretative phenomenological approach to focus group data. *Qualitative Research in Psychology, 7*, 99–121.

Parker, I. (1988). Deconstructing accounts. In C. Antaki (Ed.), *Analysing everyday explanations: A casebook of methods* (pp. 185–198). London: Sage.

Parker, I. (1989). *The crisis in modern social psychology: And how to end it*. London: Routledge.

Parker, I. (1992). *Discourse dynamics: Critical analysis for social and individual psychology*. London: Routledge.

Parker, I. (1996). Discursive complexes in material culture. In J. Hayworth (Ed.), *Psychological research: Innovative methods and strategies* (pp. 184–196). London: Routledge.

Parker, I. (2002). *Critical discursive psychology*. Houndmills: Palgrave Macmillan.

Parker, I. (2004). Discourse analysis. In U. Flick, E. von Kardorff & I. Steinke (Eds), *A Companion to qualitative research* (pp. 308–312). London: Sage.

Parker, I. (2005a). Lacanian discourse analysis in psychology: seven theoretical elements. *Theory & Psychology, 15*, 163–182.

Parker, I. (2005b). *Qualitative psychology: Introducing radical research*. Maidenhead, UK: Open University Press.

Parker, I., & the Bolton Discourse Network (1999). *Critical textwork: An introduction to the varieties of discourse and analysis*. Buckingham, UK: Open University Press.

Patton, M. Q. (1990). *Qualitative evaluation and research methods* (2nd ed.). Newbury Park, CA: Sage.

Patton, M. Q. (2002). *Qualitative research & evaluation methods* (3rd ed.). Thousand Oaks, CA: Sage.

Peace, P. (2003). Balancing power: the discursive maintenance of gender inequality by wo/men at university. *Feminism & Psychology, 13*, 159–180.

Pedersen, E., Hallberg, L.-M., & Waye, K. P. (2007). Living in the vicinity of wind turbines – a grounded theory study. *Qualitative Research in Psychology, 4*, 49–63.

Peel, E. (2001). Mundane heterosexism: understanding incidents of the everyday. *Women's Studies International Forum, 24*, 541–554.

Peräkylä, A. (2002). Agency and authority: extended responses to diagnostic statements in primary care encounters. *Research on Language & Social Interaction, 35*, 219–247.

Peräkylä, A. (2006). Observation, video and ethnography: case studies in Aids counselling and greetings. In P. Drew, G. Raymond & D. Weinberg (Eds), *Talk and interaction in social research methods* (pp. 81–96). London: Sage.

Pidgeon, N. (1996). Grounded theory: theoretical background. In J. T. E. Richardson (Ed.), *Handbook of qualitative research methods for psychology and the social sciences* (pp. 75–85). Leicester: BPS Books.

Pidgeon, N., & Henwood, K. (1996). Grounded theory: practical implementation. In J. T. E. Richardson (Ed.), *Handbook of qualitative research methods for psychology and the social sciences* (pp. 86–101). Leicester, UK: BPS Books.

Pidgeon, N., & Henwood, K. (1997). Using grounded theory in psychological research. In N. Hayes (Ed.), *Doing qualitative analysis in psychology* (pp. 245–273). Hove, UK: Psychology Press.

Pidgeon, N., & Henwood, K. (2004). Grounded theory. In M. Hardy & A. Bryman (Eds), *The handbook of data analysis* (pp. 625–648). London: Sage.

Pitts, M., & Smith, A. (Eds) (2007). *Researching the margins: Strategies for ethical and rigorous research with marginalised communities*. Houndmills, UK: Palgrave.

Poland, B. D. (2002). Transcription quality. In J. F. Gubrium & J. A. Holstein (Eds), *Handbook of interview research: Context & method* (pp. 629–649). Thousand Oaks, CA: Sage.

Popper, K. (1959). *The logic of scientific discovery*. Oxford: Basic Books.

Potter, J. (1996). Discourse analysis and constructionist approaches: theoretical background. In J. T. E. Richardson (Ed.), *Handbook of qualitative research methods for psychology and the social sciences* (pp. 125–140). Leicester, UK: BPS Books.

Potter, J. (1997). Discourse analysis as a way of analysing naturally occurring talk. In D. Silverman (Ed.), *Qualitative research: Theory, method and practice* (pp. 144–160). London: Sage.

Potter, J. (2003). Discourse analysis and discursive psychology. In P. M. Camic, J. E. Rhodes & L. Yardley (Eds), *Qualitative research in psychology: Expanding perspectives in methodology and design* (pp. 73–94). Washington, DC: American Psychological Association.

Potter, J., & Hepburn, A. (2007). Life is out there: a comment on Griffin. *Discourse Studies, 9*, 276–282.

Potter, J., & Reicher, S. (1987). Discourses of community and conflict: the organization of social categories in accounts of a 'riot'. *British Journal of Social Psychology, 26*, 25–40.

Potter, J., & Wetherell, M. (1987). *Discourse and social psychology: Beyond attitudes and behaviour*. London: Sage.

Potter, J., & Wetherell, M. (1995). Discourse analysis. In J. A. Smith, R. Harré & L. van Langenhove (Eds), *Rethinking methods in psychology* (pp. 80–92). London: Sage.

Potter, J., Wetherell, M., Gill, R., & Edwards, D. (1990). Discourse: noun, verb or social practice? *Philosophical Psychology, 3*, 205–217.

Potts, A., & Parry, J. (2010). Vegan sexuality: challenging heteronormative masculinity through meat-free sex. *Feminism & Psychology, 20,* 53–72.

Price, J. (1996). Snakes in the swamp: ethical issues in qualitative research. In R.-E. Josselson (Ed.), *Ethics and process in the narrative study of lives* (pp. 207–215). London: Sage.

Pulver, A. (2010, Friday 28 May). *Sex and the City 2* – rise of the critic proof movie. *The Guardian.* [Online: http://www.guardian.co.uk/film/2010/may/28/sex-and-the-city-2].

Pyett, P. M. (2003). Validation of qualitative research in the 'real world'. *Qualitative Health Research, 13,* 1170–1179.

Radley, A., Hodgetts, D., & Cullen, A. (2005). Visualizing homelessness: a study in photography and estrangement. *Journal of Community & Applied Social Psychology, 15,* 273–295.

Ramazanoglu, C., & Holland, J. (2002). *Feminist methodology: Challenges and choices.* London: Sage.

Reicher, S. (2000). Against methodolatry: some comments on Elliott, Fischer, and Rennie. *British Journal of Clinical Psychology, 39,* 1–6.

Reinharz, S. (1992). *Feminist methods in social research.* New York: Oxford University Press.

Reinharz, S. (1993). Neglected voices and excessive demands in feminist research. *Qualitative Sociology, 16,* 69–76.

Reinharz, S., & Chase, S. E. (2002). Interviewing women. In J. F. Gubrium & J. A. Holstein (Eds), *Handbook of interview research: Context and method* (pp. 221–238). Thousand Oaks, CA: Sage.

Renzetti, C. M., & Lee, R. M. (Eds). (1993). *Researching sensitive topics.* Newbury Park, CA: Sage.

Ribbens, J. (1989). Interviewing – an 'unnatural situation'? *Women's Studies International Forum, 12,* 579–592.

Rice, C. (2009). Imagining the other? Ethical challenges of researching and writing women's embodied lives. *Feminism & Psychology, 19,* 245–266.

Richardson, L. (2000). Writing: a method of inquiry. In N. K. Denzin & Y. S. Lincoln (Eds), *Handbook of qualitative research* (2nd ed., pp. 923–948). Thousand Oaks, CA: Sage.

Riessman, C. K. (1987). When gender is not enough: women interviewing women. *Gender & Society, 1,* 172–207.

Riessman, C. K. (2007). *Narrative methods for the human sciences.* Thousand Oaks, CA: Sage.

Riggs, D. (2006). Developmentalism and the rhetoric of 'best interests of the child': challenging heteronormative constructions of families and parenting in foster case. *Journal of GLBT Family Studies, 2,* 57–73.

Riolo, S. A., Nguyen, T. A., Greden, J. F., & King, C. A. (2005). Prevalence of depression by race/ethnicity: findings from the National Health and Nutrition Examination Survey III. *American Journal of Public Health, 95,* 998–1000.

Roberts, K. A., & Wilson, R. W. (2002). ICT and the research process: issues around the compatibility of technology with qualitative data analysis. *Forum Qualitative*

Sozialforschung/Forum: Qualitative Social Research, 3. [Online: http://www.qualitative-research.net/index.php/fqs/article/view/862/1873].

Rorty, R. (1979). *Philosophy and the mirror of nature.* Oxford: Blackwell.

Rose, L., Mallinson, R. K., & Walton-Moss, B. (2002). A grounded theory of families responding to mental illness. *Western Journal of Nursing Research, 24*, 516-536.

Rose, N. (1996). *Inventing our selves: Psychology, power, and personhood.* Cambridge: Cambridge University Press.

Roy, S. C. (2008). 'Taking charge of your health': discourses of responsibility in English–Canadian women's magazines. *Sociology of Health & Illness, 30*, 463–477.

Rubin, H. J., & Rubin, I. S. (1995). *Qualitative interviewing: The art of hearing data.* Thousand Oaks, CA: Sage.

Rúdólfsdóttir, A. G. (2000). 'I am not a patient, and I am not a child': the institutionalization and experience of pregnancy. *Feminism & Psychology, 10*, 337–350.

Russell, C. (1999). Interviewing vulnerable old people: ethical and methodological implications of imaging our subjects. *Journal of Aging Studies, 13*, 403–417.

Russell, C. K., Gregory, D. M., & Gates, M. F. (1996). Aesthetics and substance in qualitative research posters. *Qualitative Health Research, 6*, 542–552.

Sacks, H. (1992). *Lectures on conversation* (Vol. 2). Cambridge, MA: Blackwell.

Sacks, H., & Jefferson, G. (1995). *Lectures on Conversation* (Vols 1 & 2). Oxford: Blackwell.

Sacks, H., Schegloff, E. A., & Jefferson, G. (1974). A simplest systematics for the organization of turn-taking for conversation. *Language, 50*, 696–735.

Sainsbury, C. (2009). *Martian in the playground: Understanding the schoolchild with Asperger's syndrome* (Revised ed.). London: Sage.

Sandelowski, M. (1994a). Notes on qualitative methods: notes on transcription. *Research in Nursing & Health, 17*, 311–314.

Sandelowski, M. (1994b). Notes on qualitative methods: the use of quotes in qualitative research. *Research in Nursing & Health, 17*, 479–482.

Sandelowski, M. (1995). Sample size in qualitative research. *Research in Nursing & Health, 18*, 179–183.

Sandelowski, M. (2001). Real qualitative researchers do not count: the use of numbers in qualitative research. *Research in Nursing & Health, 24*, 230–240.

Sandelowski, M. (2004). Using qualitative research. *Qualitative Health Research, 14*, 1366–1386.

Sanders, S. A., & Reinisch, J. M. (1999). Would you say you 'had sex' if … . *Journal of the American Medical Association, 281*, 275–277.

Sarbin, T. R. (Ed.) (1986). *Narrative psychology: The storied nature of human conduct.* New York: Praeger.

Sawyer, L., Regev, H., Proctor, S., Nelson, M., Messias, D., Barnes, D., & Meleis, A. I. (1995). Matching versus cultural competence in research: methodological considerations. *Research in Nursing & Health, 18*, 557–567.

Schaie, K. W. (1993). Ageist language in psychological research. *American Psychologist, 48*, 49–51.

Schegloff, E. A. (2007). *Sequence organization in interaction: A primer in conversation analysis* (Vol. 1). Cambridge: Cambridge University Press.

Scheurer, M., Brauch, H. J., & Lange, F. T. (2009). Analysis and occurrence of seven artificial sweeteners in German waste water and surface water and in soil aquifer treatment (SAT). *Analytical and Bioanalytical Chemistry, 394*, 1585–1594.

Schneider, S. J., Kerwin, J., Frechtling, J., & Vivari, B. A. (2002). Characteristics of the discussion in online and face-to-face focus groups. *Social Science Computer Review, 20*, 31–42.

Schofield, J. W. (1993). Increasing the generalizability of qualitative research. In M. Hammersley (Ed.), *Social research: Philosophy, politics and practice* (pp. 200–225). London: Sage.

Schulze, B., & Angermeyer, M. C. (2003). Subjective experiences of stigma. A focus group study of schizophrenic patients, their relatives and mental health professionals. *Social Science & Medicine, 56*, 299–312.

Schwalbe, M. L., & Wolkomir, M. (2002). Interviewing men. In J. F. Gubrium & J. A. Holstein (Eds), *Handbook of interview research: Context and method* (pp. 203–219). Thousand Oaks, CA: Sage.

Schwandt, T. (2000). Three epistemological stances for qualitative inquiry: Interpretivism, hermeneutics, and social constructionism. In N. K. Denzin & Y. S. Lincoln (Eds), *The Sage Handbook of qualitative research* (2nd ed., pp. 189–213). Thousand Oaks, CA: Sage.

Schwartz, B. M., Landrum, R. R., & Gurung, R. A. R. (2012). *An easy guide to APA style*. Thousand Oaks, CA: Sage.

Scully, D. (1994). *Understanding sexual violence: A study of convicted rapists*. New York: Routledge.

Seale, C. (1999). *The quality of qualitative research*. London: Sage.

Seely, J. (2009). *Oxford A–Z of grammar and punctuation*. Oxford: Oxford University Press.

Selltiz, C., Jahoda, M., Deutsch, M., & Cook, S. W. (1965). *Research methods in social relations*. London: Methuen.

Shaw, R. L., & Giles, D. C. (2009). Motherhood on ice? A media framing analysis of older mothers in the UK news. *Psychology & Health, 24*, 221–236.

Shaw, R. L., Dyson, P. O., & Peel, E. (2008). Qualitative psychology at M level: a dialogue between learner and teacher. *Qualitative Research in Psychology, 5*, 179 – 191.

Sheriff, M., & Weatherall, A. (2009). A feminist discourse analysis of popular-press accounts of postmaternity. *Feminism & Psychology, 191*, 89–108.

Shuy, R. W. (2002). In-person versus telephone interviews. In J. F. Gubrium & J. A. Holstein (Eds), *Handbook of interview research: Context and methods* (pp. 537–555). Thousand Oaks, CA: Sage.

Silver, C., & Fielding, N. (2008). Using computer packages in qualitative research. In C. Willig & W. Stainton Rogers (Eds), *The Sage handbook of qualitative research in psychology* (pp. 334–351). Los Angeles: Sage.

Silverman, D. (1993). *Interpreting qualitative data: Methods for analysing talk, text and interaction*. London: Sage.

Silverman, D. (2000). *Doing qualitative research: A practice handbook*. London: Sage.

Silverman, D. (2005). *Doing qualitative research* (2nd ed.). London: Sage.

Silverman, D. (2006). *Interpreting qualitative data: Methods for analysing talk, text and interaction* (3rd ed.). London: Sage.

Silverman, G. (n.d.). Online focus groups come in a poor 2nd to telephone focus groups for hard-to-get, dispersed respondents. [Online: http://mnav.com/focus-group-center/online-focus-group-htm/].

Sims-Schouten, W., Riley, S. C. E., & Willig, C. (2007). Critical realism in discourse analysis: a presentation of a systematic method of analysis using women's talk of motherhood, childcare and female employment as an example. *Theory & Psychology, 17*, 101–124.

Singer, E., Frankel, M. R., & Glassman, M. B. (1983). The effect of interviewer characteristics and expectations on response. *Public Opinion Quarterly, 47*, 68–83.

Singer, M., Stopka, T., Siano, C., Springer, K., Barton, J., Khoshnood, K., Gorry de Puga, A., Heimer, R. (2000). The social geography of AIDS and hepatitis risk: qualitative approaches for assessing local differences in sterile-syringe access among injection drug users. *American Journal of Public Health, 90*, 1049–1056.

Sloan, C., Gough, B., & Connor, M. (2010). Healthy masculinities? How ostensibly healthy men talk about lifestyle, health and gender. *Psychology & Health, 25*, 783–803.

Smith, B., & Sparkes, A. C. (2008). Changing bodies, changing narratives and the consequences of tellability: a case study of becoming disabled through sport. *Sociology of Health and Illness, 30*, 217–236.

Smith, J. A. (1995). Semi-structured interviewing and qualitative analysis. In J. A. Smith, R. Harré & L. van Langenhove (Eds), *Rethinking methods in psychology* (pp. 9–26). London: Sage.

Smith, J. A. (1996). Evolving issues for qualitative psychology. In J. T. E. Richardson (Ed.), *Handbook of qualitative research methods for psychology and the social sciences* (pp. 189–201). Leicester: BPS Books.

Smith, J. A. (1999a). Identity development during the transition to motherhood: an interpretative phenomenological analysis. *Journal of Reproductive and Infant Psychology, 17*, 281–299.

Smith, J. A. (1999b). Towards a relational self: social engagement during pregnancy and psychological preparation for motherhood. *British Journal of Social Psychology, 38*, 409–426.

Smith, J. A., Flowers, P., & Larkin, M. (2009). *Interpretative phenomenological analysis: Theory, method and research*. London: Sage.

Smith, J. A., & Osborn, M. (2003). Interpretative phenomenological analysis. In J. A. Smith (Ed.), *Qualitative psychology: A practical guide to methods* (pp. 51–80). London: Sage.

Smith, J. A., & Osborn, M. (2007). Pain as an assault on the self: an interpretative phenomenological analysis of the psychological impact of chronic benign low back pain. *Psychology & Health, 22*, 517–534.

Smith, L. T. (1999). *Decolonizing methodologies: Research and indigenous peoples.* Dunedin: University of Otago Press.

Smith, M. W. (1995). Ethics in focus groups: a few concerns. *Qualitative Health Research, 5,* 478–486.

Sneijder, P., & te Molder, H. (2009). Normalizing ideological food choice and eating practices. Identity work in online discussions on veganism. *Appetite, 52,* 621–630.

Sparkes, A. C., & Smith, B. (2008). Narrative constructionist inquiry. In J. A. Holstein & J. F. Gubrium (Eds), *Handbook of constructionist research* (pp. 295–314). London: Guilford Publications.

Speer, S. A. (2002a). 'Natural' and 'contrived' data: a sustainable distinction? *Discourse Studies, 4,* 543–548.

Speer, S. A. (2002b). Sexist talk: gender categories, participants' orientations and irony. *Journal of Sociolinguistics, 6,* 347–377.

Speer, S. A., & Green, R. (2008). On passing: the interactional organization of appearance attributions in the psychiatric assessment of transsexual patients. In V. Clarke & E. Peel (Eds), *Out in psychology: Lesbian, gay, bisexual, trans and queer perspectives* (pp. 335–368). Chichester, UK: John Wiley & Sons, Ltd.

Speer, S. A., & Potter, J. (2000). The management of heterosexist talk: conversational resources and prejudiced claims. *Discourse & Society, 11,* 543–572.

Stainton Rogers, W. (2011). *Social Psychology* (2nd ed.). Maidenhead, UK: Open University Press.

Stainton Rogers, W., & Stainton Rogers, R. (1997). Does critical psychology mean the end of the world? In T. Ibáñez & L. Íñiguez (Eds), *Critical social psychology* (pp. 67–82). London: Sage.

Stark-Adamec, C. I., & Kimball, M. (1984). Science free of sexism: a psychologist's guide to the conduct of non-sexist research. *Canadian Psychology/Psychologie Canadienne, 25,* 23–34.

Stenner, P. (1993). Discoursing jealousy. In E. Burman & I. Parker (Eds), *Discourse analytic research: Repertoires and readings of texts in action* (pp. 94–132). London: Routledge.

Stephens, M. (1982). A question of generalizability. *Theory & Research in Social Education, 9,* 75–89.

Stewart, D. W., Shamdasani, P. N., & Rook, D. R. (2007). *Focus groups: Theory and practice.* Thousand Oaks, CA: Sage.

Stokoe, E. (2010). 'I'm not gonna hit a lady': conversation analysis, membership categorization and men's denials of violence towards women. *Discourse & Society, 21,* 59–82.

Stopka, T. J., Springer, K. W., Khoshnood, K., Shaw, S., & Singer, M. (2004). Writing about risk: use of daily diaries in understanding drug-user risk behaviours. *AIDS and Behavior, 8,* 73–85.

Storey, L. (2007). Doing interpretative phenomenological analysis. In A. Coyle & E. Lyons (Eds), *Analysing qualitative data in psychology* (pp. 51–64). London: Sage.

Story, M., & Faulkner, P. (1990). The prime time diet: a content analysis of eating behavior and food messages in television program content and commercials. *American Journal of Public Health, 80,* 738–740.

Sturge-Jacobs, M. (2002). The experience of living with fibromyalgia: confronting an invisible disability. *Research and Theory for Nursing Practice, 16*, 19–31.

Sturges, J. E., & Hanrahan, K. J. (2004). Comparing telephone and face-to-face qualitative interviewing: a research note. *Qualitative Research, 4*, 107–118.

Summers, M. (2007). Rhetorically self-sufficient arguments in Western Australian parliamentary debates on lesbian and gay law reform. *British Journal of Social Psychology, 46*, 839–858.

Suzuki, L. A., Ahluwalia, M. K., Arora, A. K., & Mattis, J. S. (2007). The pond you fish in determines the fish you catch. *The Counseling Psychologist, 35*(2), 295–327.

Swain, J., Heyman, J., & Gillman, M. (1998). Public research, private concerns: ethical issues in the use of open-ended interviews with people who have learning difficulties. *Disability & Society, 13*, 21–36.

Sweet, C. (2001). Designing and conducting virtual focus groups. *Qualitative Market Research: An International Journal, 4*, 130–135.

Sword, H. (2010). Becoming a more productive writer. *MAI Review, 2*. [Online: http://www.review.mai.ac.nz/index.php/MR/article/view/339/463].

Taggart, C., & Wines, J. A. (2008). *My grammar and I (or should that be 'me'?): Old-school ways to sharpen your English.* London: Michael O'Mara Books Ltd.

Tasker, F., & Golombok, S. (1997). *Growing up in a lesbian family: Effects on child development.* New York: Guilford Press.

Taylor, G. W., & Ussher, J. M. (2001). Making sense of S&M: a discourse analytic account. *Sexualities, 4*, 293–314.

Taylor, S. (2001). Evaluating and applying discourse analytic research. In M. Wetherell, S. Taylor & S. Yates (Eds), *Discourse as data: A guide for analysis* (pp. 311–330). London: Sage.

Tebes, J. K. (2005). Community science, philosophy of science, and the practice of research. *American Journal of Community Psychology, 35*, 213–230.

Tee, N., & Hegarty, P. (2006). Predicting opposition to the civil rights of trans persons in the United Kingdom. *Journal of Community & Applied Social Psychology, 16*, 70–80.

Terry, G. (2010). *Men, masculinity and vasectomy in New Zealand.* PhD, The University of Auckland, Auckland, New Zealand.

Terry, G., & Braun, V. (2009). 'When I was a bastard': constructions of maturity in men's accounts of masculinity. *Journal of Gender Studies, 18*, 165–178.

Terry, G., & Braun, V. (2011a). 'I'm committed to her and the family': positive accounts of vasectomy among New Zealand men. *Journal of Reproductive and Infant Psychology, 29*, 276–291.

Terry, G., & Braun, V. (2011b). 'It's kind of me taking responsibility for these things': men, vasectomy and 'contraceptive economies'. *Feminism & Psychology, 21*, 477–495.

Terry, G., & Braun, V. (2011c). Sticking my finger up at evolution: unconventionality, selfishness, and choice in the talk of men who have had 'preemptive' vasectomies. *Men and Masculinities 15*, 207–229.

The Ethics Committee of the British Psychological Society (2009). *Code of ethics and conduct.* Leicester, UK: The British Psychological Society.

The Working Party on Conducting Research on the Internet (2007). *Conducting research on the internet: Guidelines for ethical practice in psychological research online.* Leicester, UK: The British Psychological Society.

Thomas, R. J. (1995). Interviewing important people in big companies. In R. Hertz & J. M. Imber (Eds), *Studying elites using qualitative methods* (pp. 3–17). Thousand Oaks, CA: Sage.

Thompson, R., & Holland, J. (2005). 'Thanks for the memory': memory books as a methodological resource in biographical research. *Qualitative Research, 5*, 201–219.

Tischner, I., & Malson, H. (2008). Exploring the politics of women's in/visible 'large' bodies. *Feminism & Psychology, 18*, 260–267.

Toerien, M., & Durrheim, K. (2001). Power through knowledge: ignorance and the 'real man'. *Feminism & Psychology, 11*, 35–54.

Toerien, M., & Wilkinson, S. (2004). Exploring the depilation norm: a qualitative questionnaire study of women's body hair removal. *Qualitative Research in Psychology, 1*, 69–92.

Toerien, M., Wilkinson, S., & Choi, P. Y. L. (2005). Body hair removal: the 'mundane' production of normative femininity. *Sex Roles, 52*, 399–406.

Tolich, M., & Davidson, C. (2003). Collecting the data. In C. Davidson & M. Tolich (Eds), *Social science research in New Zealand* (2nd ed., pp. 121–153). Auckland: Pearson Education.

Toner, J. (2009). Small is not too small: reflections concerning the validity of very small focus groups. *Qualitative Social Work, 8*, 179–192.

Torre, M. E., & Fine, M. (2005). Bar none: extending affirmative action to higher education in prison. *Journal of Social Issues, 61*, 569–594.

Tracy, S. J. (2010). Qualitative quality: eight 'Big-Tent' criteria for excellent qualitative research. *Qualitative Inquiry, 16*, 837–851.

Treharne, G. J. (2011). Questioning sex/gender and sexuality: reflections on recruitment and stratification. *Gay & Lesbian Issues and Psychology Review, 7*, 132–154.

Truss, L. (2003). *Eats, shoots and leaves: The zero tolerance approach to punctuation.* London: Profile Books Ltd.

Tsui, A. B. M. (1991). The pragmatic functions of *I don't know. Text – Interdisciplinary Journal for the Study of Discourse, 11*, 607–622.

Underhill, C., & Olmsted, M. G. (2003). An experimental comparison of computer-mediated and face-to-face focus groups. *Social Science Computer Review, 21*, 506–512.

Ussher, J. M. (1999). Eclecticism and methodological pluralism: the way forward for feminist research. *Psychology of Women Quarterly, 23*, 41–46.

Valentine, G. (1989). The geography of women's fear. *Area, 21*, 385–390.

van Dijk, T. A. (1993). Principles of critical discourse analysis. *Discourse & Society, 4*, 249–283.

Van Emden, J., & Becker, L. (2010). *Presentation skills for students* (2nd ed.). Basingstoke: Palgrave Macmillan.

Vaughn, S., Schumm, J. S., & Sinagub, J. (1996). *Focus group interviews in education and psychology.* Thousand Oaks, CA: Sage.

Verkuyten, M. (2005). Accounting for ethnic discrimination: a discursive study among minority and majority group members. *Journal of Language and Social Psychology, 24*, 66–92.

Vidich, A. J., & Lyman, S. M. (1994). Qualitative methods: their history in sociology and anthropology. In N. K. Denzin & Y. S. Lincoln (Eds), *Handbook of qualitative research* (pp. 23–59). Thousand Oaks, CA: Sage.

Wainwright, D. (1997). Can sociological research be qualitative, critical and valid? *The Qualitative Report, 3*. [Online: http://www.nova.edu/ssss/QR/QR3–2/wain.html].

Walkerdine, V. (1987). No laughing matter: girls' comics and the preparation for adolescent sexuality. In J. M. Broughton (Ed.), *Critical theories of psychological development* (pp. 87–125). New York: Plenum Press.

Walsh, E., & Malson, H. (2010). Discursive constructions of eating disorders: a story completion task. *Feminism & Psychology, 20*, 529–537.

Wann, M. (2009). Fat studies: an invitation to revolution. In E. Rothblum & S. Solovay (Eds), *The fat studies reader* (pp. ix–xxv). New York: New York University Press.

Warner, M. (1993). *Fear of a queer planet: Queer politics and social theory*. Minneapolis: University of Minnesota Press.

Watts, S., & Stenner, P. (2005). Doing Q methodology: theory, method and interpretation. *Qualitative Research in Psychology, 2*, 67–91.

Weatherall, A., Gavey, N., & Potts, A. (2002). So whose words are they anyway? *Feminism & Psychology, 12*, 531–539.

Weatherell, C., Tregear, A., & Allinson, J. (2003). In search of the concerned consumer: UK public perceptions of food, farming and buying local. *Journal of Rural Studies, 19*, 233–244.

Webb, C., & Kevern, J. (2001). Focus groups as a research method: a critique of some aspects of their use in nursing research. *Journal of Advanced Nursing, 33*, 798–805.

Weedon, C. (1987). *Feminist practice and poststructuralist theory*. Cambridge, MA: Blackwell.

Weedon, C. (1997). *Feminist practice and poststructuralist theory* (2nd ed.). Oxford: Blackwell.

Wellings, K., Branigan, P., & Mitchell, K. (2000). Discomfort, discord and discontinuity as data: using focus groups to research sensitive topics. *Culture, Health & Sexuality, 2*, 255–267.

Wenger, G. C. (2002). Interviewing older people. In J. F. Gubrium & J. A. Holstein (Eds), *Handbook of interview research: Context and method* (pp. 259–278). Thousand Oaks, CA: Sage.

Wetherell, M. (1998). Positioning and interpretative repertoires: conversation analysis and post-structuralism in dialogue. *Discourse & Society, 9*, 387–412.

Wetherell, M. (2007). A step too far: discursive psychology, linguistic ethnography and questions of identity. *Journal of Sociolinguistics, 11*, 661–681.

Wetherell, M., & Potter, J. (1992). *Mapping the language of racism: Discourse and the legitimation of exploitation*. Hemel Hempsted, UK: Harvester.

White, C., Woodfield, K., & Ritchie, J. (2003). Reporting and presenting qualitative data. In J. Ritchie & J. Lewis (Eds), *Qualitative research practice: A guide for social science students and researchers* (pp. 287–320). London: Sage.

Whitehead, K., & Kurz, T. (2009). 'Empowerment' and the pole: a discursive investigation of the re-invention of pole dancing as a recreational activity. *Feminism & Psychology, 19*, 224–244.

Whitehead, S., & Biddle, S. (2008). Adolescent girls' perceptions of physical activity: a focus group study. *European Physical Education Review, 14*, 243–262.

Whittaker, A. (2009). *Research skills for social work*. Exeter, UK: Learning Matters.

Whitty, M. T. (2005). The realness of cybercheating: men's and women's representations of unfaithful internet relationships. *Social Science Computer Review, 23*, 57–67.

Widdicombe, S. (1995). Identity, politics and talk: a case for the mundane and the everyday. In S. Wilkinson & C. Kitzinger (Eds), *Feminism and discourse: Psychological perspectives* (pp. 106–127). London: Sage.

Wiggins, S. (2004). Good for 'you': generic and individual healthy eating advice in family mealtimes. *Journal of Health Psychology, 9*, 535–548.

Wiggins, S. (2009). Managing blame in NHS weight management treatment: psychologizing weight and 'obesity'. *Journal of Community and Applied Social Psychology, 19*, 374–387.

Wiggins, S., & Potter, J. (2010). Discursive psychology. In C. Willig & W. Stainton Rogers (Eds), *The Sage handbook of qualitative research in psychology* (pp. 73–90). London: Sage.

Wilkinson, S. (1988). The role of reflexivity in feminist psychology. *Women's Studies International Forum, 11*, 493–502.

Wilkinson, S. (1998a). Focus group methodology: a review. *International Journal of Social Research Methodology, 1*, 181–203.

Wilkinson, S. (1998b). Focus groups in feminist research: power, interaction and the co-construction of meaning. *Women's Studies International Forum, 21*, 111–125.

Wilkinson, S. (1998c). Focus groups in health research: exploring the meanings of health and illness. *Journal of Health Psychology, 3*, 329–348.

Wilkinson, S. (1999). Focus groups: a feminist method. *Psychology of Women Quarterly, 23*, 221–244.

Wilkinson, S. (2004). Focus group research. In D. Silverman (Ed.), *Qualitative research: Theory, method and practice* (2nd ed., pp. 177–199). London: Sage.

Wilkinson, S., & Kitzinger, C. (2007). Conversation analysis. In C. Willig & W. Stainton Rogers (Eds), *The Sage handbook of qualitative research in psychology* (pp. 54–72). London: Sage.

Wilkinson, S., & Kitzinger, C. (Eds) (1996). *Representing the other: A Feminism & Psychology Reader*. London: Sage.

Williams, M., & Robson, K. (2004). Reengineering focus group methodology for the online environment. In M. D. Johns, S.-L. S. Chen & G. J. Hall (Eds), *Online social research: Methods, issues, & ethics* (pp. 25–45). New York: Peter Lang.

Williams, S., & Reid, M. (2007). A grounded theory approach to the phenomenon of pro-anorexia. *Addiction Research & Theory, 15*, 141–152.

Willig, C. (2001). *Introducing qualitative research in psychology: Adventures in theory and method*. Buckingham: Open University Press.

Willig, C. (2008). *Introducing qualitative research in psychology: Adventures in theory and method* (2nd ed.). Maidenhead: Open University Press.

Willig, C., & Stainton Rogers, W. (2008). Introduction. In C. Willig & W. Stainton Rogers (Eds), *The Sage handbook of qualitative research in psychology* (pp. 1–12). London: Sage.

Willmott, J. (2000). The experiences of women with Polycystic Ovarian Syndrome. *Feminism & Psychology, 10*, 107–116.

Willott, S. (1998). An outsider within: a feminist doing research with men. In K. Henwood, C. Griffin & A. Phoenix (Eds), *Standpoints and differences: Essays in the practice of feminist psychology* (pp. 173–190). London: Sage.

Willott, S., & Griffin, C. (1997). 'Wham bam, am I a man?': Unemployed men talk about masculinities. *Feminism & Psychology, 7*, 107–128.

Wilson, H. S., & Hutchinson, S. A. (1997). Presenting qualitative research up close: visual literacy in poster presentations. In J. M. Morse (Ed.), *Completing a qualitative project: Detail and dialogue* (pp. 63–85). Thousand Oaks, CA: Sage.

Wilson, M. S., Weatherall, A., & Butler, C. (2004). A rhetorical approach to discussions about health and vegetarianism. *Journal of Health Psychology, 9*, 567–581.

Wishart, M., & Kostanski, M. (2009). First do no harm: valuing and respecting the 'person' in psychological research online. *Counselling, Psychotherapy, and Health, 5*, 300–328.

Wodak, R., & Meyer, M. (2001). *Methods of critical discourse analysis*. London: Sage.

Woods, P. (1999). *Successful writing for qualitative researchers*. London: Routledge.

Worth, N. (2009). Making use of audio diaries in research in young people: examining narrative, participation and audience. *Sociological Research Online, 14*. [Online: http://www.socresonline.org.uk/14/4/9.html].

Wyer, S. J., Earll, L., Joseph, S., & Harrison, J. (2001). Deciding whether to attend a cardiac rehabilitation programme: an interpretative phenomenological analysis. *Coronary Health Care, 5*, 178–188.

Yardley, L. (2000). Dilemmas in qualitative health research. *Psychology & Health, 15*, 215–228.

Yardley, L. (2008). Demonstrating validity in qualitative psychology. In J. A. Smith (Ed.), *Qualitative psychology: A practical guide to research methods* (2nd ed., pp. 235–251). London: Sage.

Yip, A. K. T. (2008). Researching lesbian, gay, and bisexual Christians and Muslims: Some thematic reflections. *Sociological Research Online, 13*. [Online: http://www.socresonline.org.uk/13/1/5.html].

Zimmerman, D. H., & Wieder, D. L. (1977). The diary: diary-interview method. *Urban Life, 5*, 479–498.

Index

References in **bold** are to tables, in *italics* are to boxes, followed by a letter f are to figures and followed by a letter g are to glossary items.

PRINCIPLES AND METHODS IN LANDSCAPE ECOLOGY

**Published by Chapman & Hall, an imprint of Thomson Science,
2–6 Boundary Row, London SE1 8HN, UK**

Thomson Science, 2–6 Boundary Row, London SE1 8HN, UK

Thomson Science, 115 Fifth Avenue, New York, NY 10003, USA

Thomson Science, Suite 750, 400 Market Street, Philadelphia, PA 19106, USA

Thomson Science, Pappelallee 3, 69469 Weinheim, Germany

First edition 1998

© 1998 Chapman & Hall Ltd

Thomson Science is a division of International Thomson Publishing **I(T)P**

Typeset in 10/11 pt Times by Saxon Graphics Ltd, Derby

Printed in Great Britain at the University Press, Cambridge

ISBN   0 412 73030 8 (HB)   0 412 73040 5 (PB)

A catalogue record for this book is available from the British Library